Prentice Hall Advanced Reference Series

Computer Science

DUBES AND JAIN *Algorithms for Clustering Data*
SHERE *Software Engineering and Management*

Engineering

FERRY, AKERS, AND GREENEICH *Ultra Large Scale Integrated Microelectronics*
JOHNSON *Lectures on Adaptive Parameter Estimation*
MILUTINOVIC *Microprocessor System Design GaAs Technology*
WALRAND *Introduction to Queueing Networks*

Science

BINKLEY *The Pineal: Endocrine and Nonendocrine Function*
CAROZZI *Carbonate Depositional Systems*
EISEN *Mathematical Methods for Biology, Bioengineering, and Medicine*
FRASER *Event Stratigraphy*
WARREN *Evaporite Sedimentology*

SOFTWARE ENGINEERING AND MANAGEMENT

KENNETH D. SHERE

Avtec Systems, Inc.

PRENTICE HALL, Englewood Cliffs, New Jersey 07632

Library of Congress Cataloging-in-Publication Data

SHERE, KENNETH D., (date)
   Software engineering and management.

   Bibliography.
   Includes index.
      1. Computer software—Development.   2. Software
maintenance.   I. Title.
QA76.76.D47S49 1988   005   87-3578
ISBN 0-13-822081-6

Editorial/production supervision
   and interior design: *Joan McCulley*
Manufacturing buyer: *Gordon Osbourne and Paula Benevento*
Cover design: *Karen Stephens*

 © 1988 by Prentice Hall
A Division of Simon & Schuster, Inc.
Englewood Cliffs, New Jersey 07632

The Publisher offers discounts on this book when ordered in bulk
quantities. For more information write:

   Special Sales/College Marketing
   Prentice-Hall
   College Technical and Reference Division
   Englewood Cliffs, New Jersey 07632

The author and publisher of this book have used their best efforts in preparing
this book. These efforts include the development, research, and testing of the
theories and programs to determine their effectiveness. The author and
publisher make no warranty of any kind, expressed or implied, with regard to
these programs or the documentation contained in this book. The author and
publisher shall not be liable in any event for incidental or consequential
damages in connection with, or arising out of, the furnishing, performance, or
use of these programs.

Printed in the United States of America
10   9   8   7   6   5   4   3   2   1

ISBN   0-13-822081-6   025

Prentice-Hall International (UK) Limited, *London*
Prentice-Hall of Australia Pty. Limited, *Sydney*
Prentice-Hall Canada Inc., *Toronto*
Prentice-Hall Hispanoamericana, S. A., *Mexico*
Prentice-Hall of India Private Limited, *New Delhi*
Prentice-Hall of Japan, Inc., *Tokyo*
Simon & Schuster Asia Pte. Ltd., *Singapore*
Editora Prentice-Hall do Brasil, Ltda., *Rio de Janeiro*

Contents

Preface

This book is intended for the computer professional who needs to gain a system-level perspective of software development. This person may have a B.S. degree in computer science, work experience in a special area (such as data bases or operating systems), or responsibility for managing software-related products. The approach taken is very pragmatic.

There are a few unique features of this book. These include a new concept for a software development and maintenance environment and a new method for applying the concepts of expert systems to conventional data bases. Most importantly, this book offers guidance not generally included as part of on-the-job training or in university curricula.

After reading and studying this book, technical staff will have a better understanding of how their technical tasks fit into the larger scheme of software development and maintenance. Managers and task leaders will be better able to control their software projects. Insights into technical and management risk, cost estimation, the utilization of a system's legacy, and other aspects of the development process are provided.

The first seven chapters are intended to provide an understanding of the system development life cycle. After studying these seven chapters, you should be able to think at the system level. On the surface, this seems simple, but it isn't. If you have been working in the details of one (or a few) specific areas, it is very difficult to suddenly be able to step back and view the entire system. Planning the activities needed to develop or integrate an entire system is not an obvious process.

Recent college graduates may know a great deal about languages and may have built compilers in a class, but performing a requirements analysis, estimating costs, and determining risks are beyond the information presented in undergraduate curricula. A substantial amount of time is wasted because even experienced professionals frequently do not know what they are expected to produce. When you understand the life cycle, you also have a reasonable understanding of what products need to be produced and when they need to be produced. This understanding helps to eliminate floundering time at the beginning of many tasks

Chapter 8 is a case study. It serves as an introduction to the structured design techniques and data-base design, the subjects of Chapters 9 and 10, respectively. Because of the system-level orientation of this book, techniques related to quality assurance (which includes configuration management and testing), capacity planning, and reliability are discussed in Chapters 11 and 12. Having devoted most of this book to processes associated with software development, a case study of a systems engineering and integration job is presented in Chapter 13.

This sudden change in orientation emphasizes that:

- The project management procedures discussed in this book apply to all systems jobs.
- Taking existing software into account is becoming standard operating procedures; in the years to come, this case study will become the typical way of building systems.
- Once you have begun thinking at the system level, you really are a systems (or software) engineer.

Most of the chapters (and many of the sections) of this book could easily be expanded into an entire book. Consequently, it has been necessary to blend an overview of the topic with some depth. I have tried to make this blend appropriate by using practical examples of how the techniques are applied.

This book is suitable for use as a reference in a training course on software engineering. A syllabus for a very fast moving three-day training course could cover most of the material in Chapters 1, 3 to 9, 13, and 14. The target audience for this type of training course is directors of software, project managers, task leaders, and software users and developers.

This book is also suitable for use as a textbook for graduate courses on either software project management or software engineering. The manuscript for this book was used to teach software engineering to graduate students at George Mason University. We generally covered one chapter per week. It was usually impossible to lecture on all the information in a chapter in one week. This approach required the students to read each chapter in advance of the lecture. The lecture then covered the highlights of the chapter and answered students' questions. This approach is suitable for a class of good engineers who are generally at the level of a Ph.D. candidate. Most of the students worked full time and had their own experience on which to draw.

In the case of a software project management course, the pace would have to be slower. Significant portions of the manuscript for this book were used in a course with that title at the University of Maryland. The recommended chapters would be the same as the chapters covered in the training course described previously, plus Chapter 2. The pace would be slower than the pace for the software engineering course, and the instructor should cover the chapters more thoroughly. In this case, the instructor needs to emphasize the management aspects of these chapters. I would recommend that the instructor of a project management course digress from this book occasionally to discuss problems involved with managing people.

Exercises are scattered throughout this book. They are designed to evoke thought. The reader should work the exercises as he or she comes to them. Sometimes the exercises do not have a unique answer. By skipping the exercises and reading my answer, the reader may deprive himself or herself of the chance for independent thinking. Some of the exercises may take an excessive amount of time to answer completely. I suggest that time limits be imposed by the instructor. For those exercises, the final answer is not what counts, but rather the class discussions they elicit.

Each instructor is left to his own devices to generate examinations. I have assigned projects based on Chapter 14 as a final exam. During the semester I give two examinations. For the first one, each student is required to go to the library and find an article that he or she thinks can be applied. After I approve of the article, the student is required to write a short paper (and give a 10 minute presentation) that demonstrates understanding and shows how he or she would apply the concepts at work. For the second examination, the students are required to write a software development plan for the final project.

Many of the ideas in this book were developed while I was at Planning Research Corporation (PRC). PRC is one of the largest suppliers of software services to the government. At PRC, I helped organize their systems engineering organization and managed one of its two departments. My group developed and implemented that company's software engineering methodology.

We produced their software standards and procedures and a software development plan that could be tailored to any company project. We also developed and taught a training course on software engineering. The primary contributors to those ideas were W. Barrie Wilkinson, Neil McDermott, C. Randy Allen, Charles Shartsis, and J. Kendrick Williams. Many of the ideas on knowledge data bases (in Chapter 10) were due to Charles Shartsis.

The encouragement and support of my partners at Avtec Systems, Inc., Ron Hirsch, Steve Mellman, and Jay Schwartz, are also acknowledged. Most of the material on fault tolerance in Chapter 12 was taken from a report by Jay Schwartz.

I thank my children, Reenie, Elisa, and Jeremy, for giving up so much of the time that they should have had with me. Their sacrifice is realized in subtle ways, like Jeremy's occasional question, "Daddy, when will you be finished with your story?" Most of all, I need to thank my wife, Madeline Zoberman Shere. Over two decades ago my research professor said to me, "I'm glad you married Maddy. She is good for you." I keep finding more reasons why he was correct.

SOFTWARE ENGINEERING AND MANAGEMENT

CHAPTER 1

Introduction

Software engineering is not a single process, instruction manual, or organization. It is the systematic use of many disciplines, tools, and resources for the practical application of computer hardware. In the 1930s, engineering was defined in Webster's (1936) as "the art and science of managing engines for practical application." If we consider our engines to be computers, this definition seems especially appropriate to software engineering.

This definition of software engineering is very broad; it includes almost everything except hardware. As we shall see during the discussion of the system development life cycle, in Chapter 3, many people consider software engineering to be those activities beginning with the analysis of software requirements. The viewpoint of this book is that software engineering begins with the system concept definition. Concept definition and system requirements have frequently been determined by hardware personnel with no input from software personnel. People performing these activities should include both software-oriented people and hardware-oriented people. They should also include expected system users. This team is needed to avoid imposing unrealistic performance requirements on either the hardware or the software.

To manage these engines, we have to consider all aspects of the intended application. These aspects include operational concepts, requirements, design, development, and maintenance. An aspect of managing engines that is generally ignored in the computer industry is developing criteria for determining when a system is no longer useful. That is, when should the system be replaced, and how do we retire the existing system?

Usually we consider this aspect of software engineering (and system engineering) only when developing a plan for transition from the existing system or procedures to the system we are going to develop. We don't plan for the death of the new system. Some people claim that systems don't die—they evolve. If that is the case, then why is it neces-

1

sary to spend billions of dollars to replace existing systems? In the case of the FAA Air Traffic Control System, the Government has committed an expenditure in excess of $1 billion dollars during a very tight budget period to redesign the system and to replace the hardware and software. This project was expected to cover an eight-year period from its inception in 1983.

This book is not a book on either structured programming or structured analysis. There are other books devoted to those subjects. Some of those books are cited in the bibliography. The subject of this book is software engineering. Software engineering is a superset of structured programming and structured analysis. For example, structured analysis techniques exclude from their scope cost analyses, simulations, legacy assessments, and a host of other analyses necessary for the design and development of a software system. This book describes what you need to do to plan, manage, and develop software systems and discusses some techniques for how to do it. The intent is to provide the reader with a system-level view of systems.

The system development life cycle is discussed in detail. Products associated with each phase of the life cycle are described. These descriptions are important because knowing the phase of the life cycle in which your task occurs and the products of that phase enables you to determine what you need to produce; your task becomes bounded. You may still need to determine how you will obtain the products, but you have eliminated the floundering time—time spent trying to figure out what to do.

In other engineering disciplines, there are handbooks, standards, and professional engineer examinations. The handbooks help us define our problems and serve as a reference for how to solve problems. The standards provide professional judgment on procedures. The professional engineer examination is used to certify that engineers are familiar with these handbooks and standards. Unfortunately, the software engineering discipline is just emerging. These handbooks, standards, and certification procedures do not yet exist for our industry, although some progress has been accomplished.

The greatest progress has been in the area of standards. The lead in developing and establishing standards has been the Department of Defense. There are extensive military standards related to software development. Many other agencies and many companies use these standards as the basis for their internal software standards and procedures. There are computer programmer examinations, but these are generally ignored. There is also a lack of conviction in the industry that these examinations reflect ability in software engineering.

Some companies have taken it upon themselves to develop their own standards and to "certify" their engineers by providing training courses. Significant portions of this book are based on the software methodology developed by and under the direction of the author for Planning Research Corporation (PRC), one of the largest suppliers of software services to the government.

In this introduction we discuss the need for a formal approach to software engineering, the applicability of a formal approach, and the institutionalization of a standard methodology. The reader who is working on small projects, who is a student, or who is not in a position to change the way his or her company does business should not jump to the conclusion that this introduction does not apply. This conclusion would be false. Company

operating committees may pontificate and pronounce policy, but it is the project managers, task leaders, and people who work for them that implement things.

A formal approach is presented to establish an attitude, a plan of attack, a way of thinking. That is what software engineering is all about.

1.1 DO I NEED A FORMAL SOFTWARE METHODOLOGY?

Why do we need a formal software engineering methodology? Either we can answer this question to the satisfaction of line management, key marketing personnel, and the vast majority of the technical staff, or we do not need a formal methodology.

To line management and marketing, the justification must be in terms of the bottom line, dollars and cents. For example, at PRC Government Information Systems the need was recognized by executive management. One of that company's strategic goals has been to move from a software company, with considerable work in facilities management and coding, to a systems engineering and integration company. As one step toward accomplishing this goal, a systems engineering group was formed. A primary objective of this group was to develop and implement a software methodology that would enhance the company's vitality and performance.

There was no intent for that group (or this book) to present a new structured technique. Over a half-dozen different techniques are discussed in subsequent sections. These are good enough, there is no need for another. The methodology presented here is a practical approach for managing, designing, building, and maintaining systems. It is based on things that are known to work because they have been used. Any structured technique can be used with this methodology.

Being able to use any structured technique is a requirement of methodologies used by companies performing software engineering for many clients. Some clients have very strong opinions about structured techniques. Some company field offices have been using specific structured techniques for many years; it would be foolish to tell them that they can no longer use these techniques. If you did, you could be assured that your new method would not be implemented.

Other companies or organizations are in a position to specify a single structured approach. Depending on the circumstances, it may also be advantageous to use a very formal, rigid approach. For example, an organization that runs a large software operation for a single corporation may insist that all documentation be of a specified format. A single approach to structured diagrams is important. This is also true of small companies producing business applications that must be tailored to the customer. Each applications programmer should use a similar approach to lessen confusion when reading another person's documentation.

As a first step toward developing a corporate methodology, a generic Software Development Plan (SDP, pronounced *ess dee pee*) that would be applicable to all software development should be produced. An SDP tells us what to do from a variety of perspectives. It includes a description of the development organization and schedule and an explanation of the company's or organization's software development methodology. By nature, an SDP must be project specific to be completely useful. Thus, the generic SDP should include instructions for tailoring it to specific projects.

Next a generic Software Standards and Procedures (SSP, pronounced *ess ess pee*) should be produced. Sometimes the standards and procedures are included as part of the software development plan. When this is done, the combined document tends to be thick, so I recommend that these be written as two different documents. Writing the software standards and procedures could be done concurrently with the development of the SDP. Whereas the SDP tells us what to do, the SSP tells us how to do it. At PRC, these two documents have proved to be extraordinarily useful.

We had no trouble convincing top line and marketing management that our approach should be implemented. We provided internal consulting and temporary staffing for projects that had had problems. We delivered top-quality products to the delight of the client and line management. Applying the methodology paid off.

For marketing, we wrote the technical approach on proposals and provided easy-to-read documentation. Our approach won or helped win major contracts (valued in excess of $10 million each). In large companies working on systems development contracts, it is important to specify the technical approach in proposals. When the proposed work is won, the company is obligated to use the approach it espoused. This approach is key to changing the way a mid-sized or large company does business.

Some details of the implementation approach will be discussed later. The pace at which the software methodology was adopted throughout the company was only limited by the availability of personnel for training the staff and by the development of some of the tools needed to implement the methodology.

The line manager needs to be convinced that using the standardized approach increases the likelihood that his or her projects will be completed on schedule and within cost. Key marketing managers (who may be the same people as the line managers) have to be convinced that the formal technique will help sell jobs. These sales may be to other companies, to the government, or to other organizations within the company. Task leaders, analysts, designers, and programmers all need to be convinced that it is good for their careers.

In the training course on Software Engineering mentioned previously, the trainees were asked to specify what they thought were the pros and cons of a formal methodology. Their answers are given in Table 1-1.

The primary objections were fears that the client would prefer some other design technique and that the approach might be too rigid. The latter fear was expressed by someone who had just taken a five-day course on a particular structured design approach. When he left the course, he had fourteen thick notebooks and did not have enough shelf space in his office to store them.

When they were told that the standardized approach given here could accommodate all the well-known structured techniques, there was enthusiastic endorsement. The reasons soon became clear. Everybody could speak a common language and could describe

TABLE 1-1 Benefits of a Standardized Approach

Pros	Cons
Improved management control	Too rigid
Credibility of work plans	Oversegmentation
Ease of personnel transition among projects	We never before did it this way
Avoiding work loss due to	Limits innovation
Promotions	Could standardize on a bad standard
Illnesses	Hard to change a standard (inhibits
Employment changes	technology-stimulated improvements)
Guidance for junior level personnel	
Helps establish career paths	
Marketing	
Standard products help retain corporate memory	
Tells us what *not* to do	
Easier to maintain	

their career accomplishments in terms of products that are understood in all divisions of the company. A standard methodology can be used to help generate career paths!

It was interesting that the greatest enthusiasm for a standardized methodology came from junior personnel. These people typically were college graduates with computer science degrees and three or fewer years experience. They were all familiar with a couple of structured analysis techniques and a variety of computer languages. Despite a good education, they felt limited in their career. Very little guidance had been received when they entered the "real world."

They understood their jobs and were performing well; however, they had trouble relating to how their jobs fit into the total development effort. They also had trouble relating to a career path. In the absence of an identifiable career path, immediate financial gain becomes a primary motivator. Keeping employees happy with their current tasks becomes the only way to retain them. As evidenced by the huge turnover rate in the computer industry, nearly all companies have been unsuccessful in providing the proper motivation.

Task managers were almost as enthusiastic as junior-level people. Their "pro" was the fact that it would be much easier to bring up to speed people who had been assigned to their task. As people are assigned to the project, they still have to learn about the user's environment and problems. They do not have to spend time learning new software methodologies.

Program managers liked the idea of having a formal life cycle with products defined for each phase of the life cycle. They could relate the company life cycle to their client's life cycle. With this relationship, they could tell the client what information they need and what products the client should expect. This approach has gotten out of trouble many projects that had gotten into trouble by doing software "the old-fashioned way."

1.2 IS A FORMAL METHODOLOGY REALLY APPLICABLE
TO MY PROJECT?

Many people respond to discussions about software methodologies by agreeing that they are really necessary for large jobs, but not for small jobs. Indeed, most of us think of our own project as a small one—even if it is part of a large system.

To make matters worse, we usually justify the funding for new system developments by showing that the system provides many benefits at low risk. In the government, people often play games with cost estimates to have a system designated as a minor system rather than a major system. The minor system designation greatly reduces bureaucracy.

In industry, the justification for funding is frequently done in terms of return on investment. Under some circumstances, the employees are with the company long enough to demonstrate the real return on investment. This justification is easier to measure than many government justifications.

I was involved in the design of an interactive system with the following parameters:

- Over 200 concurrent users armed with microcomputers.
- A distributed data base in excess of 20 gigabytes.

A distributed data base is a data base in which the data are stored in multiple locations. A 300-page book without pictures is about 180,000 words or 1 megabyte (1 character = 1 byte). Thus, this data base is equivalent to 20,000 such books located in various places. The client considered this a simple system because each individual process was well understood. It required a bit of discussion about risk to convince this client that those two parameters alone were adequate for the system to be considered complex.

There are misconceptions concerning complexity; these misconceptions influence our viewpoints regarding the need for a formal methodology. In the next section, various viewpoints of complexity are given.

Some of us, perhaps most of us, really are working on small projects. It seems silly to discuss a formal preliminary design review for a project that will last two months and will be staffed by one or two people. Indeed, when we compare productivity, the idea of a formal methodology at first blush seems absurd. Productivity for large jobs typically ranges from six to fifteen executable lines of code per day per person. A good programmer writing in Pascal can generate up to 200 executable lines of code per day.

The difference in productivity is basically due to the large number of people on big projects who do not produce code, the larger number of meetings and reviews, the larger number of documents that must be produced, and the greater likelihood of misunderstood requirements and specifications. For example, ''Brooks' law'' (Brooks, 1975) tells us that the number of interfaces increases as $n * (n + 1)/2$, where n is the number of people.

Trying to determine whether the need for following a formal methodology varies with the size of the task is equivalent to trying to determine whether the need for maintaining a formal project book varies with the size of the task. In each case, the answer is no. The need for using good project management practices and good engineering practices does not vary with the size of the job. If you expect to be able to maintain a program and to reuse it at some unanticipated time, it must be well documented and it must be built properly.

Another aspect of this book that may cause some concern about its applicability to your job is the obvious influence of military standards on its format and approach. Some of us may question whether these documents are relevant to our commercial or nonmilitary government projects. This influence exists because of historical reasons. The military has been the primary financier for the development of software engineering practices.

The development of ADA, the ADA Program Support Environment (APSE) concept, the Software Technology for Adaptable, Reliable Systems (STARS) program, the ARPA Advanced Computer Program, and the development of the trusted computer base are just a few examples of this effort. The military standards themselves are very good documents. Many nonmilitary agencies, including FAA and NASA, use them.

Any major commercial producer of software would be foolish to ignore this resource. As in any other engineering field, the discipline, tools, and resources (i.e., the art and science) that comprise the practice do not depend on the application. Of course, it is true that the particular tools and resources used may be project dependent.

In summary, the methodology described here is applicable to all software projects.

1.3 WHAT IS A COMPLEX SYSTEM?

One of the pitfalls of systems engineering is to think that a system is simple (i.e., not complex) when we have a very good understanding of its (application) functions. An example of such a system is a banking system visualized by the users as a set of automatic teller machines (ATMs). The functions of an ATM are extremely well understood; its applications are trivial transactions. From a system viewpoint, however, we have to worry about a system with a large data base of sensitive information with hundreds to thousands of users. With this system come problems related to security (literally millions of dollars are at risk) and data-base concurrency.

Virtually all real-time systems are complex because of the constraints on both cycle time and memory resources. It is not unusual to have to deviate from structured programming standards during programming of real-time systems. Smart and creative programmers will frequently tinker with chips to determine their operating characteristics. These characteristics include operations that are not published or supported by the chip manufacturer. When a real-time programmer utilizes these unsupported operations, she or he creates a time bomb.

Consider the situation, for example, in which a manufacturer decides to transfer his manufacturing from the United States to a third world country. In doing so, he may change his manufacturing procedures. This could affect the unsupported operations of the chip. From the manufacturer's viewpoint, there is no need for an announcement because the supported operations are unchanged—*from the manufacturer's viewpoint, the chip looks the same to the user.* Now, the problem is, "How do you find the bug in your real-time software?" From a logical viewpoint the software is correct and has been running fine. Suddenly, the new chips don't work.

Unfortunately, there are no commonly accepted metrics for measuring software complexity. However, considerable attention has been devoted to determining a method for measuring complexity by well-known authorities in software engineering.

E. Yourdon (1975) considers a system to be complex if most of the following features apply to that system:

- $10,000 \leq$ SLOC $\leq 100,000$
- Five to twenty programmers over a two- to three-year period
- Several subsystems
- $100 \leq$ number of modules $\leq 1,000$

where SLOC is defined as the delivered source lines of code. He considers a system *nearly impossible* (this could be read as very complex) if it has the following attributes:

- Real-time processing, telecommunications, and multitasking
- Complex interactions between subsystems and/or other separately developed systems
- Requires continuing development and maintenance by somebody other than the original development team
- $1,000 \leq$ number of modules $\leq 10,000$
- 100 to 1,000 programmers over several years
- $100,000 \leq$ SLOC $\leq 1,000,000$

For either of these cases, Yourdon concludes that the end result of the effort is largely dependent on the use of modern, formal techniques of design and management.

The second source on complexity referenced is the USAF Space Division "Management Guide for IV&V" (1980). IV&V is an acronym for independent validation and verification. These terms are used by the government to represent various aspects of system testing. Verification is the process of "verifying" that the software meets the specifications. In a top-down design process, we verify that the software at any particular level of specification satisfies the preceding, higher level of specification. For example, we verify that the code satisfies the detailed program design. Validation is the process in which the system requirements are validated. That is, we "validate" that the end system satisfies the requirements. The term independent is used to emphasize that the validation and verification testing should be done by a group that is independent of the development group.

This guide provides a mechanism for measuring the criticality of software and gives guidance on the amount of money (as a percentage of development costs) that should be spent on IV&V.

Four criticality classes are defined. The two most severe are *critical* and *cata-*

strophic. Critical software is defined to be modules that, upon failure, would cause degradation of the operational mission. Catastrophic software is defined to be modules that, upon failure, would cause mission failure, critical equipment loss, or excessive cost overrun.

This guide specifies seventeen required IV&V activities for modules satisfying either of these two categories. Some of these activities are:

- Critique the developer's documentation, design, reviews, and milestone reviews
- Identify critical requirements and design problems
- Spot-check design performance
- Conduct limited testing
- Perform selected audits
- Independently analyze requirements and design
- Rederive key algorithms

The point is that many software efforts that we would like to think of as being simple and straightforward satisfy these criteria for complexity. Experts in the field have concluded that formal methodology is needed for complex software.

1.4 HOW DO I INSTITUTIONALIZE A STANDARDIZED APPROACH?

The answer to this question could constitute a book on organizational behavior. Rather than attempting to answer this question for all organizations, some ground rules that have been used successfully at two companies are provided. These ground rules are:

- Each plan or standard document must not exceed 150 pages.
- It is preferable that the length of a document be about 50 pages.
- Each document should be able to be tailored to any specific project.
- Tailoring instructions should be included with each document.
- Each document should be easy to use.
  - If project engineers have readily available terminals, documents should be in digital form and available in an interactive mode.
  - Guidelines should be available so that the project engineer need read only the sections applicable to his or her task.
- The approach must be flexible enough to accommodate client preferences; many clients are knowledgeable about software!
- The approach must be flexible enough to accommodate task-leader preferences.
- A three- to five-day training course should be developed and regularly taught.
- The approach should initially be used on a few key (and preferably small) projects—quick, visible success is needed.

- It is necessary for a high-level committee, such as a company's Operating Committee, to pontificate and to pronounce a policy of accepting the method.
- Most importantly, lead engineers, task managers, and project managers must be convinced to use the method.

1.5 A ROADMAP TO THIS BOOK

Historically, the discipline of software engineering began with the introduction of structured programming in the late 1960s. We follow this pattern by beginning our technical discussion in Chapter 2 with structured programming. We include coding standards in that discussion.

If this book is used for a training course, Chapter 2 is a good way to start. Most software people are aware of structured programming and this chapter can be used to get the class to work together as a group. Chapter 2 includes material on standardizing approaches to ''work-arounds.'' This approach illustrates the relationship between ''program design languages'' and programming languages. By standardizing work-arounds, systems are easier to maintain.

As mentioned previously, a key attribute of the methods discussed here is the elimination of floundering time by maintaining a life-cycle view of software engineering. Thus, the software life cycle is discussed next in Chapter 3. This discussion introduces a data approach to the life cycle. This approach is used to debunk various myths about the life cycle. Understanding what to do is influenced by our knowledge of the responsibilities of various organizational components throughout the life cycle. Consequently, this life-cycle discussion includes that topic.

Chapters 4 through 6 focus on some activities that are considered in all phases of the life cycle. These sections are devoted to risk analyses, cost estimation, and legacy assessments, respectively. A risk analysis should be part of every software development plan, but frequently it is omitted. Cost estimation is a perennial problem. As the design progresses, more accurate cost estimates could and should be made. Legacy assessments are used to determine what existing software is reusable and to locate sources of information that are useful to the design. For example, when redesigning an existing system, the code may be useless, but the documentation may indicate how many special situations were resolved. These intricacies may be omitted from the program design if the legacy assessment was not done. Legacy assessments are generally not done, but they should be. A case study is used in Chapter 5 to illustrate the benefits of a legacy assessment.

The products of each life-cycle phase are discussed in further detail in Chapter 7. Then, in Chapter 8, a case study illustrating some requirements analysis and design techniques is presented. Structured analysis techniques are described in further detail in Chapter 9. Chapter 10 is a brief introduction to data-base design. Chapters 8 to 10 illustrate the connection between a system's functional hierarchy and its data structure. This connection is usually either omitted or not clearly discussed in books advocating a particular structured technique.

Quality assurance is discussed in Chapter 11. This discussion includes sections on configuration management and control, and checklists for reviews and testing. Chapter 12 discusses some analytical techniques that are generally ignored in software engineering books. Specifically, this chapter discusses capacity planning, reliability, and fault tolerance.

Chapters 9 to 12 clearly do not describe their topics in depth. Entire books are devoted to each of those topics.

A second case study is presented in Chapter 13. This case study is a systems engineering and integration problem. It illustrates the way many systems will be built in the future and how some systems (such as office automation systems) are currently built. This book then closes with a challenge to the reader(s) in Chapter 14 to design an integrated computer for the home. This challenge was the subject of a six-hour workshop. It requires the use of much of the information in this book.

REFERENCES

USAF Space Division, ''Management Guide for Independent Verification and Validation,'' Aug. 1980.

Yourdon, E., *Techniques of Program Structure and Design*, Prentice-Hall, Inc., Englewood Cliffs, N.J., 1975.

CHAPTER 2

Structured Programming

To effectively manage software projects and to practice software engineering, it is necessary to have both a system perspective and a life-cycle perspective of software development. In this chapter, these perspectives are introduced by turning our attention to a topic with which we have some familiarity—structured programming. Most of the sections of this chapter are written as if they were part of a software standards and procedures document. Note the awareness in this discussion of the need to maintain the software. It is a good practice to always write software with an eye on maintaining it. You will find the impact of this attitude on the code you write very significant.

With this perspective, Section 2.1 leads us to the topic of implementing standard "work-arounds." A work-around is a procedure for getting a language to utilize a construct that is not native to the language. Details on these procedures are given in Section 2.1.3. In Sections 2.2 to 2.5, the discussion focuses on dividing a large program into small bits of code that are easy to maintain and to understand. In Section 2.6, deviations from programming standards are discussed. It is important on even small jobs to keep standards in mind. If you need to be convinced about the importance of thinking maintenance while programming, take a look at any code that you have written over six months ago. Ask yourself the following questions:

- How easy is it to understand this code?
- Can I still use the code?

If you are happy with your answer, then I congratulate you; you are the exception.

In the final section, Section 2.7, the concept of a software development environment is introduced. We will return to this concept periodically throughout this book. It is a key to the production of quality software and to potentially significant savings in production costs.

2.1 STRUCTURED PROGRAMMING PHILOSOPHY

By the late 1960s, large operational computer systems were a fact. We began to realize that the cost of maintaining a system exceeds the cost of building the system. Furthermore, attempts to enhance system applications and performance were very difficult. The philosophy that *programming is a black art* was becoming financially unacceptable. Although creative programming (as opposed to creative design) was not yet being condemned, articles decrying "spaghetti" code and advocating GOTOless code appeared (e.g., Dijkstra, 1968).

The structure theorem was proved in 1966 by Bohm and Jacopini. They defined a proper program to be any program with one entry, one exit, no unreachable code, and no infinite loops. Unreachable code (also called "dead code") is code that cannot be executed by any path that goes through the program from the entry point to the exit point. The structured theorem states that *any* proper program is functionally equivalent to a program containing only the following three structures:

- Sequences of two or more operations
- Conditional branch to one or more operations, and then return (e.g., IF a THEN b ELSE c)
- Repetition of a set of operations while a condition is true (e.g., DO WHILE p)

Any program with only these structures is called a structured program. These structures are called the primitive constructs of structured programming. Two other constructs, the "DO UNTIL p" and the "DO a WHILE p DO b" (called the DO WHILE DO), are equivalent to the DO WHILE. These two constructs are also considered primitive constructs.

The repetition structure could be replaced by a recursion structure. Recursion permits a program to call itself. An example of this construct is given in the next section. Recursion is more elegant than repetition, but it is also not as well understood; you should use this structure with caution. The ability to repeat operations is the key feature of the third structure.

2.1.1 Allowable Constructs

Unless there exists substantial justification for deviating from structured code, the only constructs allowed shall be the primitive structured constructs, the CASE statement and the IF THEN ELSEIF THEN ELSE statement.

The primitive constructs are described in Figure 2-1 by using both flow charts and Warnier–Orr charts. When Warnier–Orr charts are used, the flow of control is specified by brackets. Each element of the Warnier–Orr chart is either a datum or a process; in a

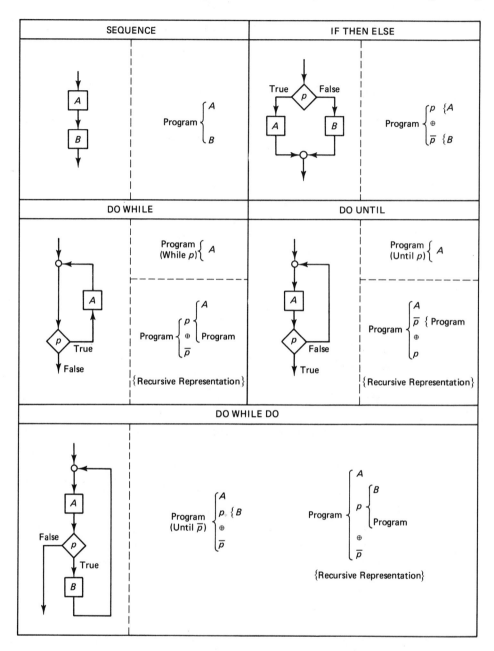

Figure 2-1 Primitive constructs of structured programming.

single chart, data and processes are not mixed. The element may then be partitioned into a more detailed structure by specifying another bracket. Figure 2-1 can also be viewed as the definition of Warnier–Orr charts.

An advantage of Warnier–Orr charts is that programmers can easily code from these charts. This statement is not obvious if you have never before seen a Warnier–Orr chart, but after you use them once or twice the statement becomes clear. Another advantage to Warnier–Orr charts is that unstructured constructs cannot be used.

When people first see Warnier–Orr charts, they frequently ask whether calls to subroutines can be performed. The answer is yes. Simply let one of the elements be "CALL [SUBROUTINE NAME]" if the element were a process, or "[SUBROUTINE NAME]" if the element were a datum.

The Warnier–Orr representation of DO WHILE, DO UNTIL, and DO WHILE DO is given in two ways: the traditional loop representation, and the recursive representation. When converting directly from Warnier–Orr diagrams to code, the traditional representation is easier for programmers to use. The recursive representation is closer to the thinking involved in artificial intelligence processing, such as performed with LISP.

Structured programming eliminates the need to write explicit GOTOs; however, it is not intended to eliminate the use of subroutines invoked by "CALL/RETURN" logic. It is the intent of structured programming to make programs easy to read. Saying that a 10,000-line program of structured code is easier to read than a 10,000-line program of unstructured code is like saying that it is easier to walk up the steps of a 100-story building than to walk up a 1,200-foot rock pile. Thus, structure programming also encourages the use of subroutines.

A program may be subdivided into subroutines, which may in turn be partitioned into units and then modules. The hierarchical structure of programs is given in Section 2.2.

2.1.2 Prohibited Constructs

Three basic constructs are prohibited: explicit branching, multiple entry or exit points, and self-modifying code. To implement structured programming in some languages, it is necessary to use the GOTO statement. Only branching instructions necessary to simulate structured constructs are permitted. All other explicit branching is prohibited.

Each module should have a single entry point and, except for error exits, each module should have a single exit. Some languages, such as FORTRAN, permit multiple entry and exit points. When these are used, it is necessary for the calling module to know the internal structure of the called module. This fact violates good design principles. These design principles are discussed in Section 2.5.

Self-modifying code is confusing and is extremely difficult to maintain. Errors are hard to locate because we may not be able to determine the state of the code at the time of the error.

2.1.3 Implementation of Standard Constructs

The primitive structured constructs are not features of all programming languages; they are probably not even features of most programming languages. For example, in COBOL the PERFORM UNTIL structure is actually a DO WHILE. There is no DO UNTIL construct, although this can be simulated.

The implementation of a language characteristic that is not present in a language as a construct is called a *work-around*. Using work-arounds is common to virtually all coding tasks. Traditionally, the use of work-arounds has not been controlled.

Work-arounds have probably been used by everyone with a reasonable amount of programming experience. On a large project, there may be 100 programmers, each implementing the same work-arounds fifteen different ways. This process is confusing. The maintenance programmer frequently has difficulty determining what is being done by the code. By specifying a standard way of implementing these features, the maintenance problem is greatly simplified. People doing the maintenance quickly learn to recognize these work-arounds; this effectively creates an additional characteristic for the implementation language.

In Figure 2-2, standard procedures for implementing the primitive structured constructs in each of four languages are given. These languages range from assembly language to ADA. Standard work-arounds could, of course, be specified for other constructs also. In Figure 2-2, the capital letters A through D represent executable statements, or groups of statements, in the language under consideration. Lower case p represents a logical condition. In the assembly language examples, specific executable statements are used. In the higher-order languages, more general examples are used. It seems rather uninformative to give an example of a sequence as simply A and B written on successive lines.

In some cases, there is more than one standard implementation of a construct. The DO loop in FORTRAN is the standard implementation of a DO UNTIL (p) if the condition ''p'' is ''any integer from a to b.'' If p were a general logical expression, then the implementation would involve an 'IF (.NOT.p) GOTO' statement, as shown in Figure 2-2.

Similarly, when executing a CASE construct in which the condition is a low natural number, the directed GOTO in FORTRAN is an acceptable implementation. If the condition were not a natural number, it would be desirable to simulate the CASE construct by using a set of nested IF statements. In the case of an assembly language, like the Honeywell GMAP, it would be desirable to construct code to convert a more general condition to a condition involving integers, and to use the 'TSX1*' command (i.e., to transfer a specified number of lines or commands down from where you are).

A list of ninety-eight higher-order language requirements is given in the *DOD Requirements for Higher Order Computer Language 'STEELMAN'* (June 1978) report. A sample of some of these requirements together with some examples of languages that do not satisfy these requirements is given in Table 2-1. Determining whether or not a given development needs these features is a nontrivial problem. In fact, understanding the ninety-eight requirements is a nontrivial problem.

The ninety-eight language constructs given in the STEELMAN report are not the easiest to use and understand. It may be desirable to evaluate language features needed by a system using a simpler list. During the competition for building a very large system, we evaluated its system requirements specification to determine a required set of language characteristics. A sample set of characteristics for a specific process is given in Table 2-2. Some of these characteristics were explicitly referenced in the requirements specification;

TABLE 2-1   Sample Language Features Specified in STEELMAN

Feature	Description of Requirement
Syntactic extensions	Inability of the user to modify source language syntax (e.g., FORTRAN IV violated this by permitting the user to change the value of constants, like making a 1 have the value 0).
Mnemonic identifiers	Significant identifiers shall be allowed with a "break character" for use within the identifier (e.g., DAY_OF_WEEK; the initial versions of BASIC violated this feature by permitting parameter names to contain only two characters).
Strong typing	Determine the type of data item during translation.
Type definitions	Define new types of data in programs (e.g., TYPE DAY_OF_WEEK = (SUNDAY, MONDAY, . . . , SATURDAY); DEFINE TODAY OF TYPE DAY_OF_WEEK).
Form of expressions	The parsing of correct expressions shall not depend on the types of their operands.
Resource control	Presence of low-level operations to interrogate and control physical resources (e.g., memory) that are managed (e.g., allocated) by built-in features of the language.

other characteristics were derived from the requirements. The overall characteristics needed for applications programs are given in Figure 2-3.

We could then evaluate the standard languages in terms of these requirements and determine, from a technical viewpoint, a ranking of these languages. Figure 2-3 is a copy

TABLE 2-2   Language Characteristics Needed by the Surveillance Process (§3.7.1.1.3.1 of the Specification)

Language Characteristic	Description
Constants	Whenever dealing with numbers implies use of unchanging types
Strong typing	Accepting various types of data
Type checking	Accepting various types of data
Variable range definition	Specifies parameter range
Variable range checking	Checks the defined range
Interface to assembly	Because data accepted from someplace else may have to go into compiler
Communication between compilation modules	Two modules (in separate programs) may have to communicate
Optimization control	Optimize code in compiler or not (there may be a need to not optimize an on-line processing application for code V&V)
Tasking	Prioritizing processing order
Exception handling	Parity check; input data check
Parallel processing	Tasks using multiple processors
Real-time processing	Ability to handle data at any input speed without a buffer and without loss of data
Reentrant	Processing more than one type of data; may need same code in more than one place

Construct	ADA	COBOL	FORTRAN	GMAP
Sequence: Process { A B }	X:= X + 1; PUT (X);	MOVE A to B ADD C to D	X = X + 1 A = 3.2	LDA THIS STA THAT
Do While: Process (p) — p ⊕ {A, p̄ {Exit	WHILE p LOOP A; END LOOP	PERFORM A UNTIL p	10 IF (.NOT.p) GOTO 99 A GO TO 10 99 CONTINUE	LUPCNT ZERO / COUNT ZERO / STZ COUNT / LDA −11, DL / STA WPCNT / LOOP AOS LUPCNT / TZE ENDLUP / AOS COUNT / TRA LOOP / ENDLUP NULL
Process — {A, p ⊕ {Process, p̄				
Do Until: Process (p) — {A, p̄ ⊕ {Exit, p	LOOP A; EXIT WHEN p; END LOOP	PERFORM A UNTIL p	If p is an integer between a and b, then the standard is: DO 10 I = a,b / A / 10 CONTINUE ——— For any logical condition p, the standard is / 10 A / If (.NOT.p) / GO TO 10 / CONTINUE	LUPCNT ZERO / COUNT ZERO / STZ COUNT / LDA −10, DL / STA LUPCNT / LOOP AOS COUNT / AOS LUPCNT / TNZ LOOP
Process — {A, p̄ ⊕ {Process, p				

If-Then-Else:

Process: $p \oplus \bar{p} \begin{cases} B \\ C \end{cases}$

```
IF p THEN          IF p              IF (p) GO TO 20         LDA    Y
  B;                 PERFORM B         C                     CMPA   X
ELSE               ELSE              20  GO TO 30            TZE    VALUEX
  C;                 PERFORM C        20  B                  CALL   B
END IF;                                30  CONTINUE          TRA    VAL
                                                             CALL   C
                                                      VALUEX  NULL
                                                      VAL
```

Case:

Process: $\begin{cases} 1 = 1 \\ \oplus \; 1 = 2 \\ \oplus \; 1 = 3 \\ \oplus \; 1 = 4 \end{cases} \begin{cases} A \\ B \\ C \\ D \end{cases}$

```
CASE I IS           IF I = 1 THEN          GO TO (I)              Calculate OFFSET
 WHEN 1 = > A;        PERFORM A             100,200,300,400       TSX1*, OFFSET
 WHEN 2 = > B;      ELSE                100  CONTINUE       TAG 1:  NULL
 WHEN 3 = > C;        IF I = 2 THEN          A                     A
 WHEN 4 = > D;          PERFORM B            GO TO 500             TRA ECASE
END CASE;           ELSE                200  CONTINUE       TAG 2:  NULL
                      IF I = 3 THEN          B                     B
                        PERFORM C            GO TO 500             TRA ECASE
                    ELSE                300  CONTINUE       TAG 3:  NULL
                      IF I = 4 THEN          C                     C
                        PERFORM D            GO TO 500             TRA ECASE
                                        400  CONTINUE       TAG 4:  NULL
                                             D                     D
                                        500  CONTINUE       ECASE   NULL
```

Figure 2-2 Examples of allowable program constructs

19

LANGUAGE FEATURES	SYMBOL	COMMENTS
Structures (records, lists, sets, etc.)		
Multidimensional arrays		
IF-THEN-ELSE		
Iterative DO		
DO WHILE		
Modular segmentation		
Block scope		
Visibility of declarations		
Comment convention (clear, easy to distinguish, etc.)		
Clear diagnostic messages		
Individual compilation of modules		
Constants		
Strong typing		
Type checking		
Variable range definition		
Variable range checking		
Character manipulation		
Interface to Assembly language		
Communication between compilation modules		
Optimization control		
Conditional compilation		
Tasking (synchronization)		
Exception handling		
Recursion		
Parallel processing		
Real-time processing		
Reentrant code		

√ = Fully satifies requirement   ● = Partially satisfies requirement   = Does not satisfy requirement

Figure 2-3 Sample language evaluation form.

of the form we used for this evaluation. This information enables us to specify, in advance, work-arounds for requirements that were not satisfied. This evaluation is shown in Figure 2-4.

This procedure is general. It is possible to evaluate languages in terms of the STEELMAN language constructs and to store the results in a data base. A program can then be written for the user to specify which of the language characteristics are required

Language	Advantages	Disadvantages	Requirements Satisfied
ADA	Standardized DOD supported Leading-edge technology	Untested Few programmers	27/28
PASCAL	Widely taught Standardized Simple, clear	Designed as teaching tool Not portable	20/28
PL/1	Standardized Vendor supported Well known	Difficult to debug	17/28
ALGOL 60	Widely taught	Implementation-dependent features Supported only by Burroughs	14/28
C	Can be used in systems programming design Widely available Supports UNIX development system	Medium level language	13/28
CMS-2	DOD approved	Not hardware-vendor supported Relatively unknown Few software development tools Few programmers	10/28
JOVIAL	AF pays support		10/28
COBOL	Well known Standardized Vendor supported	Mostly business applications	9/28
BASIC	Development oriented Interpreted	Not production oriented	6/28
FORTRAN	Vendor supported Standardized	Outmoded structure	6/28

Figure 2-4 Results of a language comparison exercise.

for his job. The output of the program would be a ranking of the languages in the data base and an indication of the unsatisfied language requirements. This was actually done at PRC.

2.2 SOFTWARE HIERARCHY AND THE LEVELING PRINCIPLE

When we first start programming, one of the first things we learn about is subroutines. We learn that there is a library of support software, such as the trigonometric functions, that we can use in our programs. We also learn to partition the program into parts that are small enough to be easily understood.

One of the reasons for doing this is to have a main program that clearly defines the flow of information. It is undesirable to cloud the flow with a bunch of detail on how a particular parameter is calculated. Those details are specified in subroutines. This reasoning is similar to the process used to write a paper. Detailed explanations are frequently placed in an appendix.

Likewise, systems are subdivided into subsystems, configuration items (both hardware and software), components, units, and modules, in that order. This hierarchy is illustrated in Figure 2-5. Note that there may be several layers of components between configuration items and units. When we limit our attention to software, the configuration items are called computer software configuration items (CSCIs) and the components are called computer software components (CSCs).

To digress for a moment, working with large systems and using formal methodologies has one big drawback. There is a multitude of acronyms. I will try to keep these to a minimum and I will try to spell them out occasionally. Whenever you see an acronym, it is pronounced one letter at a time unless I specify to the contrary. CSC is pronounced *see-ess-see*. Later I will point out that a system engineering master plan is represented by SEMP, pronounced *semp* (which rhymes with hemp).

Referring to Figure 2-5, a system is divided into subsystems. Subsystems generally include both hardware and software. Each subsystem is partitioned into a group of configuration items. Some of these configuration items are composed of software (the CSCIs); other configuration items are composed of hardware. We do not mix hardware and software at the configuration item level. As we progress in this book, there will be a variety of examples of software configuration items. Hardware configuration items may be a console configuration. A console configuration could consist of a Microvax II microcomputer, a MEGATEK B color graphic terminal, and a VT241 terminal (the Microvax II and VT241 are products of Digital Equipment Corporation). Other examples of hardware configuration items are given in Chapter 13.

The configuration item level is the level at which we have formal reviews for large systems. We shall discuss various aspects of this level in future chapters. Depending on the size of the software, it is further subdivided as shown in Figure 2-5. There may be several layers of levels at the component (or CSC) level.

Unfortunately, no standard set of terms is used to describe the software hierarchy.

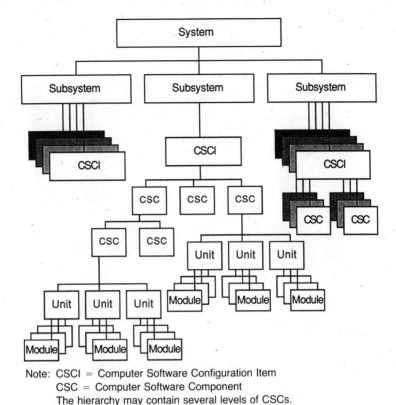

Note: CSCI = Computer Software Configuration Item
CSC = Computer Software Component
The hierarchy may contain several levels of CSCs.

Figure 2-5 System hierarchy.

The terms used in this book correspond to the software hierarchy defined in military standards DOD-STD 2167/2168. Other names for these items are given in Table 2-3.

After reading Table 2-3, it seems that the terminology in the right column (program, subroutine, module, unit) is simplest. In many regards, I prefer this terminology and would recommend using it for smaller companies doing commercial software. I will stay with the terminology in the left column because this is the terminology I use daily. Other terminology would result in an inconsistent book. The rationale behind the long-winded "computer software configuration item" is as follows. Configuration item is used to make terminology consistent with hardware. Computer software is used to emphasize that we are controlling documentation as well as code.

TABLE 2-3 Alternate Names for the Software Hierarchy

Computer software configuration item	Computer program configuration item	Program
Computer software component	Computer program component	Subroutine
Unit	Unit	Module
Module	Module	Unit

A unit should not exceed 200 executable source lines of code and should average about 100 source lines of code. If a component consists of about 3 units, it should average somewhat over 300 lines of code. It would not be unusual for a CSC to have 600 lines of code. The size of a single CSCI depends on several parameters.

These parameters are briefly discussed here and are discussed in greater detail in other chapters. One parameter is the fact that each CSCI is reviewed separately and has a separate set of documentation (such as specifications). Another issue is the physical location of the CSCI. Generally, a CSCI should not be constructed so that its components are

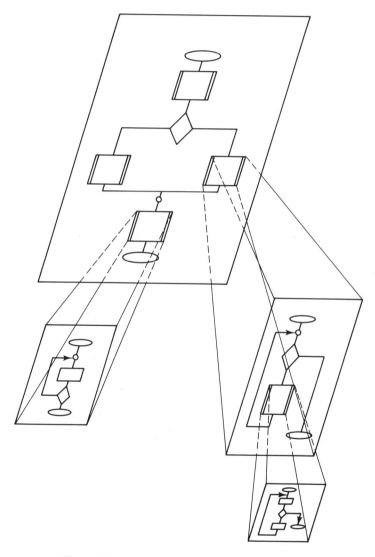

Figure 2-6 Example of leveling applied to flow charts.

located on more than one machine. Another issue is the number of lines of code. A CSCI should be limited to not more than 15,000 executable source lines of code.

If a unit consisted of two modules, each module would be about fifty lines of code, the number of lines that could fit on a single sheet of paper. This notion is the key. It is necessary to present concepts on a single sheet of paper. Thus, for example, a flow chart should not be longer than one page; to accomplish this limitation, some of the processes named in the flow chart require further description. Each of these processes is in turn described on a single page. This process is iterative and is illustrated in Figure 2-6. As we shall see when we discuss various structured analysis techniques, the concept of leveling is a general principle and has many applications.

2.3 TOP-DOWN VERSUS BOTTOM-UP PROGRAMMING

A comparison of top-down to bottom-up programming is illustrated in Figure 2-7. In the case of bottom-up programming, the modules are built first. These are tested and then integrated into units. To test this lower-level software, it is necessary to build other software (or hardware) to simulate its surrounding environment. This test software is generally called a *driver* because it drives the lower-level software by providing inputs that this software would expect to receive from its environment.

In the case of top-down programming, the high-level structure is built first. Interfaces are tested by implementing *stubs* that emulate the lower-level software. A stub may represent any block of code, such as a configuration software component. A stub generally consists of code with the same inputs and outputs as the code it represents, but may perform no other processing.

In practice, the primary sources of errors are changing requirements and inadequate interfaces. Since top-down programming attacks interface problems as early as possible (when they are cheapest to fix), it is no wonder that so many people espouse top-down programming. In theory, a system that has been developed using a top-down programming procedure will have a very short and smooth test and integration phase. There are actually a few cases in which this has happened.

In practice, it is necessary to do both. If we take system software into account, nearly every software development includes commercial off-the-shelf (COTS, rhymes with ''pots'') software. Even if the operating system were excluded from this discussion, most medium and large software developments use either existing applications software or commercial software.

For configuration management purposes, it is not desirable to separate an existing subprogram into units belonging to two or more programs (i.e., CSCIs). This configuration management criterion may conflict with a logical structure of the system functions based on a structured analysis of the applications. That is, the functions performed by a single existing software package may have not been a priori grouped together in a single program (or computer software configuration item) before the ''buy'' or ''reuse'' decision had been made. In this case it is necessary to redefine the programs so that the configuration management requirement is satisfied.

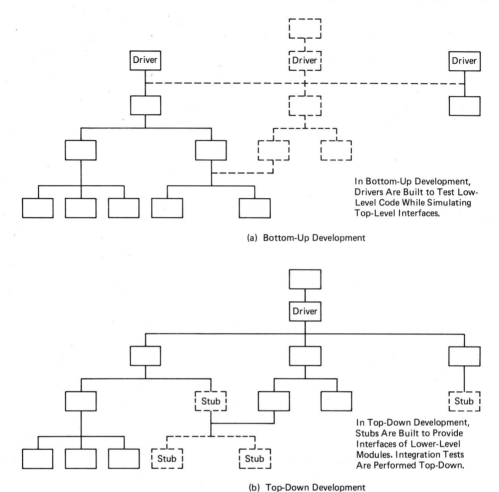

(a) Bottom-Up Development

In Bottom-Up Development,
Drivers Are Built to Test Low-
Level Code While Simulating
Top-Level Interfaces.

In Top-Down Development,
Stubs Are Built to Provide
Interfaces of Lower-Level
Modules. Integration Tests
Are Performed Top-Down.

(b) Top-Down Development

Figure 2-7 Top-down versus bottom-up development.

Thus, reusing existing code has a bottom-up impact on the design of a system. It is generally the logical design of the system that is impacted. The affect should occur before work on the physical design has begun. The concepts of logical and physical design are discussed further, in Section 3.3 and Chapters 8 through 10.

Having digressed from programming to design, let us return to the former. Before specifying the use (or reuse) of existing code or of commercial code, it is good practice to make sure that this code is understood. Both the functionality and interfaces should be tested and incorporated into the design. Thus, reusable and commercial code should be tested in a bottom-up manner, even if the rest of programming is being accomplished in a top-down manner.

The testing of existing code should not be underestimated. The fact that code has been running for a long time is not sufficient to conclude that the code is error free. Furthermore, interfaces and (design) assumptions are not always clearly transferred with the code. While bottom-up test and integration is a practical reality, it is not sufficient to ensure system integrity.

EXERCISE 2.1   List the advantages and disadvantages of both bottom-up and top-down testing.

In Chapters 5 and 11, some guidelines are presented on the amount of testing needed.

2.4 COMMENTING STANDARDS

Despite the bureaucracy imposed by requirements documents, program specifications, and other documentation, the most useful program documentation is the source code comments. This fact should be kept in mind whenever code is being written. If you have doubts, take a look at any code you have written and not looked at for at least six months. Can the code be understood?

When structured design techniques are being used, code is written by following a program specification. The algorithms given in a program specification are typically in the form of a program design language (PDL), Warnier–Orr diagrams, or other equivalent format.

Depending on personal preferences, program design languages are sometimes called structured English or pseudocode. Some people prefer to distinguish between these terms. Modern PDLs are based on a higher-order language, such as ADA, and can be compiled.

In the case of PDL, the PDL is typically embedded in the code. Warnier–Orr diagrams can be directly converted to code. The design aspects of the Warnier–Orr diagrams can be embedded as comments in the code.

There are two types of commenting standards: preface commenting standards and in-line commenting standards. The preface commenting standards are:

- *Name:* Identify the module, specify its version, and specify its entry point.
- *Purpose:* A brief description of the purpose or function of the module shall be given.
- *Input/output:* Specify here the name of each I/O file. Indicate whether it is input, output, or both.
- *Parameter:* Define all input, internal, and output parameters. Specify their domains of definition and the range of values of any functions.
- *Restrictions:* Describe any special or unusual features that restrict module performance characteristics.

- *Abnormal end:* Describe any abnormal end conditions and actions.
- *Method:* Provide a detailed description of the methods used; specify reference documents, tables, algorithms or other pertinent information.

In addition to the preface commenting standards, commentary within the body of the source code shall define the processing to be performed. These comments should describe the reasons for tests and actions. They should be placed before logically grouped blocks of statements. Generally, in-line comments should precede statements containing IF, DO, CASE, CALL, or Input/Output.

2.5 SOFTWARE MODULE DESIGN*

The intent of modularity is to develop code that is easy to understand, maintain, and reuse. For these reasons, each module should perform a single function. As we consider the cohesiveness of each module and coupling among modules, the theme of performing an independent single function permeates the discussion.

The notion of how big a single function can be is fuzzy. To place a bound on this definition, the average number of executable source lines of code (in a high-order language) of a system's modules should not exceed 100. No individual module should have in excess of 200 executable lines of code.

By using subroutines and nested CALLs, very complex functions can be programmed.

Coupling is a measure of the dependence of one module on another module. It may be thought of as the relationship among modules. Cohesion is the substance of a single module. Cohesion relates to the nature of the structure within a module. These two concepts are discussed next.

The five levels of coupling in decreasing order of preference are:

- Data (preferred)
- Common data (undesirable)
- Control (undesirable)
- External (forbidden)
- Content (forbidden)

Data coupling occurs when inputs are passed as explicit parameters. The "CALL f(a,b)" in FORTRAN is an example of data coupling. This is the cleanest boundary and is preferred. When data coupling exists, a module can be thought of as a "black box." A black box consists of a process, input data, and output data. To the world outside the box, data can be inserted and output can be received without any knowledge of how the process is performed. Very complex functions, such as the stress on an aircraft as a function of

---

*There is some inconsistency in terminology in Section 2.5. The term *module* described here corresponds to the term *units* in other sections.

altitude, speed, and load (weight), may be determined totally experimentally. The function may exist as a table of thousands or millions of points with no analytical description.

Passing data from one module to another through common data is possible in many languages. Examples are labeled or global common in FORTRAN and compool tables in JOVIAL. This mechanism of passing data is undesirable. Depending on the sequencing of operations, data in common can be altered by a third module before the intended module reads the information. These errors are difficult to locate and can cause disastrous results. This approach should be forbidden for real-time systems.

A control variable determines the type of processing to be performed. Two modules are control coupled if one of the modules passes or sends a control variable to the other module. The determination of whether or not data passed are control variables or external data depends solely on the perception of the sending module. If module A is control coupled to module B, then, from the viewpoint of module B, module A is not an independent function because module B knows something about the processing of module A; that is, module A is not a black box. If the control variable were passed by using common data, the problem is compounded. Because of possible erroneous changes in the common data, incorrect processing may occur. Errors of this nature are significantly more difficult to locate, or determine, than errors involving an incorrect calculation.

External coupling is the interface level in which a module receives its input data by inspecting and using variables that are defined and reside in another module. This type of coupling is very bad because changes in one module cannot be made without inspecting other modules for unintentional effects. Maintenance becomes very expensive and difficult. External coupling should be forbidden from all programming practices.

Content coupling is the worst of all types of coupling. Content coupling requires one module to understand the internal mechanics of another module. Examples of content coupling are sharing code (but not in a subroutine relationship), using a set of internal data (not externally declared) of another module, and knowing internal switch settings of another module. With content coupling, a change in code of one module can change the function of another module. Content coupling should also be forbidden in all programming practices.

EXERCISE 2.2   Using any programming language that you desire, write a series of programs that provide examples of each type of coupling.

The second attribute of module design is cohesion, or binding. Cohesion is a measure of the association of the elements within a module. There are six types of cohesion. These are listed, roughly from best to worst:

- Functional (required)
- Sequential
- Communicational
- Temporal

- Logical

- Coincidental

The premise of structured programming is that each module should perform a single function or logical transformation. Each statement within the module should contribute to this process. Generally, a module has functional cohesion if its purpose can be described in English using a simple declarative sentence. An example is "REMOVE ADDRESSES WITHOUT ZIP CODES FROM THE FILE."

Functional cohesion is the strongest form of cohesion. Most company and government standards require functional cohesion. As long as a module exhibits functional cohesion, it is irrelevant whether it also exhibits other types of cohesion.

Any module with multiple entry points or multiple exit points (except for exit points resulting from error conditions) either violates functional cohesion or possesses an unacceptable form of coupling with another module. Thus, these should be avoided. That is, each module should have a single entry point and a single exit point.

A module is said to have sequential cohesion if it is based on the control structure organization. This typically results when a problem is flow charted and the modules are then specified from the flow chart. For example, the module whose description is "SEARCH ADDRESS FILE. ELIMINATE DUPLICATES." illustrates a simple sequence of two functions. Other clues of sequential cohesion are module descriptions that are either conditional or iterative. Examples are, respectively, "ADD ADDRESS TO FILE UNLESS ZIP CODE IS ABSENT" and "UPDATE TRAFFIC FILE UNTIL OPERATOR INTERRUPT."

Communicational cohesion has at least two definitions. One definition is modularization of a program based on grouping input and output activities in the same module. A module that performs all I/O operations on a data base exemplifies this definition. Some people will argue that this type of cohesion is good. By isolating all DBMS I/O operations to a single module, it is possible to limit the effort required to change DBMS interfaces. Unless this approach is used, one is tied to a particular vendor for a long period of time.

The other definition (Tausworthe, 1979) of communicational cohesion is a module with sequential cohesion and whose components communicate with each other. The submodules either reference the same data or communicate among one another. An example of this type of cohesion is a module whose description is "RETRIEVE COST DATA AND PLOT RESULTS." Using this definition, communicational cohesion is fairly strong.

A module whose basis is temporal is designed to handle time-oriented activities, such as initialization or termination. In this case, specific actions needed by a group of modules are grouped together and performed at one time by a single module. For example, a module whose description is "RESET ALL FLAGS" or "DOWNLOAD ALL FILES" has temporal cohesion.

Modularizing a program by grouping logically similar activities is termed logical cohesion. An example is a module that prints error messages originating in various segments. This type of module typically induces control coupling of modules.

Coincidental cohesion occurs when the elements of the module have little or no relationship to one another. Sometimes coincidental cohesion results when someone overzealously limits the number of statements in a module. This can also result from attempts to eliminate duplicate code by creating modules of convenience.

Relationships among modules in real-time systems are discussed by Gomaa (1984). He describes loosely coupled and tightly coupled message communication modules; he also describes synchronization among modules. Some design techniques he defines are given in Chapter 9.

2.6 DEVIATIONS FROM PROGRAMMING STANDARDS

Suppose a system has been built the old-fashioned way. The code is "classic spaghetti." Let us next suppose that our job is to convert this to structured code. What is the relationship between the number of lines of executable code in these two systems? *Guess the answer before continuing.* Based on the results we had in converting a major Air Force system (in COBOL), the ratio of structured code to spaghetti code is the same as the ratio of the number of words in the third sentence of this paragraph to the number of words in the first sentence of this paragraph.

The problem with structured code is that it is significantly longer than unstructured code. The most common reasons for deviating from structured code are that the code either is not fast enough or takes up too much room; that is, structured code cannot be written to satisfy the required function within the allocated resources. Sometimes these problems can be avoided by having software engineers involved in the requirements and design process when these allocations are being decided. Generally, this is not the case.

The need to deviate from structured programming is most likely to arise in real-time systems. As it is used here, we distinguish between real-time and near-real-time systems. A near-real-time system is one that, on the average, needs to keep up with live data, but it has a buffer so that it can occasionally fall slightly behind. A radar position processor is generally near real time. It needs to keep up with the "pings." The radar communications processor is real time; it must process the first ping before receiving the signal from the second ping.

It is important to note that we are discussing deviation from structured programming here, not deviations from structured design. When a deviation is going to occur, it should first be approved by appropriate management. When these deviations are made, they should not be done in such a way as to make the code machine dependent. Sometimes programmers play games with chips to determine operations that are not officially part of the manufacturer's operating system. If these neat tricks are used, you may have code that is undocumented and nearly impossible to maintain. If the manufacturer subsequently updates the chip design and uses that "operation" to mean something else, then the code may need major rewrites to be usable. That is, a long gap in operational ability may occur.

An extensive discussion of real time and multiprogrammed structure programs is given by Tausworthe (1979). That reference is recommended for further reading on this subject. Gomaa (1984) discusses the design of real-time systems.

EXERCISE 2.3   The computer program given in Figure 2-8 was written in 1973 using CDC FORTRAN IV Extended. Evaluate this program against modern programming practices and module construction. Extract the essentials of this program into a design using any technique desired (a flow chart is acceptable). Rewrite this program using modern practices.

```
       SUBROUTINE CNTROID(N,M,K,IEV1,I,XC,X,K1,G,H,KDIM,CNSTR1),
    ,                     RETURNS(VIOLATE)
C PURPOSE
C   TO CALCULATE THE CENTROID OF POINTS
C SUBROUTINES REQUIRED
C   CNSTR1
C DESCRIPTION OF PARAMETERS
C   MOST HAVE BEEN PREVIOUSLY DEFINED IN SUBROUTINE BOX OPT
C   K1    THE FIRST K1-1 POINTS ARE COMPUTED FOR THE CENTROID WITH THE
C         EXCEPTION , IF I.GT.0, OF THE ITH POINT.  THIS IS USED WITH
C         K1.NE.K+1 IN A VERSION OF INITIAL (NOT VERSION 8).
C NONSTANDARD RETURN
C   USED TO INDICATE THAT THE COMPUTED CENTROID VIOLATES THE CONSTRAINTS
        DIMENSION X(KDIM,M),XC(M)
        DIMENSION G(M),H(M)
        K2 = K1 - 1
        DO 20 J = 1,N
         XC(J) = 0.
         DO 10 IL = 1,K2
          XC(J) = XC(J) + X(IL,J)
10       CONTINUE
         RK = K2
        IF(I.EQ.0) GO TO 21
        XC(J) = (XC(J)-X(IEV1,J))/(RK - 1.)
        GO TO 20
21      XC(J) = XC(J)/RK
20      CONTINUE
        II = 0
        CALL CNSTR1(N,M,KDIM,X,G,H,II,XC)
        DO 30 J = 1,M
        IF (XC(J).LT.G(J).OR.XC(J).GT.H(J))  GO TO 40
30      CONTINUE
        RETURN
40      PRINT 1,(XC(J),J=1,M)
        RETURN VIOLATE
1       FORMAT(* THE CENTROID LISTED BELOW DOES NOT SATISFY THE CONSTRAINT
       *S*/10F12.3))
C
        END
```

Figure 2-8 Sample program written in 1973 CDC FORTRAN.

2.7 ELECTRONIC UNIT DEVELOPMENT FOLDERS

A unit development folder (UDF) contains all the information about a software unit that is needed to determine the status of the unit and to maintain the unit. The purpose of the UDF is to make the software both more visible and easier to audit.

This information is generally kept in a notebook. Consequently, another name for the UDF is the software development notebook. The problem with UDFs is that they are difficult to control and onerous to maintain. Thus, many large projects do not keep them.

In the following paragraphs, the contents of a unit development folder are described. Next we discuss the concept of an electronic unit development folder (EUDF). The purpose of the EUDF is ostensibly to make it convenient to maintain the folder and easy to control it. This purpose itself is important enough, but, as we shall see in the next chapter, the EUDF actually has the kernel of a state-of-the-art software development facility.

A typical outline for the UDF is:

- Status sheets
- Requirements
- Detailed design descriptions
- Functional capabilities
- Code
- Test case descriptions
- Test case results
- Software problem report log
- Software change order log
- Miscellaneous

The UDF contains a separate section of each for these items. It also contains all information associated with its modules. Thus, this outline is repeated and sections exist on a module basis as well as on a unit basis.

The unit development folder is critical to the development of large or complex systems. These folders should exist in some form for all such developments. People who become accustomed to using them do not see how projects can survive without them. The absence of unit development folders is a major contributor to the loss of control of a system.

The amazing part about their lack of use is the ease with which they can be (at least partially) developed in electronic form. Major computer manufacturers have relational data bases and software packages to track versions of code. System requirements can be associated with units using a relational data base, and code can be associated with units using another (file management) package. By placing both under the control of a system librarian, a rudimentary EUDF is established.

A sample status sheet for a unit development folder is given in Figure 2-9. The requirements section contains a list of requirements specified in the System Requirements Specification that are addressed by this unit. In an electronic UDF, the requirements would be stored in a file, and the contents of this section would simply be requirement identifier numbers. If the programmer wanted to see the requirements, the software would automatically retrieve the referenced requirements from the requirements file.

Detailed design descriptions include data-flow diagrams, process descriptions, program design language, and all other design descriptors. Descriptions of the input and out-

Module Name: _____ CI #: _____
Unit Name: _____ CI #: _____

Responsible Person: _____
Tel: _____ Organization: _____

Section Number	Description	Date Due	Date Complete	Originator	Reviewer	Date Reviewed
1	Requirements					
2a	Preliminary design					
2b	Detailed design					
2c	Walkthrough					
2d	As built					
2e	Message flow analysis					
3	Functional capabilities list					
4	Code					
5	Test plan and Procedure					
6	Test cases					
7	Problem reports					
8	Notes					
9	Reviewer's comments					

Comments: _____
_____
_____
_____

Figure 2-9 Sample status sheet for a unit development folder.

put data are also contained in this section. In an electronic version of the UDF, the metadata (i.e., the data about the system data) would probably be stored in the data dictionary. Unit-related data could be retrieved by means of DBMS searches.

Sample problem report logs and change logs are given in Figure 2-10. Again, the

Date Submitted	Form Identification	Problem Description	Affected Items	Urgency	Status	Reviewer	Date Review	Recertification Method

Figure 2-10   Software problem report and change request log.

process would be simplified with an electronic UDF. Most of the data in the problem report log would be automatically retrieved from the entries to a software problem report form (a sample problem report form and a sample software change request form are given in Chapter 11). Changes to code could be captured automatically using commercial packages. Code version control packages are available for all minicomputers and mainframes produced by major manufacturers. The electronic UDF needs to interact with these tools to automatically create a log. Changes to design may have to be entered manually.

So far, the electronic software development folder seems like a simple thing to implement. Unfortunately, the difficult part has not been discussed. In a multiuser environment, it is necessary to impose controls on who is able to change data in the unit development folder. These authorizations vary with the status of the unit.

If you want to build an electronic unit development folder, you should do it using extensive prototyping. First build a simplified single-user version of the EUDF. Use a microcomputer with the capabilities of at least an Apple MacIntosh and a data base with the capabilities of at least DBase /// or Omnis 3 Plus. This approach will enable you to define all the needed relationships. It also will provide time to think about and resolve many of the problems involved with a multiuser environment. For example, how does a requirements file get updated if a change is made to a UDF at a remote location?

Next, implement a version of the EUDF on a mainframe or minicomputer. Continue to revise and enhance the EUDF until you are satisfied with it.

REFERENCES

BOHM C., and G. JACOPINI, "Flow Diagrams, Turing Machines, and Languages with only Two Formation Rules," *Communications of the ACM*, vol. 9, May 1966, pp. 366–371.

DEPARTMENT OF DEFENSE, "Requirements for Higher Order Computer Programming Languages: 'STEELMAN'," June 1978 (available from Defense Technical Information Center, AD# A059444).

DIJKSTRA, R. W., "GOTO Statement Considered Harmful," *Communications of the ACM*, vol. 11, March 1968, pp. 147–148 (also, cf. pp. 538 and 541).

GOMAA, H., "A Software Design Method for Real Time Systems," *Communications of the ACM*, vol. 27, no. 9, Sept. 1984, pp. 938–949.

TAUSWORTHE, R. C., *Standardized Development of Computer Software*, Parts I and II, Prentice-Hall, Inc., Englewood Cliffs, N.J., 1979.

CHAPTER 3

A Life-Cycle Approach to Software Engineering

We defined software engineering as the art and science of managing the operations of computers. The software engineering process is divided into a sequence of phases ranging from concept definition to maintenance. As a whole, this range is called the software life cycle.

While discussing the software life cycle, we also present an overview of our approach to software engineering. Part of the discussion of this approach will seem more like a discussion of management than technical work. Actually, that perception is in keeping with our definition of engineering.

Many good technical people do not want to "do management." Actually, they do not want the aggravation of being involved with personnel problems, and they prefer not to spend their time in lengthy policy meetings. It is not possible to be a senior technical person without being a good task manager. A chief scientist frequently is able to set her or his own schedule. Other senior technical staff are generally expected to serve as task leaders and to provide technical guidance to more junior personnel. This guidance and leadership must take into account schedules, budget, deliverables, and dependencies.

Another attribute of doing good quality work is understanding the environment in which you work. Part of that environment is your supervisor. By understanding your supervisor's job, you will be able to perform your own tasks more effectively.

The individual phases that comprise the software life cycle are shown in Figure 3-1. The software life cycle is given in the middle row of this figure. Also shown in this illustration are the system engineering life cycle (the top row) and the hardware engineering life cycle (the bottom row). It is usually necessary to view software engineering as part of a complete system that includes hardware.

Each major phase ends with a review of its products, with the exception of the plan-

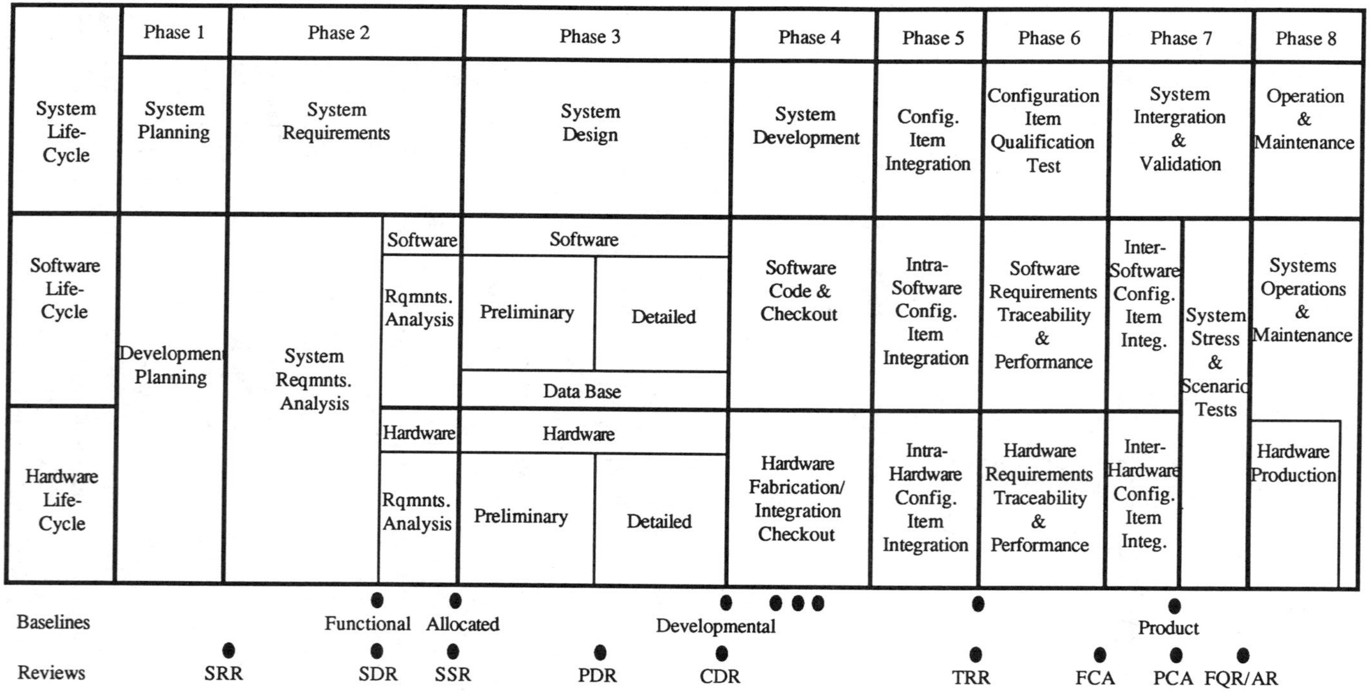

Figure 3-1 Phases of the software development life cycle.

	Phase 1	Phase 2	Phase 3	Phase 4	Phase 5	Phase 6	Phase 7	Phase 8
System Life-Cycle	System Planning	System Requirements	System Design	System Development	Config. Item Integration	Configuration Item Qualification Test	System Integration & Validation	Operation & Maintenance
Software Life-Cycle	Development Planning	System Reqmnts. Analysis — Software Rqmnts. Analysis	Software (Preliminary / Detailed); Data Base	Software Code & Checkout	Intra-Software Config. Item Integration	Software Requirements Traceability & Performance	Inter-Software Config. Item Integ.; System Stress & Scenario Tests	Systems Operations & Maintenance
Hardware Life-Cycle		Hardware Rqmnts. Analysis	Hardware (Preliminary / Detailed)	Hardware Fabrication/Integration Checkout	Intra-Hardware Config. Item Integration	Hardware Requirements Traceability & Performance	Inter-Hardware Config. Item Integ.	Hardware Production
Baselines		Functional Allocated		Developmental			Product	
Reviews	SRR	SDR SSR	PDR CDR	CDR	TRR	FCA	PCA FQR/AR	

AR — Acceptance Review
CDR — Critical Design Review
FCA — Functional Configuration Audit
FQR — Formal Qualification Review
FQT — Formal Qualification Test

PCA — Physical Configuration Audit
PDR — Preliminary Design Review
PQT — Preliminary Qualification Test
SDP — Software Development Plan
SDR — Systems Design Review

SRR — System Requirements Review
SSP — Software Standards and Procedures
SSR — Software Specification Review
TRR — Test Readiness Review

38

ning phase. A review of the products of the planning phase occurs during the early part of the requirements phase. This delay in the review occurs because it is important to review the requirements specified from a user's perspective in the operational concept, test concept, and maintenance concept (products of system planning) together with some system-level requirements (derived from the user's requirements by the system engineers).

The reviews specified in Figure 3-1 all have long names and are referred to by their acronyms. These names are the ones used by the Department of Defense. For large projects, it is necessary to have all these reviews. In nongovernment work, you may want to call them by other names that are more meaningful to your industry. The content of the reviews should remain unchanged. For smaller projects, it may not be necessary to have all these formal reviews. However, at a minimum, there should be informal reviews covering much of the material that would be presented in formal reviews of larger products. The reviews that could be skipped depend on both the environment and the nature of the problem.

Associated with each review is a system baseline or an update of a system baseline. The purpose of these baselines is to capture the system data and control these data. Activities associated with the control and management of the system data are called configuration management activities. These activities are discussed in Chapter 11.

Those of you who have worked with system developments may be accustomed to working with a life cycle that differs from the one given in Figure 3-1. The life cycle presented here is compliant with military standards DOD-STD 2167 and 2168. As we shall see in Section 3.2, the fact that there are many different system life cycles is really not a problem. The same data need to be produced, independently of how the phases are defined. The baselines and reviews are included on the figure because they are useful in calibrating this life cycle with other definitions of the life cycle.

Understanding the life cycle is a key to our approach. *You should never be lost if you understand the life cycle and if you know the phase in which your task resides.* With a knowledge of the life cycle, you should be able to deduce the information you need and the products you need to produce. In the following subsections, we show why this is true.

3.1 WHAT GOALS WILL THIS METHODOLOGY HELP ACHIEVE?

The underlying idea of the software engineering approach is to view the life cycle from a data viewpoint rather than an activities viewpoint. Think of each phase of the life cycle as a black box (in the classical electrical engineering sense). A black box is opaque to the outside observer. This observer can measure the data going into the box and measure the data produced by the box. The data produced by each phase include system design data (such as requirements, data-flow diagrams, and code), management data (such as documentation, schedules, and milestones), financial data, and maintenance data. As we shall see, a focus on the system data will enable us to develop new concepts for software support environments that include other advanced concepts, like the ADA Program Support Environment (APSE), as a subset.

The goals of the methodology described in this book are enhanced productivity and increased management control. These goals are common to most, if not all, methodologies. The features of this methodology aimed at enhancing productivity are:

- Focus on design information, rather than presentation format
- Criteria for selecting design techniques tailored to the project
- Life-cycle traceability of requirements
- On-line access to management and development tools

The focus on design information rather than presentation format allows us to use any structured analysis or design technique. For example, programmers might like to use Nassi–Shneiderman charts (described in Section 9.1). These structured flow charts graphically highlight program flow. However, in the event that you are maintaining a large system and storing system documentation on line, or in digital form, this technique is inefficient.

The charts are cumbersome to maintain, and they must be entered into the computer by programmers; they are too complicated for data-entry clerks. Warnier–Orr diagrams (discussed in Section 9.6) are much simpler to draw and can be entered by data-entry clerks. In this case, significant cost savings can be achieved by using the simpler presentation technique.

Another alternative to flow charts is to use a program design language. Several commercial program design languages are available. The information specified with program design languages is easy to maintain and to store on line.

As an aid to selecting analysis and design techniques to be used on the project, we have developed tables that show usage characteristics and information captured for each technique. Usage characteristics include the ability to model existing systems, ease of communication with client, and notational simplicity. Information captured includes functional hierarchy, data flow, and event sequencing. These tables are given in Section 7.3.

In addition to providing characteristics of techniques as a function of the life cycle, an inventory of requirements and design techniques is presented in Chapter 9. Each technique is described to the level of detail expected of a standards document. That is, the graphical representation procedures are described.

There are books thicker than this one devoted to individual structured analysis techniques. For some of these techniques, there are training courses in which over a half-dozen thick notebooks are distributed to each student. The level of detail presented in Chapter 9 is generally not really adequate for teaching how to use a method (unless you are already familiar with structured analyses and have used similar methods). References are provided in the bibliography for the reader who needs greater detail.

Life-cycle traceability of requirements is key to the development of systems. It is the requirements that the final product is measured against. Simply put, if we don't know what the system is required to do, we cannot say that it does its job. This traceability is a primary reason that it is necessary to use a System Design Data Base (SDDB) and why the System Design Data Base is a cornerstone of the methodology described here.

On-line access to management and development tools is the direction that the industry is taking. To put this in perspective, systems engineers are probably the last working group that still does its job without the aid of computers. It is a classic case of "the shoe-maker's son."

Nearly everybody who has worked as a computer industry professional has in her or his bookcase a 3-inch thick standards document, configuration management document, or project document that has never been opened. Software tools and documentation will simply not be used unless they are easy to use. This is human nature and our software methodology must take it into account.

On-line access helps, but by itself does not make documentation and tools easy to use. One technique to enhance the use of the documentation is to generate a mapping of the sections of each project document (e.g., software development plan or software standards and procedures) to the phases of the life cycle. This chart will enable the user to focus more easily on the sections that apply to her or his particular task.

Features aimed at improving management control are:

- Integration of project monitoring with software development
- Plans and standards that are easy to use
- Total systems view of the software development process
- Development of test requirements and plans independently of the development group

The integration of project monitoring with software development can be achieved by designing the System Design Data Base in a broad enough manner. This integration is helpful to both project managers and the technical staff. The project manager can relate specific tasks to products and schedules. The system design is available for her or his inspection. Most technical staff are interested in the overall status of their project and in what their next task will be. This knowledge helps motivate them. Just as project managers cringe at the "95% done" rule, the technical staff cringes at the "this urgent three-week task is due on Monday" rule.

Your project plans and standards should be easy to use if you expect anyone to use them. They should be reasonably short, 50 to 150 pages, even for large projects.

If project engineers have ready access to terminals, project documentation should be stored on line. This way it is possible for them to review documentation without searching bookcases, going to the project library, or returning to their office (as the case might be).

The total systems view of the software development process is discussed in Section 3.2, where the life cycle is also described. In Section 3.3 the System Design Data Base (SDDB) is discussed in greater detail. It is shown how the SDDB can be used to keep track of the system design and project data. The SDDB permits us to focus on design and maintenance information and to use any structured technique or software tool that is convenient. It is also used to integrate project monitoring with software development.

A view of an ideal software support facility is presented in Section 3.4. It is ideal because we all wish we had it but nobody does. By the time you read this book, some companies may have such a facility. PRC has already developed a product control environment. This is a significant step toward establishing the ideal environment. Teledyne Brown Engineering has an environment in which structured analysis techniques have been combined with configuration management and simulations. This is another significant step forward. At Avtec Systems, we have developed a prototype electronic unit development folder and have integrated it with configuration management tools.

Most major aerospace companies have invested a significant amount of money developing their own software development environment. These vary widely in terms of the tools they provide and the control they impose on the development process. These environments are considered proprietary and very little information about them is published. Even when you are given a tour of their facility, it is hard to get answers to key questions regarding the capabilities of these environments.

After a data base that captures the system design data is built, it should be enhanced to permit the specification of dynamic relationships. This capability is very useful for maintenance. The combination of the ability to provide relationships dynamically with relational data bases provides a data base that we call a *knowledge data base*. The relation of knowledge data bases to expert systems is discussed in Chapter 10. An example of how a knowledge data base can be used for maintenance is also given in Chapter 10.

The ideal software support facility is discussed here because it gives an idea of the direction in which the practice of software engineering is developing.

The final topic discussed in this overview is metrics and statistics. At this time virtually no company in the United States publishes statistics on software development that it maintains at a corporate level. There are few accepted metrics used to estimate the cost or schedule for producing a system, for estimating the progress during production of a system, or for evaluating the quality of a system after it is produced. Section 3.5 is devoted to this topic because of the need to elevate our awareness of metrics and statistics.

3.2 SOFTWARE ENGINEERING LIFE CYCLE

The software development life cycle is given in Figure 3-1. It consists of 12 phases and subphases. In theory, a development begins in system planning and proceeds sequentially through the phases to operations and maintenance. The last phase should be retirement. We should develop a set of criteria so that we will know when it is no longer feasible to continue the evolutionary process; that is, we need to predict when a redesign is needed. The criteria are application and industry dependent. They are generally expressed in terms of return on investment and the design limits of the existing or planned system.

I have never seen the retirement phase included in a description of the system life cycle. The government ignores it.

The process of analyzing design limits and planning for increased capacity or the redesign of systems is called *capacity management*. A brief overview of capacity management is given in Chapter 12.

Decisions to develop new automation capabilities are based similarly on return on investment. For example, the Japanese auto makers (cf. *High Technology*, August 1986) do not permit the development of any manufacturing automation (i.e., new robotic capability) unless it can be demonstrated that a net savings of $90,000 will be realized. The exact dollar required varies from company to company. The Japanese account for retirement of equipment in the manufacturing plant through a vigorous program of determining how all aspects of the process can be automated. This criterion results in the continuous introduction of new technology and removal of older, less productive, systems.

Some commonly accepted myths about the life cycle are:

- A life cycle approach is strictly sequential.
- The use of prototypes cannot be accommodated by the life cycle.
- Top-down testing contradicts the life-cycle approach because integration is listed after coding and unit test.
- Expert systems (alias artificial intelligence) cannot be developed in accordance with the life cycle (snide remark overheard at least once: this is a black art too sophisticated for engineers to understand).
- Using the life-cycle approach imposes a large bureaucracy.

Each of these myths will be briefly discussed. The life cycle is listed in a sequential manner because the baselines and reviews are sequential in time. Systems requirements do change throughout the system life. In maintenance, we call the subsequent actions enhancements. When the system requirements review is held, an agreement is reached about the requirements at that time. A baseline is formed and the contractor is asked to build to those requirements.

During system design, new requirements are frequently imposed. It is necessary to do a *requirements analysis* to determine their impact, even though we are still in the design phase of the life cycle. As we shall see, one of the benefits of the ideal environment is that it includes a requirements traceability matrix that permits the program manager to determine which parts of the system (to the unit level) are affected by the changes. This knowledge of the units affected is critical to the quantitative determination of cost and schedule changes.

Another aspect of the sequential life cycle is that the phases are defined sequentially in terms of baseline products and reviews; we have not specified the activities. It is perfectly reasonable to build test plans and procedures during the design and coding phases. In fact, a primary criterion to be applied to specifying a requirement is that the requirement should be testable. One should consider designing and building test materials in the requirements phase.

It is also reasonable to use a development process that follows a *build a little, test a little* approach. Not only is this reasonable, but it is actually required in cases where we are utilizing reusable or commercial code. This code affects our design; it would be unprofessional to specify its use without testing it to make sure that the interfaces and functions are really understood.

Similar statements could be used about prototypes. Prototypes are used to evaluate design concepts and to determine requirements. When built, they need to be controlled just like any other portion of the system (but they do not need formal review like the operational software would need). If prototype software becomes operational software, it needs to be tested and subjected to the same standards and quality assurance processes as the other software.

Another type of system whose formulation is very dynamic is an expert system. Expert systems generally use a LISP-based (or type) language to dynamically establish relationships among objects. Their purpose is to capture the decision-making skills of experts and to then use these decisions to process data. The currently successful applications of expert systems have been in fields with well-established diagnostic procedures. These fields include medicine and mineral exploration.

Expert systems are especially amenable to rapid prototyping. It is easy to build relationships and to "put software together." It is also easy not to document or have the same type of formal reviews required of other software. When the computer interface looks reasonable, it is conducive for everybody to nod their heads in approval. Meanwhile, the behavior of the software may not be documented; assumptions may not have been scrutinized.

It is critical to avoid slipping into the modus operandi of the 1960s, when FORTRAN programming was treated the same way. Claims that the process is too dynamic to control and document properly are simply wrong. Expert system software can be delivered, within the context of the software environment described later, in the same way that conventional software can be delivered. Requirements and specifications for expert systems are appropriate; only the actual specification of relationships among objects is dynamic. These relationships can be specified a posteriori. Since these relationships are subject to change as operational knowledge increases, these relationships are often treated as data items.

The most difficult myth to debunk is that the imposition of the life cycle goes hand in hand with the imposition of a large bureaucracy. Part of the difficulty with this myth is that many people think that all configuration management is bureaucracy. It is true that some formalism is introduced, but with the proper environment this formalism can be constructed in a way that limits its bureaucratic aspects. The way to accomplish this goal is to make the controls mostly transparent to the user.

Most people define the beginning of the software life cycle to be the Software Requirements Analysis phase. (This notion is so ingrained in the profession that even the new military standard on software development, DOD-STD 2167, specifies the beginning of the software life cycle this way.) This phase seems like a reasonable place to start until you live through a few horror stories. After the scars heal, one concludes that the software engineers should be involved with all the early phases of development. Many problems and risks are mitigated by including the software engineers in decisions related to allocating performance requirements to software modules.

I strongly recommend that the project-specific software development plan be developed during Phase 1. As the project progresses, the software development plan can be updated. Unfortunately, a project usually begins in the middle of the life cycle. In this event, the software development plan should be developed either as part of a proposal (for those of us in the contracting business) or at the very beginning of the project.

The need for a software development plan is independent of the size of the project.

For small projects of short duration, the software development plan could be only a few pages thick. It is still needed because the software development plan specifies the schedule, what is to be produced, organizational responsibility, and the approach to accomplishing the tasks.

For larger projects, we should approach each task from the following viewpoints:

- Where are we in the life cycle?
- What products must we produce?
- What reviews do we have to prepare?
- What items of the work breakdown structure (WBS) apply to this phase?

In other words, this approach to software engineering requires systemic planning for each task. When competing for work from the government, the planning is generally done during the preparation of a proposal in response to a solicitation. An example of this type of planning for a large technical support project is now given.

The purpose of the solicitation was to state requirements for systems engineering support in a general subject area. The types of tasks included performing requirements analyses, developing small systems, maintaining existing systems, and providing independent testing of systems under development by other contractors.

Included in the solicitation was a work breakdown structure. Tasks beginning anyplace in the life cycle would be placed under this contract. One of the things we did to demonstrate that we understand the systems engineering process was to graph the top levels of the work breakdown structure as a function of the life cycle. This graph is given in Figure 3-2. It tells us what types of tasks need to be performed during any specified phase of the life cycle.

Figure 3-2 shows the relationship between the life cycle and:

- Program reviews specified in MIL-STD 1521
- Program baselines specified in MIL-STD 1521
- A typical work breakdown structure
- Project documentation

A work breakdown structure is a hierarchical structure in which the nodes are tasks. The sum total of these tasks corresponds to all the work that needs to be done for the job under consideration. It is not unusual for a work breakdown structure to have a dozen levels of hierarchy in the case of large jobs. For graphical presentations, as in Figure 3-2, the third level of the work breakdown structure is usually adequate. As we see, this graph is a mapping of the tasks to the life cycle. Thus, if I am given a task associated with work breakdown structure (WBS) element 252, Data Base Design, I know that I am in either the preliminary design phase or the requirements phase. By asking whether the CSCI in question has passed its system design review (SDR) or software specification review (SSR), I can narrow the position of the task in the life cycle to a particular phase.

Also shown in the very complicated Figure 3-2 is a documentation schedule. The

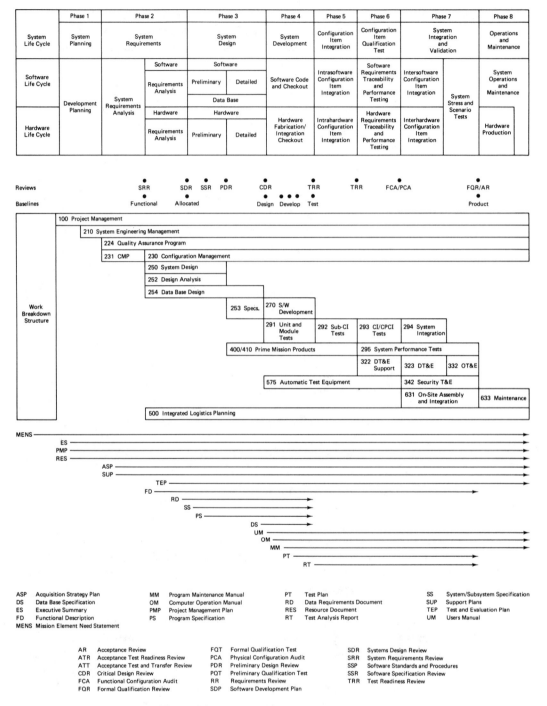

Figure 3-2 Mapping tasks and deliverables to the life cycle.

documentation acronym is positioned at the place of the life cycle when a draft version should be completed. The arrows denote the fact that these documents are revised as the system is being developed. The arrowhead denotes the time of the life cycle at which the final document should be delivered. This documentation schedule is based on a Naval Electronics Systems Command (now the Naval Space and Warfare Command) instruction.

All this may seem fine, but you probably don't work on military projects or, more specifically, on projects that require compliance with the standards selected here. Figure 3-3 compares the software life cycle used in this book with other software life cycles. Since you probably also do not work for NSA, EPA, nor HHS (née HEW), I have left two rows blank.

EXERCISE 3.1   Before continuing to read, use one of the blank rows in Figure 3-3 to try to fill in the life-cycle phases for a project on which you are currently working. After you read Chapter 7, come back to this figure and use the second row to fill in the life cycle correctly. If you are like me, you won't get it right the first time.

Although a strong emphasis has been placed on government standards, the methods apply to all systems development, including industrial environments.

Program reviews are both very formal and very costly for large programs. For programs costing over $20 million, it is not unusual for 125 people to attend each review. If you start counting the client (e.g., the government personnel), an independent testing contractor, and the key people from the developer's organization, it really adds up. The cost for such a review is about $4 per second for the duration of the review.

If you discount the cost of people who are not in the developer's organization, but include the cost of preparation, the number remains unchanged. Thus, if the review lasts for one week, the cost should be about $580,000. That is a lot of money. When bidding on contracts and trying to price low enough to win, the real budgetary and schedule cost of the reviews is often underestimated or simply ignored. Note that the danger of a cost overrun on large programs increases before you start.

On smaller jobs (e.g., $1 million to $7 million), the cost of a formal review may drop to as low as $1 per second, or to about $85,000 for a three-day review. There is a moral here: even if you are working on small jobs with informal reviews, the review process is expensive and takes time. It should be included in your cost and schedule estimate.

Program baselines are key to the configuration management process. They are generally established at reviews and updated as necessary by configuration management personnel.

Work breakdown structures are discussed as part of project management in Section 7.2. At first glance they seem like an unreasonable imposition of bureaucracy. They aren't. For proper project planning and control, it is always necessary to describe the project in terms of tasks and subtasks and to plan schedules and prepare cost estimates for these tasks and subtasks. While performing the project, charges should be levied against each task so that actual costs can be compared to budgeted cost. The use of a standardized

DOD-STD 2167/2168 Compliant

System Planning	System Requirements Analysis	S/W Requirements Analysis	Software Design		Code and Checkout	Intra-CSCI Integration	S/W Validation and Performance Testing	Inter-CSCI Integration	Stress and Scenario Tests	Operations and Maintenance
			Preliminary	Detailed						

AF Reg 300-15

Conceptual	Definition	Development		Test and Operation	

DOD-STD 7935.1-S

Initiation	Definition	Development		Integration, Test, and Installation	Evaluation	O&M	Revised Operations
		Design	Programming				

NSA

System Requirements	Top-Level System Design	Software Requirements	Software Preliminary Design	Software Detailed Design	Software System Build and Integrate	Software System DT and E Testing

HEW ADP STD

Concept Definition	Requirements Definition	Design	Programming and Checkout	Implementation	Operation

EPA Minicomputer S/W Doc. L Proc. STD

Initiation		Definition	Development			Evaluation	Operation
Request	Analysis		Design	Coding	Test	Validation	

EPA ADP Manual

Feasibility		Preliminary Design	Design	Development and Implementation	Operation and Maintenance
Requirements	Alternatives				

Figure 3-3 Comparison of various system life cycles.

work breakdown structure permits us to gather statistics over a variety of projects. These statistics can subsequently be used in estimating similar jobs.

Thus, each task is subdivided into subtasks in accordance with the work breakdown structure (WBS). Technical staff assigned to a subtask can check the WBS to ascertain the phase of the life cycle in which they are working. Using the System Design Data Base described later, each person knows what products he or she needs to produce and what information he or she needs. Given this information, most people can figure out how to obtain the products. The key feature here is that floundering time is virtually eliminated. Floundering time is the time we spend trying to decide what to do. The absence of floundering is a major cost saver.

Figure 3-2 is also very useful in determining the products that have to be delivered for each phase because of the mapping of the required documents to the life cycle and work breakdown structure. Knowing what is expected is a key ingredient to system planning. It helps the program manager define the tasks. Thus the relationship between the work breakdown structure and the products is important to understand.

All the documents mentioned in Figure 3-2 give a frightening appearance. Under what circumstances do we really need all this paper work? To answer this question, two figures have been reproduced from "Guidelines for Documentation of Computer Programs and Automated Data Systems," FIPS PUB 38. Figure 3-4 gives documentation requirements versus *total weighted criteria* (sic). The total weighted criteria is calculated by adding the weights determined from Figure 3-5.

Total Weighted Criteria	Software summary	User's manual	Operations manual	Program maintenance manual	Test plan	Functional requirements document	System/subsystem specification	Test analysis report	Program specification	Data requirements document	Data base specification
0–12*	×										
12–15*	×	×									
12–26	×	×	×	×	×			†		‡	‡
24–38	×	×	×	×	×	×		†		‡	‡
36–50	×	×	×	×	×	×	×	×		‡	‡
48–60	×	×	×	×	×	×	×	×	×	‡	‡

Notes: *Additional document types may be required at lower weighted criteria totals to satisfy local requirements.

†The Test Analysis Report logically should be prepared, but may be informal.

‡Preparation of the Data Requirements Document and Data Base Specification is situationally dependent.

Figure 3-4 Required documentation versus weights. (Reproduced from FIPS PUB 38)

Criteria	1	2	3	4	5
1. Originality required	None—reprogram on different equipment	Minimum—more stringent requirements	Limited—new interfaces	Considerable—apply existing state of art to environment	Extensive—requires advances in state of the art
2. Degree of generality	Highly restricted. Single purpose	Restricted—parameterized for a range of capacities	Limited flexibility. Allows some change in format	Multi-purpose. Flexible format. Range of subjects	Very flexible—able to handle a broad range of subject matter on different equipment
3. Span of operation	Local or utility	Component command	Single command	Multi-command	Defense Department. World wide
4. Change in scope and objective	None	Infrequent	Occasional	Frequent	Continuous
5. Equipment complexity	Single machine. Routine processing	Single machine. Routine processing. Extended peripheral system	Multi-computer. Standard peripheral system	Multi-computer. Advanced programming. Complex peripheral system	Master control system. Multi-computer auto input/output and display equipment
6. Personnel assigned	1–2	3–5	5–10	10–18	18 and over
7. Developmental cost	1–10k	10–50k	50–200k	200–500k	Over 500k
8. Criticality	Data processing	Routine operations	Personnel safety	Unit survival	National defense
9. Average response time to program change	2 or more weeks	1–2 weeks	3–7 days	1–3 days	1–24 hours
10. Average response time to data inputs	2 or more weeks	1–2 weeks	1–7 days	1–24 hours	0–60 minutes
11. Programming languages	High level language	High level and limited assembly language	High level and extensive assembly language	Assembly language	Machine language
12. Concurrent software development	None	Limited	Moderate	Extensive	Exhaustive

Figure 3-5   Sample weighting criteria. (Reproduced from FIPS Pub 38)

3.3 SYSTEM DESIGN DATA BASE

As indicated previously, each phase of the system development life cycle is treated like a black box, in the electrical engineering sense. We specify the input data and the output data (i.e., the products) to be produced. Any existing technique needed to produce these products can be incorporated into this methodology.

These data are stored in the System Design Data Base (SDDB). The top two levels of the logical design of the SDDB are partially shown in Figure 3-6. This figure illustrates both the contents of the SDDB and the phases in which these data elements are input or output.

An initial conceptual design of the design data for the System Design Data Base is given in Appendix A. This structure is not the conceptual design for a complete System Design Data Base because it does not include maintenance data, management data, or financial data.

Knowledge of the System Design Data Base permits you to assess the state of a project when the beginning of a task is in the middle of the life cycle. This situation is the norm, not the exception. At the beginning of the task, we have a systematic means of determining the data that we should have. If these data are unavailable, we can ask the client to either provide these data or initiate an effort to obtain the data.

If the problem of missing data is not addressed in the beginning of the task, implicit assumptions are frequently made by analysts and programmers. These assumptions lead to design flaws that are very expensive to correct in later phases of the life cycle.

Typically, assumptions relate to:

- Missing or poorly defined requirements
- Data-base access (because no logical data-base design exists)
- The person–machine interface (because no concept of operations exists)

The list is really quite long, but three examples suffice. Can you think of other areas in which design assumptions are made in the absence of missing input data? How do these assumptions vary with life cycle phase?

The SDDB has many different uses. For example, it provides traceability of requirements throughout the life cycle. This is achieved by associating requirements with every configuration item from subsystem to module source code. This association includes the functional hierarchy, data-flow charts, and program design language. These associations are illustrated in Figure 3-7.

How these associations are achieved is illustrated in Figure 3-8, which shows a typical report generated from the SDDB by a data-base management system. This report shows data associated with a computer software configuration item (CSCI; see Figure 2-5 for a description of the software hierarchy) and a computer software component (CSC). Observe that one of the data elements is "requirements." The values of this data element are paragraph numbers in the System Requirements Specification, or the Functional Description (FD) of Figure 3-2.

Phase / SDDB Items	Planning Output	Requirements		Design		Development		CI Integration		CI Qualification Test		System Integration		O&M	
		I	O	I	O	I	O	I	O	I	O	I	O	I	O
• CSCI Level															
Data Flow			•	•	•			•		•		•		•	•
Mini-Specs.			•	•	•			•		•		•		•	•
CSC I/F Document			•	•	•			•		•		•		•	•
I/F Code								•						•	•
Data Store			•	•	•	•	•	•	•					•	•
Est. LOC			•	•	•	•	•	•						•	•
Alloc. LOC			•	•	•	•	•	•	•	•				•	•
Actual LOC						•	•	•						•	•
Sub. CSCs			•	•	•			•							•
• CSC Level															

Figure 3-6 A partial look at the SDDB.

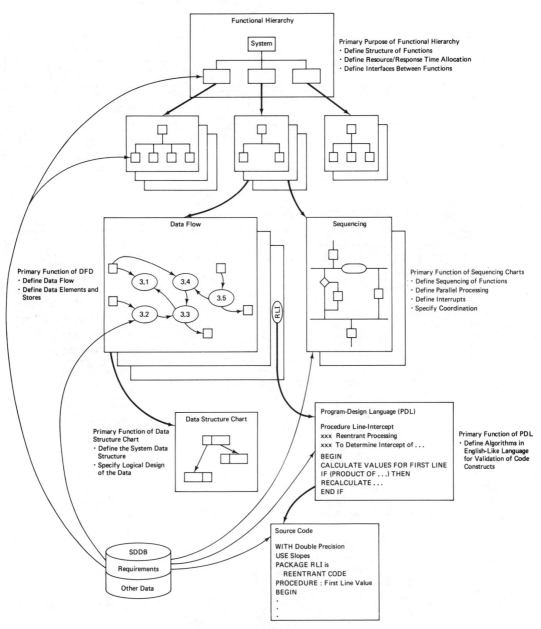

Figure 3-7   Traceability of software requirements for large, complex systems.

The prefixes used in Figure 3-8 are defined in Table 3-1. These alphanumeric references to documentation should be implemented as file references so that it is easy to access the reference.

COMPUTER SOFTWARE CONFIGURATION ITEM REPORT

IDENTIFIER		HIERARCHY		FILES	
CI NUMBER	DESCRIPTIVE NAME	PARENT SYSTEM	SUBORD TLCSCs	TYPE	UNIQUE NAME
01_ABC_01_01_I02000	LAUNCH_GROUND_TEST	01	C02004	DFD001	LGTS_DATA_FLOW
			C02005	SDP002	LGTS_SW_DEVEL_PLAN
			C02012	TEC001	PERFORMANCE_STUDY
				TEC002	LGTS_DB_TRADE_OFF
				REQ	REQUIREMENTS

LOWER LEVEL COMPUTER SOFTWARE COMPONENT REPORT

IDENTIFIER		HIERARCHY		FILES	
CI NUMBER	DESCRIPTIVE NAME	PARENT TLCSC	CHILDREN	TYPE	UNIQUE NAME
01_ABC_01_01_C02017	COMM_SIMULATOR	C02004	C02035	DFD001	LGTS_DATA_FLOW
			C02036	TEC001	PERFORMANCE_STUDY
			U02012	TEC002	RESOURCE_EST_BASIS
			U02013	SEQ001	SEQUENCING_CHART
				REQ	REQUIREMENTS

Figure 3-8 Typical report generated from the SDDB.

TABLE 3-1 SDDB Prefixes

Prefix	Meaning
CSCI	Computer Software Configuration Item
CSC	Computer Software Component
CSM	Computer Software Module
DF	Data flow
DS	Data store
DB	Data base
DT	Data structure
PDE	Primitive data element
DFD	Data-flow diagram
WO	Warnier–Orr diagram
PDL	Program design language
HP	HIPO chart
N2	N2, or input–output, chart
NS	Nassi–Shneiderman flow chart
FLC	Flow chart
DMD	De Marco structure diagram
SE	Structured English

EXERCISE 3.2   What is the relationship between the System Design Data Base and the Electronic Unit Development Folder (discussed at the end of Chapter 2)?

3.4 AN IDEAL SOFTWARE SUPPORT FACILITY

Describing the ideal software support facility (SSF) is somewhat like describing a man for all seasons. It needs to be all things to all people. In the case of software engineering, this utopia is not impossible to achieve, but it doesn't exist today. What does exist is a considerable amount of confusion caused by overzealous advertising and a lack of distinction between research ideas and operational capabilities. Some positive steps toward building a software support facility with the characteristics described next have been made.

The current software support facility state of the art is analogous to the state of the art of computers in the mid-1960s when our mainframes had 32 kilobytes of memory and we dreamed of a computer that was unbounded by on-line memory limitations. Infinity cannot be achieved, but virtual memory has been here for a long time. On-line memory limitations are a major concern today only for systems whose size and processing requirements exceed our imaginations of that time.

In recent years it has been fashionable to talk about software engineering and programming environments in terms of toolkits and structured methodologies. There are currently a host of software development tools, some integrated collections of tools, and a variety of structured methodologies available as commercial software. Government jargon for commercial software is *commercial off-the-shelf software* (COTS, rhymes with pots). Toolkits and structured methodologies are both fundamental parts of software engineering and of programming environments, but they do not represent all the levels of abstraction required of a software support facility.

Computer jargon, like other technical jargon, probably adds more confusion than clarity. A programming environment, envisioned here, is a misnomer. It is intended to be a facility that provides the tools needed for efficient production of high-quality software. This is more than a set of tools to be used when coding. This facility should be used throughout the life cycle of system development and maintenance. This is part of the reason that within the first paragraph we use the term software support facility rather than programming environment.

EXERCISE 3.3   A name that may be even more descriptive than software support facility would be *systems engineering factory*. Which name do you prefer? Describe your rationale.

There are several different names for the systems engineering factory that will be used interchangeably. These are software engineering factory, software support facility, software support environment, and systems engineering environment. The most appropriate name is probably the last. What is being described is really a systems engineering environment in scope. The term factory conjures images of production, so that is also appropriate, especially when considering reusable software. Because of the emphasis of this book on software, the term software support facility will most often be used.

Commercially available toolkits and structured methodologies have generally been built by viewing the software development process from *the inside out*, that is, from the perspective of what is required to produce code efficiently. This viewpoint is limited because it does not provide the controls needed for large multiperson projects. These controls include project management, configuration management, and test and evaluation. Furthermore, the inherent limitations of this bottom-up approach make it difficult to expand the scope of these methodologies to include the appropriate controls.

The level of abstraction needed to provide these controls requires us to view the development process from *the outside in*. It is necessary to get our arms around the whole problem. This is obtained by adopting a system-level approach. More specifically, the first step is to analyze the data that define the state of a system, the same way the design of a transaction-based system would begin. This permits the identification of the products and the required controls. By beginning with a data viewpoint, we think in terms of storing the data in a data base and in terms of the relations needed to extract the data needed. Next, a facility is built for keeping track of these products, enforcing configuration management, and aiding test and evaluation. Given this framework, it is easy to add both structured methodologies and toolkits.

There are in essence three levels of abstraction of software tools. These levels, illustrated in Figure 3-9, are complementary to one another. Specification of the tools at one level of abstraction should have no impact on the specification of tools at the other levels of abstraction.

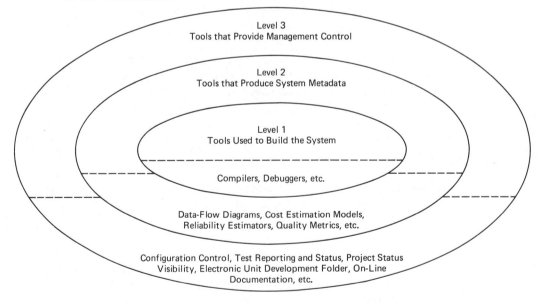

Figure 3-9 Three levels of abstraction needed to design in quality.

At the most detailed level of abstraction are the tools that are used by programmers and testers. These tools include code generators (such as report generators that produce COBOL code), file comparators, test tools, and compilation checkers.

The second level of abstraction consists of tools typically used to determine system metadata (i.e., data about the system data). Examples of such tools are structured analysis techniques like the Ganes and Sarson approach or the Warnier–Orr approach, capacity planning tools like BEST/1 (a product of BGS, Inc.) or SCERT II (a product of Performance Systems, Inc.), and cost-estimating tools like SLIM (a product of Quantitative Software Management, Inc.) or COCOMO (Boehm, 1981).

The third or most abstract level of software development tools is related to the control of the software development and maintenance process. It is at this third level of abstraction that no commercial tools exist, although two companies have produced tools at the "2.5 level" of abstraction. These tools are TAGS, produced by Teledyne Brown Engineering, and APCE, produced by Planning Research Corporation. Major manufacturers like Digital Equipment Corporation have produced a wide variety of tools at the first two levels, but have not integrated them into a single package.

TAGS was developed by engineers from the bottom up. In addition to providing a structured design approach, it is capable of system sequencing and capacity management. It also includes configuration management controls. It does not include the program management controls that are needed.

The APCE stands for Automated Product Control Environment, and it is well titled. It provides the visibility needed by the project manager and provides many of the controls needed by configuration management and testing groups, but it is not integrated well with other tools. APCE is a good first step and is based on some of the concepts of the ideal environment presented later.

The logical design of the system design data base (SDDB) forms the basis for developing the ideal software support facility. When fully implemented, the SDDB becomes a repository for all system data. Building a software box around this repository enables us to:

- Capture these data
- Control access to the data
- Monitor the progress of development efforts

The software support facility expands on the concept of a virtual machine. It is essentially a virtual environment. We do not have to allocate all the resources of this environment in advance; it adapts to the needs of the users. This concept is illustrated in Figure 3-10.

When a user logs onto a terminal, the software support facility automatically determines from the user's identification in which phase of the life cycle and on what tasks the user is working. Note the dependence here on the work breakdown structure and its relation to the life cycle.

The environment created for the software designer includes a design data base, rele-

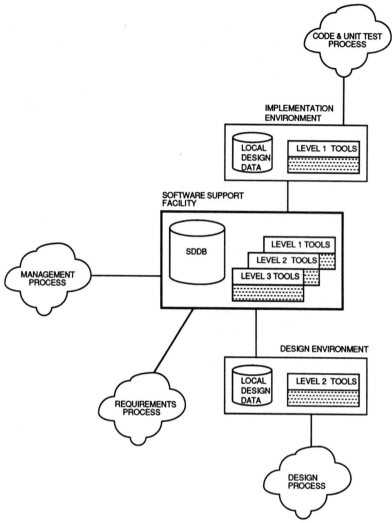

Figure 3-10   Each user of the software support facility has an environment that relates to its job.

vant requirements, a toolkit, and other needed data (such as the standards and proce-dures). Working with a graphics terminal, the designer could, for example, develop data-flow diagrams. These diagrams would be stored for on-line access. The data would be extracted automatically from the diagrams and added to the data dictionary. Of course, consistency checks would be made. These diagrams are used in detailed design where they become part of an electronic unit development folder.

From a programmer's viewpoint, some of the features of the ideal environment in-clude the availability of support tools and on-line documentation. The support tools may include file comparators, debuggers, and version control packages (so that an earlier version of a program can be reconstructed). If the programmer is doing maintenance, he needs access to system design data, trouble reports, and a mechanism for searching data on recent software changes and previous problems and solutions.

It is a real hassle to look through a bookcase for a document and to then search that document for applicable requirements or standards. It is also a hassle to have to maintain a unit development folder, or equivalently a software development notebook. Thus the environment should permit the programmer to have on-line access to the contents of the unit development folder; this includes requirements and design information for his or her particular unit or module. It also includes various versions of the software unit (and indicators of how they differ). When a programmer has completed coding and testing a unit, he or she would like to indicate this by simply entering a command to the system. The programmer's *electronic unit development folder* would then be automatically placed under configuration management control and would be made available to the testing group for intra-CSCI testing.

To members of the configuration control board (CCB), the software support facility looks like a big configuration management tool. The configuration control board is able to control each version of the software; in fact, no software unit can be released, revised, or inserted into the system under development or maintenance without approval of the CCB. The configuration of each release, or multiple releases prepared concurrently, of a system is tracked automatically and passively through the software support facility.

The preceding paragraph makes the control process seem very bureaucratic and foreboding. This situation is really not the case. Programmers can get copies of code and other system data upon request. They simply cannot update controlled software without approval. To update software, they submit a software change request. This change request is typically coordinated by the configuration manager who becomes responsible for advising people designing components of the system that may be impacted by the change request. This process should normally be achieved informally, without formal CCB review, by using electronic mail, brief meetings or other techniques. Changes need to be brought to the attention of the CCB only when objections to the change are raised.

To the test group the SSF environment is a dream. The software support facility is designed to track the status of products and reports at the individual work package level. When a software module or unit is completed, the developer transmits this information to the system design data base, which is resident in the software support facility. Among other benefits, this means that progress is visible. It will be harder to squeeze the time available for testing and simply rush improperly tested software to the field. The test tracking aspect of the software support facility is so powerful that, when this idea for a control environment was described to test engineers at a major aerospace company, their reaction was to insist that it should also be applied to hardware (with manual input of test results).

Testing of this software begins in a layered semiautomated manner. The first layer of tests checks the software for conformance with standards and procedures. For example, any unit exceeding 200 executable lines of code is rejected and sent back to the developer. Other quality assurance tests are also performed.

The number of layers of testing depends on the system's functional hierarchy. The first two layers are at the functional level and are defined in the Software Test Plans (STPs). One possible division of this testing is static testing for layer 1 and dynamic testing for layer 2. Higher layers of testing are devoted to the integration of software components.

The project manager uses the software support facility to monitor the status of each task. For example, at the beginning of the day, the project manager can query the SSF to determine which tasks are behind schedule and what products are due that week. He or she can also review the status of each configuration item. The project manager can determine whether any specified unit has been completed by a programmer and how well it has performed in testing.

If the software support facility can communicate with the organization's accounting system, the project manager can also monitor the financial status of each task defined in the work breakdown structure. If it cannot, a special effort is needed to ensure that all relevant costs are related to each unit at each phase. Otherwise, future cost estimates can continue to be plagued by recurring errors or perception on the part of estimators. For example, we need to know (for the next project) when a module estimated at five worker-days takes six weeks to complete. This module may be on the critical path, causing a five-week slip in the schedule.

EXERCISE 3.4   Which aspects of the software support facility described here apply to hardware development? How would you modify this concept to make it more suitable for hardware engineering? You may give several answers to the preceding question, depending upon your assumptions related to the type of hardware being developed.

3.5 ENVIRONMENTAL IMPACT ON MAINTENANCE

Talking about how to build new systems is fun. We can begin with a clean slate and take the approach of how things should be done. Deviations from the theoretical approach are described in terms of horror stories. Most computer books do not consider maintenance. Even in this book, maintenance is relegated to occasional comments and a couple of sections. Generally, maintenance activities have much lower status in organizations than development of new software.

This is unfortunate because most of the money spent on software is spent on maintenance. According to FIPS PUB 106 (National Bureau of Standards, 1984), approximately 60% to 70% of the money spent on software by the federal government is spent on maintenance. Furthermore, this percentage is increasing.

The distribution of maintenance activities is given in Table 3-2. Note that 20% of the maintenance cost, or approximately 13% of *all* dollars expended, is devoted to correcting errors.

By analogy, let's consider the cost of owning an automobile. It costs about 40 cents per mile to own and operate a typical car. If the car is driven 10,000 miles per year, then the annual cost is $4,000. If cars were sold like software is sold, the average consumer

TABLE 3-2   Distribution of Software Maintenance Activities

Maintenance Type	Purpose	Percent of Software Maintenance Activity
Perfective	To meet evolving needs of the user	60
Adaptive	Result of changes to the environment	20
Corrective	Error correction	20

would be spending approximately \$520/year (which is 13% of \$4,000) for each car to correct errors in manufacturing.

This expense is not due to parts wearing out. The automobile industry covers this expense under its product warranty. In fact, even when the stated warranty does not cover a defect, the courts have ruled that the manufacturer is responsible for major design errors. An example of this liability is the hundreds of millions of dollars that General Motors spent because of class action suits and customer demand resulting from poor design of the diesel engine for cars of model years 1978–1982.

The question remains, why do we buy errors when we purchase software? The practice of paying developers to fix errors simply encourages them to produce low-quality software. Contracts should require the software developer to fix errors free of charge. Commercial off-the-shelf software works that way. The word processor used to type the manuscript for this book worked error free.

These statements sound good for small systems, but do they apply to a \$10 million weapon system involving very complex software? I think that they should. The software builder should guarantee the product for a fixed period of time. Surely, Boeing Aircraft guarantees their commercial aircraft. Each of these aircraft costs well over \$10 million. These aircraft have complex avionics systems. Errors in the avionics could result in the death of hundreds of people. The liability to Boeing would be severe if a crash were traced to a software error.

The practice of encouraging poor quality is also a result of the other 80% of the software activities. These activities result from changing user needs and the changing system environment. When systems are poorly designed and documented, we have job security. If only one person knows how to maintain a system, and much of the system is undocumented, that person becomes irreplaceable.

In the case of a contracting environment, quality software can be encouraged by writing conditions into the contract. These conditions should include complete documentation and incentives based on product performance. In-house environments should be modeled after contracts to be sure that products exist and can be tracked.

In the following paragraphs, maintenance problems are described. After this description, it is shown how a software environment based on the concepts described in Section 3.4 can be used to mitigate some of these maintenance problems.

The basic problem areas associated with maintenance are cost, management, technical approaches, and unavailability of tools. Many of the problems associated with the cost of maintenance are due to the other problem areas; however, a significant cause for high cost is the fact that most software is not built for simple or low-cost maintenance.

Delivered software is frequently poorly documented and noncompliant with any standards. The environment discussion that follows indicates a way of building software for maintenance.

These problem areas are discussed in detail in McCall, Herndon, and Osborne (1985). They are summarized here.

Virtually all aspects of managing software maintenance are problem areas. Many people view maintenance activities as simply finding bugs or performing enhancements (often referred to as patches). The enhancements are considered to be composed of the same type of activities as those for software development, but on a smaller and less organized scale.

This viewpoint is incorrect. The enhancement activity accounts for over 50% of the total software cost. Also, there are fundamental differences between software maintenance activities and software development activities.

Maintenance personnel need to learn how software produced by somebody else works. This activity does not exist in software development. Also, contrary to popular belief, maintenance personnel need to be very creative people and need to understand all aspects of systems engineering. A software development person may be an expert in detailed design or in requirements analysis. Maintenance personnel need to understand the entire life cycle. Each person needs to be able to perform requirements analysis and to design, code, and test software. That is, maintenance personnel need to have skills in both software engineering and problem solving.

One of the problems with being a jack of all trades is that maintenance personnel perform their tasks without receiving appropriate visibility. It is difficult to develop procedures for evaluating their performance. This facet is compounded by the lack of career planning for maintenance staff in most organizations.

Some of these problems of control are mitigated through the use of work breakdown structures and formal procedures for reviewing enhancements. This way, a significant portion of the work results in identifiable products.

The technical approach for maintenance should be given in a Software Maintenance Plan. Procedures for implementing the plan, given by McCall, Herndon, and Osborn (1985), are:

- Establish physical control over the software (this activity includes developing an inventory).
- Develop a common work flow.
- Specify maintenance management plans for each application (this is done at the configuration item level).
- For each key functional area (configuration management, quality assurance, user interface, and testing), assign responsibility to one person—be able to point a finger at someone.
- Establish standards and conventions.
- Log all changes to documentation and code.
- Develop a plan for building or purchasing maintenance support tools.

- Train your personnel.
- Keep upper management informed of accomplishments and problems.
- Talk to developers and users.

A software support environment, such as the one depicted in Section 3.4, can be used to accomplish many of these procedures. The data contents of the system design data base include the data normally found in a software development notebook. Furthermore, by including commercially available packages like the DEC VAX/VMS CMS product in the support environment, versions of the code and documentation are controlled and easy to maintain.

In addition to the control and on-line documentation aspects of the software support environment, there are a large number of tools that can be incorporated into it. Many of these tools can be applied both to development and maintenance. For example, some tools can be used to enforce standards. It is fairly simple to count the number of lines of code to determine whether the total number in a module exceeds 100, whether more than ten sequential lines of code are written without a comment, or whether McCabe's complexity metric (described in Section 3.6) is violated.

One of the most important aspects of a software support environment with the characteristics described previously is the need for specifying relationships dynamically and storing these relationships in the data base. In essence, this approach brings some characteristics of an expert system to a conventional data base. The relationships stored provide information on problem areas and fixes. They should enable a person performing maintenance to take advantage of the relationships learned by somebody else.

EXERCISE 3.5   The purpose of this exercise is to specify files, or records, in such a way that the relationships (specified by one maintenance person) can be read in somewhat stilted English (by another maintenance person). One should be able to search the relationships for key words such as relation (verb) or subject. Assume that you have at your disposal a modern relational data base such as Model 204, Oracle, or RDB. Develop files for *topics, relationships,* and the structure of these files. Suppose that the file containing these structures is called the *control* file. Note that this exercise is not easy. It requires some background in relational data bases and may not be appropriate to all readers. A solution of this problem is the subject on Section 10.3.

3.6 METRICS

Metrics are the criteria used to determine the attributes of our software engineering project. These attributes include reliability, maintainability, estimated cost, and estimated progress. The absence of metrics leads to lack of control over systems and to their failure.

The need for meaningful metrics has been recognized for over twenty years. Major software companies (such as IBM, TRW, Boeing, and McDonnell Douglas) have periodically performed studies on metrics. Their efforts, however, have not resulted in systematic use of accepted metrics, either in industry or within these companies.

It is amazing how major corporations are thrown into a tizzy when they have to address software reliability or fault-tolerant software in a proposal. Typically, the reliability group is hardware oriented. They do not know how to develop plans that assure software delivery at a certain level of reliability.

It is not intended to single out reliability engineers. Try asking a manager to estimate the software development costs for a new system. True, there are some good cost estimating models in existence whose input parameters include estimated lines of code. These models include SLIM, PRICE, and COCOMO. Unfortunately, these models require an estimate of the lines of code to be produced plus estimates of various attributes of the system, such as ''complexity.''

The glitch in using these models is that they all depend on a data base of historical data. That is good if you are producing a system of the type included in their data base and if you are using a similar technology. The problem is that many of these estimates are for high-technology jobs in which we claim to have new and superior ways of doing systems engineering. If these claims are true, then why is the historical data base valid for cost estimating? It seems that your estimates would be too high. This logic related to cost estimating is especially perplexing because the average software system is delivered one year late and at double the estimated cost.

Some people use models such as SLIM only as a sanity check. They estimate costs by first analyzing the required functions by grouping them into functional configuration items (FCIs). These FCIs are then divided into subfunctions to the individual unit level. They then analyze the cost of each unit, computing total cost in a bottom-up manner.

Another difficulty is deciding whether lines of code are an appropriate metric. Halstead's work on software science (1977) provides metrics for estimating cost based on the number of operators and operands in an algorithm. His work also produces a metric for the complexity of a program. This metric is useful for predicting reliability. It is discussed in depth later in this chapter.

To date, there has been an appalling lack of accepted metrics. Even as we define metrics and develop procedures to measure them, their use is limited by lack of statistical data for comparative purposes. If we can measure the complexity of a program and arrive at the number 0.8, is that good?

In a recent speech to an IEEE/ACM joint meeting on software tools, B. O. Smith, corporate vice-president of IBM, discussed the results of a study commissioned by IBM. The results did not find a single American company that gathered statistics on systems development at the corporate level. A number of companies gathered statistics at the program level. They found that very little data exist on quality, error detection, or numbers of errors over the life cycle.

Tool use was shockingly low. For example, no organization used formal verification tools and only 27% of the organizations ever used test generators.

There have been a couple of books devoted to metrics. These include Gilb's *Software Metrics* (1977) and Halstead's *Elements of Software Science* (1977). Although these books are well known, they have been used only sporadically.

The STARS joint task force has devoted a functional task area to measurement. This task force was formed at the direction of the Deputy Under Secretary of Defense for Research and Engineering with direct support from assistant secretaries of each of the military services. For those who are unfamiliar with the Department of Defense hierarchy, it suffices to say that the issue of measurement has received visibility at the highest levels of government.

The STARS committee has established goals for the establishment of fully supported releases of metrics and models for calculating them in fiscal years 1986 and 1988. They are also funding the validation of these metrics.

The visibility that metrics is receiving at major corporations and in the government is symptomatic of the maturation of the software engineering discipline.

Having described the general state of metrics, this section will be concluded by describing a few specific metrics.

McCabe's complexity measure.

Thomas McCabe (1980) defined the complexity of a program to be the "cyclomatic number of the digraph corresponding to that program." A graph consists of nodes (or vertices) and branches (or arcs). A directed graph, or digraph, is a graph in which each of the branches is assigned a direction.

If we represent a program by a flow chart, then the digraph is constructed by replacing each process box and decision box by a node and by specifying directed branches to be the flow of control. Figure 3-11 illustrates the construction of a graph corresponding to a computer program. Note that none of the branches of the graph cross one another. A graph that has this property is called a planar graph. All structured programs have planar graphs.

A graph is called strongly connected if there exists a path to each node from each other node. To achieve this property for graphs of programs, "phantom branches" are added. The addition of a phantom branch is also indicated in Figure 3-11(c). The cyclomatic number of a strongly connected graph is

$$v(G) = b - n + p$$

where $v(G)$ is the cyclomatic number, b is the number of branches, n is the number of nodes, and p is the number of separate parts of graph G. In the case of a planar graph, $p = 1$.

McCabe's complexity measure is the cyclomatic number of a graph. A physical way of viewing the cyclomatic number is to draw a circle or cycle in each enclosed part of the graph. The number of circles equals the cyclomatic number. This is shown in Figure 3-11(d). McCabe has recommended that units with complexity measure greater than 12 should be rejected.

Number of bugs in a program.

Having an estimate of the number of bugs remaining in a program is inherently useful. This estimate can be used to determine program quality for acceptance purposes. For example, a criterion for accepting a program is that 95% of the bugs have been detected.

The problem is to determine how to estimate the number of remaining bugs. A tech-

```
BEGIN
SUM := 0
I := 0
DO WHILE .NOT. END_OF_FILE
     READ GRADE_FILE (RETURNS GRADE)
     SUM = SUM + GRADE
     INCREMENT I BY 1
   END DO
IF (I ≠ 0) THEN
        AVE := SUM/I
        PRINT "AVERAGE GRADE = " ; AVE
     ELSE
        PRINT "GRADES ARE NOT RECORDED"
   END IF
END
```

(a) Program for Computing Average Grade

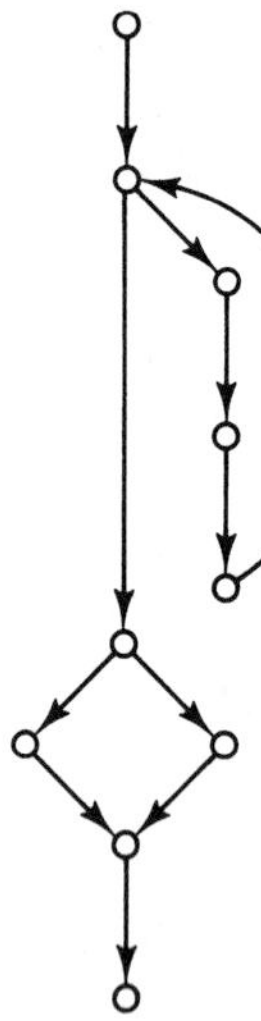

(b) Directed Graph for Program

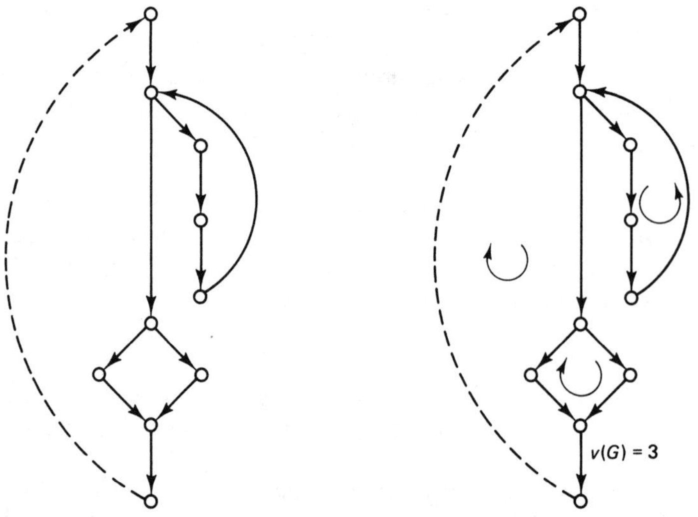

(c) Strongly Connected Digraph

(d) Calculation of Cyclomatic Number

$v(G) = 3$

Figure 3-11 Graph of a computer program.

nique for determining the size of deer populations, for example, is to catch and tag a certain number of deer, say 100. The deer are then released and allowed to mingle with the deer population in a specified forest. The next year, the foresters will count groups of deer, indicating how many of them have tags. If 1,000 deer were counted and 20 of them had tags, then the total deer population is estimated at 5000 (20 : 100 = 1000 : X implies X = 5000).

Using a similar technique, a set of bugs could be artificially created and inserted into the code before testing. We then measure both the total number of bugs (by category) and the number of artificial bugs (by category) found by the testing group. This approach is limited by how well the selected artificial bugs and categories are representative of the actual population of errors. It is also limited by the fears people have that the artificial bugs will never be removed. While this technique is mentioned in several books (such as Gilb, 1977), I am unaware of specific projects in which this technique has been used. I am reluctant to recommend this approach to error estimation.

The Halstead error equation.   Maurice Halstead (1977) studied the properties of software in a truly scientific manner. His book is very appropriately titled *Elements of Software Science*. In this treatise, he speculated that the basic parameters of software are operators and operands. He then developed a series of empirical formulas using analogies to thermodynamics and drawing from psychological studies. Having achieved a theory, he proceeded in a scientific manner to validate his theory.

Halstead used these empirical formulas to determine a variety of metrics. In Chapter 5, his approach is applied to a cost-estimation problem. Here we present Halstead's metric for determining the number of errors in a program.

Halstead showed that the number of predicted errors in a program is

$$B = \frac{V}{3000}$$

where

$$V = N \log_2 n$$

V is called the volume of a program; N is called the length of a program and is defined as the sum of the total number of operators and operands in the program; n is called the vocabulary size of the program and is defined to be the sum of the distinct operators and distinct operands. Each of these quantities is known after the program is completed.

The parameter 3000 is derived from several assumptions. One of these is that "the human brain can handle five 'chunks' in its high-speed memory." Another assumption concerns the complexity level of the English language. B is the number of estimated bugs in the program when it is delivered to the test group by the programmer (i.e., after code and unit test).

More recent work by Lipow (1986) has shown that Halstead's predictor for the number of faults in a module containing LOC lines of code is

$$B = 16.24 + 0.000933 \; LOC^{4/3}$$

This equation is a correction to the equation in Halstead's book (1977).

Lipow also shows that you can expect a 3 : 1 reduction in the total number of faults when a higher-order language is used to program an algorithm instead of assembly language. These results take into account both the differences in lines of code among languages (e.g., one line of code in higher-order language is about four lines of code in assembly language) and statistical data on the number of operators and operands per line of code per language.

Program conciseness metric.   This metric is based on Halstead's estimates for program length. For a given program, we can measure the total number of operators and operands, the number of distinct operators, $n1$, and the number of distinct operators, $n2$. Halstead estimates the length of the program to be

$$N' = n1 \log_2 n1 + n2 \log_2 n2$$

A measure of the conciseness of a module is

$$\text{Module conciseness} = \frac{1 - (N' - N)}{N}$$

while N remains the actual length of the module. A measure of the conciseness of a system could be the average module conciseness.

McCabe's quality assurance metrics.　　Each of the preceding metrics focuses on programs. McCabe (1980) chose a different focus. He specified the factors that affect software quality. These factors are correctness, reliability, efficiency, integrity, usability, maintainability, flexibility, testability, portability, reusability, and interoperability. Each of these terms was defined. Next, a set of criteria was selected to quantify each of these factors.

These criteria are presented in Figure 3-12. This figure indicates the phases of the life cycle in which the criteria should be measured and the impact of not applying criteria in specifying software quality. By comparing the criteria to the factors, it is clear that some criteria apply to more than one factor. For example, modularity helps quantify interoperability, reusability, testability, and flexibility.

McCabe then specifies metrics for each of these criteria. Some of the metrics are in the form of checklists where a value of 1 is assigned whenever the item is satisfied and a value of 0 is assigned otherwise. His completeness checklist is given in Table 3-3.

Other criteria are partitioned into a set of module attributes. A formula used to measure many of these attributes is

$$1 - \frac{\text{number of modules that violate rule}}{\text{total number of modules}}$$

Having evaluated the attributes for a criterion, the metric for that criterion is the average value of the attributes. If a manager did not think that the attributes were of equal value, a weighted average could be used.

Samples of the attributes, grouped by criteria, measured with this formula are (McCabe, 1980):

- Consistency (of procedures)
  - Standard design representation
  - Calling sequence conventions
  - Input/output conventions
  - Error-handling conventions
- Simplicity of the design structure
  - Independence of the module
  - Module processing not dependent on prior processing

TABLE 3-3 McCabe's Module Completeness Checklist

Factor(S): Correctness

Criterion/ Subcriterion	Metric	Requirements Yes/No 1 or 0	Requirements Value	Design Yes/No 1 or 0	Design Value	Implementation Yes/No 1 or 0	Implementation Value
Completeness	CP. 1 Completeness Checklist:						
	(1) Unambiguous references (input, function, output).	☐☐		☐☐		☐☐	
	(2) All data references defined, computed, or obtained from an external source.						
	(3) All defined functions used.	☐☐☐		☐☐☐		☐☐☐	
	(4) All referenced functions defined.						
	(5) All conditions and processing defined for each decision point.						
	(6) All defined and referenced calling sequence parameters agree.	☐		☐		☐	
	(7) All problem reports resolved.			☐☐		☐	
	(8) Design agrees with requirements.					☐	
	(9) Code agrees with design.						
	System metric value = $\dfrac{\sum\limits_{1}^{9} \text{score for element i}}{9}$		☐		☐		☐

Reprinted with permission of McCabe & Associates.

Life-cycle Phases	Development			Evaluation		Operation	
Criteria	Requirements Analysis	Design	Code and Debug	System Test	Operation	Maintenance	Transition
Traceability	△	△	△	×	×	×	
Completeness	△	△	△	×	×		
Consistency		△	△	×	×	×	
Accuracy	△	△	△	×	×		
Error tolerance	△	△	△	×	×		
Simplicity		△	△	×	×	×	×
Modularity		△	△	×	×	×	×
Generality		△	△			×	×
Expandability		△	△			×	×
Instrumentation		△	△	×	×	×	×
Self-descriptiveness			△	×		×	×

Criterion							
Execution efficiency			×		△	△	
Storage efficiency			×		△	△	
Access control			×		△	△	△
Access audit			×		△	△	△
Operability			×	×	△	△	△
Training			×		△	△	
Communicativeness		×		×	△	△	
Software system independence	×	×			△	△	
Machine independence	×				△	△	
Communications commonality	×				△	△	△
Data commonality	×	×			△	△	△
Conciseness	×				△	△	

Legend: △, where criteria should be measured; ×, where impact of poor quality is realized.

Figure 3-12 Impact of not applying criteria in specifying software quality. (Reprinted with permission of McCabe & Associates)

- Module description includes input, output, and processing limitations
- Modular implementation
  - Hierarchical structure
  - Module size standard
  - Module represents one function
  - Controlling parameters defined by calling module
  - Input data controlled by calling module
  - Output data controlled by calling module
  - Control returned to calling module
- Implementation generality
  - Application and machine-dependent functions are not mixed in a single module
  - Processing not data volume limited
  - Processing not data value limited
  - All constants defined precisely once
  - Input, processing, and output functions are not mixed in a single module

The applicability of the criteria to any specific module or system should be determined before the criteria are used. For example, the data value limitation under the implementation generality criteria may not be valid for edit modules. Likewise, some criteria not mentioned here may be imposed for a specific set of domain-dependent software.

A similar approach is taken by McCall and Matsumato (1980) of General Electric and by Bowen and others (1983) of Boeing Aerospace.

By inspecting this list, it is seen that not all attributes of a category apply to all phases of the life cycle, nor do all the attributes of a single criterion necessarily apply to the same phases of the life cycle. The attributes depend on the phase.

EXERCISE 3.6   Create a matrix of criterion/attribute versus phases of the life cycle. Enter an *x* as the value of the matrix element whenever an attribute is applicable to a phase.

EXERCISE 3.7   Generate at least one metric for each criterion listed in Figure 3-12. You may skip the criteria for which examples have been given.

EXERCISE 3.8   For each of the examples given in this section and for each metric specified in the preceding exercise, answer the following questions:

- Can it be applied to existing software?
- Is documentation required during design that is not normally available?
- Can the criterion metric be automated? If it can only be partially automated, provide further details.

EXERCISE 3.9   Refer to the computer program given in Figure 2-8:

- Develop a directed graph or digraph for this program.
- Use phantom branches as necessary to make this graph strongly connected.
- What is the numerical value of McCabe's complexity metric?
- Compute the number of operations $N1$, the number of operands $N2$, the number of distinct operations $n1$, and the number of distinct operands $n2$.
- Compute the length N of the program and the predicted length (using Halstead's estimator) N'. Next compute the program conciseness metric m. [Hint: $m = 1 + (N - N')/N'$.]

Hall and Preiser metric.   Hall and Preiser (1984) recognized that the available set of metrics for measuring complexity of code were not directly applicable to measuring the system complexity. They recognized that there is a trade-off between program complexity and system complexity. For example, a strategy of extreme modularization may be used. The result could be a system in which no module has a cyclomatic number in excess of 3, but the system communications is a nightmare.

Hall and Preiser have represented a system as a network of modules. This representation is applicable to MIS systems, concurrent processing, and real-time considerations. They evaluated McCabe's complexity measure, source lines of code, Halstead's complexity measure, and others. Only McCabe's metric was found to be both suitable for networks of modules and easy to apply.

EXERCISE 3.10   Develop network control graphs for Figures 8-4 and 8-7. Approach this problem in the same way you would develop a graph for a program. It may be necessary to add phantom nodes and phantom branches for input processing and output processing. Develop the cyclomatic number, C_N, for this network.

A problem mentioned earlier is the coupling of network complexity with module or unit complexity. The Hall and Preiser complexity metric is

$$C = w_1 C_N + w_2 \sum_{i=1}^{k} C_i$$

where w_1 and w_2 are weighting factors (i.e., they are positive numbers whose sum is 1) and C_i is the complexity of the ith module.

A difficulty with this metric is its level of application. Do we consider a module to be the lowest level or a unit? Should the complexity be applied at the component, configuration item, or system level? If a component has four modules, each with complexity $C_i = 8$, and a network complexity of $C_N = 6$, and if equal weights are assumed, then the component complexity is

$$C = \frac{6}{2} + \frac{8 + 8 + 8 + 8}{2} = 19$$

A complexity of 19 would be considered too high for a module, but it may be good for a component. It remains to determine guidelines for weighting factors and system complexity numbers.

This dependency on the number of modules could be removed by normalizing the metric; that is, replace the preceding complexity equation by

$$C = w_1 C_N + \frac{w_2}{k} \sum_{i=1}^{k} C_i$$

In this case, the preceding example yields a complexity coefficient of $C = 7$.

This approach enables us to consider the component network complexity measure, the module or unit complexity measure, and the combined measures in a consistent manner. It also provides a consistent extension to configuration items and systems.

REFERENCES

BOEHM, B., *Software Engineering Economics*, Prentice-Hall, Inc., Englewood Cliffs, N.J., 1981.

BOWEN, T. P., AND OTHERS, "Software Quality Measurement for Distributed Systems: Guidebook for Software Quality Measurement," Boeing Aerospace Company, RADC-TR-83-175, Vol. II, July 1983.

DEPARTMENT OF DEFENSE, "Software Technology for Adaptable, Reliable Systems (STARS)," a series of twelve reports, March 1983.

DEPARTMENT OF DEFENSE, "Defense System Software Development," Military Standard, DOD-STD-2167.

DEPARTMENT OF DEFENSE, "Technical Reviews and Audits for Systems, Equipment and Computer Programs," Military Standard, MIL-STD-1521A.

GILB, T., *Software Metrics*, Winthrop Publishers, Inc., Cambridge, Mass., 1977.

HALL, N. R., and S. PREISER, "Combined Network Complexity Measures," *IBM Journal of Research and Development*, Vol. 28, No. 1, Jan. 1984, pp. 15–27.

HALSTEAD, M. H., *Elements of Software Science*, Elsevier North-Holland, Inc., New York, 1977.

LIPOW, M., "Comments on 'Estimating the Number of Faults in Code' and Two Corrections to Published Data," *IEEE Transactions on Software Engineering*, Vol. SE-12, No. 4, Apr. 1986, pp. 584–585.

McCABE, T., *Software Quality Assurance: A Survey*, McCabe & Associates, Columbia, MD, 1980.

McCALL, J. A., M. A. HERNDON, and W. M. OSBORNE, "Software Maintenance Management," National Bureau of Standards, NBS Special Pub 500-129, 1985.

McCALL, J. A., and M. MATSUMOTO, "Software Quality Metrics Enhancements," General Electric Company, RADC-TR-80-109, Vol. I, Apr. 1980.

NATIONAL BUREAU OF STANDARDS, FIPS PUB 38, "Guidelines for Documentation of Computer Programs and Automated Data Systems," Feb. 1976.

NATIONAL BUREAU OF STANDARDS, FIPS PUB 106, "Guidance on Software Maintenance," June 1983.

CHAPTER 4

Risk Management

Chapters 4 to 6 are devoted to subjects that need to be considered in all phases of the life cycle. The discussion in this chapter is about determining risk and risk-mitigation techniques. Next, in Chapter 5, software cost estimating is discussed. Chapter 6 focuses on a subject that is frequently ignored, the system legacy. Only rarely do we encounter a system, like the first time a satellite was launched in 1958, whose primary functions are not currently being performed. Even if these functions are being performed manually, there is a legacy that the designers of the new system can exploit.

There are also other types of analyses performed throughout the life cycle, such as simulations, buy or build decisions, and security analyses. These analyses are frequently done in response to specific issues. Generally, these issues surface during risk and cost analyses.

Simulations are a valuable tool used in capacity planning. They are also valuable for developing concepts. This is especially true in cases where the system is not viewed as an information system. These systems often consist of a network of machinery for which the computers are one component.

For example, when viewed in its broadest sense, a military command and control system consists of sensors, vehicles on which the sensors are mounted, a communications network, and a data-processing and analysis center. Each of these components can be thought of as systems. Each is very expensive, and new components are frequently designed and built with little consideration of their impact on other components. Before making a major investment in any one component of this system, an analysis of the entire system would be useful. A basic criterion that could be used is the resulting improvement in the military's capability of placing metal on targets.

Should improvements go toward improved sensors? If the improvement places a processing load on the data-processing center that cannot be handled, there may be a decrease in overall performance. Maybe the improved sensor needs to be accompanied with improved processing at the sensor (i.e., on the vehicle housing the sensor). The impact on the entire system needs to be evaluated during the system concept phase for a new or improved subsystem.

Several simulations of computer systems are currently available. Two widely used simulations are SCERT II (produced by Performance Systems, Inc., of Rockville, Maryland) and BEST/1 (produced by BGS Systems of Boston). Surveys of available simulations that indicate producer, cost, and required hardware regularly appear in trade magazines such as *Datamation* or *Computer Decisions*. Discussions of how to build simulation models involve either queuing theory or detailed modeling of hardware and system software. Detailed mathematical discussions of both of these topics are beyond the scope of this book; however, an introduction to the concepts is given in Chapter 12.

Build or buy decisions are issue oriented. Consequently, they are not amenable to a general discussion. As a general rule, it is cheaper and less risky to buy than to build. Most engineers prefer to build, so project managers have to closely evaluate the analyses of these options. When a decision is made to buy software, it is important to look at the seller. Is there more than one source for the software? What happens if the seller goes out of business? What happens if the seller decides to no longer support the software? These are all risks that have to be evaluated. One potential mitigating approach (for a large buy) is to require the software developer to place all the source code and documentation into an escrow account that will be made available to the buyer if any of the preceding events occur.

Many systems contain extremely sensitive data. If an unauthorized intruder could gain access to these data, he may be able to steal huge amounts of money, gain proprietary information that gives his company a competitive edge, or obtain data that would adversely affect national security. A lot of research is currently being done on computer security analysis. The question of how much security your system needs is addressed commercially by companies that publish questionnaires designed to make you conclude that you need their product. The literature and newspapers have a smattering of articles on computer theft. This is not a subject that the victims (usually financial institutions) like to talk about.

The Department of Defense has published a set of criteria for establishing a "trusted computer base (TCB)" (DOD, 1983). This publication specifies the criteria that must be satisfied for various levels of security, depending on need. The government is certifying some systems at various lower levels of security (i.e., less protected levels). Certification at the most secure levels (B2 or A1) cannot be achieved with any existing mainframe operation system. The Honeywell SCOMP system has been certified at the A1 level. This computer is designed as a front-end processor. It is useful for protecting a system during its communications with external systems and for protecting system data in a multilevel security network. The SCOMP is the first system to achieve this certification.

A description of various methods for measuring the level of computer security in computer applications, systems, and installations is given in NBS Special Publication 500-133 (Neugent and others, 1985).

4.1 HOW DO YOU DETERMINE RISK?

Risk is determined and evaluated at a variety of levels. On one level, it is necessary to determine the cost and schedule risks associated with each task of a project. At another level, it is necessary to determine the performance risks associated with a project. Performance risks range from unsatisfied requirements that are "nice to have" to system failure. These performance risks should be expressed in terms of their impact. Terms such as equipment damage, personal injury, and loss of life are appropriate.

A risk matrix should be developed for each project. An example of a general risk matrix is given in Table 4-1. Some typical critical areas of risk are included in this figure for illustrative purposes. The assessment of the impact of these critical areas should be as specific as possible. But sometimes the impact is fairly general. When working with business applications, risk should be expressed in terms of dollar loss whenever possible.

The approach to risk mitigation should never be general. Concrete actions should be specified. The project software development plan should include a detailed discussion of risk-mitigation techniques.

Risk should be approached like driving a car. It is wise to drive defensively, but this is inadequate. Even with this approach, the statistics show that you will have an accident sometime within the next 10 years. The nature of risk is that things do go wrong. A technique for mitigating the impact of the accident is to wear seatbelts.

TABLE 4-1 Risk Matrix

Critical Area	Assessment		Risk Mitigation
	Performance	Delivery	
Changing requirements	Failure to perform needed functions	Cost and schedule overrun	Visits with users; documented concept of operations; validate requirements in terms of feasibility and user needs
Lack of documentation	Enhancements and patches cause major failure due to unknown attributes	Steep learning curve (costly maintenance)	Document units while performing maintenance; build central repository for documentation; CM audits
Lack of definitive requirements	Misinterpretation of requirements resulting in implementation of wrong functions	Cannot justify budget nor measure progress; poor relations with customers	Specify measurable requirements before design; use rapid prototype
Nonstandard interfaces	Probability of failure significantly increases	Severe cost penalties; CM problems; new hardware could require new design	Support standard interfaces; impose strict configuration control

In Section 4.2 we discuss how the criticality of each major system component can be calculated and we present a risk matrix using a different format. Matrices with the format of Table 4-1 are easily understood and have been very successfully used in management reviews. These matrices should be discussed at every project progress review.

While planning a project, place a huge blank matrix of this form on a wall. When this planning is done as part of a proposal, the matrix should appear in the proposal room. While working on projects, the matrix should be placed on a wall that is convenient to the key people. One of the best ways of determining the risk is to simply write it down whenever people think of it. This is a spontaneous process that occurs during discussions and while concentrating on a specific problem or task. Many people do not want to write down these "concerns" because they have not yet evaluated the risk or because they might be able to think of a way to avoid the problem. Most people are optimists; they tend to underestimate the chances of the downside occurring. Even if they are pessimists, something totally unforeseen will cause "pain."

The actual determination of risk should be done by a team of people that includes system engineers, operational personnel (i.e., people who use, or will use, the system), and consultants. Some risk determination and mitigation techniques are presented in Table 4-2. Observe that each of the general methods for determining risk involves a group of people. A more detailed discussion of these techniques is given in Delp and others, 1977.

The risk-mitigation techniques typically involve the practice of software engineering. This practice includes modeling, testing, and product control (such as requiring documentation). One aspect of risk mitigation that should not be overlooked is the determination of backup solutions in the event of program trauma (i.e., in the event that things go wrong despite our efforts to minimize the risk).

An approach used by Perry (1985) is to divide risk into structural risk, technical risk, and size risk. He then specifies a group of criteria for each category. Each criterion is then evaluated by selecting the "rating" as a multiple choice. The score for that criterion is the product of the rating and a preassigned weight. An example of this process is given next.

Structural risk refers to management, environmental, and project issues. Some of these are:

- Time since last major change
- Project performance site
- Critical staffing
- Documentation status
- Availability of test facilities
- Commitment of senior users

The rating scheme used by Perry for critical staffing is as follows: in house $= 1$, sole source $= 2$, competitive bid $= 6$. Perry rates developments using the competitive bidding process espoused by the government as much more risky than an in-house development. The total structural risk is the weighted sum of the ratings. Decisions regarding the weights and the rating scheme are based on judgment.

TABLE 4-2   Risk Determination and Mitigation Techniques

Technique	Description
Brainstorming	A group creative process used to generate solutions and approaches to problems and to identify experts on specific problem areas. This approach is relatively unstructured, but responds to a central theme.
Synectics	A group approach to problem solving. The focus is on identifying possible solutions by infusing technology transfer from one discipline to another.
Nominal group technique	The nominal group technique (NGT) is similar to the Delphi technique. It is a group process for eliciting opinions and aggregating judgments. It is used to identify and rank goals or priorities and to involve personnel in the decision-making process (thereby increasing likelihood of final product acceptance).
Morphological analysis	Morphological analysis decomposes a problem into its basic elements. Attributes of each element are identified. Alternative solutions are obtained by combining attributes in various ways.
Prototyping	A prototype is a system that produces the same outputs from the same inputs as the intended system. It either uses a different process or does not have to satisfy all requirements. A typical use is to evaluate high-risk areas of the system build process.
Simulation	A simulation is a model of the intended system used to predict system performance. It is used to evaluate the design in terms of the risk of specifying inadequate system resources (CPU, storage, memory, etc.).
Training	Training is a risk-mitigation technique. By developing training manuals and performing (partial) training on prototypes and emulators, the risk of not satisfying user requirements and being unaware of changing requirements is mitigated.
Documentation	Documentation is frequently downplayed as too costly, in both time and dollars, and too hard to maintain. Cost and performance risks associated with undocumented systems are extreme. Easy to maintain (e.g., stored on line) documentation written in *English* is required for risk mitigation.
Better testing	Use the USAF Space Division ''Management Guide to V&V'' (1980) to determine program criticality and as a guide to the amount of testing required.

EXERCISE 4.1   Select at least two more criteria for the structural risk of a project. Next, develop a rating scheme for each of the criteria. Specify the weight of each criterion. For example, evaluate the importance of each criterion by specifying a number between 1 and 3 (inclusive). Apply these criteria to any project on which you have worked. How would you normalize this process?

Sample criteria for technical risk are:

• Dependency of mission on software
• Required availability
• Familiarity with hardware architecture
• Degree of pioneering

Sample criteria for size risk are:

• Project phasing

* Organizational experience with projects of this size
* Adherence to schedules

EXERCISE 4.2 Repeat Exercise 4.1 for technical risk and size risk.

4.2 DETERMINING FUNCTIONAL CRITICALITY

In this section we present a method developed by the USAF Space Division for determining the level of funding that should be committed to independent validation and verification (IV&V) of a system. IV&V activities include:

* Verifying that requirements can be tested
* Reviewing specifications
* Tracing requirements
* Participating in design reviews
* Checking correctness of algorithms
* Testing software

These activities are intended to reduce the risk of failure to critical system components by making sure that the software both performs the intended functions and does not perform any unintended functions.

Independent validation and verification is a concept that is generally limited to government contracts. In private industry, this group is an independent testing group. I generally recommend organizing independent testing as part of quality assurance. The quality assurance group would then include configuration management, independent testing, quality control, and the development of quality assurance tools. This combination of functions should be sufficient to encourage experienced systems engineers to join the group. The IV&V effort described here should simply be thought of as independent testing in a commercial environment.

The criticality analysis is generally performed on the highest level of software that is or will be under configuration management control. Depending on the nomenclature selected, this level of software is called the computer program, computer program configuration item (CPCI), or computer software configuration item (CSCI). Sometimes preliminary analyses are performed before the system functions are allocated to software or hardware. In this case, the criticality analysis is performed on the functional configuration items or the functional areas.

The first step of the criticality analysis is to determine the critical factors. These depend on the nature of the system. If one were building an air traffic control system, the performance factors might be loss of life, personal injury, equipment and/or property damage, and primary system functional failure. The system delivery factors might be economic impact and schedule impact.

Next, the criticality class and the probability (of failure) class are determined for each system component being evaluated and for each criticality factor. The criticality classes and values are, respectively:

- Catastrophic   4
- Critical   3
- Marginal   2
- Negligible   1

These terms are reasonably self-explanatory. When failures result in loss of life, mission failure, or excessive cost overrun, the criticality class is catastrophic. If failure results in some equipment loss, substantial cost overrun, or a degraded mission capability, it is critical. If secondary functions, such as planning, fail or if some schedule slippage occurs, the failure is marginal. The criticality class for failures resulting in inconvenience or minor cost overrun is negligible.

The probability class for a failure is determined from the following listing:

- Frequent   3
- Probable   2
- Improbable   1
- Impossible   0

Generally, any newly developed software would be assigned probability class ''frequent'' for the likelihood of an error occurring. Reusable software would probably be assigned the class of ''probable.'' Commercial off-the-shelf software is normally assigned the value of 1. If it has been *proved* that there are no errors in the software, then it is assigned probability class ''impossible.'' Proof of correctness is very difficult to achieve. The ''impossible'' rating is sometimes given to software that has been extensively used over a long period of time without error.

The criticality factor is the product of the value of the criticality class and the value of the probability class. Figure 4-1 is part of a criticality factor matrix for an air traffic control system. In this illustration, the criticality factor has been calculated for three of the functional areas.

CRITICALITY FACTOR / CONFIGURATION ELEMENT	PERFORMANCE FACTORS				DELIVERY FACTORS		TOTAL POINTS	CRITICALITY VALUE
	LOSS OF LIFE	PERSONAL INJURY	EQUIPMENT DAMAGE	MISSION FAILURE	EXCESSIVE COST OVERRUN	MAJOR SCHEDULE SLIPPAGE		
FLIGHT DATA PROCESSOR	4 X 3	4 X 3	4 X 3	4 X 3	4 X 3	4 X 3	72	12
WEATHER PROCESSOR	4 X 2	4 X 3	4 X 3	2 X 3	3 X 3	3 X 3	56	9
PLANNING AIDS	4 X 1	4 X 1	4 X 1	3 X 3	3 X 2	2 X 1	36	6

Figure 4-1   Criticality factor evaluation matrix.

The Flight Data Processing area has a criticality class of catastrophic for all factors. A software error could result in mid-air collisions. Although there is a strong legacy of existing software, that software contains many patches and must be rewritten. It is complicated software requiring extreme accuracy. The probability class is "frequent." From a delivery point of view, this functional area is also of catastrophic criticality class. The

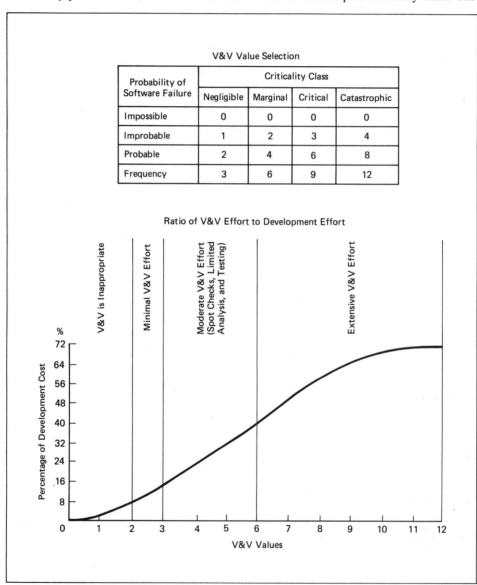

V&V Value Selection

Probability of Software Failure	Criticality Class			
	Negligible	Marginal	Critical	Catastrophic
Impossible	0	0	0	0
Improbable	1	2	3	4
Probable	2	4	6	8
Frequency	3	6	9	12

Ratio of V&V Effort to Development Effort

Figure 4-2 Validation and verification application guidelines. (From USAF Space Division, Management Guide for IV&V, 1980.)

software must be part of the initial operating capability, and it must be fault tolerant. Failures could affect delivery schedule and cost severely.

The planning aid area is designed to schedule flights so that the work load on air traffic controllers is reasonable and to plan fuel-efficient flight paths. An error in planning aid could result in an accident because a controller is trying to handle too many aircraft (criticality class value = 4 for life, injury, and damage), but this is improbable because the controller can simply refuse to accept aircraft into his or her sector (probability class = 1). This action would very likely cause airborne aircraft to either change their flight path to avoid that sector or fly in circles until the controller is ready to receive them. These actions result in large fuel costs (mission failure criticality class = 3, probability class = 3).

The calculation of criticality value is illustrated in Figure 4-1. Note that the criticality value of the functional area is simply the average value of the individual factors. If desired, a weighted average could be used in lieu of the simple average. Next, referring to Figure 4-2, guidance is provided for the amount of money that should be spent on IV&V as a function of the development cost for each functional area.

In the extreme (such as for Flight Data Processing), about 60% of the software development cost should be spent on IV&V. This IV&V activity should be fairly complete. Algorithms should be checked, software tested, and so on. In the case of the planning aid, about 30% to 35% of the software development cost should be spent on IV&V. Note that development cost here means the cost to design and code the software; it excludes costs for requirements analyses and system integration.

A word of caution is in order. Software buyers normally shudder at the thought of spending the amount on IV&V that is suggested by this procedure. People do not like to pay for testing and documentation. This reluctance, however, does not change the lessons learned by the USAF Space Division.

While independent testing, or IV&V, is difficult to ''sell'' to a commercial customer, it can frequently be buried in development cost. This may significantly increase development costs over a competitor's stated bid. If the customer requires a full life-cycle cost estimate, this difference can sometimes be offset by an extended warranty period. If the customer is unwilling to pay for independent testing, the development contractor has to decide whether the job is worth the risk and whether he is willing to produce a system of lower quality than could be produced. Most software development companies will accept work under these conditions. I recommend refusing work when the result is unlikely to be of high quality.

REFERENCES

Delp, P., and others, ''System Tools for Project Planning,'' Program of Advanced Studies in Institution Building and Technical Assistance Methodology (PATSITAM), 1977 (ISBN# 0-89249-021-7).

Department of Defense Computer Security Center, ''Trusted Computer System Evaluation Criteria,'' CSC-STD-001-83, Aug. 15, 1983.

NEUGENT, W., AND OTHERS, "Technology Assessment: Methods for Measuring the Level of Computer Security," National Bureau of Standards, NBS Special Pub. 500-133, Oct. 1985.

PERRY, W. E., *A Standard for Testing Applications Software*, Auerbach Publishers, Inc., Pennsauken, N.J., 1985.

USAF SPACE DIVISION, "Management Guide for Independent Verification and Validation," Aug. 1980.

CHAPTER 5

Cost Estimation

I was once asked on a job interview, "What is a good method for estimating the cost to produce software?" Under the pressures of the interview, I simply replied that I couldn't think of any method that was good. At that point, the job interview could have ended. That answer was truthful and correct (I still don't know of a *good* method), but it was not what the interviewer wanted to hear.

Actually, I answered the wrong question. He really wanted to know how I would estimate the cost of producing software. In this chapter, methods of analogy, parametric analysis, and industrial engineering will be discussed.

Costing software by analogy is done by:

- Determining the general functions that have to be performed
- Comparing these functions to similar functions implemented for other systems
- Using the cost for the similar function as an estimator

This method assumes that somebody knows what the cost was to build the similar function. Generally, our industry has been remiss in collecting performance and cost data. The knowledge on which this approach depends is usually based on somebody's recollection. Although I have seen this approach used for estimating the rough order of magnitude of software cost, I have rarely seen it actually used for pricing a job.

Costing by analogy has an inherent conflict. If the analogous software were close enough to the required software to provide reliable development cost estimates, then why can't some portion of the analogous software be reused in the required software? If we can modify, delete, or enhance existing software, the development costs of the required software should be significantly reduced.

Another difficulty with cost estimating by analogy is that this approach does not consider a variety of factors that affect production costs. Parametric methods attempt to account for these factors. A precise list identifying these factors depends on the parametric method used. A typical list of parameters that are evaluated for these methods is:

- Lines of code
- Programming language
- Project complexity
- Staff skill levels
- Programming environment
- Maximum time to completion

Because costing by analogy leads inherently to questions regarding the cost of changing code, as opposed to creating new code, the first section of this chapter focuses on the cost of modifying existing code. This section is followed by a discussion of parametric methods. A description of the industrial engineering method for cost estimation is embedded in the discussions of the other methods. Then, in Section 5.3, we consider what is required to significantly reduce the cost of software.

5.1 COST OF MODIFYING EXISTING CODE

Modifying existing code takes several forms. One form is the conversion of code from one language to another, such as IBM 360 COBOL to Burroughs B6700 COBOL or IBM basic assembly language (BAL) to Burroughs B7700 COBOL. Other forms of modifying existing code involve adding new functions, deleting functions, changing interfaces, and changing code.

Tausworthe (1981) has recognized problems associated with estimating the cost of producing software in an environment of a considerable amount of existing software when he developed a software cost-estimating model for the Deep Space Network developed at the Jet Propulsion Laboratory (JPL). He developed the concept of "equivalent lines of code, LEQ."

His formula for equivalent lines of code is

$$LEQ = LNEW + 0.27\ LMOD + 0.53\ LADD + 0.24\ LCHG$$
$$- 0.15\ LDEL + 0.11\ LREMOVE + 0.12\ LTEST$$

where

- LNEW is the new lines of executable source code to be developed (i.e., subject to the entire development process),
- LMOD is the lines of code in modules to be reused (but modified by additions, changes and deletions),

- LADD is the lines of added code,
- LCHG is the lines of changed code (which require less documentation and coding effort than lines of added code),
- LDEL is the lines of deleted code,
- LREMOVE is the lines of code corresponding to modules that are removed (note that testing must take place to check reused modules that interface with the removed modules),
- LTEST is the lines of code in the unmodified modules that need to be retested and validated.

The equivalent lines of code, LEQ, is the number that should be used as the lines of code estimate requested by parametric methods. Tausworthe obtained the parameters of his equation by developing a standard work breakdown structure (WBS) and by estimating the effort of each element of the work breakdown structure for a job (i.e., a new module) that could be completed in one staff year or 242 days. He then estimated the activity required for added code, deleted code, and so on.

His results, reproduced from JPL Publication 81-7, are shown in Table 5-1. The factors at the bottom of that figure correspond to the factors of the preceding equation after an adjustment to eliminate double counting of the testing effort for a changed module (0.27 LMOD). Remember, this table was developed for the software produced by JPL for a specific project, the Deep Space Network. Both the work breakdown structure and the estimated effort for each element should be adjusted to your environment before using the procedure.

The last column indicates that the cost of reusing a module that simply requires test and integration is 12% of the cost of producing a new module. Equivalently, productivity is increased by a factor of nearly 9 when a module is reused. For systems requiring less extensive testing than a space system, or for modules that are designed for reusability, this factor could increase to 10 or more.

EXERCISE 5.1   Select a work breakdown structure for a development project that you have previously worked on. If you are unable to obtain one or have not worked on a development project, use the WBS of Table 5-1. Without further consulting Table 5-1, specify the amount of time that you think each task should take for a project that could be completed in exactly one year or 242 work days. How do your results compare to Tausworthe's results? What do you think could be some of the causes of the differences?

Two sources of detailed information on the cost of software conversion are Wolberg (1983) and the Federal Conversion Support Center (1981). Wolberg's book contains the best accumulation of data, of which I am aware, on software conversion. He partitions his data in several ways. Wolberg uses the parameters of redesign, reprogramming, and straightforward conversion to distinguish among the types of activities. He also distinguishes between manual and automated conversion.

Wolberg uses the terms *redesign* to imply a software effort that includes functional

TABLE 5-1　Inherited Code Effort Requirement Estimate

Activity	New Module	Changed Module				Deleted Module	Retested Code
		Added Code	Deleted Code	Changed Code	Same Code		
Requirements and design							
FRD phase	6						
FDD phase	7						
SRD phase	10						
SDD phase	13	13	4	13	4	4	
SIS activity	10	10	3	10	3	3	
SSD phase	22	22	5	6	5	5	
Special	6	6		3			
Other	3	3		1			
Coding							
SSD phase	23	23	3	7		3	
Special	6	6		3			
Other	4	4		2			
Testing							
Integration	12	12		12	12		
Verification	12	12		12	12		
Contingency	2	2		2	2		2
Acceptance test	10	10		10	10		10
Demonstration	10	10		10	10		10
Documentation							
FRD	3						
FDD	3						
SRD	3						
SDD	3	3	1	2		1	
SSD	31	31	4	10		4	
SOM	3	3	1	2		1	
SIT	6	6	1	3		1	2
Management							
FRD review	2						
FDD review	2						
SRD review	5						
Management plan	7						
SDD review	3	3	1	1	1	1	
High-level design review	1	1	1	1	1	1	
Acceptance review	1	1	1	1	1		1
Transfer	1	1	1	1	1		1
CDF SSD phase	9	9	2	9	2	2	
CDF test phase	3	3	1	2	1		3
Total	242	194	29	123	65	26	41[sic]
Factor	1.0	0.80	0.12	0.51	0.27	0.11	0.12

From Jet Propulsion Laboratory Publication 81-7.

redesign of a system, *reprogramming* for a software effort that requires some redesign but leaves the system functionally unchanged, and *conversion* for a software effort that is limited to the recoding of software manually or the primarily automated translation of software.

Wolberg has published data on the cost of conversion, reprogramming, and redesign efforts expressed in terms of effort (staff months) and duration (calendar months) as a function of lines of code. For each category, he then assumes an exponential form:

```
E = E(i) * (L/L(i)) ** A
```

where L is thousands of lines of executable code, A is a parameter, and E(i) and L(i) are, respectively, the effort and executable lines of code for a similar type of effort. He assumes a similar formula for the duration of a program. The value of A is determined by a least-squares fit of data contained in tables published in his book. E(i) and L(i) are determined by consulting those tables for projects similar to the one under consideration. Given the value of A, the factor E(i)/L(i) could be determined from your organization's experience.

In the absence of an entry providing a direct comparison, the following formulas may be used:

```
E = 7.14 * L ** 0.47    (conversion)
E = 2.6  * L ** 0.91    (reprogramming)
E = 5.2  * L ** 0.91    (redesign)
```

The corresponding formulas for project duration are

```
D = 4.1 * L ** 0.22    (conversion)
D = 3.3 * L ** 0.36    (reprogramming)
D = 4.1 * L ** 0.36    (redesign)
```

These equations do not apply to jobs of fewer than 10,000 lines of executable code.

Wolberg continues his discussion with procedures for minimizing cost and for determining when automated conversion makes sense. Conversion costs quoted by Dataware, Inc., in 1980 range from 40 cents per line for FORTRAN-to-FORTRAN clean compile to $1.50 per line for BAL-to-COBOL clean compile. At the other extreme, the cost in 1985 of producing complex new software for space systems varies from about $80 per line (possibly real-time machine-language code) to $270 per line. Since few systems are totally new, Wolberg's book should be considered recommended reading.

The Federal Conversion Support Center (FCSC) evaluated six methods for estimating the cost of software conversion in 1981. They grouped these methods into three categories: experience, task analysis, and parametric. Note how similar these categories are to those mentioned at the start of this chapter.

The experience approach is more meaningful for software conversion than for new developments because companies in the software conversion business may have experience in similar types of jobs. In this case, similarity is measured by the nature of the conversion (e.g., COBOL to COBOL or ASM to COBOL), tools being used, and lines of code.

Within each of these categories, the FCSC evaluated two methods. The first method in the experience group was the unit costing technique. This technique uses historical data to determine the cost per line, cost per file, or other suitable parameters. Costs are then adjusted to current fiscal year dollars. Because of significant variation in salaries across municipalities, the adjustment factor takes locality into account. Parameters to be taken into account in the historical data include:

- The amount of work included in historical cost figures (e.g., just translation or all conversion activities)
- Type of work (e.g., application programs, job control language conversion, file conversion, or combinations of these)
- Personnel skill levels
- Use of automated translators

Costs published by the FCSC (in fiscal year 1980 dollars) range from 40 cents per line for a simple FORTRAN-to-FORTRAN conversion (clean compile, no documentation, no system testing) to $15 per line for complex ASM-to-ASM conversion. The FCSC does not indicate what is included in the latter cost; however, they also published costs of $10 per line for translation, clean compile, unit testing, and minimum redocumentation of a complex COBOL-to-COBOL conversion.

The second experience method is the productivity measurement technique. This technique is similar to the unit cost technique, but uses lines per day as a measure rather than cost. The factors influencing productivity include the use of automated translation, the nature of the conversion activities included (just translation or the entire process), and the environment (batch versus on line, complexity of the code, programmer skills, etc.). Productivity for COBOL-to-COBOL conversion varied from 25 to 400 lines per day. Even when we restrict attention to manual techniques, the variation in COBOL-to-COBOL conversion was 25 to 60 lines per day. Productivity for RPG-to-COBOL conversion ranged from 10.5 to 150 lines per day. Note that productivity of 10.5 lines of code per day is about what is expected for new developments using a higher-order language.

The large variation in productivity when automated tools are used is due to the variety of the available tools. Tools used in software conversion include those given in Table 5-2.

The FCSC concluded that experience can be used to estimate conversion costs when accurate historical data exist. They also concluded that this is generally not the case. Most historical data do not include a description of all the parameters affecting results. The FCSC cautions that "extreme care should be taken in analyzing historical data as to its applicability and in adjusting the historical data." They do not recommend the use of these techniques.

The task analysis techniques correspond to the approach called the "industrial engi-

TABLE 5-2 Sample Set of Software Conversion Tools

Title	Description
File generator	Test generator and extractor
File extract	Extraction of critical records that cause code activation; this permits greater test efficiency
Execution measurement	Identifies unexecuted code during testing and calculates total statements exercised
Program comparator	Compares two versions of the same program and determines the places that changes have been made
File comparator	Identifies differences in records when two files are compared
Execution trace	Flow of logic is recorded for each test data set
Translator	Translates code from one language to another
Code reformatter	Reformats source code so that it is easy to read (e.g., indents appropriately to show logic structure); may have other features such as insertion and deletion of debugging code;
Quality control	Identifies unreferenced data names and procedures
Cross-reference	Source line cross-reference map

neering method'' mentioned at the beginning of this chapter. This approach defines all the activities to be performed in terms of a work breakdown structure. Each task is then analyzed to determine the cost of personnel (in terms of staff hours per wage category), computer time, and other direct costs. One such approach was developed by Paul Oliver, who created a work breakdown structure of fifty-six categories. He developed algorithms for twenty-five of these categories and stated that the other thirty-one must be costed by the individual manager to account for their environment and experience. The underlying idea of this approach is similar to Tausworthe's approach for estimating the cost of modifying software.

The FCSC concluded that his approach was good for planning, but not costing, because of the lack of estimating rules for thirty-one categories and because of lack of sensitivity to certain parameters. To me, his approach seems pretty good; however, no final opinion is offered because I have been unable to locate the original source.

Another task analysis approach was used by Jerry Gitomer (Auerbach portfolio 2-05-04), but he defines only fifteen tasks. Generally, his approach seems too coarse for satisfactory cost estimation.

Neither these two task analysis approaches nor the two parametric approaches considered by the FCSC are discussed here. The FCSC recommended using a hybrid approach that combines features of all the approaches they considered. This hybrid approach is described later. Parametric methods are discussed in the next section.

For reference purposes, one parametric method discussed by the FCSC is the Department of Army procedure presented in Technical Bulletin TB18-122. The other procedure, developed by the Navy, is called the Project Management Control System. My only source describing this procedure is the FSCS (1981) document. The algorithms they recommend for costing the conversion planning, analysis, and preparation activities are given in Figure 5-1.

ACTIVITY	FORMULA
Planning, analysis, and work package identification	SD = 5 * S + P + F + J for a highly dissimilar environment SD = S + (P + F + J)/2 for a highly similar environment
Conversion study and inventory preparation	None, use estimator experience
Policy and procedure review and implementation	SD = [S + ((P + F + J/20) + (P/20)] * PCOR for a highly dissimilar environment SD = S * PCOR for a highly similar environment
Work package preparation	SD = (P + F)/4
Test data generation and validation	SD = 3 * P + F

Where	F = number of files	
	J = number of job streams	
	P = number of programs	
	PCOR = 1.05 (for planning coordination)	
	S = number of systems	
	SD = staff days	

Figure 5-1   Estimation of conversion planning, analysis, and preparation.

The estimation of the effort for tasks related to application program and system software conversion depend on:

- Complexity
- Documentation status
- Automatic translation percentage (T)
- Lines of code (LOC)

The total staff days is given as the sum of the staff days, SD(i), required for each complexity class, i. SD(i) is given by the formula

$$SD(i) = \{[LOC(i) * (1-T(i))] / MCPR(i)\} + [LOC(i) * T(i)] / ACPR$$

where MCPR(i) is the average manual conversion productivity rate for complexity class i, and ACPR is the automated conversion productivity rate.

The default value for ACPR is 630. The five complexity classes are defined as an ordered 5-tuple:

(reprogramming, major program logic modification, minor program logic modification, simple syntax translation, software transference)

The FCSC defines the totally new development process to consist of design analysis, programming, and testing. They then assign the percentage of effort for these tasks to be, respectively, 40, 20, and 40. These percentages are based on empirical data. The FCSC then reduces the percentages for each of the classes, again based on empirical data. In the following paragraphs, the procedures for calculating MCPR(i) and T(i) are given. When the value of a parameter is expressed as a 5-tuple, then the value of the parameter for complexity class i is given in the ith position. For example, the design effort, DE, is evaluated as DE = (30, 20, 4, 1, 0). This means that complexity class $i = 2$, or major program logic modification, has a design effort parameter of DE = 20.

T(i) is the percentage of lines of code capable of being translated automatically. Typical values range from (0, 20, 65, 80, 0) to (25, 75, 90, 100, 0). Note that T(5) = 0 because there is no automatic translation of code; the code is simply being transferred.

The value of MCPR(i) is

```
MCPR(i) = 100 * BR / {[(1 - DOC/2) * DE(i)] + PE(i) + TE(i)}
```

where BR is the baseline productivity rate for new development (default value is 12.6 lines per day), DOC is the fraction of documentation available, the design effort DE is as given previously, the programming effort is PE = (15, 10, 2, 0.5, 0), and the testing effort is TE = (35, 20, 10, 2, 0.1).

The estimated cost in staff days for data-file and data-base conversion is obtained by first calculating the staff days using the formulas for application programming and system software. During the calculation of this number, DSD(i), LOC(i) are the lines of source code for data description or data dictionary languages for each complexity class i. The staff day resources are then adjusted to account for documentation status.

The result is

```
SD(i) = DSD(i) +  {F(i) * FCF(i) * [1-DOC/2]}
```

where F(i) is the number of files to be converted for complexity class i, and FCF = (5, 3, 2, 1, 0.25) is the file-conversion complexity factor.

The formula for determining the effort required for the conversion of operation control language code is the same as the formula for application programming. A simple formula sometimes used is SD = J/8 for compatible environments and SD = J/3 for noncompatible environments, where J is the number of programs, or job streams and independent runs, to be converted.

The effort required to redocument code for a noncompatible system is estimated as the sum of the technical and clerical staff days,

```
SD = 1.1 * DOC * {[P/4 + S] + [P/2 + 2*S] }
```

where P is the number of programs to be converted and S is the number of systems to be converted.

The estimated cost of system testing is bounded by

$$[1 + RE/10] * [JPS + (P+F+J)/80] > SD > [1 + RE/10] * [JS + (P+F+J)/40]$$

where RE is the probable reruns during system testing, F is the number of files and data bases,

$$JPS = J/4 + P/2 + S/2$$

and

$$JS = S/10 + J/10$$

The left side of the inequality corresponds to a noncompatible environment, and the right side of the inequality corresponds to a compatible environment.

The estimated effort for acceptance testing is also given in terms of an inequality. A primary variable is the duration, DUR, of the acceptance test in work days; however, no relationship for duration versus complexity or system size is given by the FCSC. The inequality is

$$DUR * S/8 + \{15 * [J/4 + (P+F+J)/80] * [1 - exp(-DUR/10)]\}$$
$$> S >$$
$$DUR * S/20 + \{15 * [(P+F+J)/40] * [1 - exp(-DUR/10)]\}$$

Site preparation, dual operation, and training are mentioned as tasks that need to be estimated, but the FCSC provides no algorithms for this purpose. The FCSC spent considerable effort generating and validating this model in the early 1980s; however, before using it, you should attempt to validate it for your operations. It is suggested that you contact the Federal Conversion Software Center in Falls Church, Virginia. Any updated model and details on model validation are in the public domain and are available through them.

5.2 PARAMETRIC METHODS

The general idea behind parametrics is to first postulate a model for estimating the cost of software that includes one or more parameters and then to use historical data for evaluating the parameters. Some examples of parametric models were given in Section 5.1. Some of these models are very elementary, such as the estimate of lines of executable source code produced per day.

It is not unusual to estimate the number of lines of code (LOC) of a subsystem and then to determine a cost estimate by assuming that productivity is 10 LOC per day per programmer. Typically, some number between 7 and 15 is selected for large systems (e.g., in excess of 50,000 LOC). The number selected is frequently a compromise between the number that the estimator believes to be true and the number he or she thinks the buyer will accept.

Other parametric methods involve the development of regression formulas based on these parameters and an assumed probability distribution. For example, the Constructive Cost Model (COCOMO) developed by Barry Boehm (of TRW, Inc.) assumes that the nominal number of man-months (MM) from completed requirements specification to software acceptance test is given by

$$MM = 3.2 * KDSI ** 1.05$$

where KDSI is thousands of delivered source instructions. The parameters given assume the ''most common form of in-house, familiar software development'' (Boehm, 1981). These parameters are adjusted for the use of software tools and other parameters.

Other well-known and popular cost-estimating models include:

- SLIM, developed by Larry Putnam of Quantitative Software Management
- PRICE S, developed by RCA
- JS-2, developed by Randall Jensen of Software Engineering, Inc.
- Software Science, developed by Maurice Halstead
- Boeing Computer Services model
- Wolverton's method developed at TRW

There are many other parametric cost-estimating models. No offense is intended nor is a value judgment intended if your favorite has been omitted. Some people may have qualms about the inclusion of Software Science as a parametric method. Despite the scientific basis for this procedure, its practical application to cost estimation depends on ''engineering parameters.''

As a general rule of thumb, all the parametric methods are equally good or equally bad. By their nature, they depend on a data base of historical cost data. How applicable the data base is to your project and your development procedures is open to question. This problem is exacerbated in modern programming environments. If it is true that software development tools are being used to significantly enhance productivity, then the data base of historical costs loses its validity.

My personal experience in costing jobs has been that these parametric cost estimators are satisfactory for larger jobs. Although the deviation between predicted costs and ''believable costs'' may be large at the unit or module level, when the total development costs are computed these errors cancel one another. Company vice-presidents want to see the results of a parametric cost-estimating procedure when they are *pricing* a job, but they are generally loathe to use them. There are fundamental differences between pricing and costing. These differences are discussed next. Then two of these parametric approaches, SLIM and Software Science, are discussed in greater detail.

The industrial engineering method for cost estimation consists of specifying the system to the lowest possible level of detail—at least to the level of the CSC and the modules of which it is comprised. Additionally, this method depends on the development of a complete work breakdown structure. A work breakdown structure is a hierarchical list of activities required to produce the system. Activities in the lowest level of the work breakdown structure are called *work packages*. Ideally, a work package corresponds to a task (resulting in a product) that is performed in two weeks by an individual. Having achieved this, the cost of each work element for each module is estimated. The work element cost consists of both labor and *other direct costs* (ODCs). Other direct costs include the cost of commercial software, computer time, travel, and hardware.

This bottom-up approach to cost estimating is probably the most accurate and reliable method. It also requires the greatest effort; it may be necessary to combine this method with one of the other methods. This approach to cost estimating:

- Makes the budget visible
- Is the only method that would satisfy an auditor

In competitive environments (especially in the government contracting environment), corporate vice-presidents and presidents usually have a preconceived idea of how much the customer is willing to pay and how much the competition is likely to bid. This information is frequently obtained by the marketing staff. The pricing strategy when bidding on competitive contracts is to bid the highest cost that you think will be low enough to win. Unfortunately, this price is frequently lower than the cost estimated by the industrial engineering method. Contractors will frequently bid jobs below cost and assume that they will be able to recoup these costs and make a profit through changes in requirements of the system (and hence the contract). These changes are known as engineering change proposals.

This process differs in commercial work where the price is determined by what the manufacturer thinks the market will bear. In this case, the profit is determined strictly by the cost to produce the object. The lower the cost per unit, the higher the profit. A classic example of this practice occurs in the automobile industry. When the dollar is very low compared to the yen, Japanese cars cost more in the United States. Rather than taking advantage of the cost differential to raise their market share, American manufacturers usually raise their prices to increase their profit.

Unfortunately, most companies do not separate pricing from costing when deciding what to bid on a government contract. Consequently, the pricing exercise forces a reduction to the cost estimate. Sometimes this reduction process is real because lower vendor prices have been negotiated. Sometimes the reduction is phony. For example, the cost allocated for a preliminary design review (PDR) may be eliminated on the grounds that it was included elsewhere (despite the fact that it had not been). Depending on the size of the job, the cost of a preliminary design review varies from $1.50 to $4 per second. Given a five-day PDR (40 hours), this cost could exceed a half-million dollars.

Since this chapter is on cost estimation, and not pricing strategy, we shall proceed with a discussion of cost methods.

5.2.1 SLIM

The ideas behind SLIM were developed by Larry Putnam at the Army Computer Systems Command. Subsequently, a commercial version has been produced. The commercial version enhances the original version by accounting for more parameters, today's microcomputer environment, and a larger historical data base. It is sold by Putnam at Quantitative Software Management, Inc.

The outputs of SLIM are total development cost, development time, personnel loading, documentation estimates (size and cost), reliability, and risk estimates. Other outputs include the cost and time estimates for system functional design and system planning.

As we shall see later, the virtues of SLIM lie not in its theoretical approach—anybody who knows BASIC can easily write a program for cost estimation based on a Rayleigh distribution—but in its analytical approach and its data base of historical projects. This comment is only slightly tongue-in-cheek. The Rayleigh functions used in the current version of SLIM are somewhat more sophisticated than the two-parameter version described here; the exact form of the equation is not published for competitive reasons. Adjustments to the Rayleigh distribution were made, in part, to improve the accuracy of SLIM in regions of less than 70,000 source lines of code. Putnam had found (empirically) that the peak staffing curves for smaller projects are different than the peak staffing curves for large projects.

Currently, SLIM is available on personal computers, including the IBM PC. Its user interface combines interactive queries with graphic and tabular products. This approach permits the user to conduct trade-offs among the minimum time solution, minimum cost solution, and design to risk solution.

Perhaps the most important aspect of SLIM is its display of the *impossible region*. We are frequently placed in a position in which the client demands a development schedule that is significantly shorter than our estimated schedule. It is not unusual for the client to say that he is willing to pay a little extra for us to reach his schedule and that we should simply put more people on the project.

This logic defies the facts of life of development projects. After a certain staffing level, dependent on the specific job, productivity decreases as people are added to the job. When unrealistic demands are placed on the development team for a software project, the results of SLIM can be shown to the client, who is frequently a company vice-president demanding an instant solution to a long-term problem. The approach to take is to tell this person that you will try to meet his schedule if he insists, but based on your data base of over 1000 projects, nobody has successfully produced a similar system in less time than your minimum time.

In the following paragraphs, an overview of the analytical approach used by SLIM is presented. Next, a table of required input data is given. Finally, some sample outputs are illustrated.

An input–process–output diagram that describes the general approach is included as Figure 5-2. As implied there, SLIM cost estimates are based on the Rayleigh distribution. The Rayleigh distribution is given by

$$f(x) = \frac{x}{s^2} \exp\left(-0.5\left(\frac{x}{s}\right)^2\right), \qquad \text{for } x \geq 0$$

$$f(x) = 0, \qquad\qquad\qquad \text{for } x < 0$$

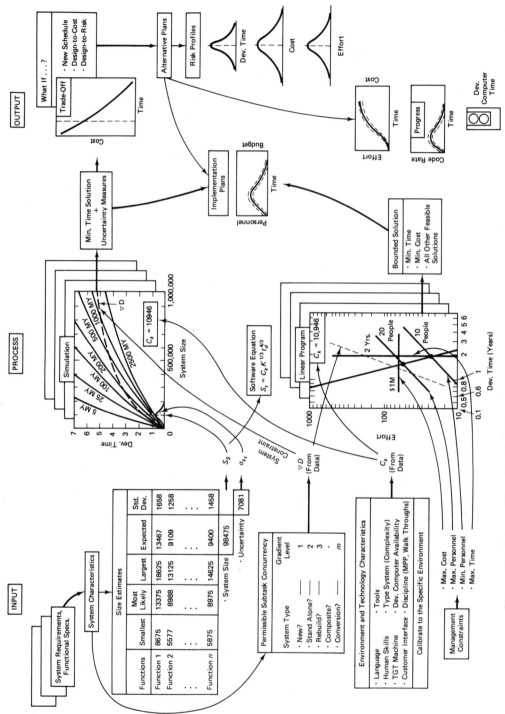

Figure 5-2 Software life-cycle methodology used in SLIM. (Courtesy of Quantitative Software Management, Inc. Reprinted by permission)

98

where s is the standard deviation. The normalized Rayleigh distribution (i.e., $s = 1$) has a maximum value of $f(x) = 0.606$ at $x = 1$. The mean value occurs at $x = 1.25$. The general shape of the Rayleigh distribution is given in Figure 5-3.

Figure 5-3 contains several overlapping Rayleigh distributions. In electrical engineering, Rayleigh distributions are used to describe the envelope function of a filter designed to eliminate broadband noise from a narrowband process. The envelope function is not sensitive to small perturbations. Physically, this seems like a good quality for a distribution used to estimate software costs.

According to Thibodeau (1981), Putnam applied a hypothesis developed by P. V. Norden of IBM that, given linear learning, the rate of expending effort on the solutions of problems follows a Rayleigh distribution function over time. For large software projects, the Rayleigh distribution was found to be applicable to the entire software development process and to its component parts by Putnam.

Specifically, Putnam demonstrated that

$$dy/dt = Kt/t_d^2 \exp\left(-0.5(t/t_d)^2\right)$$

where dy/dt is the rate of expending effort (e.g., in worker-months per month), K is the total effort expended (worker-months), t_d is the development time (months), and t is the time from the start of the development phase.

In SLIM, the development phase is defined to be from completion of the preliminary design review until completion of system installation. This corresponds to the detailed design, code and unit test, and the testing, integration, and installation phases of the software development life cycle defined in Chapter 3. Estimates for the requirements phase, which Putnam calls the feasibility phase, and the preliminary design phase, which Putnam calls the functional design phase, are derived from the results of the development phase.

This equation is graphically portrayed in Figure 5-2 under Implementation Plans. Before this equation can be calculated, it is necessary to estimate the values of K and t_d. Putnam does this by first observing that the ratio of expended effort to the square of the development time (i.e., K/t_d^2) is the difficulty, D, of the system. The difficulty is a subjectively determined parameter.

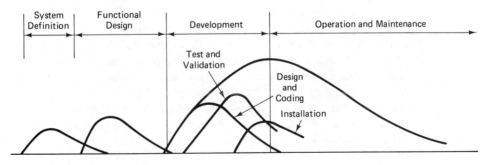

Figure 5-3 Rayleigh distributions used in SLIM. (Courtesy of Quantitative Software Management, Inc. Reprinted by permission)

The next step in this approach is the development of an empirical formula that relates the average productivity of the system to the difficulty. This formula is

$$PR = C_n D^{-2/3}$$

where PR is the average productivity and C_n is an empirical constant.

The next observation is that 95% of the code is produced during the design and code phases of the life cycle. This is what SLIM refers to as the development phase. The other 5% of the code is produced after installation. These assumptions lead to the equation

$$S_s = C_k K^{1/3} t_d^{4/3}$$

where S_s is the number of lines of source code, and C_k is a technology factor.

Again referring to Figure 5-2, observe that the formula for S_s is shown as a family of curves in the box marked Simulation. The value of C_k is obtained from the environment and technology characteristics. These characteristics are parametric input data to SLIM that describe the problem. Note that K is still unknown; this is the reason that we have a family of curves rather than a single curve.

The final equation developed by Putnam is for the gradient of the difficulty, ∇D, which he shows is related to the type of development. More specifically,

$$|\nabla D| \simeq D/t_d \simeq K/t_d^3.$$

Putnam has developed empirical data for the difficulty gradient as a function of the type of development. (The empirical data subsume the 2 from the gradient calculation.) For a given difficulty gradient, the preceding formula is plotted as a function of development time. This plot is the dashed curve shown in Figure 5-2 in the Simulation box. The simulation permits us to solve for K.

Thus far, the minimum time solution has been calculated. Plotting these curves as shown in the Linear Program box illustrates how total effort may be reduced by extending the total development time. This approach also permits the imposition of management constraints and the solution of the problem as a linear program.

It is this pragmatic approach that permits us to conduct trade-offs and to measure the sensitivity of our answer to our assumptions. SLIM is the only method that produces infeasible regions and provides a set of criteria from which the manager can choose. In the following paragraphs, we present the inputs requested by SLIM and some sample outputs.

The input data required by SLIM are given in Figure 5-4. These data are divided into three parts: calibration, new system information, and constraints and options. The calibration data enable you to calibrate your corporate data with the SLIM data base. When performing a calibration, the output data are technology factor and gradient level. Your estimation of the input of these parameters for the new system can be based on experience your company or organization has had on similar projects.

The new system information (Part 2) consists of the input parameters SLIM needs to perform its calculations. These parameters are grouped by category. Although the category is not explicitly stated, it can be determined by referral to Figure 5-2. The final part, constraints and options, consists of instructions to SLIM to perform various calculations and display various information.

PART 1: CALIBRATION

System name
System size (source statements)
Development time (months)
Development effort (worker-months)

PART 2: NEW SYSTEM INFORMATION

System name
Project start date

Fully burdened labor rate ($/worker-year)
Standard deviation of the labor rate
Inflation rate (decimal fraction)

Proportion of development in on-line, interactive mode
Proportion of development computer dedicated to effort
Proportion of development computer capacity used for other production work
Proportion of system coded in a higher-order language
Primary language

Type of system
Level of system
Proportion of memory of target machine utilized to be utilized by the software
    system
Proportion of real-time code

Use of structured programming
Use of design and code inspection
Use of top-down development
Use of chief programmer teams

Overall personnel skills
Personnel experience with development computer
Personnel experience with programming language(s)
Personnel experience with system of similar size and application

Technology factor

For each module (or once for the entire system):
    Function name
    Smallest possible number of source statements
    Most likely number of source statements
    Largest possible number of source statements

Figure 5-4   SLIM input data.

PART 3: CONSTRAINTS AND OPTIONS

Maximum development cost (dollars)
Maximum development time (months)
Minimum and maximum number of people at peak staffing time
Request for trade-off analysis
Level of accepted risk
Desired mean time to failure
Criteria for optimization (e.g., design to cost)
Output requests (e.g., for graphic displays or Gantt charts)

Figure 5-4   (continued)

The output data are given in Figure 5-5. As can be seen by inspecting the data produced by SLIM, the cost analyst can perform a number of trade-offs. The output includes statistical measures of the data. Specifically, both the standard deviation of the individual parameters is given and a consistency check of the data base against similar jobs is given. This approach instills confidence in its applicability to the user's problem.

As I indicated earlier, I think that all the more popular software cost-estimating tools are equally good for estimating total cost. They are influenced more by the historical data base than by the specific algorithm (because each of the algorithms is reasonable). SLIM has the advantage of providing a deeper view of the cost-estimating problem than other methods. Its determination of the "impossible region" is extremely useful for bargaining with clients over unreasonable demands, even if the name of the region is somewhat of an overstatement.

5.2.2 Software Science

Software Science was developed by Maurice Halstead (1977). In his classic book, Halstead follows a scientific approach in an effort to formulate a foundation for software engineering. As a scientist, he used analogies to thermodynamics to postulate the basic principles of software. He sheds the established parameters of programming, such as lines of code, in favor of "information attributes." These attributes include the length of an algorithm, N, expressed as a sum of its operators and operands, language complexity, and discriminations per second. A list of the parameters and primary relationships is given in Figure 5-6.

Having postulated these basic parameters and relationships, Halstead attempted to validate this theory by comparing theoretical results to experimental measurements taken from published programs. Correlations have been very high. Halstead's work has generated a wide variety of subsequent reports and papers. These papers tend not to have a middle ground. They either claim to support the theory or to show that it doesn't work. My personal experience tends to support the theory. I am unaware of any other (substantially different) scientific approach to software.

PART 1: CALIBRATION

Technology factor
Gradient Level

PART 2: MINIMUM TIME SOLUTION (ALL ITEMS INCLUDE STANDARD
    DEVIATION UNLESS SPECIFIED TO CONTRARY)

System size (source LOC): mean
Minimum development time (months): mean
Development effort (worker-months): mean
Development cost ($K): mean

Sensitivity profile (± 1, 2, 3 standard deviations)
    Source statements
    Months
    Worker-months

Consistency check (with other systems of same size): no standard deviation
    Total worker-months
    Project duration
    Average number of people
    Productivity

Staff loading per month
Cumulative staff loading
Labor cost per month (current or inflated)
Cumulative cost per month (current or inflated)

PART 3: OPTIONS

Gantt chart
Tabular display of major milestones
Graphical display of linear programming solution
Tabular display of minimum-cost versus minimum-time solutions
Front-end estimates of effort and duration for feasibility study and functional
    design phases
Risk profile by month
Total pages of documentation
Estimated monthly code production
Estimated monthly computer usage
Part 2 outputs for other criteria
    Design to cost
    Design to risk
    Time or staffing constraints

Figure 5-5 SLIM output data.

LIST OF SYMBOLS

E	Effort	n#	Potential vocabulary
L	Language complexity	n1#	Potential operator count
N	Program length	n2#	Potential operand count
n	Vocabulary size	P	Program level
N1	Total operators	S	Discriminations/second
n1	Unique operator count	T	Implementation time
N2	Total operands	V	Program volume
n2	Unique operand count	V#	Potential volume

BASIC EQUATIONS OF SOFTWARE SCIENCE

$$n = n1 + n2$$

$$N = N1 + N2$$

$$n\# = n1\# + n2\# = 2 + n2\#$$

$$N = n1 * \log_2 n1 + n2 * \log_2 n2$$

$$V = N \log_2 n\#$$

$$P = V\#/V = 2 * n2/(n1 * N2)$$

$$L = P^2 * V$$

$$E = V/P$$

$$T = E/S$$

Figure 5-6 Equations and notation of Software Science. (Reprinted by permission of the publisher from Maurice H. Halstead, Elements of Software Science, p. 2. Copyright 1977 by Elsevier Science Publishing Co., Inc.)

A detailed discussion of Halstead's work is presented in his book. Rather than reproducing his work, his general approach is presented by using an example. This example predicts programming time for the redesign of a large system.

Estimating the number of operators and operands in an algorithm or program is no easier than estimating the number of lines of code. If the algorithm were known in enough detail to count the number of operators and operands, we would also know enough to make a good estimate of the lines of code.

For the example of this section, the only datum at our disposal is the number of words of memory occupied by the old code. Using this information, an estimate will be made for the number of lines of executable source code required for the existing code. This estimate will then be adjusted to predict the number of lines of redesigned code.

The old hardware of this example is an IBM 9020, which is an IBM 360/50 with a few modifications to its operating system. Thus each word of memory is 32 bits and corresponds to one machine instruction, I. By counting operators and operands, and allowing for indexing, the following inequality can be derived:

$$2\,I \leq N \leq 4\,I$$

Citing a statistical study of Knuth (1971) on FORTRAN statements, Halstead then concludes that $N = \frac{8}{3}I$. Note that this result is a general engineering parameter specified without distinction to the type of application program. Whether this relationship holds for systems programs and other types of programs written in FORTRAN is unknown. The applicability of this parameter to other languages is also unknown.

A typical FORTRAN module might have a value for n between 40 and 80. For $n = 50$, $N \simeq 560$. Reverse engineering our steps yields $I = 210$. At three words of instruction per line of FORTRAN code, we get a module of about 70 lines of code.

The next assumption of our procedure involves the relationship between the number of operators and the number of operands. This assumption basically addresses the program complexity. Since we have no hard data, it is assumed that the number of operands, $n2$, equals the number of operators, $n1$. For very complex programs, another assumption (such as $n1 = 2 * n2$) may be made. For small values of n, the difference between these two assumptions is small. For example, a value of $n = 150$ yields $N = 934$ under our first assumption and $N = 946$ under the "very complex" assumption. Since programming time varies with the square of the program length (discussed later), the effect of this assumption for large programs could be significant.

Under the first assumption, the vocabulary size, n, is determined by solving the inverse equation

$$N = n \log_2 n/2$$

Recall that we can determine N from I. The easiest way to "solve" this equation is to:

- First, produce a table of N versus n by inserting values of n and calculating N.
- Next, calculate n by looking up values of N and interpolating as necessary (linearly) between table entries.

Programming time T is then expressed as the ratio of the required energy to the number of discriminations per second, S, a programmer makes. Under the preceding assumptions,

$$T = N^2 \log_2 n \,/\, 4\,S\,L^2 = E\,/S\,L^2$$

The parameter E is defined as the programming effort in units of number of discriminations needed to be made by the programmer, and S is the number of discriminations per second that a programmer makes. A table for E is given as Appendix B.

It has been determined by psychologists that the value of S is bounded between 5 and 20. Halstead uses a value of $S = 18$ for a programmer concentrating very well. This value may be fine for a bright graduate student locked in his office and working undisturbed, but for large development projects in a "typical working environment" a value of $S = 12$ seems much more realistic. This value is used in the example given next.

The language level, L, is a measure of the information content or power of a language. Experimentally determined values of language level are

- 0.88 for COMPASS
- 1.14 for FORTRAN
- 1.53 for PL/I
- 2.16 for English

The results shown in Table 5-3 use a value of 1.6, which may correspond to Pascal.

The number of lines of code can then be calculated from the programming time by assuming a productivity of k lines of debugged, executable lines of code per day. That is, $LOC = k * T$. The productivity assumed in Table 5-3 is six lines of code produced in an eight-hour day.

As a validity check to this Software Science approach, the results of this example were compared to the results obtained from an empirical ratio (used at a major aerospace firm) of three words of memory to each line of code in a higher-order language. The difference between these two approaches was only 8%, almost too small a number to believe.

TABLE 5-3   Sample Estimate of Programming Time and Lines of Code

Subsystem	Words of Memory	Programming Time (hours)	Lines of Code
Preliminary processing	2,770	255	76
Flight data processing	55,640	75,400	21,900
Route conversion	36,800	57,800	16,700
Track data processing	39,600	57,900	17,000
Flight status alert	50,200	35,300	10,300
Posting determination	34,200	40,500	11,900
Supervisory	15,000	12,800	3,750
Inquiry processing	46,306	44,000	12,900
Display channel output	40,084	89,400	26,200
Radar processing and track	20,880	15,200	4,500
Flight plan analysis	2,720	950	270
Real-time quality control	4,628	3,100	900
Totals	348,800	437,000	126,500

N.B.: The programming time was computed using $L = 1.0$. For a language such as Pascal, $L = 1.6$. Therefore, the programming time is reduced by a factor of 2.56. To obtain the lines of code, divide the time by 2.56 and then multiply the result by 0.75 line per hour.

The estimated lines of code and programming time need to be adjusted to account for the following factors:

- The redesigned applications will have greater functionality, thereby increasing the amount of code.
- The existing code was written in an unstructured manner using either JOVIAL or Basic Assembly Language; conversion to structured code may increase the amount of code by 40%.
- A considerable amount of the logic of the old code is reusable, thereby decreasing some of the development time.

5.3 POTENTIAL GAINS IN PRODUCTIVITY

Cost estimating is somewhat depressing. The cost estimation methodologies are not very good and experience shows that software costs too much. A variety of studies have estimated the amount of software needed in the years 2000 and 2010. The answers are staggering. There will not be enough programmers available to develop the software, let alone maintain it. Unless dramatic improvements in productivity are achieved, there will not be enough money to produce the software.

We begin by estimating the potential for increasing productivity by improving management. Suppose that a programmer is locked in a room for one day with a personal computer and with a specification that is clear. Also suppose that the programmer understands the problem. The maximum number of debugged, executable lines of code that can be produced is about 100. Responses to a survey of dozens of programmers yielded a range of 50 to 200 lines of code. Those people who specified the high side (100 to 200) said that, if they could do it, they would be "wiped out the next day."

Further suppose that code and unit tests take 15% of the software development life cycle. In this case the total project takes 6.7 days (1/0.15), and the productivity is 15 LOC per day. Thus, the greatest productivity gain that we can expect from good management is from approximately 8 to 15 LOC per day. Since we have not accounted for interruptions, we can expect a gain of not more than 50% due to ideal management.

We will briefly digress to determine the impact of working on jobs involving more than one person. If there were N people with whom the programmer must interface, then the programmer has 2^{N-1} interfaces with other people. If we assume that the productivity drops with some power of the number of interfaces, then

$$P = K[2^{-c(N-1)}]$$

where K and c are constants.

EXERCISE 5.2   Specify the maximum number of interfaces that a programmer is likely to have on a very large project. Next, specify a reasonable productivity (LOC per day) for a very large project. Determine K and c. Finally, calculate P for $N = 4$. Complete this exercise before proceeding to avoid being influenced by my opinion.

Since $P(1) = 15$, we see that $K = 15$. For this calculation, assume that $P(N_{max}) = 8$ lines of code per day. Now, what is a practical limit for the number of interfaces? I think that people generally work in groups of not more than eight people. Add to this number three levels of management, configuration management, testing, and three miscellaneous people to get $N_{max} = 16$. This assumption yields a value of $c = 0.06$; thus

$$P = 15 \, [2^{-0.06(N-1)}]$$

Since ideal management produces a maximum increase in productivity of about 50%, we can save substantial money, but we cannot meet the needs of the twenty-first century. What we need is order(s) of magnitude increase in productivity.

Some of these productivity increases have been achieved for special applications. COBOL generators produce report generators and other established applications at rates of hundreds or thousands of LOC per day. These tools cannot produce the type of complicated code needed for scientific, military, and complex commercial application.

There is considerable work underway in the field of very high order languages. Some of this work is oriented toward building requirements languages that will generate code directly from requirements specification. This work is in its early stages of research. In twenty years, this area may yield results beyond our current imagination.

Another technology area whose impact is difficult to assess is the increase in machine computational speed. As hardware improves, higher-order languages can be used to solve problems that currently require assembly language code. Programming a given algorithm in assembly language takes at least twice as long as in a high-order language. Some major companies estimate software costs at seven worker-months per 1000 lines of code for assembly language and 3.5 worker-months per 1000 lines of code for high-order languages. This increase is still well below an order of magnitude.

Another approach is to reuse existing code. As was indicated in Section 5.1, Tausworthe estimated that the equivalent lines of code for a module that is to be reused is 12% of the lines of code in that module. This number measured the effort needed to retest this code for integration with the system. In this case, reusing software increases productivity by a factor of 8 (1/0.12). This near order of magnitude increase in productivity is significant. This estimator does not take into account the extra time required to determine whether reusable software exists and the impact of this activity on design.

Another factor that needs to be considered is the additional time it takes to design modules for reusability. If that time were taken, the initial development might take slightly longer (and cost a little more), but the testing time for the reusable module may be significantly decreased. It may also be more likely that a module is reused. Capturing software so that it is reusable could be achieved by using a software support environment similar to the one discussed in Chapter 3.

There are no validated software cost estimators for reusable software at the time of this writing; however, Lockheed Missile and Space Company (LMSC, 1987) is in the process of developing one for the Department of the Navy. This effort is part of the Reusable Software Implementation Program (RSIP). Its existence is indicative of the fact that we cannot produce the software needed in twenty years unless we fundamentally change the way we do business.

LMSC (1987) used an approach that combines the industrial engineering and parametric methods. They developed a detailed generic work breakdown structure for software development and maintenance. This work breakdown structure includes tasks required to reuse software, such as searching a library, that are excluded in traditional methods. For each element of the work breakdown structure LMSC developed a cost estimating relationship. Many of these cost estimating relationships are based on COCOMO.

While a reusable library is being established, no cost advantages are realized. It may actually cost a little extra to develop the code in a format that is suitable for deposit in a library. During subsequent reuse, substantial saving should be realized. Some quantitative estimates of these savings were obtained by Lockhead based on assumptions related to the software environments and analyses of percentage of reuseable code for various command and control systems.

Better management is important, but it is not the answer. Order of magnitude improvements are achievable only through reusing software and software development facilities that provide needed tools and capture software.

REFERENCES

BOEHM, B., *Software Engineering Economics*, Prentice-Hall, Inc., Englewood Cliffs, N.J., 1981.

FEDERAL CONVERSION SUPPORT CENTER, "Review and Analysis of Conversion Cost-Estimating Techniques," GSA/FCSC-81/001 (NTIS# PB81-207854), Apr. 1981.

HALSTEAD, M. H., *Elements of Software Science*, Elsevier North-Holland, Inc., New York, 1977.

LOCKHEED MISSILE AND SPACE COMPANY, ADA Technology Support Lab, "Description of the SPAWAR RSIP Cost Comparison Model," 1987.

TAUSWORTHE, R. C., "Deep Space Network Software Cost Estimation Model," Jet Propulsion Laboratory, JPL Publication 81-7 (also NASA-CR-164277), Apr. 15, 1981.

THIBODEAU, R. "An Evaluation of Software Cost Estimating Models," Rome Air Development Center, RADC-TR-81-144, June 1981.

WOLBERG, J. R., *Conversion of Computer Software*, Prentice-Hall Inc., Englewood Cliffs, N.J., 1983.

CHAPTER 6

Determining the System Legacy

Large-scale systems generally come into being by an evolutionary process over many years. This process is not systematic and the resulting system architecture may be called a "default architecture." Eventually, system limits implicitly imposed by this default architecture are reached.

This architectural limit is frequently realized through loss of control of the software, increasing maintenance problems, and high computer processor utilization. Capacity problems can sometimes be corrected through the purchase of a faster computer for which the current software instruction set is either compatible or nearly compatible. Major manufacturers are generally careful to make their machines upward compatible. That is, software that runs on an older or smaller member of a computer family (such as the DEC VAX family) will run without modification on the newer, faster machine.

When switching to a new machine, software conversion can sometimes effectively be accomplished by using language translators (such as Burroughs COBOL to IBM COBOL, or vice versa). This normally works best when the capacity growth was planned. Sometimes, when the capacity growth has not been planned, this approach is also effective. In this case, simply using the existing software on a faster machine just delays the inevitable redesign. The increased throughput capacity does nothing to solve maintenance problems or to enable the system functions to be enhanced, although, depending on the circumstances, the primary problem may be solved.

Thus, the purpose of very large jobs is frequently to redesign and redevelop systems having a substantial legacy of operational procedures and software. When companies are competing for these jobs, a legacy assessment affects several criteria normally used to evaluate proposals and could be a discriminating factor. Information obtained from a legacy assessment is also important in noncompetitive situations. Specifically, the legacy assessment is used to:

- Demonstrate (or gain) understanding of the existing system and procedures.
- Show that the proposed system addresses the appropriate problems; for example, the proposed design addresses the functional components with the greatest potential increase in operator productivity.
- Partially justify the cost estimate on the basis that existing system capabilities are being used whenever feasible.
- Provide traceability of existing system functions to the proposed system design.

Theoretically, an operational concept is written before a system (requirements) specification is completed. In practice, this is frequently not done. For example, many government ''request for proposals'' are released for bid with a requirements specification attached, but without any concept of operations. The assessment of the current system provides the basis for an operational concept for the proposed system.

While performing a legacy assessment, it is important to keep in mind all aspects of the system—the people, facilities, hardware, code, and documentation.

In this chapter we present a heuristic methodology for performing a legacy assessment and an example of a legacy assessment. In Section 6.1 we show how to identify the functional components in which system automation provides the greatest potential pay-off. This pay-off is expressed in terms of increased operator efficiency. Then, in Section 6.2, we provide a scheme for tracing the existing system capabilities to the required functions. We then show how to use this scheme to determine the software legacy.

The procedure given here is simple and straightforward. More sophisticated approaches can be taken by using task (or time and motion) analysis methods developed by industrial engineers. There are some systems planning packages available that may be of use in capturing the legacy also.

The example used in each section is the FAA Advanced Automation System (AAS). The AAS, which is currently under development, is a redesign of the existing Air Traffic Control (ATC) system.

6.1 DETERMINING WHERE AUTOMATION PAYS OFF

The methodology consists of two general steps:

- Identifying functional components of the current system that are primarily manual and could be automated in the future.
- Relating those components to elements of the future system.

These two general steps are iterated to accommodate both analytically derived information and user-supplied information.

Using a top-down approach, the major functions of the system are defined from an operational point of view. This approach requires that the overall functions of the system be defined first. The system is then decomposed into components with progressively greater functional detail.

Once the current system has been subdivided into major functional components, we determine whether these components are primarily manual or automated. The manual functional components are further categorized in accordance with their susceptibility to automation.

The operational viewpoint should reflect all aspects of system operations. These aspects include:

- Applying the system by users or operators
- Maintaining the system by local and/or remote systems engineering and facility personnel
- Operating the system by local systems personnel

Next, a design for the future system is developed in as much detail as practical. Usually a top-down approach is used, and the planned system is decomposed into units performing distinct functions.

Using top-down analysis, the current air traffic control system was decomposed into components with progressively greater functional detail. For illustrative purposes, the ensuing discussion will focus on air traffic control applications functions (as opposed to system functions such as security, training, or data-base services). At the top level, the system was subdivided into six major functional components:

- *Manage Flight Plans:* To receive, validate, and modify flight plans in accordance with aircraft needs, traffic conditions, weather, and so on.
- *Traffic Flow Management:* To multiplex airspace and develop usage patterns in accordance with flight plan requirements.
- *Terminal Departure:* To monitor and control aircraft from the runway into the air for hand-off to an en route center.
- *Terminal Traffic Management:* To multiplex ground space and local airspace associated with terminals.
- *En Route Control:* To monitor and control aircraft from the vicinity of departure terminals to the vicinity of arrival terminals (or adjacent en route control).
- *Terminal Arrival:* To receive (from en route control), monitor, and control aircraft during approach and landing at terminals.

A determination was then made whether these components are primarily manual or automated. It was found that all six major functional components are primarily manual, or controller intensive, in the current air traffic control system. The results and rationale are given in Figure 6-1. Analysis was then performed to see which of these primarily manual functions could be automated in a future air traffic control system. Based on current tech-

Functional Component	Controller Intensive	Rationale
Manage flight plans	Yes	Controller makes modifications, validations, updates to the data base manually.
Traffic flow management	Yes	Airspace structuring, flow control, and traffic management is almost totally manual.
Terminal departure	Yes	Departure clearances are issued verbally by the controller. • Voice communication • Radar display monitoring
Terminal traffic management	Yes	Controller is responsible for departure/ arrival airspace traffic management.
En route control	Yes	Controller is responsible for maintaining separation, traffic flow, handoffs. • Voice communications • Radar display monitoring
Terminal arrival	Yes	Arrival clearances issued by the control, separation, and landing guidance. • Voice communication • Radar display monitoring

Figure 6-1   Current domain of the controller.

nology, it was evident that three functional components, Manage Flight Plans, Traffic Flow Management, and Terminal Traffic Management, are most amenable to automation. The rationale is given in Figure 6-2.

Now the first step has been completed. Next, the functional components are related to the elements of the future system. Following this comparison, user input is obtained and the process is iterated.

The elements, or required capabilities, of the future system were obtained from a draft FAA System Requirements Specification for the Advanced Automation System. These capabilities were then partitioned into a preliminary set of functional configuration items (FCIs) and were further divided into functional components (FCs). (The term ''functional'' is being used here rather than ''software'' because the functions have not yet been allocated to software and hardware. It is a good idea to categorize these functions in a way that is compatible with configuration management terminology so that the development team thinks in terms of configuration control from the beginning of the project.) This partition is based on a logical grouping of the functions and on an analysis of the communication between those functions.

Functional Component	Controller Intensive	Rationale
Manage flight plans	No	Computer is capable of assistance in areas such as: • Flight plan probe, verification, validation • ETABS • Flight plan modification and update
Traffic flow management	No	AERA is capable of assistance in areas such as: • Automatic conflict probe and resolution • En route metering • Trajectory modeling, etc.
Terminal departure	Yes	Controller is required for: • Voice communication • Radar display monitoring • Review of computer outputs Computer-assisted clearances
Terminal traffic management	No	Computer capable of assistance in areas such as: • En route metering • Separation, flow management • Landing sequencing, etc. Computer-assisted clearances
En route control	Yes	Controller is required for: • Voice communication • Radar display monitoring • Review of computer outputs
Terminal arrival	Yes	Controller is required for: • Voice communication • Radar display monitoring • Review of computer outputs Computer-assisted clearances

Figure 6-2 Future domain of the controller.

The preliminary functional configuration items for the AAS include fourteen functional configuration items. The five functional configuration items that comprise the Application Subsystem and their associated functional components are shown in Figure 6-3. When we discuss structured analysis techniques, this figure will be called a *hierarchical function chart* or *function tree*.

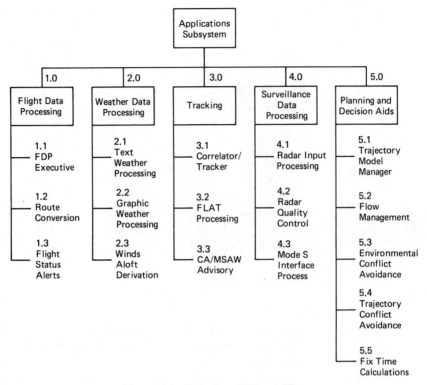

Figure 6-3 Preliminary FCIs and FCs.

The functional descriptions of the Applications Subsystem FCIs and FCs were examined to see which of these subsystem components (for the new system) could provide the capabilities furnished by the functional elements (determined from an operational viewpoint): Manage Flight Plans, Traffic Flow Management, and Terminal Traffic Management. After examining these descriptions, it was apparent that four functional configuration items of the Advanced Automation System and twelve subordinate functional components could be the means for automating the three functional elements just discussed.

This matching of operator functions to system functions is illustrated in Figure 6-4. It is shown, for example, that FCI 1.0, Flight Data Processing, and FCs 1.1 through 1.3 provide future support for the functional element Manage Flight Plans. The boxes in Figure 6-4 with the darker shading denote the areas in which highest productivity gains can be realized. The boxes with lighter shading show areas where lower productivity gains can be realized.

The procedure until this point has been based on a review of documentation and on our knowledge of air traffic control operations. This knowledge was based on visits to terminals and to en route centers and the experience of some of our staff. These results were taken to a major airport terminal and an en route center to obtain inputs from air traffic controllers.

Operator Functional Elements \ Application Subsystem Functions	1.0 Flight Data Processing	1.1 FDP Executive	1.2 Route Conversion	1.3 Flight Status Alerts	2.0 Weather Data Processing	2.1 Text Weather Processing	2.2 Graphic Weather Processing	2.3 Winds Aloft Derivation	3.0 Tracking	3.1 Correlator/Tracker	3.2 FLAT Process	3.3 CA/MSAW (Collision Avoidance)	4.0 Surveillance Data Processing	4.1 Radar Input Process	4.2 Radar Quality Control	4.3 Mode 'S' Interface Processing	5.0 Planning and Decision Aids	5.1 Trajectory Model Manager	5.2 Flow Management	5.3 Environmental Conflict Avoidance	5.4 Trajectory Conflict Avoidance	5.5 Fix Time Calculations
Manage Flight Plans	▓	▓	▓																			
Traffic Flow Management					▓	▓	▓	▓									▓	▓	▓	▓	▓	
Terminal Departure					▓	▓	▓	▓									▓					
Terminal Traffic Management					▓	▓	▓	▓									▓	▓	▓	▓	▓	
En Route Control					▓	▓	▓	▓									▓	▓	▓	▓	▓	
Terminal Arrival					▓	▓	▓	▓									▓	▓	▓	▓	▓	

Figure 6-4   Functional configuration items and components.

Their inputs are included in the figures presented here. A primary input from the controllers that was not anticipated in earlier analysis is the significant increase in controller productivity expected from the Mode S communications system. This system will provide a digital link between the controllers and aircraft. Only the interface with Mode S is part of the Advance Automation System, so it was not initially considered important.

However, significant productivity gains with Mode S will be realized because a limiting factor in the number of aircraft that can currently be controlled by a single air traffic controller is the time it takes to speak with each pilot. Routine passing of clearances can be achieved digitally. The time saved by a digital transmission over a verbal transmission will permit the controller to talk to and handle more aircraft.

All the functional components listed in Figure 6-4 have to be implemented. Most of them will provide capabilities similar to those that already exist and will provide computer assistance to the controllers. The functional components specified in the columns containing the more darkly shaded boxes will provide the greatest increases in productivity.

6.2 TRACEABILITY OF CURRENT CAPABILITIES

We first provide an approach to evaluating the system legacy by establishing a traceability matrix between the existing system capabilities and the required functions. The current capabilities can then be addressed from a variety of viewpoints (e.g., hardware, software, facility) to determine the system legacy. In this section, we provide an example using a software viewpoint. Thus, we establish the software legacy.

The software legacy is the portion of the existing system that can be reused. These items, or reusable parts, consist of code, blocks of logic, design, and requirements. The requirements being reused may be special exceptions, not thought of in previous requirements documents, that are realized through the patches to the existing system. Many of these requirements are likely not to be included in the system requirements specification for the new system. The following activity is equivalent to the determination of reusable parts. In the government, this activity is required for the procurement of major systems with *mission critical software* by DOD Directive 5000.29 (June 1986).

Each of these steps should be performed in a structured analytic approach so that various levels of system capabilities and requirements are addressed. As will be shown later, this assessment of the software legacy permits the utilization of existing code, algorithms, or capabilities whenever feasible without imposing significant restrictions on the architecture or design of the new system. There is a bottom-up influence on the design that occurs whenever software is reused.

The top-level traceability matrix is illustrated in Figure 6-5. The current ATC system consists of Air Route Traffic Control Centers (ARTCC), Terminal Radar Control Centers (TRACONS), tower cabs, and supporting facilities. The support facilities include research and development and system engineering at the Technical Center in Atlantic City, and a training center in Oklahoma City. The Advanced Automation System includes the Area Control Facility (ACF), the Tower Control Facility (TCF), the Research and Development Facility (RDF), and the System Support Facility (SSF).

These facilities are further subdivided into subsystems and processing areas in Figure 6-5. These subsystems correspond to computer software configuration items (CSCIs). Figure 6-5 is abbreviated and used for illustrative purposes only. The shaded area of Figure 6-5 is expanded in Figure 6-6. Thus, Figure 6-6 is one segment of the complete top-level traceability matrix. Figure 6-6 compares the Air Route Traffic Control Center applications subsystems to the Area Control Facility basic ATC processing area. The presence of a check indicates that some of the capabilities of the current subsystem (the row) are required by the AAS processing subarea shown in the column.

The absence of a check in a column is due to either the fact that the processing area is new and does not represent a current capability or to the fact that the subsystem having the required capability is not shown. The absence of a check in a row means that the capability represented by the subsystem is required in some other processing area.

The matrix is completed by comparing the functions being performed by the current system (as described in the Subsystem Design Data documentation) with the functions specified for the Advanced Automation System. Using the software viewpoint, this process is carried to one further level of detail—a matrix of existing software modules versus planned subarea functions. By reviewing the existing modules and comparing them to the planned software, the *potential* software legacy is determined. The usefulness of the existing modules is determined separately.

As a word of caution, the logic of this top-down description is appealing but may also run contrary to the way the work is performed. It should be used as a guide (so that the analyst knows where he or she is going). The matrices are usually completed at the lowest level of detail first. The checks at the higher level are then achieved by summarizing the more detailed results.

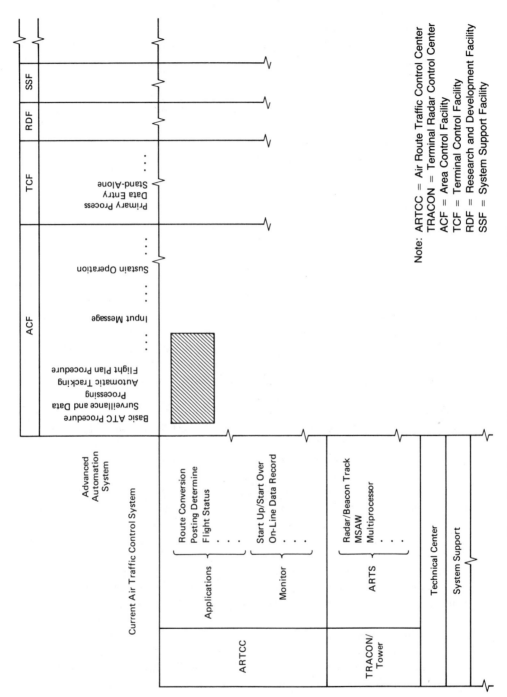

Figure 6-5 Mapping of the current capabilities into the required functions.

118

Current CCC Applications Subsystems	Surveillance and Data Processing	Automatic Tracking	Flight Plan Processing	Metering	Separation Assurance	Weather	Ancillary Processing
Route Conversion			✓				
Posting Determination			✓				
Flight Status Alerts			✓	✓			
Inquiry Processing					✓		
Track Data Processing	✓		✓	✓			
Display Channel Output							
Radar Processing and Automatic Tracking	✓	✓	✓	✓			
Real-Time Quality Control			TBD				
Preliminary Processing							
Flight Data Processing							
Supervisory			TBD				
Interfacility Outputs						✓	
Flight Plan Analysis			TBD				

(Column group heading: AAS Required Basic ATC Processing for ACF)

Figure 6-6 Relationship of required capabilities to existing subsystems (Part 1).

The actual legacy of each module is addressed by inspecting both the existing documentation and the code. The types of items that may provide useful legacy include:

- Overall program logic
- Algorithms
- Exception handling
- Detailed design
- Interface descriptions
- Code

In the case of the Advance Automation System, we first evaluated the System Design Data documentation for most applications subsystems. The documentation includes detailed flow charts and corresponds to a C5 Specification in accordance with MIL-STD 1521. This type of specification is a "code to" specification; that is, enough detail is presented for the programmers to produce code. After the code is operational and the document has been updated to reflect the actual code, this document becomes part of the

Subsystem	Code	NASP System Design Data							NAS MD-XXX
		Function	Design Considerations	Subroutine Environment	Interfaces	Start Up/Start Over	Top-Level Logic	Detailed Design Logic	
Route Conversion		✓	✓	✓	✓	N/A	✓	✓	312
Posting Determination		✓	•	•	✓		•	•	312
Flight Status Alerts		✓	•	•	✓	N/A	✓	•	311 314 315
Inquiry Processing		✓	✓	•	✓	N/A	•	•	314
Track Data Processing		✓	✓	✓	✓	✓	•	•	313
Display Channel Output		✓	•	•	✓	✓	✓	•	314
Radar Processing and Automatic Tracking		✓	✓	•	✓	✓	✓	•	320 321 316
Real-Time Quality Control		TBD							322
Preliminary Processing		•	•	•	✓	✓	•	•	311
Flight Data Processing		✓	✓	•	✓	N/A	✓	•	313
Supervisory		TBD							314
Interfacility Outputs		✓	✓	•	✓	✓	•	•	315
Flight Plan Analysis		TBD							313

Note: ✓ = mostly useful
     • = somewhat useful
       = hardly anything useful

Figure 6-7 Summary of documentation and code legacy.

product baseline, a subject we revisit in Chapters 7 and 11. A summary of the results is given in Figure 6-7.

Also given in Figure 6-7 is an indication of the applicable functional specification documentation (NAS MD-XXX). As indicated, there is no clear traceability from functional specification to subsystem for the current ATC system. Be careful about making value judgments on the existing system as a result of these charts. The existing system works very well. Also, much of this documentation predates concepts like structured programming and program modularity.

The columns under NASP System Design Data correspond to the subsections of the documentation. That is, each module of each subsystem is described in accordance with a format that has these components. The code itself was also obtained and inspected. The code is written in IBM Basic Assembly Language (BAL) and in JOVIAL.

The summary chart shows that the code itself has no useful legacy. There are many aspects of the software documentation, however, that are useful. Remember this chart is obtained by first completing a similar chart for each subsystem so that each module is inspected. The inspection is qualitative. The meaning of the check, dot, or blank must be assigned before the inspection for each column. This meaning is periodically reviewed as the tables are filled out.

A check under Design Considerations means that the documentation includes some information on special cases that should be included in the redesign. A dot means that there may be a little useful information there. Similarly, under Detailed Design Logic a check means that there are many blocks of logic that can be utilized in the redesign. A dot means that there are some useful blocks of logic.

Having achieved this level of detail, we have a qualitative assessment of the software legacy and a traceability of this legacy to the redesign system. A quantitative assessment is achieved by carrying this analysis one step further—by replacing the checks with specific algorithms and details.

The qualitative assessment should be performed during the requirements phase. A quantitative analysis should be performed during the preliminary design phase of the life cycle. If the existing system is well documented, it should take about three worker-days per subsystem or computer software configuration item for the qualitative analysis.

This qualitative legacy assessment provides an indication of the complexity and the cost of doing the job. It also provides indicators of *where* to look and *what* to look for during the system design phase.

CHAPTER 7 ⎯⎯⎯⎯⎯⎯⎯⎯⎯⎯⎯⎯⎯

Life-cycle Products

The system development life cycle was introduced in Chapter 3. When we described the life cycle, we kept emphasizing that our approach to software engineering is based on knowing what needs to be produced in each phase of the life cycle. Most programmers, systems analysts, and software engineers are good at their jobs. If they know what they need to produce, they can usually figure out how to do it. In this chapter we describe what needs to be produced in terms of the products demarcating the end of a phase.

There are three types of products that are produced during software development:

- Planning documents
- Management data and documents
- Software

Planning documents include the software development plan, the software standards and procedures, and configuration management plans. Planning documents are discussed in Section 7.1.

Planning documents are generally unpopular. They frequently are published in 3- or 4-inch notebooks and are placed on a bookshelf. I am aware of the case at a major corporation where the software configuration management/quality assurance manual was published in a 4-inch binder. Six months after it was published, a meeting was held by the senior vice-president for quality assurance. In attendance were division presidents and vice-presidents. This meeting was held in response to some quality problems on a couple of their major programs. It was clear from the comments and questions during the meeting that *none* of the line vice-presidents or presidents had read the manual. It was unlikely that they ever opened the notebook.

If these documents are expected to be read and used, they should not be longer than 150 pages; preferably, they should be under 50 pages. Anything that can enhance readability and convenience, such as on-line storage, should be done. When changes are made to documents, publish a highlight for these changes (like highlights to tax changes are published on the front of the instruction sheet for your 1040 tax form). Managers will ask their secretaries to insert the change pages and will never read them. In the case of on-line storage, page inserts are unnecessary.

Management data and documents include work breakdown structures, Gantt charts, and progress reports. These items are discussed in Section 7.2.

Software is intended to mean code and all associated documentation. We take a liberal viewpoint of documentation here. This documentation is intended to include requirements, specifications, users manuals, and test results. That is, software is the generic word for technical products. The software products are discussed by phase in Section 7.3.

Discussion of life-cycle products is inherently a dry topic. A lot of names of documents and acronyms are introduced. The terminology used here corresponds to that used by the Department of Defense. Some of it seems silly. For example, the word ''computer'' in ''computer software configuration item'' seems redundant (computer would be needed if jargon were consistent with English and we used the term ''soft goods'' for software). Many companies tailor the products to their needs and choose names that are more descriptive.

It is assumed in this chapter that we are discussing a large project. Smaller projects do not need all the documentation described here. Exactly what documentation is needed for your project depends on your customer's perception of what is needed and on your judgment. Until you obtain enough experience to make this judgment independently, documentation guidelines published by the National Bureau of Standards and other government agencies can be consulted.

7.1 PLANNING DOCUMENTS

The relationship among various project documents is given in Figure 7-1. The Program Master Plan is the governing document over the entire program development. It specifies the management organization and responsibilities, the work breakdown structure, schedules, and other program plans. These plans include the System Engineering Master Plan (SEMP), the Integrated Logistics Support Plan, the Computer Resource Management Plan, the Production Plan, and the Transition Plan.

These plans are all at the system level. On very large systems involving hundreds, or even thousands, of devices, it is important to address production capacity, second sources, and delivery schedules. These subjects are included in the production plan. Transition plans are needed whenever a system is to be installed in an existing operation. Transition plans are not always written as a separate formal document, but our planning needs to take into account factors such as:

• Training the current operators on the new system

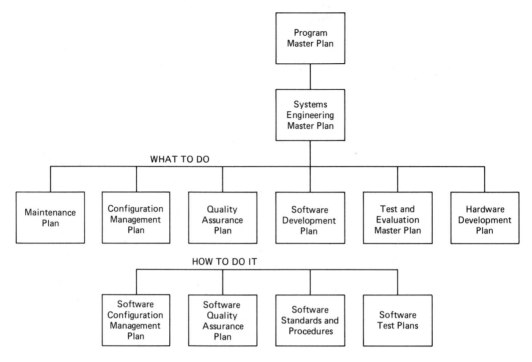

Figure 7-1 Relationship among project documents.

- The impact of installation on current operations
- The need to operate the new system and the existing system simultaneously

Some people would group the maintenance plan with the other documents at the level of the SEMP. It is listed in Figure 7-1 as subordinate to the SEMP because I think that the SEMP should account for maintenance as well as development. *Maintenance could be significantly simpler if products are developed to be maintained.*

A topical outline for a program management plan is given in Figure 7-2. This outline is based on the Data Item Description (DID) UDI-A-23972, indicated in this figure under Reference. I shall digress for a moment to explain what a DID (pronounced *did*) is. Whenever a contract is let by the government, the contract includes a table of items called the Contract Data Requirements List, or CDRL (pronounced *see-drl*). This table lists all the data deliverables. Each row of the table includes data elements, such as data title, technical office to which the data shall be delivered, how many copies of the product must be delivered, when it must be delivered, and a description of the item. The Contract Data Requirements List is a form (number DD 1423) that is completed and attached to the contract.

The description of the data to be delivered is frequently given in terms of a Data Item Description number. Published separately is a set of Data Item Descriptions that describe the deliverable in detail. For example, the Data Item Description for a software development plan is 13 pages long (single spaced). These Data Item Descriptions are available to the public.

Definition:
   The PMP is the basic documentation of the program management effort.

Top-level Outline
   • Overview of the management organization
   • Management controls
   • Schedule
      —Milestones
      —Critical Path
      —Cost
      —Work Breakdown Structure
   • Functional and Schedule Interrelationships
      —System Engineering Master Plan
      —Integrated Logistics Support Plan
      —Configuration Management Plan
      —Transition Plan

Reference
   • UDI-A-23972 Program Management Plan

Figure 7-2   Program master plan (PMP).

At other times a standard DID is not specified. In this event, a DID is written and enclosed with the contract. This DID could be the simple statement "Data to be delivered in contractor's format."

7.1.1 System Engineering Management Plan

The system engineering management plan (SEMP) is the basic plan for managing the system engineering effort. Generally, it is the first plan produced by the developer. The program management plan is frequently produced by the client. This is especially true for government procurements. For very large projects that involve hardware production, site preparation (such as construction), and other major nondevelopment activities, the program management plan is necessary. In this case, the concepts, plans, and policies in the program management plan are further defined at the system level by the SEMP.

A topical outline for the system engineering master plan is given in Figure 7-3. Note that the system development methodology is first specified in the SEMP. The methodology (i.e., procedures for what we are going to do) is given in greater detail in the system level plans of Figure 7-1 in the row labeled What to Do.

Each major system component is defined in the system engineering master plan. The hardware and software components are defined in terms of subsystems, segments, and configuration items. The SEMP provides the strategy for developing the system on a component-by-component basis. This is important because other plans, like the software

Definition:
   The SEMP specifies the plan for performing the management and systems
   engineering functions of the program.

Top-level Outline
   • Technical Program Planning and Control
      —Organization
      —Work Breakdown Structure
      —Schedules and Deliverables
      —Organizational Responsibility
      —Performance Metrics

   • Systems Engineering Process
      —Support Areas (e.g., human factors, engineering programs, configuration
        management programs)
      —Development Process (e.g., methodological approach, tools)

   • Engineering Specialty Integration
      —Intermeshing of, e.g., Safety, Reliability, Logistics Engineering
      —Site Integration

Reference
   • Mil-Std 499A Engineering Management

Figure 7-3 Systems engineering master plan (SEMP).

development plan, are often limited in scope to a single configuration item. Thus, it is the
SEMP that provides the glue. The SEMP takes into account the variations in development
schedule for configuration items.

The system development schedule is specified in the system engineering master
plan. This schedule indicates when each component must be completed, the dependencies
among these components, and the critical path. If we represent the scheduled activities as
a network in which the dependencies are indicated by the branches and the activities are
indicated by the nodes, then the critical path is the path through the network in which a
slip in the schedule at one of the nodes causes a slip in the delivery date.

The presence of performance metrics in the topical outline is emphasized. This item
is usually excluded from the SEMP. These metrics are the criteria on which the performance of the development group and the maintenance group will be measured. The criteria
should be stated in the System Requirements Specification and should be approved by the
client. The purpose of specifying these metrics in the system engineering master plan is to
evaluate the product in terms of the objectives, rather than by using ex post facto judgments. These judgments are frequently personality driven. They frequently do not account
for unplanned changes in requirements and the environment. When metrics are specified
in advance, they may form part of a basis on which the contractor's performance can be
judged in a legal sense if problems arise.

The system engineering master plan also defines the procedures to be used for integrating these components. Safety, reliability, power requirements, electromagnetic control, logistics, site integration, and human factors are just some of the disciplines that are tied together in the SEMP.

The SEMP is the cornerstone of the development effort. The software and hardware development plans only amplify and refine the principles and practices outlined in the system engineering master plan. Since the scope of this book is limited to software engineering, the only system level plan discussed here is the software development plan.

At the more detailed, "how to do it" level, each of the software-related documents is discussed. Subsequent chapters of this book are devoted to techniques for producing the required software.

7.1.2 Software Development Plan

The software development plan (SDP) outlines the software development process and explains what types of information must be collected at each phase of the development life cycle for management control. The detailed software plans and procedures, such as the software configuration management plan, are governed by the software development plan, and are frequently viewed as part of this plan. A topical outline for the SDP is given in Figure 7-4.

When large systems are being developed under contract, the development is typically performed by a team of companies. For example, the next-generation air traffic control system (called the Advanced Automation System) is being designed by two teams of companies. This competition is reminiscent of the old Air Force "fly-offs" used to purchase planes. The prime contractor for one team is IBM; the subcontractors include Computer Science Corporation. The prime contractor for the other team is Hughes Aircraft, with System Development Corporation, Burroughs, Magnavox, and others as subcontractors.

Under these circumstances, software is being designed, developed, and tested by more than one company. For large jobs, the software development plan and its subordinate documents are oriented toward specific configuration items. Any specified CSCI would be developed entirely by one company. Thus, each company may have an SDP. It is the job of the prime contractor to integrate these configuration items. The SDPs must conform with the schedule and guidelines of the system engineering master plan. There is only one SEMP, and it is the responsibility of the prime contractor to write it and to manage the entire program.

Sometimes a medium-sized system is being developed under a variety of hardware constraints that essentially converts the development into a software job. Suppose further that the entire job will be performed by a single development group (contractor, organization, etc.). In this case, there may be a single software development plan that covers all the software configuration items. Indeed, the SDP may assume the role of the system engineering master plan.

The role of the software development plan is becoming increasingly important. Historically, system developments have been driven by hardware. Hardware was very expen-

Definition
   The SDP describes the organization and procedures used to manage a
   software development activity.

Top-level Outline
   • Resources: facilities, software, hardware, people
   • Organization: responsibilities, relationships
   • Development Schedule and Milestones
   —Work Schedule
   —Activity Network
   —Risk Areas
   • Software Development Procedures
   —Software Standards and Procedures
   —Commercial and Reusable Software
   • Computer Software Design
   —Tools and Conventions (e.g., program design language and software
      development folders)
   —Critical CSC and Unit Selection Criteria
   • Configuration Management (cf. the SCMP)
   • Quality Assurance (cf. the Software Quality Assurance Plan and the
   Software Test Plan)

Reference
   DI-A-X103 Software Development Plan

Figure 7-4 Software development plan (SDP).

sive and not too flexible. People have gotten into the habit of specifying the hardware first
and then forcing the software structure to fit the hardware. It was not unusual for systems
to be unable to meet the requirements because of a poor selection of hardware. The attitude of simply buying the hardware before the software architecture is evaluated is still a
common practice. People who have to contend with massive bureaucracies sometimes do
this because of the long lead time to get approvals for purchases and to receive hardware
after purchase-orders are issued.

   This attitude is changing. DOD Directive 5000.29 (1986) mandates that hardware
shall not be purchased for mission-critical components until after software has been proto-
typed and evaluated. This directive recognizes that hardware is relatively inexpensive and
usually available commercially. Software is the current cost and performance driver.

   In the case of software for mission-critical components being developed for the government, the software development plan needs to reflect DOD Directive 5000.29. This
document is generally listed in Section 2 of the SDP under ''applicable documents.'' As a
result of this directive, some of the specific items that need to be addressed in the SDP for
this type of software are prototypes, reusable software, and placing developed software in
escrow.

   Delivered software is frequently only part of the total software. For example, only object code and a user's manual may be delivered. This event is common for commercial software. Problems arise when the software developer goes out of business or stops supporting the software for some other reason and claims to no longer have documentation, source code, or other parts of the software. The software contract should require the software developer to place all the software into a trust account managed by an impartial third party. The trust account would be blind to the purchaser until specified circumstances occur (such as the developer declares bankruptcy). Placing software in escrow could be a good marketing technique for commercial software.

7.1.3 Software Configuration Management Plan

The software configuration management plan (SCMP) describes the controls to be used to ensure the integrity of design, documentation, and delivered software. These controls provide guidelines for the establishment of baselines at major milestones in the development life cycle. The SCMP also specifies the methods to be used in controlling changes to these baselines. Configuration management is critical to both development and maintenance activities.

Although the software configuration management plan is essentially part of the software development plan, it must conform to the guidelines for configuration management specified in the system-level Configuration Management Plan. It should also be consistent with the maintenance procedures identified in the software maintenance plan. The SDP specifies the development schedule for each computer software configuration item (CSCI); the software configuration management plan explains how these CSCIs will be controlled. A topical outline for a SCMP is given in Figure 7-5.

7.1.4 Software Quality Assurance Plan

The software quality assurance plan (SQAP) describes the organization and procedures to be used by the system developer to ensure the quality of the final delivered product. This quality is measured in terms of compliance with the software requirements. For smaller projects, the SQAP may be included as a section of the software development plan. On larger projects, a separate SQAP is written.

The quality assurance function is not limited to participation in formal project reviews or to periodic audits. It is an integral part of the development activity. It involves the entire development team—not just those people designated as part of the quality assurance group.

A topical outline for a software quality assurance plan is given in Figure 7-6. The section on specification review should include procedures for determining the testability of the software and interface requirements. Procedures for reviews of the design and code should include both formal review and informal peer reviews. These procedures should be explicit. It is important to specify what documentation must be delivered before each review and to specify the amount of time required for documentation review before the formal review is permitted. Without these explicit procedures, it is difficult for the quality assurance group to control the review process.

Definition:
The SCMP describes the controls to be used to ensure the integrity of design, documentation, and delivered software.

Top-level Outline
- Organization
- Configuration Identification
  —Baselines
  —CSCI and Related Documentation
- Configuration Control
  —Forms
  —Procedures
  —Review Boards
  —Storage and Release
- Additional Control
  —Status Accounting
  —Audits

Reference
- DI-E-X104 Software Configuration Management

Figure 7-5 Software configuration management plan (SCMP).

Definition:
The SQAP describes the organization and procedures to be used to ensure that the software to be delivered complies with the requirements.

Top-level Outline
- Organizational Structure and Resources
- Critical Performance Factors Monitoring
- Quality Audits
- Reporting and Control
- Reviews
  —Specification
  —Design
  —Code
- Testing (Plans, Description, Procedures, Conducting of the Test, Reports)
  —Identify Responsible Organization
  —Quality Assurance Procedures for Reviewing Testing

Reference
- DI-R-X105 Software Quality Assurance Plan

Figure 7-6 Software quality assurance plan (SQAP).

Program organizations vary among companies and government agencies. In some organizations, the quality assurance group is responsible for independent testing, configuration management, quality control, and development of quality assurance tools. In this case, test plans and procedures are included as part of the software quality assurance plan. In the event that this is not the case, it is only necessary to establish the relationship between the quality assurance group and the testing group.

EXERCISE 7.1   In many organizations, the quality assurance group is considered a staff organization. In other organizations, the quality assurance group is responsible for independent testing and is considered a line organization. Which organization do you prefer? What are the pros and cons of each?

7.1.5 Software Maintenance Plan

As will be discussed in Section 7.3, the maintenance concept is a key part of the operational concept developed during the system planning phase. This concept influences

---

Definition:
   The software maintenance plan describes the organization, resources, and procedures for maintaining the system software, support software, and applications software.

Top-level Outline
   • System Description
   • Management
      —Identification of User, Developer, Maintainer
      —Responsibilities
      —Interfaces
   • Procedures
      —Configuration Management
      —Quality Assurance
      —Testing/Acceptance Testing
      —Maintenance Cycles
   • Resources
      —Hardware (maintenance environment)
      —Support Software
      —Personnel
      —Facilities
      —Supplies

Reference
   • NBS Special Publication 500-129

Figure 7-7   Software maintenance plan (SMP).

the design. A distributed system in which all software maintenance is performed remotely and downloaded to individual sites is designed differently from a system in which the maintenance is done locally.

The development process often involves the delivery of some configuration items while others are still under development. This means that some of the software is being used and maintained concurrently with some development activities. The maintenance plan should be produced (at least in draft form) by the time that the first computer software configuration item is in code and unit test. A topical outline of a software maintenance plan is given in Figure 7-7.

7.1.6 Software Standards and Procedures

The software standards and procedures (SSP) document establishes the standards, procedures, guidelines, and restrictions to be used during the software development and maintenance. The SSP tells us how to implement the methodology described in the software development plan. A topical outline for the SSP is given in Figure 7-8.

Coding practices discussed in Chapter 2 should be included in a standards and procedures document. This document also addresses module design and interface conventions. To the maximum extent possible, the interface conventions should conform to IEEE standards. Program interface standards are currently in a state of flux. Major efforts are

---

Definition:
    The SSP establishes the standards, procedures, guidelines and restrictions to be used in the development of CSCIs.

Top-level Outline
- Software Development
  —Requirements Analysis Tools and Techniques
  —Program Support Library
  —Commercial and Reusable Software
  —Test Tools
- Computer Software Design
  —Design Methodology for Software and Data Bases
  —Interface Conventions
  —Naming and Documenting Conventions
  —Software Design Folders
  —Critical CSC and Module Selection Criteria
  —Human Factors
- Coding Standards

Reference
    DI-M-X109 Software Standards and Procedures Manual

Figure 7-8 Software standards and procedures (SSP).

underway to determine these standards so that software fragments (ranging from units to configuration items) are reusable. It is suggested that, before you write standards for either your program or your company, you check with the IEEE to determine their latest results.

Key attributes of standards are that they be easily understood, easy to use, and easy to enforce. Whenever possible, tools should be used to automatically enforce the standards.

7.1.7 Software Test Plan

A software test plan (STP) is generally developed for each computer software configuration item. It defines the total scope of the testing effort. This includes both informal and formal tests. Each CSCI is composed of one or more Computer Software Components (CSCs). Informal testing is conducted at the CSC integration level and below. Formal testing is conducted on the integration of the full CSCI. Formal testing is also performed at the system and subsystem levels where multiple CSCIs are integrated or where CSCIs and HWCIs are integrated.

The testing methodology is discussed more fully in Chapter 11. A topical outline for a software test plan is given in Figure 7-9.

Definition:
  The STP defines the total scope of testing for a particular Computer Software Configuration Item (CSCI).

Top-level Outline
  • Assumptions, Limitations, and Traceability
  • Informal Test Plans (Requirements, Management, Schedule)
    —Unit Testing
    —CSC Integration Testing
    —Resources Required
  • Formal Test Plans
    —Requirements
    —Management
    —Classes (e.g., timing, capacity, and erroneous input)
    —Test Descriptions (for each formal test)
    —Data Reduction and Analysis
    —Test Table
    —Schedule and Deliverables
    —Resources Required

Reference
  • DI-T-X116 Software Test Plan

Figure 7-9 Software test plans (STP).

7.2 MANAGEMENT DATA AND DOCUMENTS

Sometimes project planning is confused with system planning. System planning is the first phase of the life cycle. Its products are described in Section 7.3.1. Project planning is needed for all projects, independently of the life-cycle phase in which they start. Project planning activities should be performed throughout the existence of a project.

Project planning includes:

- Establishing a project organization
- Developing a work breakdown structure (WBS)
- Creating a work schedule
- Determining the critical path
- Monitoring progress

The organizational structure depends on the specific project and the environment in which the project is being performed. This environment includes the relationship between the buyer of the software development and the developer. It also includes corporate policies, such as a preference for line organizations (as opposed to matrix organizations) and the role of corporate-level quality assurance.

Presented in Figure 7-10 is a generic project organization upon which subsequent discussion is based. When specifying an organization, it is necessary to specify the responsibilities, interfaces, primary functions, and supervisor's name and job title for each organizational entity. The responsibilities of each organizational entity are best defined by establishing the relationship between that entity and the work breakdown structure.

A work breakdown structure is a hierarchical organization of the project tasks. That is, a tree structure is imposed on the tasks. At the lowest level (the leaves), individual work packages are defined. A work package typically lasts about two weeks and is assigned to an individual. A work package should culminate in a product. For projects that last in excess of three to six months, it may not be possible to specify the WBS to this level of detail. In these cases, it is necessary to revisit the WBS periodically so that work packages are defined as far in advance as is practical.

The level of detail to which a WBS should be specified for large projects is frequently a subject of debate. This debate exists because large projects have multiple layers of management. Each manager only needs the information for monitoring progress at his or her level and for reporting progress for his or her area of responsibility.

Suppose that the WBS contained nine levels. The project manager may be required to report at the top three levels. He or she may need information for only the top five or six levels of the WBS. At the other end of the spectrum, the task manager may need information at only the eighth and ninth levels of the WBS.

A WBS dictionary should be developed for each work breakdown structure. The WBS element names are normally too short to define clearly what is intended. The WBS dictionary contains a short descriptive paragraph (one to three sentences) for each element

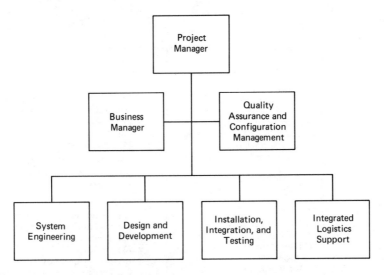

Figure 7-10 Generic project organization.

of the work breakdown structure. When a project manager receives a new task, these paragraphs help to determine the applicable WBS elements and (as we will see later) the people who should be responsible for the task.

Some organizations control money but do not actually have the people. This situation is true of matrix organizations and of organizations that use a lot of contractors. These organizations also need to perform planning and to develop work breakdown structures; however, the work packages for these organizations may be significantly bigger than the work packages described previously.

Work breakdown structures are generally determined by analyzing the work to be done. This work is specified in terms of a set of tasks and subtasks. The hierarchy continues to be refined until individual work packages are determined or until the lowest reasonable level of specificity is obtained. Numbers are assigned to these tasks and subtasks. Each item in a WBS should be assigned to a single organizational unit.

Frequently, the top three or four levels of the WBS are specified by the client. This situation is especially true in the case of government solicitations. Clients will impose this top-level structure because these are the levels of the WBS they use to monitor the contract progress. This progress is reported both in terms of the products being produced and the funds being expended for each client-specified WBS element. The developer's accounting system should be able to track the cost of the work being performed for every WBS element and should be able to compare these actual costs to the budgeted costs.

When this type of cost monitoring exists, it is possible to measure progress in terms of earned value. We say that a work package has zero earned value until it is completed. When the actual costs are subtracted from the budgeted costs, we get the variance for each completed work package. The cost progress can then be measured in terms of earned value and total variance. A positive variance means that we are under budget. Whenever the total variance is negative, costs and schedules should be reviewed. A negative variance in excess of 10% of the earned value is a warning sign of serious problems.

The Department of Defense has specified standard work breakdown structures in

100 PROJECT MANAGEMENT

110 Management Documentation
   111 Mission Element Needs Statement/
       Operational Requirements
   112 Decision Coordinating Papers
   113 Development Plan/Project Master Plan
   114 Acquisition Strategy/Plan
   115 Planning, Programming, and Budgeting
       System
   116 Briefings/Summary Reports
   117 Acquisition Documents

120 Management Data
   121 Work Breakdown Structure
   122 Project Scheduling
   123 Cost Estimates and Models
   124 Data Requirements
   125 Data Management
   126 Data Depository
   127 Contractor Reports, Reviews

130 Business and Administration
   131 Administrative Procedures
   132 Project Funded Salaries
   133 Management Reserve
   134 Undistributed Budget
   135 Negotiated Differentials
   136 Project Travel
   137 Project Security
   138 Subcontract Budgets
   139 Subcontract Management

200 SYSTEM ENGINEERING

210 System Definition
   211 Requirements Definition
   212 Baseline Definition
   213 Performance Criteria
   214 Alternatives Assessment
   215 Validation Assessment
   216 Special Concepts/Developments

220 System Design and Development
   221 System Design
   222 System Integration Requirements
   223 Data Base Design
   224 Development Model Hardware
   225 System Software Development
   226 System Data Base Development
   227 Development Model Tests/
       Demonstrations
   228 Design Enhancements

230 System Engineering Administration
   231 System Engineering Management Plan
   232 Design Development Reviews
   233 Engineering Data

240 System Engineering Support
   241 Value Engineering Program
   242 Survivability/Vulnerability Analyses
   243 Production Engineering Analyses
   244 Quality Assurance Program
   245 Safety Program
   246 Human Factors Engineering
   247 Security Engineering Program

250 System Data Base Management
   251 System Data Element Directory
   252 System Data Library

260 Configuration Management
   261 Configuration Management Plan
   262 Configuration Item Identification
   263 Specification Tree
   264 Configuration Control
   265 Configuration Audits
   266 Configuration Status Accounting

300 SYSTEM TEST AND EVALUATION

310 Test and Evaluation Planning
   311 Test and Evaluation Concept
   312 Test and Evaluation Master Plan
   313 Test and Evaluation Plan
   314 Test Plans and Procedures

320 Development Test and Evaluation
   321 Facilities/Mockups
   322 Support
   323 Test Operations and Data Collection
   324 Test Data Reduction and Analysis

330 Operational Test and Evaluation
   331 Facilities
   332 Support
   333 Test Operations and Data Collection
   334 Test Data Reduction and Analysis

340 Security Test and Evaluation
   341 Facilities/Mockups
   342 Support
   343 Test Operations and Data Collection
   344 Test Data Reduction and Analysis

350 Approval for Use

**400 PROGRAM EQUIPMENT AND
SOFTWARE**

410 Program Equipment and Software
   411 ADP Hardware
   412 ADP Software
   413 Displays Printers
   414 Communications
   415 Sensors
   416 Auxiliary Equipment

Figure 7-11 System under development program work breakdown structure.

420 Hardware Enhancements

430 Project Integration and Assembly

440 Program Integration and Assembly

500 INTEGRATION LOGISTICS SUPPORT

510 Logistics Management
  511 Administration
  512 System Design Support
  513 Production/Acquisition Support
  514 Support Management
  515 Technical Reviews

520 Documentation
  521 Logistics Plans
  522 Technical Data

530 Logistics Engineering
  531 Reliability, Maintainability and Availability
  532 Logistic Support Analysis
  533 Level of Repair Analysis
  534 Other Related Logistic Analysis
  535 Logistic Design Reviews

540 Manpower and Personnel
  541 M&P Concepts and Requirements Determination
  542 M&P Requirements Analysis
  543 Manpower Acquisition Planning

550 Training
  551 Training Concepts and Requirements Determination
  552 Training Coordination
  553 Training Materials and Service
  554 Training Equipment
  555 Training Program
  556 Follow-on Training
  557 Performing Activity Training

560 Supply Support
  561 Supply Support Concepts and Requirements Determination
  562 Provisioning Criteria and Initial Spares and Repair Parts
  563 Spares and Repair Parts

570 Support and Test Equipment
  571 Support and Test Equipment Concepts and Requirements Determination
  572 Common Support Equipment
  573 Unique Support Equipment
  574 Software Support Programs

580 Transportation and Handling
  581 T&H Concepts and Requirements Determination
  582 Handling

590 Support Facilities
  591 Support Facilities Concept and Determination
  592 Maintenance Facilities
  593 Supply Support Facilities
  594 Training Facilities
  595 Data Activity

600 SITE/PLATFORM INTEGRATION

610 Site/Platform Identification and Planning
  611 Site Platform Surveys
  612 Electron System Engineering Plan
  613 Site/Platform Test Planning

620 Site/Platform Construction Conversion
  621 Site Construction
  622 Site/Platform Conversion

630 System Assembly Installation and Checkout (On-Site)
  631 Assembly Installation and Checkout
  632 Performing Activity Standby Services
  633 Temporary Performing Activity Activation Maintenance

640 Site/Platform Acceptance Test and Turnover

700 PRODUCTION FACILITIES

710 Facility Development
  711 Construction/Conversion/Expansion
  712 Equipment Modernization

720 Facilities Maintenance

730 Inventory
  731 Spares Inventory
  732 Replacement Parts Inventory

800 OPERATIONS AND MAINTENANCE

810 Operational Maintenance
  811 Organization Level Maintenance
  812 Intermediate Level Maintenance
  813 Depot Level Maintenance

820 Operational System Activities

Figure 7-11   (continued)

Military Standard MIL-STD 481. A WBS based on this military standard is given in Figure 7-11. This WBS is specified to three levels of detail. For large projects it is not unusual for the WBS to have seven to ten levels of detail.

Using a standard work breakdown structure for each project enables us to compare costs among projects and for estimating similar types of work. This is useful information, but a standard has the disadvantage of fitting the project planning to a given structure rather than fitting the structure of the project planning to the nature of the problem at hand. Both approaches have their merits. If the second approach is used, a standard like the one given in Figure 7-11 is still useful as a checklist. Without a good checklist it is easy to neglect some key activities in your work breakdown structure.

EXERCISE 7.2   Write one- or two-sentence definitions for at least five of the elements of the work breakdown structure given in Figure 7-11.

It is a good idea to map at least the top two to three levels of your WBS to the software development life cycle. An illustration of such a mapping is given in Figure 7-12. Do not attempt to "understand" this work breakdown structure. To do so requires a review of its WBS dictionary (which is not given here). This particular work breakdown structure was taken from a government solicitation.

In Figure 7-13, we show an example of a WBS that has been assigned to organizational units. Thus, when a task is assigned to a project, it is defined in terms of WBS numbers. Organizational responsibility is clear from Figure 7-13. Using a figure like Figure 7-12, we can then narrow each WBS item within the task to a single life-cycle phase.

As indicated in Section 3.1, we consider each phase of the life cycle a black box. We know what the outputs (i.e., the products) are and we know what the required inputs are. With this information, we define the WBS items needed to obtain the products. In doing so, we specify a schedule and deliverables for each WBS element. This work schedule should be expressed graphically as a Gantt chart.

A typical Gantt chart is shown in Figure 7-14. Gantt charts traditionally show only schedule information. Some people like to show the critical path and slack on Gantt charts. Schedule charts produced by most computer program management packages, such as VISISCHEDULE, have this information. The terms "critical path" and "slack" are defined in the next few paragraphs.

After we define the work schedule in terms of individual processes or subtasks, the time it takes to complete each subtask, and the dependencies among the subtasks, we can express the set of tasks as an activity network. A typical network is shown in Figure 7-15. Having achieved this network, the critical path is the *longest path through the network*. This longest path through the network corresponds to the *shortest* time required to complete the task.

Remember, we have to complete all the activities, and because of dependencies we cannot begin some activities until others are completed. The time that we can afford to wait without interrupting the final delivery date is called the *slack*. That is, we have to wait until the longest path through the network is achieved.

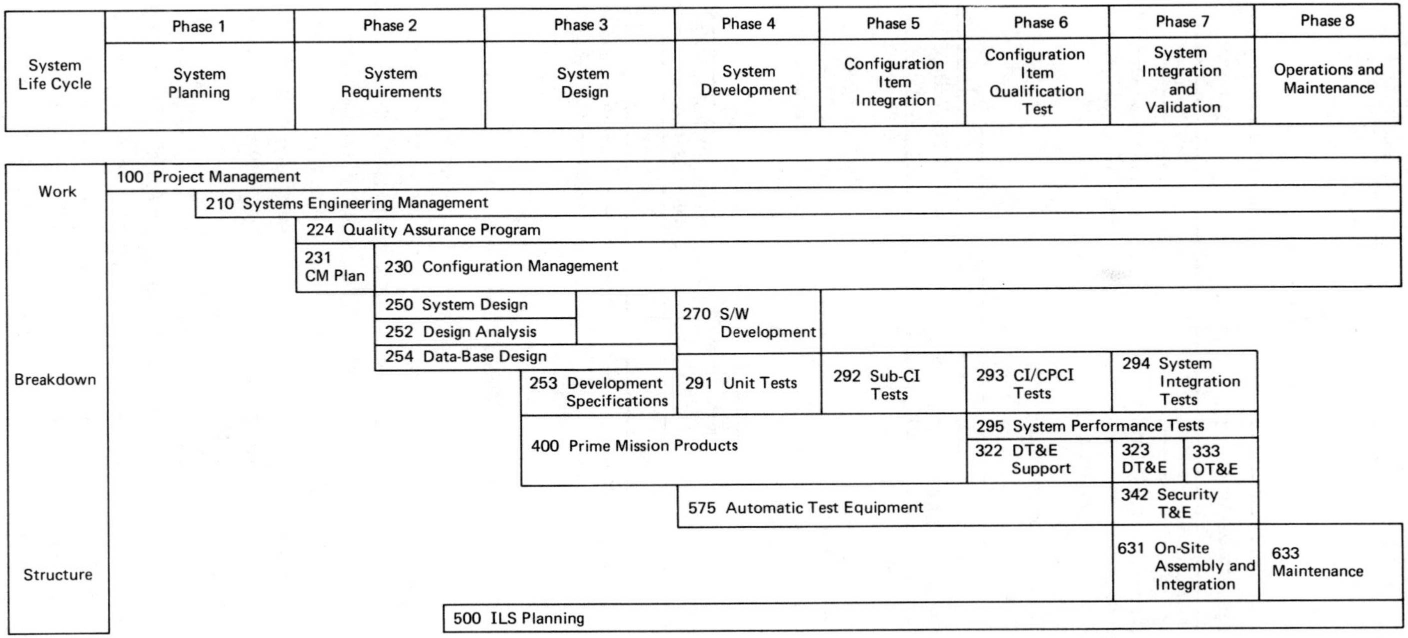

Figure 7-12 Mapping of the WBS to the life cycle.

Note: To understand this WBS allocation, you need to read the WBS dictionary.

139

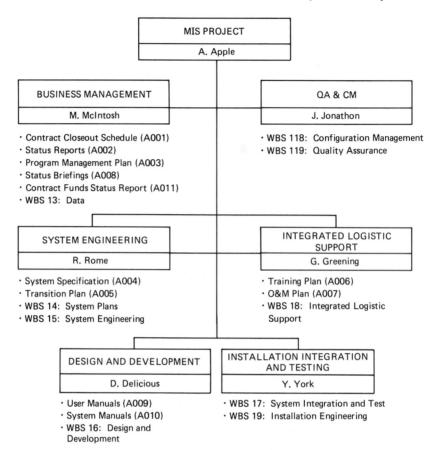

Figure 7-13 Mapping of the WBS and deliverables to organizational units.

In Figure 7-15, the critical path is indicated by the bold lines. This type of network is called a PERT chart. PERT is an acronym for Program Evaluation and Review Technique. It was developed by the Navy under the direction of Admiral Rickover for the Polaris submarine project. That was a remarkable systems engineering project that involved the development of a new class of submarine, a new type of power plant (based on nuclear energy), and a new type of missile (a submarine-launched ballistic missile or SLBM). Using PERT as a management tool, the Polaris project was actually delivered ahead of schedule and under cost.

EXERCISE 7.3   Select a project on which you have worked. Job experience is preferable, but you may select a "senior project" in the absence of work experience. Quantify this project in terms of its size and complexity. What documentation was required for this project? What documentation do you think should have been required? Using the metrics you selected to quantify the project, what documentation do you think should be required for a project that is twice (half) the size and/or complexity?

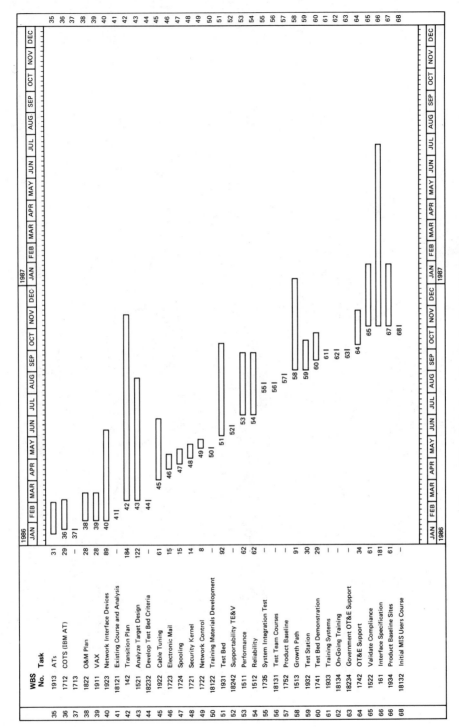

Figure 7-14 Gantt chart with critical path superimposed.

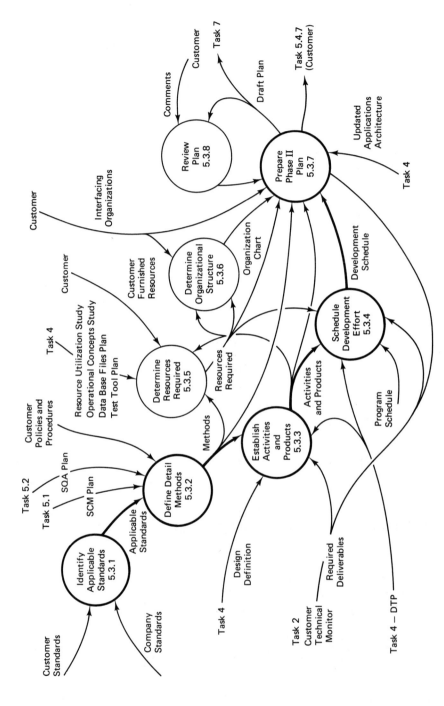

Figure 7-15 Network PERT chart of implementation plan activities.

7.3 SOFTWARE PRODUCTS

In this section we shall proceed through the life cycle, defining the technical products for each phase.

7.3.1 System Planning Phase

The system planning phase is sometimes called the system concept phase. It is a period in which various systems concepts should be explored and evaluated. Classical operations research analysis should be performed during this phase. The question to answer is, "How do we improve our operations most efficiently?"

Some of these analyses may include time and motion studies. Automation for its own sake is seldom beneficial. It is also important to avoid simply automating functions that have hitherto been performed manually. It is necessary to determine the actual purpose of the system. It is also necessary to determine what the people will do now that they should have more time available.

Once the system concept has been defined, a concept of operations should be written. The topics to be included in the concept of operations are:

- Current operational environment
- Deficiencies
- New system enhancements
- Reliability and maintainability requirements
- Conceptual approach to how the new system will operate
- Conceptual approach to maintenance
- Probable approach to training
- Predicted system workload
- Operational requirements
- Related developments and their status
- Schedule items
- User interface

To justify the need for a new system, we should be able to calculate the return on investment. To do so, it is necessary to estimate life-cycle costs and savings and to continuously revise these estimates. These estimates cannot be made without an understanding of how the system will be maintained and how people will be trained to use the system.

The approach to maintenance for some systems may be to purchase a contract from the vendor. For a large distributed system, the approach may be to perform all software maintenance at a single site and to download corrections and enhancements electronically. These decisions affect both the requirements and the design for the system. They have major impacts on system operational and development cost.

Some people claim that the operational concept, the training concept, and the maintenance concept are three separate documents. In this book they were treated as one document because it is difficult to get people to write a single document that specifies the operational concept. Getting them to write three documents may be impossible.

7.3.2 Requirements Phase

The system requirements phase is divided into three subphases: system requirements analysis, requirements allocation, and software requirements analysis. The latter two subphases are sometimes called either the logical requirements phase or the demonstration and validation phase. Another name used for the requirements phase is the system definition phase.

The latter name is descriptive of the purpose of the requirements phase. In this phase we define *what* the system is supposed to do. In subsequent phases we define *how* the system does it. During the planning phase, the system requirements were specified from the viewpoint of the user. These requirements may be called user-oriented requirements. During the requirements phase, the user-oriented requirements are transitioned into system-oriented requirements.

When first organizing requirements and trying to obtain a system orientation, it is frequently convenient to begin by appending to the user-oriented requirements or applications functions the following list:

- Security
- User interface
- Training
- Data communications
- Maintenance diagnostics
- Data-base services
- Configuration management
- Development and maintenance tools
- System resource management

This list should be thought of as a group of categories, not frequently addressed by users, that are useful for determining system-oriented requirements. Each of these categories should be analyzed from the viewpoint of the system being considered and how this system will have to be implemented. Examples of system-oriented requirements for each of these categories are given in Table 7-1.

EXERCISE 7.4   Is this set of categories adequate? If not, what categories would you add? Provide at least one example of a system-oriented requirement for each category listed previously and in the first part of this exercise. None of your examples should be the same as those given in Table 7-1. Critique the examples given in Table 7-1.

TABLE 7-1 Examples of Systems-oriented Requirements

Requirement Category	Example
Security	The system shall satisfy the B2 class of requirements for a trusted computer system specified in CSC-STD-001-83.
User interface	
Physical interface	The display must be able to be partitioned into at least four windows.
	There shall be three levels of tones, varying according to urgency, to alert the user of errors.
	Both English and Cyrillic characters shall be permanently inscribed on keycaps.
Functional interface	The HELP facility shall be structured to accommodate at least two levels of user proficiency.
	Electronic mail service shall be provided, including notifying user of mail arrival, storing mail until requested, send messages, create messages, forward messages, file messages, distribution lists for messages, bulletin board, scan mailbox, delivery confirmation, and correspondence forms.
Communications	It shall not be necessary for the user to learn any operating system (e.g., UNIX) commands.
	Except for files stored on the user's workstation, the user shall not need to know file structure or location of data.
Data-base management	
Mainframe	The DBMS shall be at least as capable as Model 204.
Workstation	It shall be able to contain formatted data and free-form text.
	Numeric, alphanumeric, and logical data fields shall be allowed.
	Interactive (nonprocedural) queries or commands equivalent to "select and print all records where [condition] is met," where [condition] can be a complex logical expression, and other data-base manipulation commands shall be allowed.
	Multikey access to data with capabilities for concatenated keys, partial keys, and "wild-card" keys shall be allowed.
Data communications	
Internal	Establish workstation-to-workstation and workstation-to-host connections.
	Support the following activity profile for each shift: . . . .
	Each workstation shall have a split screen capability and allow the user to have four simultaneous sessions.
	Provide the capability to enact moves and changes while the network is operational.
	The network control center shall maintain the network directory, set access restrictions and privileges, monitor and archive connection requests, ...
External	Establish connections with other systems that use SNA interfaces.
	Provide protection against other systems gaining access to certain types of data (this example needs to be tailored to the system).
Maintenance diagnostics	Hardware diagnostic tools shall be provided for each major subsystem or component.

TABLE 7-1   (Continued)

	DASD disaster recovery from data check, track overrun, equipment check, checksum errors, etc. BIU diagnostic routines. Audit trail of information on tape usage.
Configuration management Software	Automate capture of software metrics. Configuration status accounting shall be automated, including version control of all products in the life cycle and status of all development and redevelopment efforts.
Data	Allow "roll back" to prior releases. Allow "roll forward" of archived data. Control the data dictionary.
Hardware	Develop and maintain configuration diagrams. Cable segment diagrams shall depict the location of each cable segment, each BIU, processor, or other device connected to the segment, and the means of attachment.
Development and maintenance tools Specific tools	File and source code comparators. BEST/1 capacity planning tool. SofTool CSS or equivalent capability.
Project management	Status of tasks to be provided automatically and upon request. Provide test and development control by allowing definition of test and integration levels by authorized personnel, ...
System resource management	Information shall be provided in the following areas: CPU utilization, memory utilization, paging rate, channel queue utilization, number of users, ... Workstation backup and recovery system shall be able to transfer all data files to the backup computer, recover named files from the backup computer, maintain an audit trail of backup and recovery activities, ...
Training	Pocket-sized training aids shall be provided. On-line tutorials shall be provided.

Typical analyses performed during this phase include:

- Rapid prototyping
- Performance modeling and estimation
- Cost estimation
- Reliability modeling
- Interface definition
- Structured (functional) analysis

- Data storage requirements
- Trade-offs among candidate configurations

There are two primary dangers of the requirements phase. The first is a narrowing of the scope of this phase to simply a structured analysis. The second danger is that buyers and many builders are very anxious to *see results*. The mentality of "build, don't think" is prevalent in our industry. This attitude frequently results in imposing artificial requirements on the system design.

Examples of artificial requirements include:

- Premature specification of hardware
- Requiring all commands, even retrievals from an archived data base, to be completed within 3 seconds
- Embedding design in requirements, such as choosing data structures or allocating functions to modules
- Embedding project requirements such as software development methodology

---

EXERCISE 7.5   Using your own experience, provide four examples of artificial requirements and of assumptions that designers make in the absence of a good system-oriented requirements document.

Performance modeling is a typical activity that is omitted. This omission has two major impacts. It could result in a system that simply has inadequate capacity. The less important, but still significant, impact is on the morale of the system builders. When the system engineers have little confidence that the system will work, the quality of their product goes down, if for no other reason than the fact that the smarter engineers will figure out how to work on a different project.

A second major pitfall involves rapid prototyping. Many people do not realize that the rapid prototype is not the system. Buyers, when confronted by a prototype, will frequently respond by stating that the prototype is good enough. It does most of what they want, so why bother spending the money on the rest of the system—it doesn't seem cost effective.

System developers frequently view prototyping as a way to bypass the bureaucracy of the system life cycle. They can focus on creative design and producing the system.

EXERCISE 7.6   Both of these viewpoints are wrong. It is left as an exercise to the reader to determine why. (I do not like this technique, but, in this case, your serious thoughts on the subject are more important than my serious writing.)

The requirements analysis phase is divided into either two or three phases. Here it is divided into the system requirements subphase, the allocation of requirements subphase, and the software requirements subphase. This decision was made because it corresponded to an early version of the life cycle specified in draft copies of DOD-STD 2167. Subsequently, this life cycle was revised. In the approved version of DOD-STD 2167, the first two subphases are combined. The approved version is illustrated in Chapter 3. In this section, the earlier version is used because there are distinct orientations in the first two subphases. In the first subphase the system's perspective is added to the users' requirements. The second subphase addresses issues related to determining whether certain items should be done in hardware, firmware, or software.

The products produced during the system requirements subphase are the System Requirements Specification (SRS) and the System Requirements Review (SRR). A recommended reference on this subject is the ANSI/IEEE Standard 830, "IEEE Guide to Software Requirements Specifications." The technical tasks required to produce a system requirements specification are:

- Functional definition
  - Functional characteristics
  - System diagrams
  - Functional configuration items
- Design data base
  - What information is required
  - How do you get the information
  - Data security
- Communications
  - Logical requirements
  - Physical requirements
  - Security and performance requirements
- Revised operational concept
- Reliability, maintainability, and availability (RMA) analysis
- Transition plans
  - Development
  - Maintenance
- Logistics
  - Maintenance
  - Supply
  - Support (e.g., training)
- Test and evaluation (T&E) requirements
- Personnel and training
  - Startup
  - Operation

The second subphase is allocation of requirements to hardware and software. It is during this phase that the functional configuration items begin to take the form of hardware configuration items (HWCIs) and computer software configuration items (CSCIs).

The general products are data flows, functional decomposition, functional interface specifications, and test requirements.

The functional decomposition results in data flows, a functional hierarchy, CSCI identification, inter-CSCI interface specifications, and inter-CSCI test requirements. This subphase results in a deeper understanding of the flow of information and sequencing of operations and a grouping of functions into software or hardware. At this point, firmware is grouped with software. It does not get grouped with hardware until production.

The final subphase is software requirements analysis. The product of this subphase is the Software Requirements Specification. When combined with the Hardware Requirements Specification, these documents form the allocated baseline. This is the baseline to which we design. A Software Requirements Specification should include the following information:

- Functional hierarchy
- Data flows
- Data hierarchical relations and access paths
  - Data stores
  - Data bases
- Event sequencing
- Process descriptions
- Interface specifications
- CSCI test requirements and plans
- Cost and schedule estimates

The activities during this subphase are basically the same as in the preceding subphases. There are numerous trade-offs and analyses. These include cost analyses, performance analyses, RMA analyses, and training analyses. These analytical processes are iterative. As we know more about the system, the analyses involve greater levels of detail.

Various structured analysis techniques are discussed in Chapter 9. Structured techniques are generally useful for obtaining data during the requirements phase related to functional hierarchy, data flow, event sequencing, interface specification, data hierarchy, and data access paths. A comparison of how many of these data items are collected by each of six structured techniques is given in Figure 7-16.

Each of these structured techniques is useful for modeling the existing system. They vary somewhat in how well they facilitate communications and how easy they are to use. A quantitative comparison of features relating to the use of these techniques for requirements analysis is given in Figure 7-17.

Whether or not automated tools are used to prepare and maintain structured analysis diagrams heavily influences the last two columns of Figure 7-17. In that figure, I have assumed that no automated tools are being used. Currently, tools either exist or are under development for most of these structured techniques. For example, PROMOD, marketed by Gesellschaft fuer Elektronische Informationverarbeitung m.b.H. (GEI) of West

Techniques \ SDDB Information	Functional Hierarchy	Data Flow	Event Sequencing	Interface Specification	Process Description	Data Hierarchy, Relationships	Data Access Paths
Functional relationship charts	Yes						
Structured analysis (DeMarco)	• Leveled data-flow diagrams	• Data-flow diagrams	• Structured English	• Context diagrams (external) • Data-flow diagrams	• Structured English • Decision tables • Decision trees	• DeMarco data structure diagrams	• DeMarco data structure diagrams
Data structured systems design (uses Warnier–Orr diagrams)	• Functional flow diagrams	• Entity diagrams • In/out data-flow diagrams	• Assembly-line diagrams • Event frequency diagrams	• Entity diagrams (external) • In/out data-flow diagrams	• Assembly-line diagrams	• Data structure diagrams	
HIPO diagrams (IBM)	Yes	Yes	Yes	Yes	Yes		
N2 Charts	• Leveled N2 charts	Yes	• Step-sequenced charts • Loop charts	Yes			
SADT™ (SofTech)		• Data-flow diagrams		• Data-flow diagram • Data structure	• English description • Indicates mechanisms	• Data structure diagrams	

Figure 7-16 Information captured by software requirements analysis techniques.

Note: A "Yes" denotes the fact that the information is captured; however, no special name has been given to the form or subprocedure used. A "blank" means that the information is not captured.

Criteria / Techniques	Modeling Existing System	Communication with Client	Notational Simplicity	Ease of Use or Preparation	Ease of Maintaining Documentation
Functional relationship charts	Low	High	High	High	High
Structured analysis	Moderate	High	High	Moderate to high	Low
Data structured systems design (uses Warnier–Orr diagrams)	Moderate	Moderate to high	Moderate	Moderate	Low to moderate
HIPO diagrams	Moderate to low	High	High	High	Low
N2 charts	Moderate	Low	Low to high	High	High
SADT	Moderate to high	Moderate	Low	Moderate to high	Low

Figure 7-17 Usage characteristics of software requirements analysis techniques.

Germany, is designed to automate and maintain DeMarco's structured analysis method. The GEI product is implemented on an IBM PC. Both Warnier–Orr diagrams and DeMarco diagrams are easily prepared and maintained using software packages produced by Nastec of Ann Arbor, Michigan. Nastec's system was originally limited to Convergent Technology equipment, but now also runs on other equipment.

Two major reviews occur during the requirements phase. These are the system requirements review (SRR) and the system design review (SDR). The system requirements review occurs at the conclusion of the system requirements subphase. It is a review of requirements expressed primarily in user terms. Upon completion of the system requirements review, the functional baseline is established and placed under configuration management control. The software requirements are then assessed from a software engineer's viewpoint and derived requirements, or system-oriented requirements, are determined. For larger projects, an independent testing team can begin to formulate test plans for system validation and acceptance when the functional baseline is established.

Upon completion of these requirements analysis activities, a system design review is held. After a successful system design review, the allocated baseline is established and placed under configuration management control. We are then ready to proceed with the design.

A checklist of items covered in the system requirements review and the system design review is provided in Figure 7-18.

7.3.3 Design Phase

The design phase is partitioned into two subphases, preliminary design and detailed design. The primary products of the preliminary design phase are:

- Software top-level design
- Software test plan
- Computer system operator's manual
- Software user's manual
- Computer system diagnostic manual

The primary products of the detailed design phase are:

- Software detailed design
- Interface design
- Data-base design
- Software test description
- Software development folders
- Updates to preliminary design documents
- Software programmer's manual
- Firmware support manual

Checklist of items to Be Covered at the System Requirements Review or the System Design Review (based on MIL-STD 1521B, Dec. 1983)	SRR	SDR
Mission and requirements analysis (deficiencies, users' viewpoint)	×	×
Functional flow analysis	×	×
Requirements allocation	×	×
System cost/effectiveness analysis (including life-cycle costs)	×	×
Logistics support analysis	×	×
Reliability, maintainability, and availability (RMA)	×	×
Vulnerability	—	×
Interface studies	×	—
Generation of specifications	×	—
Program risk analysis and mitigation	×	×
Integrated test planning	×	—
Technical performance measurement planning	×	×
Engineering integration	×	—
Transition plan	×	—
Configuration management plan	×	—
Human factors analysis	×	×
Personnel requirements and personnel analysis	×	—
Training and training support	—	×
Quality assurance program	—	×
System growth capability	—	×
Security (physical, TEMPEST, data)	×	×
Trade studies	×	—
Sensitivity of cost to requirements	—	×
Operations design versus maintenance design	—	×
Architecture trade-offs	—	×
New development versus vendor-supplied and reusable software	—	×
Testability studies (e.g., fault detection equipment)	—	×
Performance versus logistics	—	×
Functional allocation between hardware, software, firmware and people	—	×
Cost versus performance	—	×
Make versus buy	—	×
Software development schedule analysis	—	×
Logical design of the system data	—	×
Description of the operational concept (users' viewpoint)	×	—
Description of the maintenance concept	×	—
Description of the training concept	×	—
Recommendations	×	×
Cryptographic requirements, characteristics, etc.	×	×

Figure 7-18 Checklist of items to be reviewed at system requirements reviews and system design reviews.

Most of these documents are discussed in the following. Not all these products are needed for all development projects. The product requirements depend largely on the size and nature of the configuration item. For example, a user's manual is unnecessary for a configuration item that will operate autonomously as a black box. Likewise, a firmware support manual presupposes that the configuration item includes firmware.

The content of software test plans is discussed in Section 7.1.7; other test documents are discussed in Chapter 11. Software development folders are discussed in Section 2.7. The top-level design document differs from the detailed design document only in the level of detail provided. Generally, the top-level design specifies the software hierarchy to the CSC or component level; this process generally requires a knowledge to one greater level of detail, the unit level. The detailed design document is often referred to as the ''code to'' specification (or spec). This is the document to which programmers can produce code.

A topical outline for the top-level design document is:

- Allocation
- Functional flow
- Interrupts
- Special control features
- Global data
- Detailed CSC requirements
  - Functional
  - Interfaces
  - Inputs
  - Local data
  - Interrupts
  - Timing and sequencing
  - Processing
  - Outputs
  - Adaptation data

As we read through these lists, it seems like a lot of data are being requested. There is. If you expect to build code that is maintainable and modules that are reusable, then they have to be documented. Try looking at some code you have written and not inspected for at least six months.

Among the worst offenders of good documentation are scientists who think they are just building some code for their own use. It is common for scientific code, such as numerical hydrodynamic code, to take over four boxes of computer cards (i.e., about 10,000 lines of code). Years ago, when I managed an applied mathematics group at a government laboratory, I used to have nightmares about the health and continued employment of my employees. Despite my efforts, we had several large numerical codes that were essentially undocumented. If any of those people had left the laboratory, we would have lost a minimum investment of three staff-years. (Fortunately for me, I changed jobs before any of them left the laboratory.)

It is important for the design documentation to include information that is useful for testing and maintenance. For example, if the system can be described in terms of a finite number of states, then there should be a matrix of state versus CSCs. Thus, if an error occurs while the system is in a given state, we can determine from the state matrix the candidate CSCs in which the error could have occurred.

Many systems can be described in terms of a finite number of states. These states are sometimes described at a very high level. For example, the states of a multipurpose radar may be search, tracking, and ready. The states of transaction-based systems could include editing, updating, and posting. Whenever it is possible to partition a system by describing its states, this should be done. It is easier to maintain a system that is divided into a set of states.

The design documentation should also include data tables for global data, local data, input data, and output data. These tables should contain the following information on each data element:

- Data item number
- Description
- Data type (e.g., real, Boolean, ASCII integer)
- Data representation (e.g., 10 × 10 array, constant, file of 10 records, variable)
- Size (e.g., 1 word, 3 bytes, 200 words at 6 bytes per word)
- Unit of measure
- Limit or range of values
- Accuracy or precision

As appropriate, the tables should also include location in memory, applicable CSCs, source CSC, or destination CSC.

For larger systems, the detailed interface and data-base design descriptions are frequently given in separate documents. The interface design or specification is called an Interface Control Document (ICD). Interface control documents are used to specify how systems communicate with one another and to specify the communications within a system (i.e., hardware configuration item to software configuration item interfaces and CSCI to CSCI interfaces).

External interfaces are specified in terms of the seven layers defined by the International Organization for Standards (ISO). Internal interfaces are defined in terms of block diagrams and interface requirements. The interface requirements include information such as:

- Concurrent or sequential execution
- Data or signal transmission format (and source identification)
- Priority of interrupts or signals
- Maximum time to respond to an interrupt or signal
- Transfer protocols for signal interface (e.g., handshaking)

A topical outline for a data-base design document is as follows:

- *Overview of the data-base management system* (DBMS): This includes a description of and references for the data-base manager (DBM), data-base definition language (DBDL), and the data-base query language (DBQL).

- *Data-base structure*: The data-base structure section should be described in terms of diagrams and file interrelationships. The diagrams should illustrate the relationships between files and records. Herein, we define a file as a set of records, a record as a set of consecutive fields, a field as a set of items, and an item as a primitive parameter. The file interrelationships define the association among files and how the files interact with the data-base management system (i.e., its DBM, DBD, and DBQL).
- *Physical data-base file design*: The contents and size of each file, record, field, and item should be described.

The data-base design document should also include a matrix that provides traceability of each file to a set of one or more requirements.

Much of this design information is captured using structured design techniques. These are illustrated in the case study of Chapter 8 and are discussed in more detail in Chapter 9. Figure 7-19 shows the type of data captured by structured design techniques and compares the abilities of twelve different techniques to capture these data. Figure 7-20 compares how well these structured techniques facilitate communications with clients and among designers.

The last document that should be produced on a routine basis during software design is the software user's manual. A draft version of this document should be produced as early as possible. Like rapid prototyping, this product enables the users of the CSCI to review the practical application of the product and to respond to the designers while it is still relatively inexpensive to make changes.

Contrary to common practice, the user's manual should be written in plain English. Computer jargon should be strictly forbidden. Sometimes this rule is ignored on the basis that the user is sophisticated and knows quite a bit about computers. This may be true of the people who sit at the terminals, but not true of their second- or third-level supervisors who may be the "real" users of the system. The purpose of the user's manual is not to discuss the theory of computer science; its purpose is to provide instructions for people to execute the software.

A topical outline of the software user's manual follows:

- *Scope*: Identify the system, subsystem, or configuration item being described by name and number; describe its purpose and the operating environment; briefly summarize the functions performed.
- *Applicable documents.*
- *Operating instructions*: Describe the initialization procedures (i.e., how the user can get started), the options, the execution procedures (i.e., user inputs, system inputs, and system outputs in human readable form), termination procedures, and restart procedures. Formats for all inputs and outputs should be included in the descriptions.

- *Interrelationships*: Specify the relationship of the functions performed in this CSCI to the functions performed elsewhere in the system; also specify the relationships among the functions within this CSCI.
- *Error messages*: A description of each possible error message output should be provided. This description should be in plain English and should include instructions for corrective action. "Error Number 345" is not an acceptable error message. If the error is not correctable by the user, the message should include information on whom to contact and how the "software repairman" can be reached.

The other products of the software design phase are not always needed. These products are the Computer System Diagnostics Manual (CSDM), the Firmware Support Manual, and the Software Programmers Manual. The Computer System Diagnostics Manual is a reference manual for hardware maintenance personnel. It specifies how to identify hardware malfunctions. The Software Programmers Manual provides the information needed for programmers to produce assembly-language or machine-language code. This information includes program instructions, input/output control programming, and error-detection and diagnostics features.

7.3.4 Code and Checkout Phase

As its name implies, the primary product of this phase is code that has been checked out by the developer. Other products of this phase include revisions of some of the design documents, operators manuals, and users manuals. By the time that code and unit test are completed, test plans and procedures should exist for both intra-CSCI and inter-CSCI or system-level testing. At the conclusion of code and checkout, a test readiness review (TRR) is held. There may be several test readiness reviews, depending on the size of the system and the levels of testing required.

As in each of the other phases, the development process continues to be iterative. Some of the activities of this phase include modifications to the requirements. These modifications cause perturbations throughout the other aspects of the system.

Formerly, the coding phase took a large portion of the development effort, typically 50%. This percentage is rapidly decreasing. With the use of rapid prototyping and structured design techniques, the coding phase should be about 20% of the development effort. As programs that develop code from program design languages and reusable code become a reality, the programming effort will greatly diminish.

The case study of Chapter 13 illustrates how systems can be developed with very little coding. Development of those systems primarily consist of system engineering and integration activities. The system of this case study is an administrative management information system that involves over 300 intelligent terminals, four minicomputers, and over 5 gigabytes of disk storage. Nearly all the software used is commercial off the shelf. The only software that needed to be written were packages that convert the data format used by individual packages to and from a standard data interchange format. This was done to permit the various software packages to be used in an integrated manner.

SDDB Information / Techniques	Functional Hierarchy	Data Flow	Event Sequencing	Interface Specification	Process Description	Data Hierarchy, Relationships	Data Access Paths
Structured design	• Leveled data-flow diagrams	• Data-flow diagrams	• Structure charts	• Data-flow diagrams	• Structure charts	• DeMarco data structure diagrams	• DeMarco data structure diagrams
Jackson design method	• Jackson program structure chart		• Jackson program structure chart		• Jackson program structure chart	• Jackson data structure chart	
Warnier's LCP	• Warnier diagrams		• Warnier flow chart		• Warnier flow chart	• Warnier diagrams	
Data structured systems design (Warnier–Orr diagrams)	• Functional flow diagrams	• In/out data-flow diagrams	• Assembly-line diagrams • Event frequency diagrams	• In/out data-flow diagrams	• Assembly-line diagrams	• Data structure diagrams	
Flow charts	• Leveled flow chart		Yes		Yes		

Figure 7-19 Information captured by structured design techniques.

Structured-flow charts (Nassi–Shneiderman)	• Leveled flow chart		Yes		Yes		
Program design language			Yes		Yes		
HIPO	Yes	Yes	Yes		Yes		
Decision tables/decision trees					Yes		
Program description document			Yes		Yes		
N2 charts	• Leveled N2 chart	Yes	• Step-sequenced charts • Loop charts	Yes			
SADT	Yes	• Data-flow diagrams	• Data-flow diagrams • Data structure	• English description indicates process mechanism	• Data structure diagrams		

Figure 7-19 (continued)

Criteria / Techniques	Modeling Existing System	Communication with Client	Notational Simplicity	Ease of Use or Preparation	Ease of Maintaining Documentation	Direct Correspondence to Structured Programming Constructs
Structured design	Yes	High	High	Moderate	Low	
Jackson design method		Low	Moderate	Low to high (high under ideal conditions)	Low	
Warnier's LCP		Moderate	Moderate	Low to high (high under ideal conditions)	Low to moderate	Yes
DSSD		Moderate to high	Moderate	Moderate to high	Moderate to high	Yes
Flow charts		Low	Low	Low	Low	
Structured flow charts (Nassi–Shneiderman)		Moderate to high	Moderate	High	Moderate	Yes
Program design language		Moderate	High	High	High	Yes
HIPO	Yes	Low to moderate	High	Moderate	Low	
Decision tables/decision trees	Yes	Moderate to high	High	High	Low to moderate	
Program description document		Low to moderate	High	High	High	
N2 charts	Yes	Low	Low to high	High	High	
SADT	Yes	Moderate	Low	Moderate to high	Low	

Figure 7-20 Usage characteristics of structured design techniques.

7.3.5 Test, Integration, and Installation

The end product of this phase is the delivered system. Interim products include test reports and the final version of all documentation that will be delivered with the system. Statistical data should be gathered during testing to determine the types of errors to expect and the modules that seem to be error prone.

REFERENCE

IEEE, "IEEE Guide to Software Requirements Specifications," ANSI/IEEE STD 830-1984, July 1984.

CHAPTER 8

Case Study: Design of a Large, Complex System

8.1 INTRODUCTION TO STRUCTURED DECOMPOSITION

As indicated in Chapter 1, the purpose of this book is to help students and computer professionals to gain a system-level perspective of software engineering. An important aspect of this discipline is the understanding of the life cycle. The first seven chapters should have provided that understanding.

The remaining chapters focus on technical approaches to systems engineering and integration. We begin with a case study that illustrates structured analysis.

We shall use some structured techniques to develop a top-level design for the Advanced Automation System (AAS). The AAS is currently being developed by the FAA. Its purpose is to replace the hardware and software used by air traffic controllers for en route and terminal control. The material is adapted from some preproposal activities conducted jointly by a major aerospace company and by one of the biggest suppliers of software to the government.

Because this material is based on a real analysis, it will not be "clean." At times I will criticize the results being presented. Do not mistake the criticism for meaning that the analysis was bad. It wasn't. Actually, I think that it was fairly good, but it wasn't perfect. A case study based on real analyses is being presented because I think it is more meaningful than any that I could create from scratch. If you want to attribute flaws to anyone, then attribute them to the author.

Several structured techniques will be used. These techniques are subsequently discussed in somewhat greater detail in Chapter 9. For detailed discussions of any particular structured technique, you should read a book dedicated to that technique. Structured analysis books are included in the bibliography. Also presented in this case study is an approach to producing a logical design for the system data base. Data base design is discussed more fully in Chapter 10. Since some techniques are being used before they are systematically discussed, some explanations will be given as we proceed. Trade-off studies and other nonstructured analyses are ignored in this chapter.

A *functional hierarchy chart* is the system engineering name for an organization chart. In the functional hierarchy chart, the system functions are partitioned into subfunctions; the subfunctions are further partitioned into subsubfunctions. This process continues until either we reach the lowest (or primitive) function level, or we cannot fit any more information on a page. In the latter case, we can continue the decomposition process by treating a subsubfunction as a function on a fresh piece of paper and continuing this process. The idea of describing the entire system or function on a single page is known as *leveling*.

A functional decomposition of the air traffic control Advanced Automation System (ATC AAS) is given in Figure 8-1. Here the system or primary overall function is partitioned into four subsystems. The two subsystems that are operating on line, all the time, are grouped together at an intermediate level called *operational software*. This intermediate step was used solely because the design team felt that the FAA liked to think of this type of software as the operational software. Beneath these subsystems is a tentative list of functional configuration items (FCIs).

This division was done by software engineers, not systems engineers. Thus, the division of the functions are being thought of as software even though the analysis was being performed in the system requirements phase, before an allocation of functions to hardware and software was made. In fact a functional baseline has not yet been established.

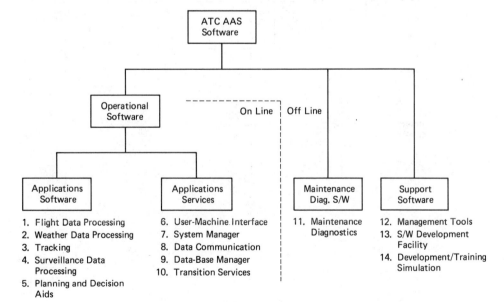

Figure 8-1 System level view of the ATC AAS.

It is generally unwise to specify hardware before the system software is considered. Likewise, an overemphasis on software is not good. The logical grouping of the software functions may be influenced by system requirements for real-time processing, security, or fault tolerance. For example, where do we introduce and how do we treat the concept of *failure-free modules*?

It is a good idea to think of these groupings as FCIs because that is what they will become when the functional baseline is established and placed under control of the configuration management group. Thinking in terms of items that will be controlled by configuration management is a good practice.

The applications software subsystem is further partitioned in Figure 8-2. In this figure the FCIs are labeled 1.0 to 5.0. These FCIs are partitioned into functional components (FCs). These two figures illustrate the leveling concept for functional hierarchy charts.

Leveling is a simple concept to understand, and people who have not worked on large projects may have difficulty imagining that leveling has its drawbacks. For large projects, it is easy to lose one's chain of thought while shuffling the stacks of paper (or while shuffling the pages on a computer terminal) required to describe the job. It may actually be easier to devote a wall of a room to one data-flow diagram of the entire system.

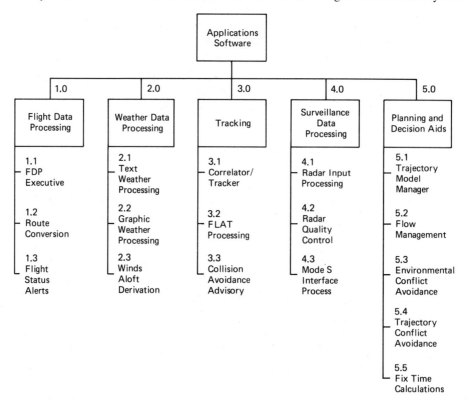

Figure 8-2 Decomposition of the applications subsystem into FCIs and FCs.

For this particular case study, we actually built an N2 chart (a technique described in Chapter 9) that was *8 feet by 10 feet.*

This functional partition illustrated in Figures 8-1 and 8-2 is obtained through a variety of iterative steps. First, applications specialists analyze the purpose of the system and the functions it performs. Next these functions are grouped logically. In the case of government procurements, the first cut at this partition is usually provided in either an operational concept or a requirements document. This logical grouping of functions is then analyzed in terms of the number of interfaces among the functions, the volume of data flowing over these interfaces, and the existence of reusable and commercial software.

The data flow is typically specified in terms of a data-flow diagram. Before proceeding with an explanation and example of data-flow diagrams (DFDs), it is necessary to momentarily digress. Some systems, such as scientifically oriented systems, are thought about and described in terms of their functions. Other systems, such as business systems, are thought about and described in terms of their data structure. For data-oriented systems, we begin by creating a logical partition of the data into a hierarchical structure. Next we generate data-state diagrams. Data-state diagrams describe the transformation of data.

As emphasized throughout the next three chapters of this book, these two approaches are equivalent. The data should be structured into a logical hierarchy simultaneously with the development of a functional hierarchy, and vice versa. When analyzing an MIS system or an office automation system, the functional hierarchy is generally very shallow. Thus the data structure is emphasized in this case. In MIS systems, the functions are somewhat independent of one another. Their dependency occurs because of the need to integrate activities.

For example, when writing a report, a system user needs to intermingle graphics results, spread sheets, and word processing. These data are generally obtained by separate applications programs and stored in files. Either the files need to use compatible formats or there needs to be a format conversion program embedded in the system to permit the files to be intermingled as needed.

The notation used in data-flow diagrams is presented in Figure 8-3. Referring to this

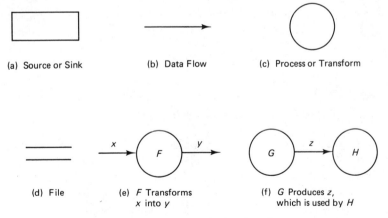

Figure 8-3   Notation used in data-flow diagrams.

figure, a rectangle denotes a source or a sink. A *source* is a place in which data originates. A *sink* is a place in which data terminates. It is important to specify all sources and sinks because these items define the boundaries of the system. The format of the data crossing some of these boundaries may already be specified in other systems (in their interface control documentation). This situation represents a constraint on the system being developed. In other cases, the format of the boundary data is not specified and we must specify this format as part of the design process.

Data flow is generally denoted by a vector. Here we define a vector to be a directed line or arc. The tail of the vector indicates the source of the data or the process that produces the data; the head (or arrow) points to the sink of the data or the process that uses the data (as input). Processes or transforms are represented by bubbles. A file, or a store in which data are kept, is represented by a straight line or a set of two parallel lines as shown.

At the early stages of requirements analysis and design, the use of the file notation should be avoided. (This philosophy is counter to the philosophy espoused by DeMarco.) When improperly used, the file notation can lead to confusion and misunderstanding. This is easy to do if the designer is inexperienced. As the design expands in detail, the use of files is necessary.

A sample data-flow diagram is given in Figure 8-4 for the Surveillance Data Processing configuration item (functional configuration item FCI 4.0). Note that each functional component (FC) is represented as a process and is numbered. Each data element shown in this figure is defined in a data dictionary. Next to each data element or file is a number in a small circle. This number is an identification number for the data element used in the data dictionary. All sources and sinks that are external to this functional configuration item are identified. For instance, the source of the Barometric Pressure file, data number 202, is FC 2.1, Text Weather Processing (TWP).

Note that the external sources and sinks are not enclosed in boxes in this figure. If they were, an unnecessary amount of clutter would be added. The purpose of these structured tools is to serve us. They should be modified as necessary to accomplish this goal. Any modifications, however, should be treated with care. For any given project, there should be a standard approach to structured analysis and documentation techniques.

8.2 ANALYZING A DATA-FLOW DIAGRAM

EXERCISE 8.1   For those of you who are already familiar with structured analysis, I pose a challenge. What is wrong with Figure 8-4?

We shall return to this figure later, and I will answer the question.

We shall proceed by performing an exercise. The purpose of this exercise is to help you analyze data-flow diagrams and subsequently to analyze the current functional decomposition.

Associated with data-flow diagrams are process descriptions and a data dictionary. A process description is written for each process or function of the data-flow diagram. The

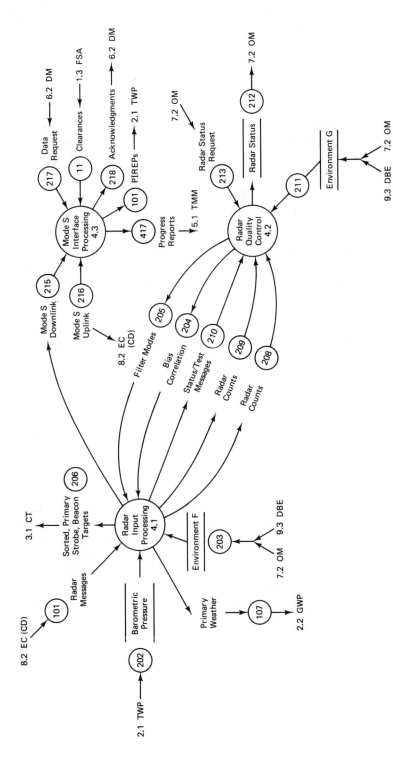

Figure 8-4 Surveillance data processing.

process description is typically one or two paragraphs long. It describes the functions that are performed by that process in terms of the system requirements. If there is a requirements specification, then the traceability to that specification should be provided, for example, by paragraph number. DeMarco refers to the process description as a "mini-spec."

A data dictionary is a *metadata base*; that is, it provides data about data. Elements in a data dictionary include:

- Data element number
- Data element identifier or name
- Source–sink pairs
- Definition or description of the data element
- Type (e.g., Boolean, ASCII, real)
- Size
- Unit of measure
- Range of values
- Accuracy
- Frequency of transmission (mean, variation, peak times, other statistical parameters)

EXERCISE 8.2   What is the relationship of data-flow diagrams, process descriptions, and data dictionaries to the electronic unit development folder described in Chapter 3?

A partial data dictionary is given in Figure 8-5.

EXERCISE 8.3   Using the more complete, albeit still partial, data dictionary of Appendix C, complete Figure 8-6 according to the following rules and guidance. The intent is to show the gross data flow among the applications processes or FCIs. Rather than drawing an arrow for each data flow indicated in the data dictionary, draw a single arrow to represent all the data flowing from a specified source to a specified sink. Next, using the data dictionary, count the number of data elements being transferred and write that number next to the arrow. In Figure 8-6, an example is given. There is precisely one data element whose source is 1.0 and whose sink is 4.0. Note that it happens to be data element 11, Clearance, which flows from 1.3 (a subfunction of 1.0) to 4.3 (a subfunction of 4.0). All sources and sinks numbered 6.0 or higher are external to the applications subsystem represented in this figure and should be treated as such.

When you finish this exercise, you should have determined:

- The number of message types transmitted among the top-level applications processes

ID No.	Identifier	Source	Sink	Description
1	Departure	6.2	1.1	Input after takeoff, absence causes FP drop
2	Amendment, FP	8.2	1.1	Altitude, aircraft type, beacon code, equipment, airspeed, 3D trajectory
3	Flight plan	6.2	1.1	Filed flight plan: beacon code, filed route, . . .
3	Flight plan	8.2	1.1	Filed flight plan: beacon code, filed route, . . .
4	Bulk FP	1.3	1.1	As ID no. 3, but without souls on board, used for regularly scheduled flights
5	Handoff FP	1.3	8.2	As ID no. 3, but only route remaining portion of filed route
.				
.				
.				

Figure 8-5   Partial data dictionary.

- The number of message types that are input from or output to external sources or sinks, respectively
- A critique of the top-level flow
- A critique of the data dictionary

EXERCISE 8.4   What have you observed? Do the application processes show cohesion? What types of coupling among the FCIs are present? (To answer this question, you need to inspect the external data types.) Are there a lot of data types being transmitted among these processes?

Note that one attribute of a good design is that there should not be too many data types being transmitted among processes. This is qualitative, not quantitative, so "too many" is undefined. Another attribute to evaluate is the data rate or volume of data being transmitted. You cannot perform this evaluation for this exercise because I have not given you the message traffic.

Generally, high message traffic between top-level processes is to be avoided. A CSCI is generally resident on a single machine. Since communication among machines is considerably slower than communication within a machine, a high-volume data flow among CSCIs could be a choke point and could significantly limit processing time. If the CSCIs were resident on the same machine, the functional structure could be realized in swapping programs in and out of memory. This data flow (depending on sequencing) could result in excessive reading and writing to disk, again artificially limiting capacity.

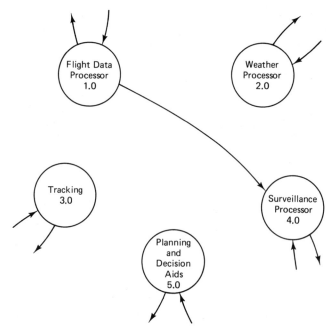

Note: As an example, the number of data or message types flowing
from 1.0 to 4.0 is given.

Figure 8-6   Gross data flow among applications processes.

The point being made here is that the structure of the CSCIs is derived from the functional (and data) hierarchy. This structure exists before the system design is achieved. The quality of the design depends on this structure, so the structure should be analyzed carefully before being accepted.

Do not read further in this chapter until you have completed the preceding exercises, unless you do not intend to think about these exercises. None of the questions posed in this chapter are intended to be rhetorical. When you see a question, stop reading and answer the question. If you continue to read without answering the questions, you will generally see the answer without benefit of thought.

In Figure 8-7, the top-level data-flow diagram for this case is presented. It shows the flow among the functional configuration items.

EXERCISE 8.5   Do you think that anything is wrong with this data flow? If so, explain.

This figure is especially interesting because the analysis done for the case study was good. The first impression is one of utter horror. I couldn't even draw all the arrows that are needed. Note the multiple data-element numbers associated with many of the arrows.

The biggest problem with this figure is that the data representation is neither consistent from a data hierarchical viewpoint nor consistent with the level of detail of the processes. Some of the data items are data bases, such as Environment F. Other data items are primitive data elements. The functions are all represented at the FCI level.

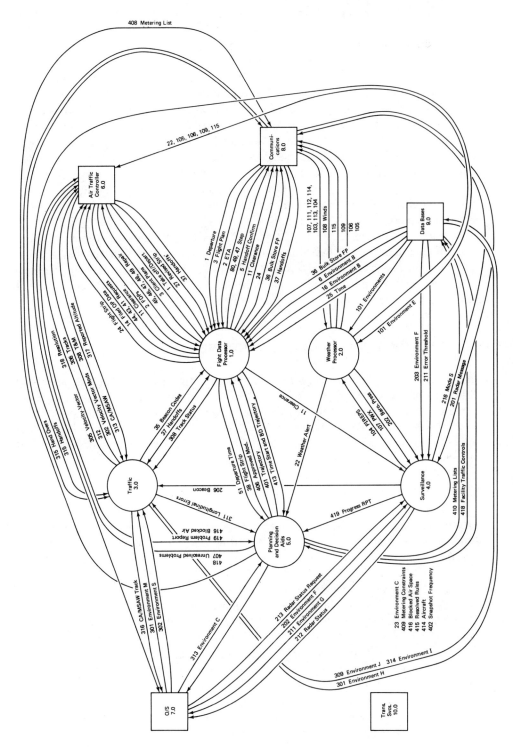

Figure 8-7 What is wrong with the data flow?.

171

This problem is a common one. People have a tendency to treat any particular design from either a data viewpoint or a functional viewpoint. To the maximum extent possible, these viewpoints should be used together. If we group the data logically, in accordance with their meaning and use, we can develop the logical design of the system data base at the same time that we are developing a logical structure for the system processes. We will soon be presenting an example of this approach. Subsequently, we will return to this approach in the chapter on data-base design.

Observe that the software has been divided between applications software and applications services. This drives, for example, all communications to one process. Figure 8-7 indicates that this may be a choke point. We cannot tell whether it actually is a choke point without an analysis of the message traffic to and from this configuration item and an estimate of processing time for each type of message.

Both the data-base configuration item (FCI 9.0) and the communications configuration item (FCI 8.0) exhibit communicational cohesion. Whether they also exhibit functional cohesion depends on their definitions, which are not given here. The purpose of this discussion has not been to critique this case study, but to illustrate the type of information we should look for when examining data-flow diagrams.

8.3 DEVELOPING THE LOGICAL DATA STRUCTURE

In this section a logical structure for the data associated with the weather data processing will be constructed. The main point of this exercise will be realized in Chapter 10 when we return to the results of this case study to "normalize the logical structure."

The data-flow diagram for the Weather Data Processing configuration item is presented in Figure 8-8, where we see that it is partitioned into two components, Text Weather Processor and Graphic Weather Processor.

EXERCISE 8.6   Using the descriptions of the data elements given in Appendix C, develop a logical grouping of the weather data. Do this by imagining that the system consists of the Weather Data Processor. Draw a single circle and label it "Weather Data Processor." Next draw the input and output arrows for this process. Group your data so that the picture you draw is a simple one.

An answer to this exercise is given in Figure 8-9. There is no unique answer; it depends on your viewpoint. People who are either meteorologists or pilots are likely to choose the grouping depicted in Figure 8-9. These people think in terms of bulk weather reports generated by the National Weather Service and in-situ weather reports typically generated by pilots. They also think in terms of text versus graphics data.

It is important during the initial analysis of processes and data to work closely with the people who will be the system users. These processes are part of the user requirements; the conceptual structure of the data base, which is where we are heading, is the structure of the data base from the user's perspective.

The in-situ reports and bulk weather reports could be further partitioned as follows:

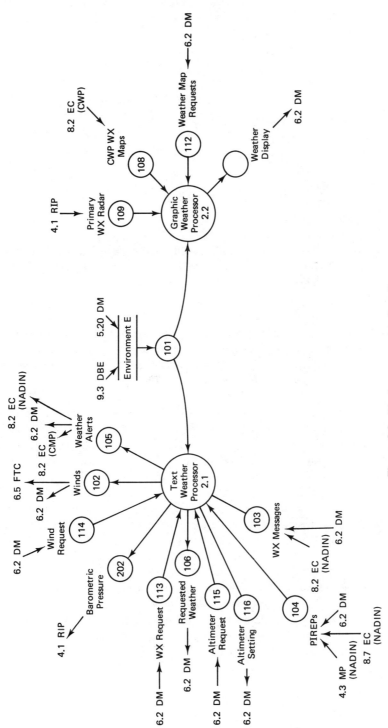

Figure 8-8 Weather process data-flow diagram.

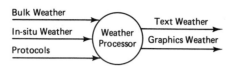

Figure 8-9   Structure of the weather data.

- In-situ reports
  - PIREPS (pilot reports)
  - Observed radar data
  - SIGMETS
  - Other observations
- Bulk weather
  - Forecasts
  - Weather reports

The bulk weather reports are generally updated at four-hour intervals. The main point of these figures is to illustrate a partitioning of the processes and data using a consistent level of detail. Compare Figure 8-9 with the Weather Processor area of Figure 8-7. Even in the simplest case, the improvement is dramatic.

EXERCISE 8.7   If you were to construct a weather report, what data elements should be in it? Make a list and keep this list. In Chapter 10, you will need to use your list. You will also be shown a list developed by a training class. This list will then be analyzed for anomalies and the data will be "normalized."

In the next chapter, structured analysis techniques are discussed. Those of you who are already familiar with the Structured Analysis and Design Technique (SADT) (a registered trademark of Softech, Inc.) should recognize that the idea being conveyed in this chapter is used in the original description of the SADT procedure. Softech recommends that you produce a data decomposition concurrently with a functional decomposition. Some of their documents are included in the bibliography at the end of this book.

This idea is extremely useful. It frees you, for example, from thinking in terms of a specific data-base management system. People who have been extensively using a data base for their applications (such as Model 204) are sometimes unable to break from that mode of thought when asked to design an enhancement or a new system. The approach given here returns to the basics. Given the logical design, the system designers can then use a suitable method of implementation; this could lead to a restructuring of the data base when somebody is trying to enhance an existing system.

This idea is simple to describe, but not often used. I have personally reviewed about ten Softech projects (none conducted by their headquarters staff); Softech did *not* implement this idea in any of those projects.

CHAPTER 9

Overview of Structured Techniques

The purpose of this chapter is to present the basic ideas behind the most popular structured techniques. It is necessary to keep in mind that the discussion is truly an overview. Most of these techniques have books devoted to them. Some techniques, such as the DSSD approach sold by Ken Orr Associates or SDM/70 sold by Atlantic Management Systems, are described in a series of notebooks that occupy at least half a bookshelf. Sources of thorough discussions of these techniques are given in the references.

I have personally used all the techniques described here, except for TAGS, a Teledyne Brown Engineering product, and SREM, a (TRW, Inc.) product in the public sector, on system development projects. TAGS and SREM are included because they are useful tools and I feel comfortable discussing them. I have had discussions with their developers and have seen demonstrations of their use. TAGS is an automated tool. SREM includes techniques that are manual, but also has an automated requirements language associated with it. The primary method omitted from this section is Jackson's technique. I am somewhat familiar with this technique and have occasionally used a Jackson-style diagram. It is excluded because of my lack of project experience with it.

I generally like all these structured techniques, but have some preferences as a function of the life-cycle phase and the nature of the problem. If the client has a preference, I simply use the tool he or she likes, and supplement it with other tools as necessary. After reading this chapter, you may want to refer back to Figures 7-15, 7-16, 7-19, and 7-20. Those figures discuss the information captured by various structured analysis techniques and the ease of use of these techniques. At that time, ask yourself whether you agree with those figures.

These techniques are all good tools. As such, it may be necessary to combine the techniques or slightly abuse them. Good tools can take some abuse, but it is necessary to be careful. For example, it is generally OK to abuse a screwdriver by opening a paint can with it, but it is not a good idea to use a screwdriver as a chisel. When software is going to be maintained for many years or when many people are working on a project, care must be taken to maintain a standard approach. The meaning of each design diagram should be unambiguous.

9.1 FLOW CHARTS

Flow charts are probably the most widely used procedure for documenting the logic of computer programs. Flow-chart symbols are also widely used in drawing system configurations. The standard set of flow-chart symbols is defined in the American National Standards (ANSI) X3.5-1970, "Flowchart Symbols and Their Usage in Information Processing." This publication has also been issued as Federal Information Processing Standard Publication 24 (FIPS Pub 24). A set of the more popular symbols is given in Figure 9-1.

If you either started programming in the 1960s, or have attempted to maintain systems that were built before 1980, or have simply been unlucky, then you have probably seen a machine-generated flow chart. Upon seeing one, the typical reaction is to generate an immediate, intense dislike for flow charts. For a large system, these machine-generated charts are measured by the foot—the parameter measured is the thickness of the document, not its length. These charts are a line by line mapping of the code. The code is typically spaghetti, and the flow charts cannot be read.

Despite the fact that I have just berated flow charts, I still use them. When used with care, they can be very effective. Flow charts permit us to indicate both sequencing and control. As we shall see in Section 9.8, they are especially useful for designing real-time code and for specifying sequencing of systems with concurrent processes. Flow charts can also be used to represent system configurations and processes that are not programs.

With the advent of structured programming, attempts have been made to develop structured flow charts. The most popular of these are Nassi–Shneiderman charts, also known as Chapin diagrams. Structured flow charts are designed to eliminate the GOTO instruction, or unstructured branching. They also encourage single exit and entry points and enhance modularity. The latter property is qualitative rather than quantitative.

Nassi–Shneiderman diagrams are constructed by enclosing a process or module in a box. To represent a process that consists of a sequence of N steps, the box is divided into a set of N rows or rectangles that are stacked horizontally. The first step of the sequence is given in the top rectangle, and subsequent steps are given in lower rectangles, respectively.

The standard representation of structured constructs is given in Figure 9-2. The decision symbol [Figure 9-2(b) and (c)] used to represent IF-THEN-ELSE and CASE constructs consists of a logical expression followed by a set of columns. Each possible alternative is represented by a column. Processing proceeds in the column corresponding to the selected alternative.

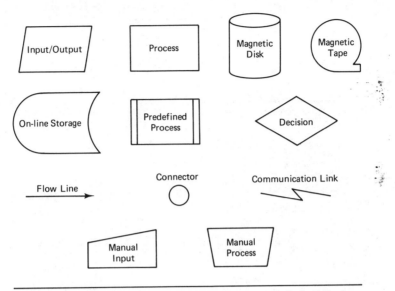

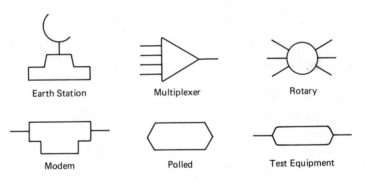

Figure 9-1   Some standard flow-chart symbols.

The iteration symbol [Figure 9-2(d) and (e)] is used to represent the DO-WHILE and DO-UNTIL constructs. This symbol includes an L-shaped area to define the boundary of the iteration. The "inside" of the L is filled in with the process being iterated.

An example of a Nassi–Shneiderman chart is given as Figure 9-3. The algorithm depicted in this figure can be programmed and used to test a child on his or her multiplication tables.

The advantages of Nassi–Shneiderman charts are:

- The structure of the program is graphically represented (and easy to read).
- The basis of alternatives and their effects are explicitly defined.
- The scope of iterations are well defined.

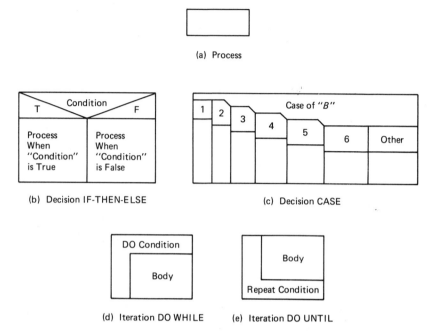

Figure 9-2 Symbols used in Nassi–Shneiderman structured flow charts.

The disadvantages of Nassi–Shneiderman charts are:

- Maintenance is not simple.
- Generally, data-entry clerks cannot understand or draw these charts.

The fact that data-entry clerks have difficulties with these charts means that they normally have to be maintained by programmers. This is a disadvantage because it is more expensive to use a programmer than a data-entry clerk. As a rule, secretaries cannot draw these diagrams from the programmers notes. There are exceptions to this; good administrative assistants (who also do not tremble at the sight of a template) can draw these charts.

9.2 N2 CHARTS

N2 charts, pronounced "N squared charts" or input–output charts were, I think, originally defined by R. L. Lano of TRW. These charts provide the same information as data-flow diagrams and can be used in lieu of them. There are two formats for drawing N2 (also written N^2) charts; both of them are described here.

First I will describe the simpler format, the one that I prefer. Imagine a matrix of squares as shown in Figure 9-4. Processes are specified along the diagonal; input and output data are specified in off-diagonal positions. Data are considered output from a process if they appear in the same row as the process; data are considered input to a process if they

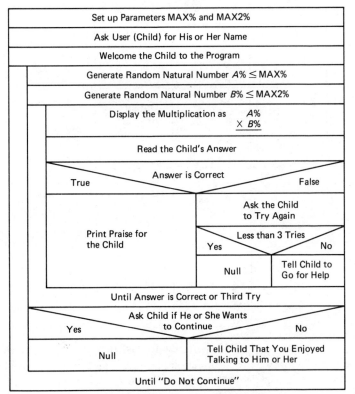

Top-Level Design for a Program That Enables a
Child to Practice Multiplication Tables

Figure 9-3 Example of a Nassi–Shneiderman structured flow chart.

appear in the same column as the process. For example, the data in (row 3, column 2) are output from process 3 and input to process 2.

The same principle of leveling that we use on data-flow diagrams and flow charts can be used with N2 charts. I like to abuse the notion of N2 charts somewhat by adding external sources and sinks to the chart. This is done by adding the sources and sinks along the diagonal and applying the same rules for data input and output to these items.

When you are managing a project, N2 charts are very useful for describing the work to be done. The tasks (your processes) are given along the diagonal. For convenience, specify your client (the source for some information and the sink for all deliverables) in (row 1, column 1).

For example, the data produced by task 1 that is used by task 2 is indicated in (row 2, column 3). These off-diagonal data show graphically the dependencies among the tasks. Along the top row, the data that must be provided by the client are specified. If the client were the government, this would be GFD (government furnished data). The data entries in the first column correspond to the task deliverables (i.e., the items delivered to the client). This information can be embellished by also specifying the due dates in the box.

Process 1			
	Process 2		Output from 2 and input to 4
Output from 3 and input to 1		Process 3	
			Process 4

Figure 9-4 Data flow represented in the form of an N2 chart.

An example of an N2 chart used for task management is shown in Figure 9-5. These N2 charts portray more information per page than can be conveyed using data-flow diagrams. The downside of N2 diagrams is the size of the boxes in which you write. These boxes are small; very few data can be written in them. That property is both a blessing and a curse.

It is a blessing because it provides an automatic warning for you. Is the reason that the data do not fit in the box because there are too many data or because the level of detail specified by the data is greater than the level of detail specified by the function? It is a curse when the answer is that you simply cannot fit the data into the box. In this event, you can use another form for the N2 charts, as shown in Figure 9-6.

The advantage of the second form over the first form is that the dependencies among processes are easier to see. The disadvantage is that the data being transmitted are not necessarily presented on the same piece of paper. You may simply specify a reference to the data, with the data themselves being given someplace else.

EXERCISE 9.1   A data-flow diagram is presented in Figure 9-7. At first glance, does it seem reasonable? Convert this data-flow diagram into an N2 chart. Do you still think that the data-flow diagram is correct?

Do not read further until you finish the exercise.

The problems you may have with this exercise arise from the fact that the data-flow diagram has numerous errors in it. These include unknown sources, unknown sinks, unknown data being transmitted, and improper leveling (why?). In general, I do not like to

Client	• Interface with external system • User requirements		• H/W and S/W constraints (3/30/84)		
	Design definition 1	• Top-level system functions			• Top-level functions
		System-level configurations 2	• H/W subsystem • S/W subsystem • Trade-off analyses		• H/W subsystem • S/W subsystem • Trade-off analyses
			Allocated baseline 3	• Requirements allocation	• Requirements allocation
			• Requirements allocation	Design budgets 4	• Performance descriptions
• Architecture design report (4/30/84)					Architecture task documentation 5

Figure 9-5 Example of project dependencies and products described using an N2 chart.

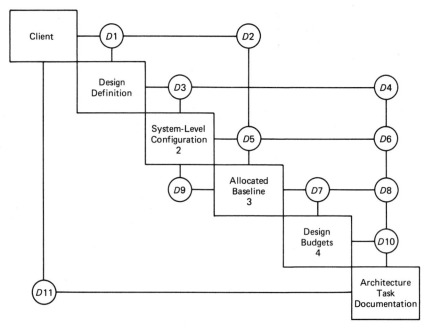

Note: 1. Data nodes are defined separately.
2. Other symbols or meanings can be attached to the nodes to identify control.
3. By specifying the boxes to represent data and the nodes to represent activities, the system data structure can be represented.

Figure 9-6 Second form of the N2 chart.

use files in high-level data-flow diagrams. The use of files tends to obscure the interface between processes. There are times, however, when file notation is very appropriate; for example, a file (like archived messages) may be a key source of data for a given process.

Note the usefulness of using one structured technique (in this case N2 charts) to check the correctness of a product produced using another structured technique (in this case a DeMarco-style data-flow diagram).

Although I do not necessarily recommend it, the complete data flow for large systems can be portrayed on a single N2 chart. Such a chart could occupy a wall of a large room. There are several reasons why a large N2 chart is very useful. Because of its graphic representation, it is easy to see whether processes have been reasonably grouped and defined. The modularity of the design is related to "how diagonal" the matrix appears. If data elements are scattered all over the matrix, then the interfaces between the modules are probably not clean, and the general structure is probably too complicated. This also has implications about module cohesiveness and coupling.

One design principle that should be followed is to minimize communication among configuration items. One reason that this principle should be followed is that communications between software configuration items frequently involve transmitting data between

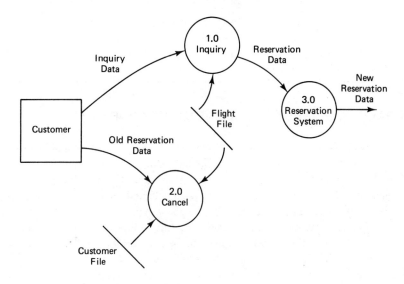

(a) Level 0 of an Airline Reservation System

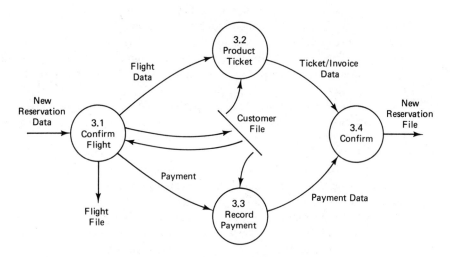

(b) Level 1 of Process 3.0 Reservation System

Figure 9-7   Data-flow diagram for an airline reservation system.

machines or reading and writing to disk. These types of operations are inherently slower than internal communications within a processor. Communications among CSCIs are graphically shown in N2 charts, but N2 charts say nothing about the communications load.

EXERCISE 9.2   Application of N2 charts is not limited to data-flow diagrams. Entire methodologies based on N2 charts have been developed. In this exercise you are to determine how to represent control structures using N2 charts. Specifically, represent the flow chart given in Figure 9-3 by an N2 chart. A *little* creativity will be necessary to accomplish this exercise successfully.

9.3 HIERARCHICAL INPUT-PROCESS-OUTPUT CHARTS

The hierarchical input-process-output (HIPO) is the first structured analysis method popularized in the United States. It was developed in the early 1970s by H. D. Mills of IBM. HIPO is a procedure for organizing a system in a top-down functional manner. The primary contribution of HIPO is that it raised data and interfaces to a high level of visibility in system design. For example, input data and output data are considered at the same level of importance as processes. At the time, this notion was revolutionary.

HIPO uses three types of charts to describe each process or system. First, there is a preamble. This is a free-form chart that includes a visual table of contents. More specifically, it includes a functional hierarchy chart and a short description of each process. A typical preamble is shown in Figure 9-8. At the module or unit levels, the preamble may consist of algorithms or other data that define the process.

The second type of chart is called an input-process-output chart. This chart, illustrated in Figure 9-9, demonstrates control flow, the process description, and data flow. There is no formal mechanism for describing the process. Thus, the process may be presented using structured English, a program design language (PDL), Warnier–Orr diagrams, or other methods. HIPO also permits the specification of notes and description of a data dictionary.

These notes and descriptions are presented in the third type of chart, which is also free form. A typical appendix chart is shown in Figure 9-10. Observe that Figures 9-8 to 9-10 must be produced for every software element at every level. HIPO quickly generates a large amount of paper that must be maintained. On the other hand, all the information required by HIPO is needed in the design. The biggest drawback to HIPO is that it is labor intensive. The means of capturing this design data on line, in an automated fashion, still do not exist.

HIPO is generally very useful for describing functional requirements, for writing specifications in the design phase, and for reference in subsequent phases. A more detailed description of HIPO is given by Katzen (1976).

9.4 STRUCTURED ANALYSIS AND DESIGN TECHNIQUE

The Structured Analysis and Design Technique (SADT), a trademark of SofTech, is useful for describing an existing system and for performing requirements analysis and top-level design. This method is based on the leveling principle introduced in Section 2.4. It begins by describing an entire system on a single page. On subsequent pages, the components of the system are described in a hierarchical fashion.

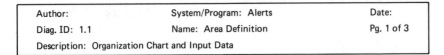

Author:	System/Program: Alerts	Date:
Diag. ID: 1.1	Name: Area Definition	Pg. 1 of 3
Description: Organization Chart and Input Data		

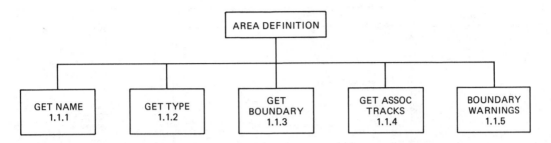

Remark: This process is used to define geographic areas. The operator must specify an area name, shape, reference track (if the area is moving with a vessel), boundaries of the area, tracks associated with the area, criterion for generating an "alerts message," and the contents of this message.

Variable Name	Type	Unit	Accuracy	Source	Definition
REF TRACK	Integer	—	—	1.1.2	Track Number to Which Area is Referenced, if the Area Moves
AREA TYPE	Integer	—	—	1.1.2	Type (Shape) of Area; Code Given in Figure . . .
AREA NAME	Alphanum	—	—	1.1.1	Name of the Area
VERTEX	Array 11 X 2	dec. deg.	0.01	1.1.3	For AREA TYPE = 2 (Polygon), Contents are (lat, lon) of Vertices
OUTER ZONE	F.P.	nm	0.1	1.1.5	Width of Outer Buffer Zone
TIME ON	Alphanum	DTG	—	1.1.3	Date-Time-Group (DTG) when Area Becomes Effective
TIME OFF	Alphanum	DTG	—	1.1.3	Time After Which Area is Ignored
. . .					

Figure 9-8   Example of a HIPO preamble.

A primary feature of SADT is that it permits the description of the system from either a functional viewpoint or a data viewpoint. If the SADT is used as recommended by SofTech, these two viewpoints are employed concurrently. That is, a conceptual design of the system data base is developed together with a logical design of the system functional structure. Unfortunately, this is not generally done, even by SofTech. Of a dozen SofTech

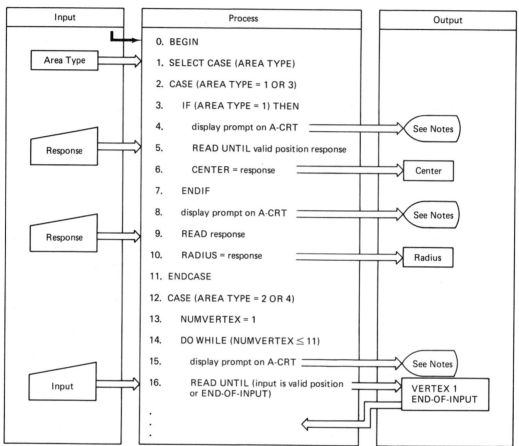

Author:	System/Program: Alerts	Date:
Diag. ID: 1.1.3	Name: Get Boundary	Pg. 3 of 12
Description: Algorithm Definition		

Input	Process	Output

0. BEGIN

Area Type

1. SELECT CASE (AREA TYPE)

2. CASE (AREA TYPE = 1 OR 3)

3.   IF (AREA TYPE = 1) THEN

4.   display prompt on A-CRT → See Notes

5.   READ UNTIL valid position response

Response

6.   CENTER = response → Center

7.   ENDIF

8.   display prompt on A-CRT → See Notes

9.   READ response

Response

10.   RADIUS = response → Radius

11. ENDCASE

12. CASE (AREA TYPE = 2 OR 4)

13.   NUMVERTEX = 1

14.   DO WHILE (NUMVERTEX ≤ 11)

15.   display prompt on A-CRT → See Notes

Input

16.   READ UNTIL (input is valid position
        or END-OF-INPUT) → VERTEX 1 END-OF-INPUT

Note: Standard data-flow symbols may be used to describe data.
Open arrows (⇒) show data flow; closed arrows (→)
show control.

Figure 9-9 Example of an input-process-output chart.

reports I have read, which use this technique, only one (Feldman, Schoman, and Snyder, 1975) actually constructed charts using both viewpoints.

The basic conventions of SADT are shown in Figure 9-11. These conventions are used to construct, depending on the viewpoint, data-flow diagrams or data-state diagrams, as shown in Figure 9-12. Figure 9-12 illustrates a two-page approach to documentation of SADT. The data-flow diagram, for example, is given on one page and a brief description

Author:	System/Program: ALERTS	Date:
Diag. ID: 1.1.3	Name: AREA BOUNDARIES	Pg. 8 of 12
Description: EXTENDED DEFINITION		

Line No.	Notes
4	prompt "ENTER POSITION OF CIRCLE CENTER (LAT/LON):"
5, 16	It is assumed that software exists to check that position inputs are valid. If an input is not valid, the operator is prompted to try again.
6	CENTER is a 1 × 2 array in decimal degrees; a conversion from the alphanumeric numbers entered is assumed.
8	prompt "ENTER RADIUS (NM):"
15	prompt "PROCEEDING CLOCKWISE, ENTER POSITION OF VERTEX (LAT/LON): *WHEN DONE, JUST DEPRESS 'RETURN' "
.	
.	
.	

Figure 9-10   Example of a HIPO appendix chart.

of its parent is given on the facing page. SADT also uses either functional hierarchy charts or a treelike table of contents to illustrate the overall system structure.

SADT data-flow diagrams differ from DeMarco data-flow diagrams (discussed in Sections 9.5 and 8.2) in the following ways:

- Processes are represented by rectangles rather than bubbles.
- All input data enter from the left and all output data exit from the right, as opposed to entering and exiting anywhere.
- Arrows entering from below are mechanisms. In the case of data-flow diagrams, the mechanism is the entity that performs the function. In the case of data-state diagrams, the mechanism is the entity that stores the data. This concept is not present in DeMarco data-flow diagrams.
- Arrows entering from above are constraint data; this concept is not present in DeMarco data-flow diagrams.

The mechanism arrows are especially useful when describing interactive processes. These arrows provide a clear indication of whether a specified function is to be automated or to be performed manually. When a network is being described, the mechanism arrow permits us to specify which functions are performed on a mainframe and which functions are performed on a microcomputer (workstation).

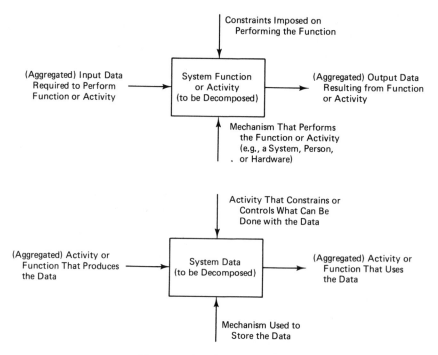

Figure 9-11   SADT conventions.

The constraint arrows cause more confusion than help. They are not well defined by SofTech documentation, and practitioners of SADT tend to use them nearly interchangeably with input arrows. Constraint data in engineering are well defined; boundary conditions are examples of such data. Constraints do exist for software processes. Examples of these are:

- Processing must be completed within a specified time.
- A certain process may have to be completed before another process can be completed, even though the first process may not produce data that are used by the second process (a process that writes data into a file assumes that the file has been initiated by another process).
- A process may be constrained to be performed in accordance with certain standards or within specified tolerance.

Generally, I do not recommend the use of constraint arrows. The difficulty with constraint arrows arises from the fact that SADT does not clearly distinguish between constraint data and input data. If constraint data were defined properly, as they are used in SYSREM (discussed at the end of this chapter), the objection to constraint arrows mentioned here would be removed.

A host of other notation has also been developed for SADT. Ross (1977), the founder of SofTech and a developer of SADT, published a paper on a structured analysis

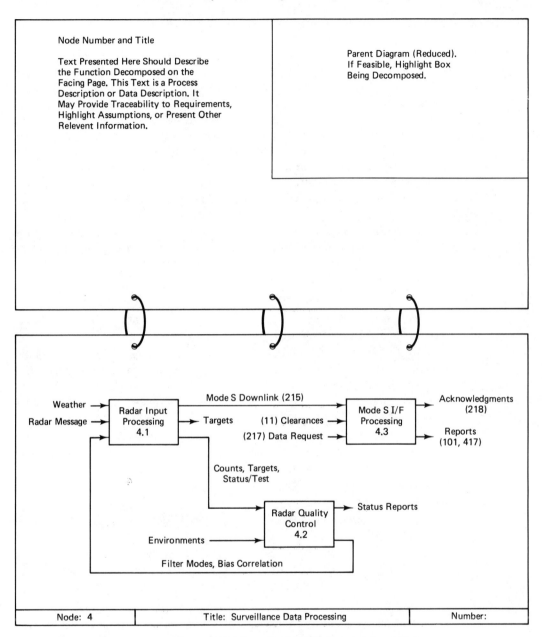

Node Number and Title

Text Presented Here Should Describe
the Function Decomposed on the
Facing Page. This Text is a Process
Description or Data Description. It
May Provide Traceability to Requirements,
Highlight Assumptions, or Present Other
Relevent Information.

Parent Diagram (Reduced).
If Feasible, Highlight Box
Being Decomposed.

Weather →
Radar Message →

Radar Input
Processing
4.1

Mode S Downlink (215)

→ Targets   (11) Clearances →
              (217) Data Request →

Mode S I/F
Processing
4.3

Acknowledgments
(218)

Reports
(101, 417)

Counts, Targets,
Status/Test

Radar Quality
Control
4.2

→ Status Reports

Environments ————→

Filter Modes, Bias Correlation

| Node: 4 | Title: Surveillance Data Processing | Number: |

Figure 9-12   Example of SADT documentation format.

language containing forty-three symbols. In other writings on the use of SADT, SofTech recommends using no more than six boxes per page, and no more than six arrows per box. Generally, they feel that the diagrams should be kept simple. This is good advice. It may also be wise to limit notation to six kinds of objects.

9.5 DEMARCO, GANE AND SARSON, YOURDON APPROACH

The method discussed in this section is popularly known as the DeMarco method. I have grouped his method with the methods of C. Gane and T. Sarson and E. Yourdon because DeMarco, Gane, and Sarson worked for Yourdon. I am not really certain how to separate the three methods without carefully reviewing each, so I don't try.

Complete discussions of this general approach to structured analysis are given in DeMarco (1979) and Gane and Sarson (1979). The general strategy of this approach, and other structured techniques, is to manage the project size by partitioning the system. Both the DeMarco approach and the Orr approach, discussed in section 9.6, emphasize that a logical design should be completed before starting the physical design. This distinction between a logical design and a physical design had not been clearly enunciated in older techniques; however, SADT does emphasize that the viewpoint with which diagrams are drawn must be clear. The viewpoint aspect allows us to specify a user's viewpoint or a system engineer's viewpoint. This difference is at the heart of the distinction between logical and physical designs.

The basic tools of the DeMarco technique are:

- *Data-flow diagrams* (DFDs): a graphic partitioning of the system portraying all interfaces involved between processes.
- *Process description* (PD): a short description of a process mentioned in a data-flow diagram. A process description should be written for each process. The process description should relate the process to system requirements. DeMarco calls these descriptions ''mini-specs.'' I prefer the term process description only because I used it before reading DeMarco's work.
- *Data dictionary (DD)*: a store to maintain all needed information about the data elements mentioned in the data-flow diagrams. In a software support facility, the data dictionary would be part of the system design data base discussed in Section 3.3.
- *Data structure diagrams (DSDs)*: a graphic tool for portraying the logical design of the data-base structure.
- *Structured English, decision matrix, decision trees*: tools used to describe process logic concisely. Sometimes a program design language (PDL) is used to describe the process. ADA-based PDLs are becoming increasingly popular because of their compilation capabilities, required use of ADA by the Department of Defense (and use of ADA in Europe), and the relation of ADA to reusability issues.

Data-flow diagrams consists of five basic elements: sources, sinks, data flows, processes, and files. We have already been using data-flow diagrams. In the previous examples, the use of data files has been discouraged. When dealing with a process-oriented system, the use of files can obscure the true data flow. In the case of a data-oriented system, the use of files is critical to the system description because files indicate the top-level data architecture. An example of a data-flow diagram for an office automation system is given in Figure 9-13.

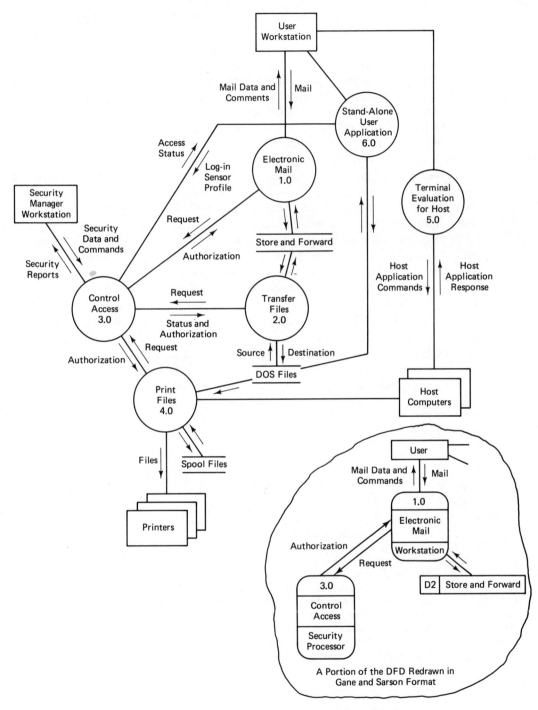

Figure 9-13 Data-flow diagram for an office automation system.

Shown as a cutout in Figure 9-13 is a portion of the data-flow diagram redrawn using the Gane and Sarson format. Note that the Gane and Sarson formats permit the specification of the physical location of the process (i.e., the mechanism of SADT). It permits the numbering of data stores. SADT also permits the numbering of all data items. These features are not available in the DeMarco method. Gane and Sarson also use *data structure charts* to define interfaces and control among the processes. An example of a data structure chart is included in the case study of Chapter 13.

In the case study of Chapter 8, a data-flow diagram for the weather data process is presented (Figure 8-8). A process description for the Text Weather Processor is given in Figure 9-14.

The specific functions given in Figure 9-14 should be traced (usually by paragraph number) to a requirements specification whenever one exists. As the structured analysis proceeds to a much greater level of detail, the process description may be given in the form of an algorithm, in structured English, or in PDL.

The data dictionary is a key aspect of this method that lends itself to automation. Data-flow diagrams can be constructed from a data dictionary. It is very helpful to have a structured analysis tool that captures information from data-flow diagrams when they are created and inserts this information into the data dictionary. CASE 2000, a product of Nastec, Inc., of Ann Arbor, Michigan, does this. When the concept of the data dictionary is extended to all system data, we get a system design data base as discussed in Chapter 3.

EXERCISE 9.3   As previously indicated, a partial data dictionary is given in Appendix C. What other elements should be included in this data dictionary to make it complete? Answer this question from at least two of the following perspectives: technical, project management, configuration management, and quality assurance.

The Text Weather Processor (TWP) is responsible for formatting and forwarding, for display or hard copy, all weather data in a textual form. Specifically its functions are to:

- Check for validity, logic, and legality of controller inputs.
- Process weather messages from:
  — Mode S
  — The central weather processor
  — Control room personnel
- Provide output data (SIGMETS, PIREPS, nonrequested alerts, requested weather data, and weather forecasts) to control room personnel.
- Maintain weather reports.
- Forward barometric pressure observations to the Radar Input Processor.
- Perform hardware and software integrity checks.
- Execute trace procedures as directed by the situation development generator.

Figure 9-14 Process description for the text weather processor.

EXERCISE 9.4   Using the partial data dictionary of Appendix C, construct the data-flow diagram for functional configuration item FCI 3.0.

Data structure diagrams are a means of simplifying complex files. These diagrams are used to construct the logical design of the data base; that is, they represent how a data base is supposed to behave and not how it is constructed. For example, a bank may wish to obtain credit information on a customer loan request if it supplies only the customer's name to the system. The analyst of this system may view the bank's data base as a rather simple file structure consisting only of credit information, indexed by customer name. In actual fact, the data base may be very complex with several intermediate accesses involved. Analysts need not worry about how the data base is organized; their only concern is that the information is available. Figure 9-15 is an example of a data structure diagram.

Having mentioned structured English, decision trees, and decision matrices on several occasions, a brief description of each will be given before proceeding to the next section. These items, although included in the DeMarco technique, are neither unique to this technique nor created for this technique.

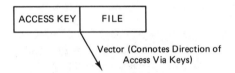

(a) Notation Used in Data Structure Diagrams

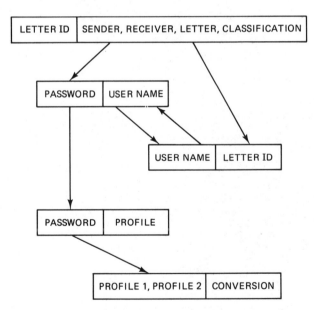

(b) Data Base Accesses Needed for the Conversion Process (1.5) to Transmit a Letter Using Electronic Mail

Figure 9-15 Example of a data structure diagram.

Structured English uses a subset of the English language. In this subset, only those constructs that are permissible in structured programming are used. Thus, this syntax permits only three linguistic constructs:

- *Sequence*: a set of one or more imperative sentences. For example:
  Calculate total assets.
  Calculate total liabilities.
  Determine net worth (= total assets − total liabilities).
- *Alternatives*: a complex sentence or sequence of sentences that defines a set of alternatives. For example:
  If (specify a logical condition)
    Then (specify result for the event that the logical condition is true),
    Otherwise (specify the result for the event that the logical condition is false).
- *Repetition*: a statement or group of statements that specify the conditions upon which a subordinate policy shall be repeated. For example:
  While (specify a logical condition) is true
    Perform (the subordinate policy).
  Proceed with the next step when the logical condition is false.

During the specification or design of low-level modules and units, structured English may take the form of looking somewhat like code. This highly detailed structured English is generally called *pseudocode*. An example of structured English (which some of you may claim is detailed enough to be called pseudocode) is given below. This example describes the algorithm for calculating the minimum time to intercept of a target by a pursuer. It assumes that the velocity of each is constant and the course of each is a rhumb line (i.e., a straight line on a mercator projection, the "usual map").

```
BEGIN Process Calculate Minimum Time to Intercept
Check for coincidence of target and pursuer
IF (target and pursuer are coincident)
    THEN Time to Intercept = 0
    ELSE Calculate course C and distance D from the target to the
              pursuer along a rhumb line
        Let the angle A be the absolute value of (C - THDG)
        where THDG is the heading of the target
        IF (speed of the target is 0)
            THEN Intercept time is D/SP where SP is the
                        speed of the pursuer
            ELSE F = (D * cos A)**2 +
                        4 * (D**2) * ((SP/ST)**2 - 1)
                    where ST = speed of target
                S = (D * cos A) - SQRT F
                IF (F.LT.0 or S.LE.0)
                    THEN Target cannot be intercepted
                    ELSE RT = (2 * D**2) / S = Distance
                                    traveled by the target
                          Minimum intercept time = RT/ST
            ENDIF
        ENDIF
ENDIF
END PROCESS
```

It is very easy to make design errors when it is necessary to implement a complex decision process. Two graphical tools used to convey decision-related information are decision tables and decision trees. A decision tree is a graphical representation of a decision table. It is a branching chart (or tree) that depicts each possible combination of conditions. An example of a decision tree is given in Figure 9-16. This example depicts a typical policy used to regulate the power bus voltage on a satellite. Note that the primary conditions are whether or not devices are turned on. The action or decision is given in terms of the set {turn a device on, turn a device off, do nothing, put the satellite in a safe mode and notify ground}.

The corresponding decision table is given as Figure 9-17. There are four parts to the decision table: (1) the set of conditions to be tested, (2) the set of possible answers or entries for each condition, (3) the set of parameters defining the action or decision, and (4) the appropriate value of each parameter for each condition. A decision rule is an ordered pair of condition and action. Decision tables and trees may have notes appended to them.

Whenever feasible, it is suggested that decision trees be used. Decision trees present a more vivid graphic presentation and are easier to understand. In those cases in which a tabular presentation is feasible but a tree presentation is not feasible, it may be necessary to use a tree representation for a portion of the decision process to resolve problems.

Decision tables and trees are limited in practice by the extremely large size they attain when a large number of conditions are involved. The size of decision tables and

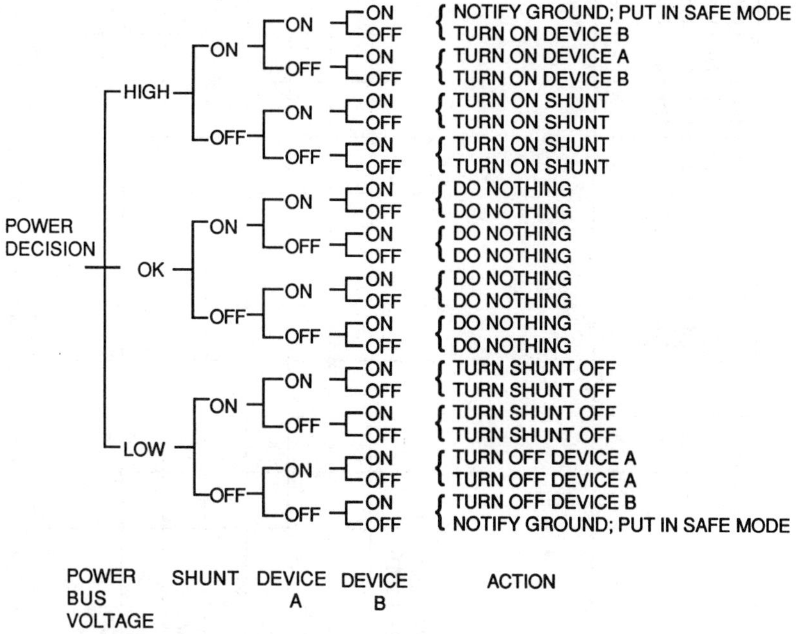

Note: Assume that Device A consumes more power than Device B. The only function of the shunt is to consume power. It consumes more power than Device A.

Figure 9-16   Decision tree for turning off the power bus on a satellite.

Condition   Condition Stub

Condition																								
Power Bus Voltage	High	High	High	High	High	High	High	High	OK	OK	OK	OK	OK	OK	OK	OK	Low	Low	Low	Low	Low	Low	Low	Low
Shunt	On	On	On	On	Off	Off	Off	Off	On	On	On	On	Off	Off	Off	Off	On	On	On	On	Off	Off	Off	Off
Device A	On	On	Off	Off	On	On	Off	Off	On	On	Off	Off	On	On	Off	Off	On	On	Off	Off	On	On	Off	Off
Device B	On	Off	On	Off	On	Off	On	Off	On	Off	On	Off	On	Off	On	Off	On	Off	On	Off	On	Off	On	Off

Action

Action																								
NOTIFY GROUND, Put Satellite in SAFE MODE	•																							•
Turn On Device A			•	•																				
Turn On Device B		•																						
Turn On Shunt					•	•	•	•																
Turn Off Device A																					•	•		
Turn Off Device B																							•	
Turn Off Shunt																	•	•	•	•				
Do Nothing									•	•	•	•	•	•	•	•								

Note: Assume that device A consumes more power than device B. The only function of the shunt is to consume power. It consumes more power than device A.

Figure 9-17 Decision table for turning off the power bus on a satellite.

trees grows exponentially with the number of conditions. For example, a decision policy having eight binary conditions requires 256 (2^8) leaves on a tree or columns of a table.

Whatever problems the size of a decision table may present, a decision table is far less ambiguous than plain English.

9.6 WARNIER–ORR APPROACH

The Warnier–Orr approach originated as the logical construction of programs. This concept was developed by Jean Warnier of Honeywell-Bull in the early 1970s, about the time that HIPO was being developed by Mills at IBM. Warnier's work was originally published in French and was not translated to English until 1976. Consequently, this approach took a long time to be accepted in the United States.

The value of Warnier's approach was recognized by Ken Orr, who expanded on the logical construction of programs and popularized this method in America. Initially, the Data Structured System Design (DSSD) method developed by Ken Orr consisted simply

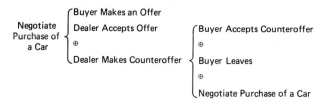

(a) Sequence with Flow of Control

(b) Exclusive OR or Case Notation with Flow of Control Indicated

(c) Repetition Using DO WHILE Construct (Recursive Representation)

(d) Repetition Using DO UNTIL Construct (Recursive Representation)

(e) Process of Negotiating the Price of a Car Expressed Using Warnier–Orr Diagrams

Figure 9-18 Symbology and examples of Warnier–Orr charts.

of Warnier–Orr diagrams. These diagrams are essentially another form of structured flow charts. They only permit structured constructs. The nomenclature for Warnier–Orr diagrams is given in Figure 9-18.

The dashed lines in Figure 9-18 indicate the flow of control; they are not physically present when Warnier–Orr diagrams are drawn. These diagrams are easily understood by users, designers, and programmers. They are very flexible. Their entries could be either data or functions. The original applications of these diagrams were business systems. These systems were data oriented and could be designed by starting with the final product and working backward until we arrive at the input data.

This approach of starting with the product, or output, and working backward is very compatible with the way problems are usually solved. In the field of mathematical optimization, the technique of dynamic programming exploits this approach. Generally, problems are solved by guessing the answer, or the form of the answer, and working backward to establish its correctness.

For system engineering purposes, the Warnier–Orr diagrams are in themselves not adequate because they do not capture all the system design data that are needed. For large

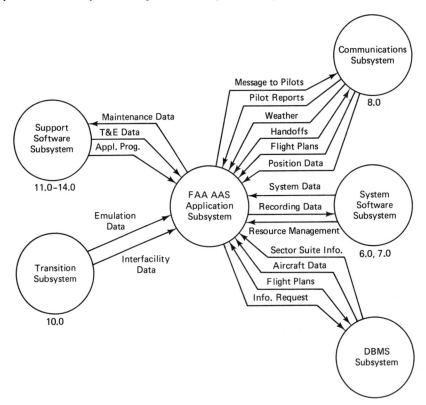

Figure 9-19 Sample entity chart.

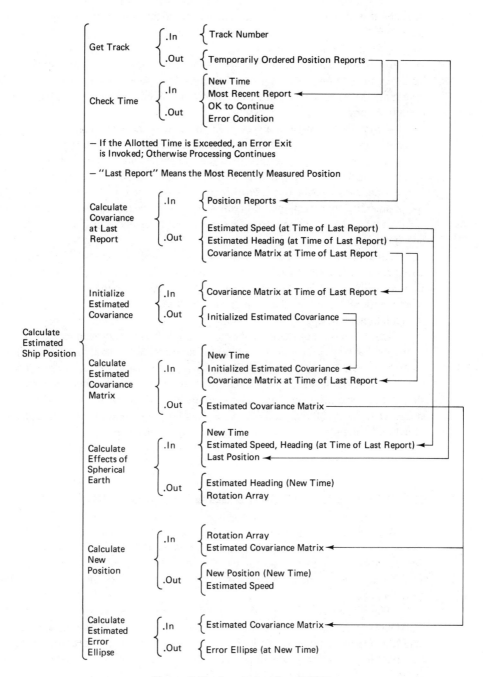

Figure 9-20   Sample data flow (DSSD).

projects, it is also necessary to establish a standardized approach that spans the life cycle.
Ken Orr's answer to this need is the Data System Structured Design (DSSD) approach.

Information not captured by Warnier–Orr diagrams includes interfaces, data flow,
sequencing, and data dictionary items (such as frequency of events, formats, and data
volume). In addition to Warnier–Orr diagrams, DSSD includes entity diagrams, data-flow
diagrams (these are *not* the same as the data-flow diagrams used by DeMarco), and output
definition forms.

Entity charts consist of a group of bubbles with the system under consideration specified in the center bubble. Other systems that interface with this system are specified in
the other bubbles. Each interface between the system in the center bubble and another
system is indicated by a spoke or arrow. The data to be passed over the interface are
labeled, and the direction of the arrow corresponds to the direction of data flow. An example of an entity chart is shown in Figure 9-19. By inserting number sequences (such as 1,
2, . . . or 1A, 2A, . . .) next to the interface data, sequences of interface interactions are
specified.

An example of a data-flow diagram is presented in Figure 9-20. Note that it looks
like a rearranged HIPO chart. Output definition forms are tables containing the information normally found in a data dictionary. These data define the output by specifying format, purpose, sample data, logical structure, volume, frequency, decision or
computational rules.

This discussion of DSSD and other methods has been limited to a description of the
charts or graphical procedures. Several of these methods, including DSSD, TAGS (discussed in the next section), and SDM 70 (not discussed here), address the complete
software development life cycle. These methods are formalized enough to permit their use
on large projects involving over a hundred people. Much greater detail is provided in the
references. These references should be read before, or at least during, the application of a
structured technique that you have not previously used.

9.7 TECHNOLOGY FOR AUTOMATED GENERATION OF SYSTEMS

The Technology for Automated Generation of Systems (TAGS) is a product of Teledyne
Brown Engineering. As we shall see, when this method is combined with procedures being developed by Siemens AG for establishing necessary control, it comes closest of any
of the structured techniques to the "third level of abstraction" needed for a software support facility.

The Siemens approach, called Computer-aided Design for Organizers and Systems
(CADOS), uses the outside-in instead of the inside-out philosophy, as described by Groh
and Lutz (1984). The policy of looking at the development process from the outside in is
identical in philosophy to the approach to building an environment advocated in Chapter
3. It is this approach that establishes the necessary controls.

TAGS has three components: the input–output requirements language (IORL), a system/software computer-based tool system, and the TAGS methodology. The IORL uses both graphical and tabular diagrams to describe the structure of a system.

The feature that distinguishes IORL from other structured analysis languages is that IORL permits the designer to specify sequences of events. This feature is evident in the symbology, described in Figure 9-21.

The "fan-in and" notation means that all incoming processes must be completed before proceeding to the outgoing process. This is a choke point. The "fan-out and" symbol has one entry; every exit path must be executed after the entry process is completed. The "fan-in or" symbol means that the output is executed after any input occurrence. The "fan-out or" symbol has a single entry with either two or three possible exits. Only one exit path is actually executed; the path selected depends on the timing. These symbols, although not commonly used for software, are included in the ANSI standards for flow charts.

The input–output requirements language uses three types of graphic diagrams to describe the system process:

- The schematic block diagram (SBD) is a data-flow diagram using blocks, or rectangles, to represent independent components of a system and arrows to represent the

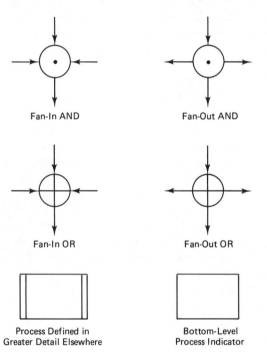

Fan-In AND   Fan-Out AND

Fan-In OR   Fan-Out OR

Process Defined in   Bottom-Level
Greater Detail Elsewhere   Process Indicator   **Figure 9-21**   IORL symbology.

data interfaces. These components are independent in the sense that the processing of one does not depend on the processing of the others. These diagrams are specified hierarchically until the components are specified to their lowest level of independence. For example, the schematic block diagram for the hardware for a computer display system may include the keyboard/display operator, the keyboard, the CPU computer, and the display system.

- The input–output relationships and timing diagrams (IORTD) are used to specify the flow of control and the sequencing of processes. All the symbols defined in Figure 9-21 are used in IORTD diagrams.

- The predefined process diagram (PPD) looks like the input–output relationships and timing diagram; however, it is used to define a single predefined process specified in either an IORTD or another PPD. The use of IORTD and PPD diagrams permits the further hierarchical structuring of processes.

Figure 9-22 illustrates these diagrams. Also shown in Figure 9-22 are parameter tables, which are used to define the data that appear in the diagrams. The parameter tables, together with the data-flow information provided by the diagrams, form a data dictionary.

The TAGS approach to design is intended to be used from top-level design through the most detailed level of design. Consequently, they also need to be able to describe the physical layout of the data. This level of description of data elements is obtained by using data structure diagrams (DSDs). The physical layout is generally described using their data structure diagram table form. The forms DSD is generally used to layout the format of a report or menu. The picture DSD is an unformatted form in which graphic data can actually be displayed.

TAGS was originally developed from a systems engineering viewpoint that included the need to apply it to real-time systems. One impact of this viewpoint is the requirement for IORL to be able to describe a communications module at the signal level of detail. More generally, IORL must be able to describe data transfers requiring critical timing control. The MACRO diagram, or MAC diagram, is devised for this purpose. A sample macro diagram is given in Figure 9-23.

The tools associated with TAGS are what elevates this approach to the "2.5 level of abstraction." These tools include a storage and retrieval package, configuration management, a diagnostic analyzer, and a simulation compiler. The diagnostic analyzer checks the ensemble of IORL diagrams for completeness and correctness. The simulation compiler checks the sequencing and timing of the diagrams for feasibility. This simulator is critical to the process of functional allocation. Making simulation an integral part of requirements analysis and design is a major step toward the design of quality systems without capacity or performance surprises late in the development cycle—when all fixes are much more expensive to accomplish. TAGS is not at level 3 of abstraction because it does not include program management tools and control.

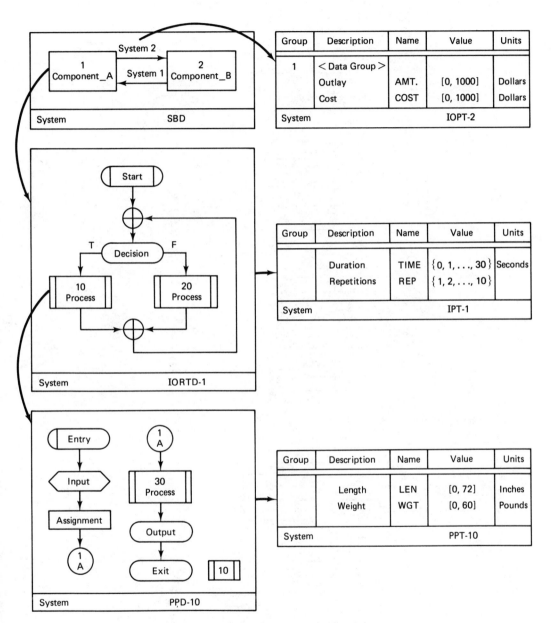

Figure 9-22 Basic IORL diagrams and parameter tables. (Courtesy of Teledyne Brown Engineering, Inc.)

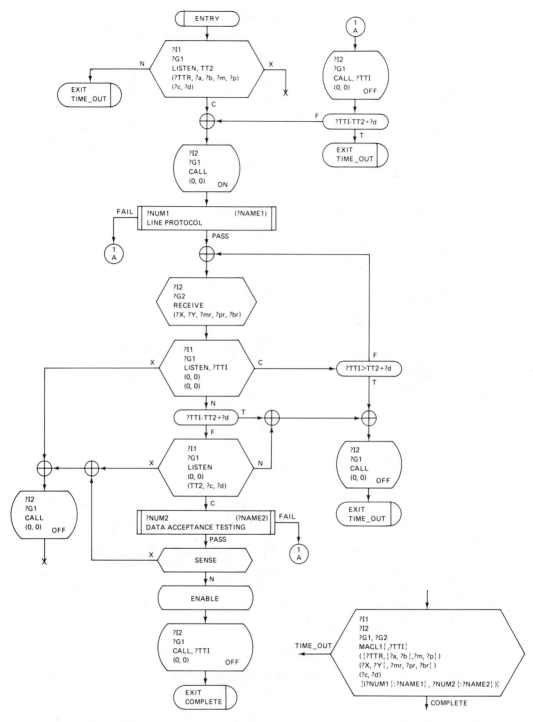

Figure 9-23 A macro to receive data (communication mode). (Courtesy of Teledyne Brown Engineering, Inc.)

204

9.8 TECHNIQUES FOR REAL-TIME STRUCTURE CHARTS

The structured analysis techniques described in Sections 9.1 to 9.7 are based on top-down, hierarchical decompositions and data-flow diagrams. With the exception of TAGS (and the more complicated structured language developed by Ross for SADT), the data-flow diagram representations do not account for sequencing of operations. Thus interrupts, concurrent processing and task synchronization cannot be easily described. In this section, some graphical techniques for representing real-time communications among modules or units are presented.

The use of FAN-IN and FAN-OUT Boolean operations in TAGS together with their requirements language permits representation of these real-time features. Other methods, like DeMarco, can claim that they are useful for real-time problems because sequencing, concurrent processing and task communication are provided in their use of process design language (PDL). This is true if the PDL is ADA based, or ADA itself. ADA pragmas permit interaction with the operating system. This feature opens the machine's entire capability to the PDL specification. This approach is not easy to understand and encourages us to think at a programming language level of detail when we should be thinking in terms of functions and their interactions.

In this section, we present some graphical methods for adding interrupts, task synchronization, and multitasking specifications to data-flow diagrams and flow charts. This discussion is based on the work of Gomaa (1984) and Tausworthe (1979). Tausworthe has an especially good discussion of real-time and multiprogrammed structured programs.

Programs may be interrupted by temporarily stopping the processing and then continuing in a planned way. This is done in time-shared systems and may be planned with a PAUSE command. An example of this circumstance occurs when a home telephone is programmed to dial a telephone number, pause (this permits the receiving number to be connected and to transmit a signal), and then enter a series of digits. This feature may be used for special long-distance service or to access a computer.

Processing of programs may also be interrupted due to the occurrence of several unscheduled external events such as a priority request, an input error, or a real-time clock. An event-driven interrupt is called a *trap*.

Data-flow diagram representation of various types of communications is given in Figure 9-24. This depiction of a navigation system (for a pilotless vehicle) uses notation

Note for Figure 9-23, page 204:

PPDs may be used to perform protocol before data are sent and to verify the data after receipt. If either test fails, the macro will attempt to receive the group again, as long as time has not run out. Pieces of data will be received until the group has been successfully transferred or until the time specified by the macro duration has expired, whichever comes first. The TIME OUT path will be taken if time runs out. The macro's time tag will be set to the time of exit from the macro.

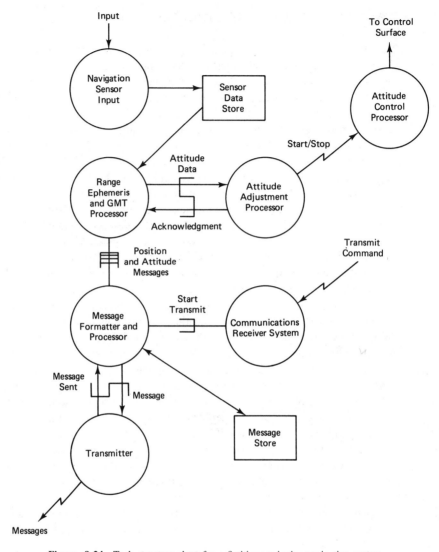

Figure 9-24 Task structure chart for a fictitious avionics navigation system.

specified by Gomaa (1984) for a robot controller system. This figure shows *loosely coupled communications, closely coupled communications*, and *task synchronization communications*.

Referring to Figure 9-24, the "Position and Attitude Messages" is an example of loose communication between the Range Ephemeris and GMT Processor and the Message Formatter and Processor. In this case, the Range Ephemeris and GMT Processor inserts data (or a message) into a queue. The Message Formatter and Processor checks the queue either periodically or at the completion of a task or both. Whenever the queue is not empty, the Message Formatter and Processor removes an item from the queue according to some scheme, such as first in, first out (FIFO). This item is the input data for the next execution of the Message Formatter and Processor.

The communication between the Transmitter and the Message Formatter and Processor is an example of tightly coupled communication. In this case, the Message Formatter and Processor expects a response (''MSG SENT'') to each message it transmits. In the absence of an acknowledgment, the Message Formatter and Processor generally takes certain actions, such as resending the message or notifying the system manager that the transmitter is not operating properly. In this case there may be a redundant transmitter; the system manager may be either a processor or a person concerned with the health and status of the vehicle. In telecommunications applications, the sender or receiver (or both) may monitor communications lines for the number of messages that need to be retransmitted. If the frequency of retransmission is too high, it may be an indicator of a problem with the communications line.

The Start/Stop message from the Attitude Adjustment Processor to the Attitude Control Processor is an example of event-driven synchronization. In this case, the message may be simply an electrical signal, as opposed to data transfer. This signal causes the Attitude Control Processor task to be executed (this may consist of the firing of a small rocket engine).

The notation introduced addresses communications synchronization but not data synchronization. Some mechanisms for data synchronization during multiprocessing are discussed in Chapter 10.

Concurrent processing and traps introduce inherently unstructured systems. A trap may require a second, nonerror exit from a program. This second exit violates structure principles. Tausworthe (1979) shows how to impose structure on concurrent programming and traps. He does this by adapting ANSI standards for flow charts and by requiring individual processing blocks to be structured. This concept is illustrated in Figure 9-25. Tausworthe uses the interrupt/terminal symbol to represent a trap and merges this symbol with the concurrent programming symbol.

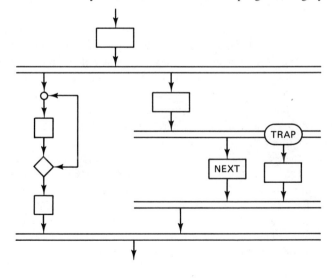

Figure 9-25 Concurrent processes with traps.

Concurrent programming is a subset of multiprogramming. In the case of concurrent programming, several tasks are being executed at once. These tasks may be accomplished by using multiple processors or by time sharing a single processor. Concurrent programming is denoted in Figure 9-25 by the separate flow charts located between the double lines. An event-driven interrupt, or trap, is denoted by the terminal symbol embedded in the double line. When the event occurs, the program beginning with TRAP is executed. At the conclusion of this program (i.e., when the lower double line is reached), the trap is cleared and processing returns to the place where the trap occurred. In Figure 9-25, the program NEXT is executed next.

EXERCISE 9.5 Is the program depicted in Figure 9-25 a proper program? If not, state why. Is this program a structured program? If not, state why. In the event that the answer to either of these questions is no, can you reformat the program so that it is structured or proper? If so, do so. If not, why?

EXERCISE 9.6 Review the discussion in Chapter 2 concerning module cohesion and coupling. How would you modify this discussion to make it applicable to real-time programs?

9.9 SYSTEM REQUIREMENTS EVALUATION METHOD

The System Requirements Evaluation Method (SYSREM, pronounced sis-rem) consists of a group of tools and a procedure for designing real-time distributed systems. SREM (for Software Requirements Evaluation Method) is an earlier version of SYSREM. SYSREM was developed by Mack Alford at TRW over a twenty-five-year period. It is available from the U.S. Army Strategic Defense Command (formerly the Ballistic Missile Defense Command) in Huntsville, Alabama, at no charge to people working on government contracts. There may be a nominal charge for other people.

SYSREM requires the specification of the system in terms of a set of inputs, a set of outputs, a set of states, and a function that maps inputs plus current state onto outputs plus updated state. An advantage of viewing real-time systems as state machines is that it highlights exception handling and sequencing. A sample graphic aid used in SYSREM is given in Figure 9-26. Here the ampersand, &, denotes the AND operation. At primary junctures, the symbol &* is used (inside a circle) to indicate that the indicated processing needs to coordinate with another process, normally a control process.

In Figure 9-26, the processing described by the net in the shaded areas (in the foreground) may correspond to processing required for an air traffic control system to process an aircraft through a given sector of airspace. Note that a variety of concurrent processes are underway. The net in the shaded area is adequate to describe the required real-time processing for that aircraft, but it is inadequate to describe the environment because there may be many aircraft in that sector. This situation is illustrated by the series of shaded areas. Each of these areas contains the status information on a single aircraft. The

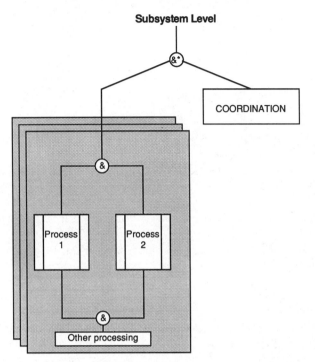

Figure 9-26 Treatment of exception handling at the subsystem level.

coordination processing is required to handle exceptions involving the multiple aircraft environment.

The primary benefit of SYSREM is that its procedures force requirements analysts and designers to consider sequencing, concurrency, and exception handling early in the life cycle. Other methods based on data-flow diagrams either cannot handle these items or do so with difficulty. SYSREM tools provide for assumptions and constraints and trace these items throughout the design. These tools include both a requirements language and graphical techniques.

The primary hindrance to using SREM is the complicated requirements language used in that process. Before using SREM it is advised that you take a two-week course on the language and methodology. Another disadvantage to SREM is that it generally requires a greater investment in up-front costs. It is likely to have lower life-cycle costs, but many people refuse to look at the total costs.

Information on exception handling and assumptions is very advantageous when system testing is being conducted. Alford (1985) claims that SREM leads to lower system test costs. The finite-state machine approach of this method is also very useful for system maintenance. Knowledge of system states can be exploited to build functions for monitoring the status and health of real-time systems. This approach can, for example, lead to the performance of some functions on board satellites that would otherwise have to be performed at a ground station.

Further information on SYSREM is provided in Paul and Siegert (1985). Alford is writing a book that should appear at about the same time as this book.

EXERCISE 9.7 Evaluate Figures 7-15, 7-16, 7-19, and 7-20. Expand those figures to account for all the structured techniques mentioned in this chapter.

REFERENCES

ALFORD, M., "SREM at the Age of Eight: The Distributed Computing Design System," *Computer*, Vol. 18, No. 4, Apr. 1985, pp. 36–46.

AMERICAN NATIONAL STANDARDS INSTITUTE, "Flow Chart Symbols and Their Usage in Information Processing," ANSI X3.5-1970 (also published by the National Bureau of Standards as FIPS PUB 24).

DEMARCO, T., *Structured Analysis and System Specification*, Prentice-Hall, Inc., Englewood Cliffs, N.J., 1979.

FELDMAN, C., K. SCHOMAN, and D. SNYDER, "Structured Analysis Model for Naval Telecommunications Procedures," Naval Research Laboratory, NRL Memorandum Report 3086, July 1975.

GANE, C., and T. SARSON, *Structured Systems Analysis: Tools and Techniques*, Prentice-Hall, Inc., Englewood Cliffs, N.J., 1979.

GOMAA, H., "A Software Design Method for Real Time Systems," *Communications of the ACM*, Vol. 27, No. 9, Sept. 1984, pp. 938–949.

GROH, H., and K. LUTZ, "Outside-in Instead of Top-down: Industrial-scale Software Production with CADOS," *Data Report*, Vol. XII, No. 4, 1984, pp. 19–25.

IBM CORPORATION, *HIPO—A Design Aid and Documentation Technique*, Manual No. GC20-1851, White Plains, N.Y., 1974.

KATZEN, H., JR., *Systems Design and Documentation; An Introduction to the HIPO Method*, Van Nostrand Reinhold Co., New York, 1976.

LANO, R. L., "The N^2 Chart," TRW-SS-77-04, Nov. 1977.

PAUL, M., and H. J. SIEGERT (EDS.), *Distributed Systems: Methods and Tools for Specification*, Lectures in Computer Science 190, Springer-Verlag Publishers, New York, 1985.

ROSS, "Structured Analysis (SA): A Language for Communicating Ideas," *IEEE Proceedings*, Vol. SE-20, Jan. 1977.

SIEVERT, G. E., and T. A. MIZELL, "Specification-based Software Engineering with TAGS," *IEEE Computer Magazine*, Apr. 1985, pp. 56–65.

TAUSWORTHE, R. C., *Standardized Development of Computer Software*, Parts I and II, Prentice-Hall, Inc., Englewood Cliffs, N.J., 1979.

WARNIER, J. -D., *Logical Construction of Programs*, 3rd ed., translated by B. Flanagan, Van Nostrand Reinhold Co., New York, 1976.

CHAPTER 10

Data-base Design

As in previous chapters, this chapter is intended to serve as an introduction to a complex subject. There are many books on data-base design. A good first book on this subject is *Data Base: Structured Techniques for Design, Performance and Management,* by S. Atre (1980). That book includes discussion of both the logical design and the physical design of a data base. Atre includes in her book the discussion of major data-base management systems (DBMSs), such as CODASYL, ADABAS, and IMS.

In this book, the discussion is limited to the conceptual and logical design of a data base. The first two sections of this chapter offer a conventional approach. Basic concepts of data bases are introduced. The categorization of data bases (as network, hierarchical, and relational) and the normalization of data bases (into first through third normal form) are discussed. The key attribute of this conventional discussion is the demonstration of the relationship between the functional design of a system and the logical design of the data base.

In Section 10.3, the concept of a knowledge data base is introduced. The knowledge data-base concept can form the basis for an expert system. If decision rules are included, it is equivalent to an expert system.

The term "expert system" will generally be avoided here because expert systems conjure images of LISP; the discussion in Section 10.3 is LISPless.

As we shall see, a knowledge data base is a relational data base with the property that the relations can be formed dynamically, after the data base is designed. In traditional relational data bases, the relations are determined during the design. They cannot be changed easily after the system is operational. Specifically, it is shown, using conventional techniques, in Section 10.3 how a "somewhat relational" data base, like M204, can be used to develop a knowledge data base.

10.1 DATA RELATIONSHIPS

10.1.1 Introduction to Data Relationships

The general classes of data are:

- *Primitive data element:* an individual data structure; the smallest element in a system; the field of a record.
- *Data structure:* a data-base component having one and only one logical access path; a record of a data base (the access key of a record is one or more fields that uniquely define a record and thereby provide the logical access path).
- *Data store:* a repository of data; also called a file.
- *Data base:* a data store having more than one logical access path.
- *Data flow:* data that are in motion between two processes.

When drawing a data-flow diagram, or its equivalent, the data that flow between the processes should be thought of as data structures rather than as primitive data elements.

Data-base models are in essence descriptions of relationships among the system data. These relationships can be categorized in a variety of ways. The first viewpoint given here is a numerical one. In this case, the data relationships are one to one, one to many, and many to many.

These data relationships are depicted in Figure 10-1. A one-to-one relationship among data is equivalent to a one-to-one discrete function, or a set of ordered pairs. Examples of this type of relationship are hospital patient to bed, and license plates to noncommercial cars (commercial vehicles, such as taxicabs, may be licensed in more than one state or in a state and the District of Columbia).

A one-to-many relationship is denoted by a double arrow in the direction of the multiple side of the relationship. Hierarchical relationships are one to many. Physical examples of a one-to-many relationship include hospital wards to beds, licensed vehicles to parking tickets, and (theoretically speaking) company organization charts.

Many-to-many relationships are by far the most common type of relationship. These relationships are networks; for ease of presentation they are represented as double arrows in both directions. Examples of many-to-many relationships include drivers to cars, inventory systems (the supplier to part relationship), and bank accounts to people.

As we begin to organize relationships among the system data, we start with the conceptual view of the data base. This viewpoint generally represents the status of the data during the planning phase of the life cycle. It is also called the user's view of the data. The logical data base is the designer's viewpoint. The physical data base is the implementer's viewpoint. During the requirements phase and the preliminary design phase, the logical design of the data base is developed.

In a world of ideal independence among data, the conceptual view would be independent of the logical view. That is, from the viewpoint of the applications programs, the logical design of the data base would be irrelevant. Changes to the logical design, such as adding fields or files and changing from a hierarchical structure to a relational structure, would have no effect on the applications.

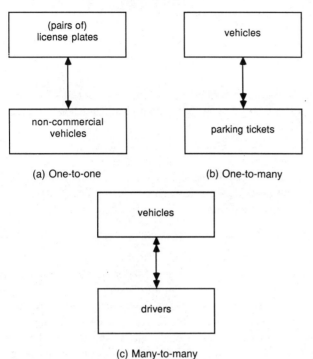

(a) One-to-one   (b) One-to-many

(c) Many-to-many

Figure 10-1 Relationships among data structures.

The physical design of the data base is the system view of the data. It is a mapping of the logical design into the hardware. In our ideal world of data independence, we would be able to change access rules and storage media, fine tune the performance, and change the physical representation of the data without affecting the logical structure of the application programs. It is a shame that this utopia doesn't exist.

To accomplish the response time required for the use of large data bases, it is generally necessary for data-base administrators and applications programmers to compromise between data independence and either storage or accessing methods. Thus it is sometimes necessary for the applications programmer to be aware of the physical representation of data and global schema (in addition to the subschema). These compromises are especially true of real-time systems.

In Section 10.2, some attributes of distributed data bases are discussed. Awareness of those attributes is required during the top-level design of systems with distributed processing. For the remainder of this section, we will be discussing dependencies among data elements, data anomalies, the normal forms of data, and models of data bases.

10.1.2 Functional Dependencies

During the conceptual design of the data base, we develop a data structure from the users' viewpoint. During the case study of Chapter 8, you were given an exercise to develop a data structure for a weather report. A typical structure might be:

```
(weather-status-text, station-identification,
message identification, effective time, ceiling,
visibility, cloud-coverage, altimeter, temperature,          (10.1)
wind direction, wind velocity, winds aloft,
activity codes, altitude, direction, velocity).
```

In the data structure (10.1), the altimeter field contains a measurement of pressure. The activity codes may be, for example, 0 for clear, 1 for light rain, 2 for heavy rain, 3 for hurricane, or 4 for severe turbulence.

EXERCISE 10.1   This record has 16 fields; if we used vector terminology, it is referred to as a 16-tuple. As we inspect this record, two immediate questions come to mind. These are: (1) what do all these data element names mean, and (2) what are the primary keys (or in mathematical terms, what are the independent variables)? Answer these questions before continuing.

Some of the data elements are clearly understood by their name. Weather-status-text is apparently the unformatted text section of the message. Station-identification leads one to think of a weather station, either a fixed ground station or a ship that maintains a fixed position to monitor weather. The question arises, "What about pilot reports of weather?"

The flight identification number (assigned by the FAA) could be used, but this is not adequate for meaningful data without an indicator of the aircraft position at the time of report. In practice, pilot reports would be verbal. The air traffic controller controlling that aircraft would make note of the weather (which would be in his sector), and he would notify other controllers as appropriate. This notification would probably be by voice.

As we inspect this message, it seems that the two fields are required to uniquely define this record. These two fields are station-identification and message-identification. The message-identification field is a number assigned by the weather station to track every outgoing message. Fields that uniquely define a record are called *access keys*.

A record that may be part of the conceptual design of an MIS system for project management is:

```
(subcontractor-number, configuration-item,                  (10.2)
subcontractor-name, subcontractor-details, price).
```

The data element subcontractor-details may include the subcontractor's address, telephone number, and point of contact.

This case again requires two access keys, configuration-item and subcontractor-number. The dependent variables are subcontractor-name and price. In this example, we could have specified the subcontractor-name to be an access key or independent variable and the subcontractor-number to be a dependent variable.

Notice that nothing has been said about the dependency of subcontractor-details yet. This field actually depends on the subcontractor name and not on the access keys we specified. It is an implicit relationship. For a better logical design, this record should be split into two records as follows:

```
1. (subcontractor-number, configuration-item, price)
```
```
2. (subcontractor-number, subcontractor-name,
   subcontractor-details)
```

Suppose that the subcontractor, who is producing 360 configuration items, changed his point of contact. In the second representation, (10.3), of the data we have to change precisely one record. In the first representation, (10.2), of the data we would have to update 360 records because the point-of-contact information is included in each record as part of the subcontractor-details.

Implicit relationships such as the one depicted in the first representation generally induce data anomalies. The anomaly illustrated in the preceding paragraph is called an *update anomaly*. An update anomaly occurs when a change in a single datum requires the update of many records. A similar anomaly is the *insertion anomaly*. An insertion anomaly occurs when the insertion of a single element must be done many times.

A more subtle anomaly is the *deletion anomaly*. This occurs when the deletion of the last record for an access key results in the loss of important information. Suppose that a record is deleted whenever a configuration item is delivered; that is, we delete the record corresponding to the *configuration-item, subcontractor-number* access key. In the first representation, when a contractor delivers the last configuration item for which he is responsible, we lose the subcontractor-details. This is probably an undesirable event; it is generally a good idea to maintain a list of subcontractors with whom you have done business.

EXERCISE 10.2   Determine the implicit relationships in (10.1). State the types of anomalies you observe and identify them.

10.1.3 Normal Form of the Data Model

The procedure for eliminating data anomalies in the structure of the logical data-base design is called *normalizing* the data. There are various normal forms of the data model. These are discussed in order.

The unnormalized data model is simply the records as they are used in the application programs. The weather report structure, (10.1), given in Section 10.1.2 is an example of an unnormalized data model.

A data set is said to be in *first normal form* if it can be represented by a two-dimensional table such as

```
RELATION (ATTR1,ATTR2,ATTR3,...,ATTRn)
```

where all repeating groups have been eliminated and each row in the table is unique. In the case of the weather report given previously, the activity codes represent a repeating group. Simply stated it is not possible to determine before a weather report is generated how many fields must be allocated for the activity codes and the subsequent description of them in terms of altitude, direction, and velocity. A single weather report may contain multiple activity codes.

If the maximum number of codes that seem reasonable is three, then a design following the conceptual layout would have multiple empty fields for most reports. Furthermore, if a fourth activity code were proved to be necessary, the data base would have to be restructured to accommodate it. Note that in first normal form all occurrences of a record type contain the same number of fields.

The second and third normal forms focus on the relationship of the nonkey fields to the key fields or the dependent variables to the independent variables. A data structure is said to be in *second normal form* when it is in first normal form and every implicit relationship has been eliminated. In other words, every nonkey field must be fully functionally dependent upon every access or candidate key.

An example of a data structure that is not in second normal form is given in (10.2). The corresponding structure, in second normal form, is given in (10.3). From the conceptual view of how the data are used, the user tries to pack as much information as possible into the data structure. These structures tend to be complicated and full of anomalies and implicit relationships. During the logical design of the data structures, the data-base designer simplifies the structures. From a logical viewpoint, these simplified structures are easy to access and the data presented are compact.

EXERCISE 10.3   Specify a first normal form for the weather report. Next develop the second normal form for this weather report.

A relation is said to be in *third normal form* if it is in second normal form and all transitive dependencies have been eliminated. As an example, consider the following structure for information related to the design of a distributed system:

$$(\text{CSCI}, \text{CSC}, \text{MACHINE})$$

where the terms CSCI and CSC refer to computer software configuration items and computer software components, respectively. One of the design rules is that each CSCI is implemented on a single machine; that is, its components are not distributed among processors.

Note that each nonkey field is fully dependent on the key field. However, for this structure, it is necessary to repeat the MACHINE entry for each CSC of a CSCI. This anomaly is eliminated by the following structure:

$$(\text{CSCI}, \text{CSC})$$
$$(\text{CSCI}, \text{MACHINE})$$

EXERCISE 10.4   Develop a structure for the third normal form of the weather report.

Kent (1983) gives a simple guide to the *five* normal forms used in relational data-base theory. The fourth and fifth forms were introduced by R. Fagin of IBM in the late

1970s. Fourth and fifth normal forms address multivalued facts. They involve composite keys and many-to-many relationships.

Suppose we consider a group of machines made up of multiple parts obtained from multiple vendors. Note that there is intentional vagueness about whether each part is obtained from multiple vendors or whether multiple vendors supply parts for each machine. A relation for this could be written as

$$\text{(MACHINE, PARTS, VENDORS)} \qquad\qquad (10.4)$$

The question is, what do the following records mean:

```
(Buick Century, steering wheel, Fisher Body)
(Buick Century, steering wheel,    )
(Buick Century,    , Fisher Body)
(Buick Century, frame, Fisher Body)
(Buick Century, steering wheel, ABC Steering)
```

Each of these records is meaningful according to the structure (10.4).

What we want to do when reviewing this information is to obtain information about the cross product; that is, who makes the steering wheel? Does this mean that we have to repeat Fisher Body's name for every part they supply to GM? Suppose they manufacture some parts that correspond to parts appearing in GM cars, but are not purchased by GM. As a supplier they would be listed for that part. They would not be listed as a vendor from whom GM purchases that part.

For this data structure to be in fourth normal form, it should be rewritten as

```
(MACHINE, PART)
(MACHINE, VENDOR)
```

The fifth normal form presents a way of dealing with the cross-product information. For example, the (MACHINE, PART, VENDOR) structure would be expressed as:

```
(MACHINE, PART)
(MACHINE, VENDOR)
(PART, VENDOR)
```

Thus, a structure is said to be in fifth normal form if its information content cannot be reconstructed from smaller record types. Note that the normalization process does not eliminate all redundancies. Certain interrecord redundancies are not addressed. For example,

```
(CSCI, CSC)
(CSCI, MACHINE)
(CSC, MACHINE)
```

is in third normal form despite obvious redundancy. A reference in which interrecord redundancy is addressed is Ling, Tompa, and Kameda (1981).

10.1.4 Data Models

Thus far we have talked about data relationships in terms of their topology (a network, a hierarchy, or one to one), functional dependencies, and anomalies (i.e., normalization). In this section we explore relationships in terms of relational, hierarchical, and network data models. It is these models on which modern data-base management systems are based.

A relational data base can be thought of as a *flat file*. A flat file is equivalent to a collection of index cards. Suppose that we are performing a requirements analysis for a major system. In the System Requirements Specification, we want to include both the data-flow diagrams for the top three levels of the user's functions and the beginning of a conceptual design for a data base (which includes a data dictionary).

Also suppose that a set of data-flow diagrams has been completed. For analytically oriented or scientifically oriented systems, it is frequently the case that the functions and their flow are better understood than the data, so these are described first. To develop the first cut at the data dictionary, we begin by getting a large stack of index cards. (A manual process is described because it is easy to understand; of course, this process could and should be automated.)

For each data-flow diagram, beginning with the first process, write each input data element and each output element on a separate index card. Indicate on the index card the name of the data element, a longer description of it, its source, and its sink. If the data element is an input to Process Alpha, then its sink is the Process Alpha, and if the data element is an output of Process Bet, then its source is the Process Bet. When you are through, repeat these steps for each process of each data-flow diagram. You can now sort these index cards any way that you desire.

This collection of index cards is a flat file. Your ability to sort it in accordance with any of the predefined fields make it equivalent to a relational data base.

EXERCISE 10.5   Perform the process just described for the data-flow diagram given in Figure 8-8.

A relational data base is visualized as a set of tables in Figure 10-2(a). Note that the relationship is stored with the data. This type of data base is what we usually prefer. Unfortunately, we have not yet been able to implement pure relational data bases and still achieve the performance we require from large commercial data-base management systems. Some DBMSs, such as Model 204, claim to be relational. Although they are not relational from a purist's viewpoint, from an applications viewpoint it can be assumed that they are relational.

The first approach to DBMS development used hierarchical data-base structures. A hierarchical or one-to-many structure is illustrated in Figure 10-2(b). The initial versions of IMS (Information Management System), CODASYL (Committee on Data System Languages), IDMS, IDS2, and DBMS were all hierarchical data bases.

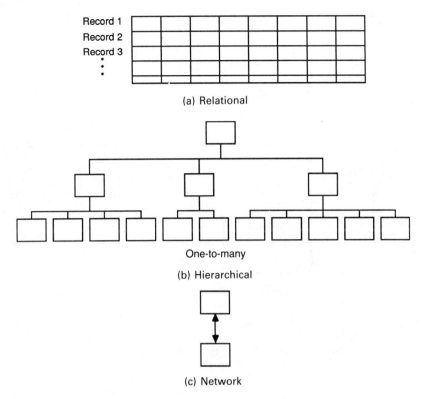

(a) Relational

One-to-many

(b) Hierarchical

(c) Network

Figure 10-2   Data-base models.

The primary advantages of hierarchical models are the existence of established DBMSs, a simple model, and the ability to provide a variety of viewpoints when multiple models are used with interconnecting fields. This concept is illustrated in Figure 10-3. The primary disadvantage arises from the fact that most real applications involve many-to-many relationships rather than one-to-many relationships.

This fact is sometimes realized in redundant physical storage of data, a generally bad feature. Insertions and deletions in hierarchical models are too complex. For example, the deletion of a parent results in deletion of all children records.

Current DBMSs based on network models include CODASYL, ADABAS, System 2000, and Model 204. These DBMSs are widely used and supported. As mentioned previously, many real-life data models involve many-to-many relationships. Network models tend to be very complex, but the DBMSs have fourth-generation languages associated with them to simplify the job of the applications programmer. When working with very large data bases, it is occasionally necessary to reorganize them. This is a complicated process and may result in loss of data independence.

Relational data bases are frequently represented by n-tuples, or records, in which the key access words are underlined. An example of this representation is given by

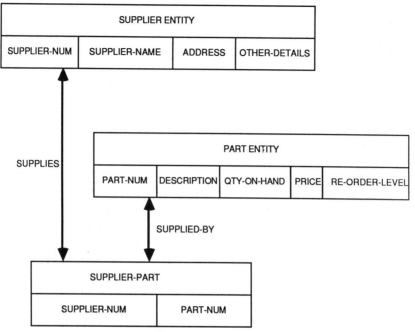

Note: An artificial entity, Supplier-Part, had to be introduced.
This entity has more than one parent.

Figure 10-3 Hierarchical model.

(SUBCONTRACTOR NUM, CONFIGURATION ITEM, SUBCONTRACTOR_NAME,
PRICE)

Hierarchical data bases are generally represented by a series of records with their structure identified by a double-headed arrow. An example of this representation is given in Figure 10-3. This figure actually shows two hierarchical structures. One is the relationship between SUPPLIER_ENTITY and the SUPPLIER_PART. In each case, the access keys are given by the top row, and the record layout is given immediately below. The first relationship has been labeled SUPPLIES. A second hierarchical relationship, SUPPLIED_BY, has also been identified. This second relationship is identical to the first relationship at the second level of the hierarchy. If thought of as a tree structure, they have a node in common.

There is a need for this second relationship because the real data that are being represented are not actually hierarchical. The supplier-part problem is actually a network. Thus, Figure 10-3 depicts how a network is represented through a series of hierarchical relationships. This problem can get quite complicated.

EXERCISE 10.6   Consider the hierarchy in which we describe the projects and resources of a department manager. This may be represented by

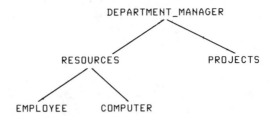

Suppose that

DEPARTMENT_MANAGER has fields NAME, EMPLOYEE_NUM and DEPT.
EMPLOYEE has fields NAME, EMPLOYEE_NUM and PAY_GRADE.
COMPUTER has fields VENDOR, MODEL and PART_NUM.
PROJECTS has fields PROJ_NAME, START, and DURATION.

Represent this structure as a relational model.

EXERCISE 10.7   For the following relationships

```
BOOK(LIBRARY, ADDRESS, TITLE, PUBLISHER, COPIES)
BKAUTH(TITLE, PUBLISHER, PUBLISHER_ADDRESS, AUTHOR,
      AUTHOR_ADDRESS)
STUDENT(NAME, ADDRESS, SEX, DATE_OF_BIRTH, TELEPHONE,
      ADVISOR)
CLASS(NAME, CLASS_NUM, TIME, DAYS, ROOM, INSTRUCTOR)
```

indicate the access keys, map the functional dependencies, indicate the highest normal form, and, if not already in third normal form, normalize to third normal form.

10.2 DATA BASES HAVING MULTIPLE USERS

In Section 10.1 some of the basic ideas underlying the conceptual and logical design of data bases were introduced. Those ideas are related to organizing and structuring the system data. Nearly all larger data bases and many small data bases are designed for use by many people simultaneously. Typical applications are office systems, automatic teller machines, and credit-card verification systems. The intent of this section is to make the reader aware of some of the problems associated with the logical and physical design of data bases on large systems involving multiple users and computer processors.

The approach to this section is based on an unpublished technical report written by Charles Shartsis.

10.2.1 Centralized Data Bases

The concepts to be discussed are concurrency (i.e., access to the data base by more than one user simultaneously), recovery from failures and abnormal termination situations, and security.

Concurrency.   There are two time-phase-related problems associated with concurrency. The long-term transaction problem occurs when one data-base user has access to a given set of data for a long time, from a few minutes to many days. Suppose that user A downloads data from a mainframe to a microcomputer and stores the data in a local data base. He makes changes over the course of the next two days and is then prepared to upload his changes to the mainframe. Now suppose that user B makes some other changes to the same data in the interim. When user A uploads his changes, the changes made by user B are lost unless there is some mechanism to trace the disposition of the data. Without such a mechanism, this sequence of steps results in an invalid update anomaly.

In the short term, data synchronization has the same problem. An example of another problem, the invalid read anomaly, is given in Figure 10-4. By permitting transaction 2 to occur before transaction 1 is completed, the incorrect value for A + B is displayed.

The synchronization of transactions is necessary to preserve the integrity of the data base. Assuming that the data base is consistent at the beginning of a transaction, it must be consistent at the end of the transaction. Each transaction may actually be a sequence of operations, such as those depicted in Figure 10-4. Transactions that exhibit the property of preserving data-base consistency are called *atomic transactions*; during an atomic transaction other transactions may not access the data base.

Two mechanisms for achieving atomic transactions are *locking* and *time stamping*. When a data base uses the locking mechanism, it requires that each transaction lock the

Transaction 1: Transfer $10K Expense from Task A to Task B			Transaction 2: Display Cumulative Charges			Charges to Each Task	
	Internal Value			Internal Value			
Operation	A	B	Operation	A	B	A	B
READ A	$75K					$75K	$40K
SUBTRACT $10K	$65K					$65K	$40K
WRITE A	$65K					$65K	$40K
			READ A	$65K		$65K	$40K
			READ B		$40K	$65K	$40K
			DISPLAY A + B ($105K)	$65K	$40K	$65K	$40K
READ B		$40K				$65K	$40K
ADD $10K		$50K				$65K	$40K
WRITE B		$50K				$65K	$50K

Figure 10-4 Cumulative task charges are incorrectly displayed as $105,000.

data objects it accesses before performing operations with these objects. This prevents other transactions from accessing objects used by the first transaction.

This approach is a viable one, but various other techniques are needed during implementation to detect and correct deadlocks. Suppose that TRANSACTION A accesses (and locks) FILE A while TRANSACTION B accesses (and locks) FILE B. Further suppose that, after accessing FILE A, TRANSACTION A wants to access FILE B. This file is locked, so TRANSACTION A must wait until TRANSACTION B is completed before continuing its processing. Now suppose that TRANSACTION B needs to access FILE A. A deadlock occurs because each transaction is waiting for files to be unlocked by another transaction.

The time-stamping approach assigns a number (which is an increasing function of time) to each transaction in order of their occurrence. Either of two policies may be implemented to handle problems of conflicts. One policy is called the *wait-die* policy. For this policy, whenever a transaction requesting data is older than a transaction currently using those data, the older transaction waits until the data are available. If the requesting transaction is younger than the transaction currently using those data, the requesting transaction is aborted and restarted.

The second policy is called the *wound-wait* policy. In this case, whenever an older transaction requests data being used by younger transactions, the younger transactions are aborted and restarted while the older transaction gains access to the data. If a younger transaction requests data being used by an older transaction, it waits. The time-stamping approach prevents deadlocks, but it requires extra storage. It also causes restarts for circumstances in which there is no possibility of a deadlock.

The techniques described for synchronization do not apply to long-term transactions. It is not feasible to lock files or records for extended periods of time. Users frequently make copies of files and keep them in local storage for further analysis. When multiple users access and change data, the data-base administration problem frequently requires human intervention. Examples of some policies are:

- Keep all data-base changes in a temporary file; at the end of each day, these suggested changes are reviewed and changes to the permanent data base are made by an authorized person.
- All changes are accepted; it is the responsibility of each user to review changes by other users. During the review process, the relevant data are locked to prevent further confusion.

Various programs can be developed to aid this review process. These policy issues need to be resolved during the system design.

Recovery.   When large data bases are maintained over a period of many years, we need to worry about the aging of data. Typically, data older than a specified time period are removed from disk storage and stored on tape as historical data. These data are seldom accessed, and when it is required, responsiveness on the order of hours or days is not uncommon. Over a period of years, systems evolve and DBMSs improve. This means that data bases are occasionally restructured. When restructuring occurs, and we want to access old data, it is necessary to build a means of recovering these data.

The need to recover data also occurs in the normal dynamic environment of data-base operations. It is not unusual for a data base to be in the middle of performing transactions when it is interrupted. Interrupts are caused by user aborts, deadlock resolution, system crashes, and other errors.

The concept of atomic transactions is critical to recovery mechanisms. If a log of these transactions is maintained, updated objects are held by the transaction until the end of the transaction, and checkpoints are periodically performed (i.e., the entire state of the system is recorded at a time when no updates are in progress), then it is possible to regenerate or recover the state of the data base after a crash or other failure.

Security.   Security is the final topic discussed relative to the design of the data base for centralized systems with multiple users. Large data bases frequently contain data that are very sensitive. These data may be highly classified from a military viewpoint, may be highly competitive information from an industrial viewpoint, or may be very sensitive from a privacy viewpoint (e.g., tax records).

Systems with these types of information frequently have many users. To complicate the matter, these users frequently are accessing the centralized computer from intelligent workstations through local area networks or telecommunications networks. These microcomputers put a large amount of computer power at the hands of a potentially hostile user. Their ability to penetrate a system is far greater than will be acknowledged by the victims. For example, banks generally refuse to discuss computer theft and data-base security or even acknowledge that a computer theft has occurred. A set of useful criteria for evaluating various levels of computer data security is given by the DOD Computer Security Center (1983).

Areas that are typically addressed during data-base security studies are given in Figure 10-5.

10.2.2 Distributed Data Bases

In the preceding section we discussed data-base systems with multiple users, but the data were physically controlled by a single processor. Here we discuss the problem of data bases that are distributed in the sense that they are controlled by many processors. This can occur in any combination of the following two ways:

- The data base may be partitioned, with each portion being controlled by a different computer (and possibly a different data-base administrator).
- Portions of the data base may be replicated and used in multiple locations.

When visualizing a distributed data base, you should think of each component as being located in a different place. These locations could be thousands of miles apart or just a few feet apart. Each location is using its own data-base management system

Security Area	Commonly Used Techniques
Identification, workstations	Port address, workstation access permission tables, monitor port connections
Identification, individual	Passwords, questions and answers, hardware device (e.g., badge readers, and keys), personal characteristic readers (voice, fingerprint readers, etc.)
Control of unattended workstations	Automatic sign-off when inactive; forced sign-off when door opens
Data-base controls	Control access to data on a file, record, or field basis; control based on password or port location
Audits and traceability	Attempted accesses and violations are recorded; all accesses to authorization tables are recorded
Special problems: Documentation and utilities available to personnel without authorization to access data	Special control of dumps, disk dynamic debugging techniques, "back-door hooks" by development personnel, program patches, test generators, etc.
Communications	Data encryption, optical fiber, monitor boxes containing twisted pair wire
Workstations, locally stored data	Removable hard disks (for storage in safes); overwrite memory upon sign-off; workstation versus approved user tables

Figure 10-5 Commonly used techniques of data protection.

(DBMS). To further complicate matters, the various DBMSs need not be the same. We can think of each location of a system as a system in its own right.

At the local level, the logical, conceptual, and physical design of its "own data base" need not be consistent with the design of the supersystem. For example, access paths to the data might be completely different. It is highly preferable to design the entire distributed data base in a consistent manner, but practical applications frequently involve existing subsystems and variations of functions that prevent this approach.

When faced with what appears to be a nightmare, we question why a distributed data base is needed in the first place. There are a variety of reasons, including response time, telecommunications costs, system availability and reliability, and data control.

In the following paragraphs, we will discuss the concepts of concurrency, recovery, and security in terms of distributed data bases.

Concurrency.   When a data base is partitioned, but not replicated, problems with concurrency are very similar to those of a centralized system. Synchronization problems are exacerbated because a user at a remote location may need to obtain the desired data through a telecommunications network. Furthermore, there is no control over the processing time required by that remote user's local computer system. To further complicate matters, the user's local system could go down without the system on which the data base is hosted being aware of this fact. Thus deadlocking problems could be severe if not managed properly.

An example of a problem that is incurred with replicated data bases is the following: suppose a user tries to access data at one location and discovers that these data are locked; the user can then try to access the same data at another location, where the data may not be locked. In the case of replicated systems, there is no hope of keeping every copy of the data base identical at all times. There is a need to keep the versions consistent; that is, after a finite known period of time, the copies should be in agreement.

As implied in the preceding, each location can be given a fully centralized locking scheme. To access data remotely, some overhead is imposed. The locking policy could restrict locking to a finite time period; decisions to unlock data being used remotely could be made by a data-base administrator (some of whose policies could be automated). In the case of replicated data, transmissions regarding the locking and unlocking of data may be made to maintain consistency. Appropriate use of journalization, file roll back and roll forward, and checkpointing could be used to determine conflicts that need resolution in the event that a remote user transmits data to a system that had been unlocked through a data-base administration policy decision.

The key point of this discussion is that networks greatly complicate data-base problems. During the requirements analysis and preliminary design phases for networks involving large data bases, experts in data-base design should have the opportunity to review results for an early determination of requirements that may be unreasonable or a design that is inadequate.

Recovery.   Recovery of replicated data could be rather simple. For the case in which the replicated data is never updated by transactions occurring at its site (i.e., updates are transmitted to another site where they are adjudicated and transmitted back to the original site and other sites), recovery could be made by simply transmitting a copy of the data from another site.

Generally, recovery is not so simple. Consider the following scenario:

- Transaction A, at site A, accesses and changes data D.
- Transaction A then sends the messages <LOCK D>, <UPDATE D TO D'>, <RELEASE D>.
- Transaction B, at site B, uses the updated version of data D after it is released by transaction A, and updates data.
- Transaction A continues to execute at site A while transaction B is executing at site B.
- Transaction A is interrupted by an abort or crash.

Now the problem is to reconstruct the data at site A. This could require an extraordinary effort, even with very careful time stamping. Depending on the nature of the transactions, many updates at many sites could occur in the interval between the update from site A and the abort at site A. In the next few paragraphs, the Two-Phase Commit Protocol (2PCP) will be described. This is an example of one of several techniques (or combinations of techniques) that is used in commercial data bases.

A scenario of transactions that define the 2PCP approach follows. Note that a central controller called the *commit coordinator* is assumed; also note that each site has an update procedure suitable for a single-site data base.

- Upon transaction initiation, the commit coordinator sends updates or initiation messages to each other site.
- Each site attempts to complete its part of the transaction (local recovery logs are used).
- Each site sends the coordinator an ABORT or SUCCESS message.
- If all sites transmit SUCCESS messages, then the coordinator writes the "commit" record to its log and sends a COMMIT message to the other sites.
- The other sites commit their changes upon receipt of the COMMIT record and send an ACKNOWLEDGMENT to the coordinator.
- Upon successful receipt of an ACKNOWLEDGMENT from all sites, the coordinator enters a COMPLETE in its log.
- If at any step all sites do not respond positively, the coordinator aborts the process and will begin recovery whenever all sites are operating properly.

EXERCISE 10.8   What are the advantages and disadvantages of the 2PCP approach? Write a description of any other approach to recovery for distributed systems. What are the advantages and disadvantages of the approach you described? Find a commercial application that uses either the 2PCP approach, the approach you described, or a hybrid approach that includes at least one of these two approaches.

Security.   The security concerns of designers of distributed systems include as a subset the security concerns associated with centralized systems. They also need to worry about host-to-host identification, access control, and communications.

This raises several other issues, such as:

- How are remote users identified?
- Who is responsible for data storage and access at remote sites?
- Are security policies and procedures at each site compatible?
- Can remote users using remote terminals gain access to combinations of data that give them (perhaps implied) information to which they are not authorized access?

10.3 KNOWLEDGE DATA BASE

10.3.1 Introductory Comments on Expert Systems

All the preceding discussion of data bases has been applied to the conventional way of thinking about data relationships. The underlying theme has been that it is necessary to understand the relationships among the data before the data base is built. That is, the relationships among the data elements are known, specified in advance, and designed into the data base.

In 1957, John McCarthy first developed LISP (LISt Processor). LISP differs from the procedural languages because it is oriented toward symbolic processing rather than numerical or transaction processing. Subsequently, LISP has been enhanced and many languages based on LISP have been developed. The key ingredient that LISP-based languages have in common is their ability to specify relationships among objects in a dynamic fashion.

The ability to specify relationships among objects dynamically forms the basis for expert systems. In this section we describe how the underlying principle of expert systems—the ability to specify relationships dynamically—can be achieved using conventional data bases, such as M204. Because of this emphasis, the term *knowledge data base* is used, rather than expert system.

A disadvantage to using the term expert system is the image that expert systems and artificial intelligence have in the applications community. Simply stated, many people have a need and desire for an *expert system,* but would not consider paying for one. Some thoughts that flash through their minds are:

- There are few successful applications.
- There are huge existing investments in conventional data bases.
- Expert systems are not well understood by laypeople (a notion promulgated by knowledge engineers).
- Conventional systems are both costly and difficult to maintain, so expert systems should have even worse problems.

Each of these objections is overcome with this knowledge data-base approach. A bit of caution is advised. The concept presented is simple to understand, but its implementation does involve some difficulties. The implementation should be done by an expert in data bases. There are questions of performance that need to be addressed. A knowledge data-base system may encourage the use of many more searches, a CPU consuming activity. Depending on performance, distributed data bases and processing may be needed. Thus implementation of a knowledge data base may also be expensive.

Exploiting the existing huge investment in conventional data bases is critical to the application of expert systems to business and government problems. For example, a data base could easily have 25 to 50 gigabytes of data. (The data base for the Patent and Trademark Office ''automated office system'' has been estimated at 40 terabytes.) The task of reformatting and restructuring a data base of this size is extremely expensive. If we could reformat and restructure data at a cost of 500 bytes per cent, it would still cost $1 million. Another, perhaps more important reason, to exploit conventional data-base technology is the time it takes to access and search large data bases. Conventional data-base technology is designed for very fast access and search of data bases. LISP-based languages could not handle the requirements of typical large data-base systems.

The approach discussed here is based on defining records in terms of grammatical syntax. This way, each relationship can be expressed in a reasonable English-like form and stored as a record. Another potential approach is to use a LISP-like language as a front end for a conventional data base. Considerable research is currently underway on the second approach.

In addition to illustrating a technique for specifying relationships dynamically, we will show how an analyst can deduce knowledge from available data (i.e., how she or he can deduce implicit relationships), how knowledge can be shared among analysts, and how to eliminate labor-intensive search techniques required when a knowledge data-base structure is not used.

The description of knowledge data bases given here is heuristic. Any relationship of the examples used to any person, organization, or system is purely coincidental. Model 204 (or M204), a commercial data base of the Computer Corporation of America, is used as a basis for discussion. The techniques apply to other commercial data bases also. M204 was selected simply because the original work on which this section is based was done for a client who was already using M204.

10.3.2 Representing Relationships

The ensuing discussion will be heuristic. The example used will be the construction of a software development support facility. The concept of a software support facility has been discussed several times in this book. A review of this concept may be useful before proceeding.

The software support facility is based on collecting all the system data into a data store, called the System Design Data Base (SDDB) and on establishing controls over the SDDB. A top-level structure for the SDDB is given in Figure 10-6.

Let us suppose that we are building a fictitious space system in this software support environment. Names for modules, subsystems, test facilities, and other components of the space system are presented as acronyms. The names and acronyms have been changed so that they do not carry significant meaning to the reader.

The capabilities of any good relational data base that runs on a machine at least as capable as a MicroVax II are adequate for most uses of the System Design Data Base (SDDB). For example, an Electronic Unit Development Folder (like the one described in Chapter 3) can be developed without using any knowledge data-base attributes. Given a knowledge data base, users of the software support facility will find ways to exploit its capabilities.

For example, the software support environment can be used to capture software

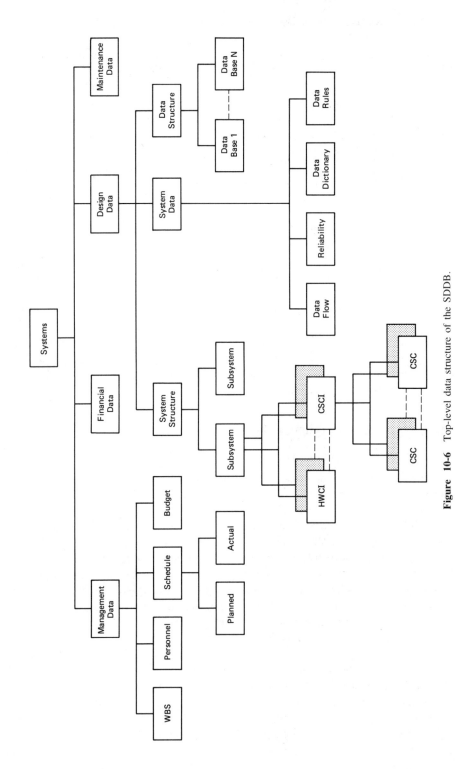

Figure 10-6 Top-level data structure of the SDDB.

products and to store them in a library. Relationships stored in a knowledge data base can be developed to help search the library for reusable software.

Actually, there are a multitude of relationships that need to be stored in the system support facility data base. These decisions and relationships occur at various levels. Some are necessary for project management. Others are needed for testing software before integration into the space vehicle. Many of these decisions are made by programmers who are trying to get everything to work. A primary area in which many relationships are developed and need to be captured is system maintenance.

Suppose that the relationships we wish to store are:

- On 2/10/86, ZDD (CSCI 0240) failed integration test 2.6 because the WDF interface was not established for specification 0240AB463.
- On 3/18/85, insert PAUSE 5 SECONDS before test call to solve ENVIRON Comm Link timing problem.
- On 1/25/86, ENVIRON Comm Link format was modified, see problem report 8.3.2-10.
- On 1/31/86, WDF procedure TEST call deleted pause 5 sec.

The difficulty addressed here is how to capture these relationships. In the following paragraphs, two standard ways of representing these relationships are discussed, and difficulties associated with these representations are described. Next the knowledge database approach to representing the data is presented.

A typical problem report file structure is shown in Figure 11-2. This type of format is useful for generating problem report forms, but it is not conducive to searching a maintenance data base of previously reported problems. Next, suppose we specify a format for describing a relationship that would be given in a problem report. For example, consider the relationship and format given in Figure 10-7(a). A difficulty with selecting a fixed format is that the events causing problems are unforeseeable. Thus, any format selected for describing a problem, such as the one in Figure 10-7(a), would be inadequate for describing other events, such as the one shown in Figure 10-7(b).

This particular example may not be exciting. Examples involving personnel files are

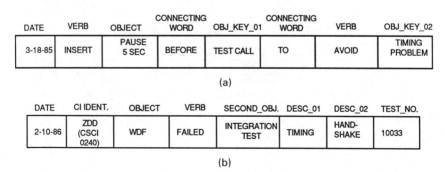

(a)

(b)

Figure 10-7 Establishing relationships with fixed formats.

more interesting because of the wide possibilities of events, such as embezzlement, that occur but affect very few people. This approach also has major applications to military intelligence and business planning.

In the case of systems, a knowledge data base can be used to store obscure facts, such as ''During test 12345, rocket engine fuel seals leaked when exposed to freezing temperatures; leaks resulted in booster rupture.'' This type of information would prevent situations in which somebody deciding whether or not to launch a space shuttle in cold weather simply calls the manufacturer and says, ''What do you think?'' It is generally not good to ask for engineering judgment about topics in which people have little or no experience. It is also not good to ask the advice of somebody who is both under contract to you and who knows the answer you want to hear. Consulting a data base of problems for cold weather effects would be more likely to bring obscure, but critical, information to the attention of the decision makers.

In the event that the fields did not exist for storing new relationships, then existing software would have to be modified to handle the new fields. The person wanting to enter the data or to evaluate other situations would have a long wait before this could be done. It is not desirable to specify new fields in a file just to accommodate special situations involving few records. If these accommodations were made, this approach results in frequent reorganization of the data and an increase in time to search fields.

Another problem with the conventional alternative for storing data is that it requires

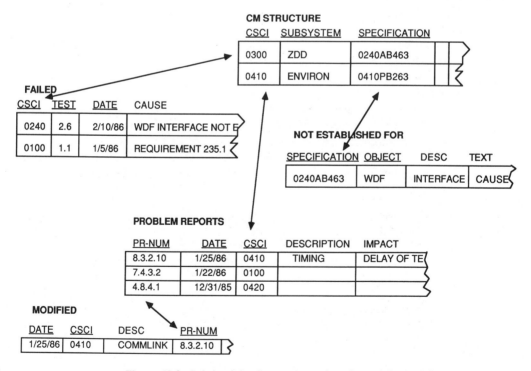

Figure 10-8 Relational data-base representation of user-defined relations.

the analyst or application program to extract information using precise data base (e.g., M204) queries. People familiar with one set of files may not be familiar with other sets of files, thus limiting their ability to get answers to difficult questions or to take advantage of implicit relationships. For example, management personnel may not be familiar enough with maintenance files to ask questions related to problems associated with the time it takes to establish communications links, or with freezing temperatures.

Another approach, using a relational equivalent to the data-base problem discussed previously, is illustrated in Figure 10-8. The underlined field names are primary keys or parts of primary keys. Arrows are drawn to show the record relationships. The arrows do not represent any kind of physical mechanism such as record pointers. All record relationships are based in the contents of the fields.

Each type of relationship is represented by a single flat file; these files usually have a compound primary key. It is just as easy (or difficult) to query for all problems reported on 3/18/85 as it is to query for all problems associated with subsystem TEST.

Relational data bases solve many problems. As we mentioned before, the relationships used in a relational data base must be known in advance because they are designed into the data base. This approach does not permit an analyst using the data base to browse relationships.

10.3.3 Knowledge Data-base Approach

Figure 10-9 shows a simplified view of the knowledge data base (KDB) for the system support facility example presented previously. The concept is explained by considering four key files: the Topics File, the Relationships File, the Topics Control File, and the Relationships Control File. Other types of files needed for implementation, such as security files, source reference files, external communications files, and candidate update files, are not discussed here.

The four primary types of files can be formed from the corresponding relational data base by the following steps:

- Put all records from the topic files (subsystem file, specification file, problem report file, etc.) into a single Topics File, as illustrated in Figure 10-9(a).

TOPIC_NAME	PRI_KEY_01		DESC_01	DESC_02	
SUBSYSTEM	NDF		0100		
SUBSYSTEM	ZDD		0200		
SUBSYSTEM	WDF		0300		
SUBSYSTEM	ENVIRON		0410		
SUBSYSTEM	TEST		0420		
SPECIFICATION	ZDD		1.0		
TEST PLAN	SUBTEST 2.6		ZDD	1.0	
REQUIREMENTS	ZDD		12	00163	
CHANGE RPT	20345		NDF	TEST PROC.	
TEST REPORT	00199		SUBTEST 2.6	FAIL	

(a) Topics File

Figure 10-9 Simplified view of the knowledge data base used for system maintenance.

TOPIC_NAME	ACTUAL FIELDS	LOGICAL FIELDS
SUBSYSTEM	PRI_KEY_01,DESC_01	SUBSYSTEM_NAME, CSCI
SPECIFICATION	PRI_KEY_01, DESC_O1	SUBSYSTEM_NAME, VERSION
TEST PLAN	PRI_KEY_01, DESC_O1, DESC_02	TP_NAME, SUBSYSTEM_NAME, VERSION
CHANGE RPT	PRI_KEY_01, DESC_O1, DESC_02	CHANGE_NUM, SUBSYSTEM_NAME, ITEM
REQIUREMENTS (C)	PRI_KEY_01, DESC_O1, DESC_02	SYSTEM_ NAME, NUM_OF_REQUIREMENTS, REQUIREMENT_ID_NUM
TEST REPORT	PRI_KEY_01, DESC_O1, DESC_02	TEST REPORT__ID SUBTEST, STATUS

(b) KDB Topics File Control File

RECORD FIELD	TEST RESULTS			CHANGE REPORT		
	ACTUAL FIELD	LOGICAL FIELD	EXAMPLE	ACTUAL FIELD	LOGICAL FIELD	EXAMPLE
SUBJ.	SUBJ_KEY_01	DATE	2/10/85	SUBJ_KEY_01	DATE	1/3/86
	SUBJ_KEY_02	SUBSYS_NAME	ZDD	SUBJ_KEY_02	SUBSYS_NAME	ENVIRON
SUBJ. DESC	SUB_DESC_01	CONFIG_ID	0240	SUB_DESC_01	CONFIG_ID	0410
	SUB_DESC_02	DESCRIPTOR		SUB_DESC_02	DESCRIPTOR	COMMLINK
VERB	VERB_1	RELATION_001	FAILED	VERB_1	RELATION_001	MODIFIED
OBJ.	OBJ_KEY_01	TEST_NAME	INTEG.TEST			
OBJ. DESC	OBJ_DESC_01	TEST_NUMBER	2.6			
CON- JUNC- TION	CONJUNCTION	CONJUNCTION	BECAUSE	CONJUNCTION	CONJUNCTION	SEE
PHRAS SUBJ.	SUBJ_KEY_03	PRASE_SUBJ.	WDF	SUBJ_KEY_03	PRASE_SUBJ.	PROB. REPORT
PHRAS SUBJ DESC	SUB_DESC_03	PHRASE_SUBJ_ DESCRIPTOR	INTERFACE	SUB_DESC_03	PHRASE_SUBJ_ DESCRIPTOR	8.3.2.10
VERB	VERB_02	VERB_02	NOT ESTAB- LISHED FOR			
PHRAS OBJ	OBJ_KEY_02	SPEC_NAME	SPECIFICATION			
PHRAS OBJ DESC	OBJ_DESC_02	SPEC_ID	0240AB463			

(c) KDB Relationships File Control File with Examples

Note: When the user enters data into a record, he sees the logical field as a prompt. The user has the option of displaying relationships in the form of stilted English, as shown below, or by using predefined report formats.
- 2/10/85 ZDD 0240 failed Integ. Test 2.6 because WDF interface not established for Specification 0240AB463.
- 1/31/85 ENVIRON 0410 COMMLINK modified. See Prob. Report 8.3.2.10.

Figure 10-9 (continued)

- Include the topic as the entry of a new field.
- Put all records from the event relationship files (pirated by, increased, etc.) in the single Relationships File.
- Include the relationship description as the entry of a new field.
- Devise a set of standardized field names for the Topics File (such as PRIMARY_ KEY_01, DESCRIPTOR_KEY_01, DESCRIPTOR_KEY_02).
- Devise a set of standardized field names for the Relationships File (such as SUBJECT_KEY, OBJECT_KEY, SECOND_OBJECT_KEY).
- Create the KDB Topics Control File and the KDB Relationships Control File. There is one record in the Control File for each topic type and relationship type, respectively. KDB control files are illustrated by Figure 10-9(b) and (c).
- Create generalized software to display, print, sort, enter, and edit Topics and Relationships records. This software displays the "logical" field names to the analyst as if they were the actual M204 field names. Logical field names are used for display, and actual field names are used for retrieving the field data.

The software described is considered part of the KDB. Using this software, new topics or relationships to the KDB can be added by changing or adding control file records. As new relationships are added, the software does not have to be modified. The software reads input data and creates actual M204 field names. From the viewpoint of the user, the data names appear to be the logical names assigned to the field or relationship. This makes it easy, for example, to scan the relationship names and their definitions.

EXERCISE 10.9   Using Figure 10-9, create new topics or relationships needed to describe traceability of requirements to specifications to configuration items.

EXERCISE 10.10   Select any other data base with which you are familiar. Apply this procedure to that data base. If you are not very familiar with any data base, then select a microcomputer-based data base, such as dBase III or Knowledgeman.

EXERCISE 10.11   Show how information can be deduced from this data base.

Using the example illustrated by Figure 10-9, suppose that an analyst working the night shift is testing subsystem NDF. Using the TEST subsystem, he invokes the simulation environment ENVIRON. He finds that his test fails because communications links cannot be established. If you look at the preceding relationships, the reason is fairly clear: the PAUSE 5 (seconds) command has been deleted from the test procedure. We previously determined that this command was necessary to fix a timing problem; the advice given by the ENVIRON developer that it is no longer necessary was not good.

Unfortunately, the person working the night shift is not the person who made the change or the person who determined the original fix. Indeed, there does not appear to be any logical reason why a Pause 5 is needed before invoking calls to ENVIRON. Furthermore, the actual relationship file would be too large for the analyst to simply look at all relationships. Since the changes to the ENVIRON subsystem, in theory, had no effect on this analyst's use of that subsystem, he or she would be unaware of those changes. Using a conventional approach, the analyst may also be unable to access test results or software change reports because he or she may be unfamiliar with the computer acronym or names assigned to those data.

Using the KDB approach, the analyst can review relationship names and topic names. Some of the logical names the analyst could look for are timing, communications lines, communications links, and transmission failures associated with ENVIRON or NDF. Perhaps the analyst searches the relationships file for object topics "comm*" where the asterisk denotes a wild card; that is, all topics beginning with "comm" would be retrieved. Of special interest is the object topic "comm link." Associated with these object topics are the relationships "modified per" and "fixed by - before." A retrieval of these relationships may yield the stilted English expressions:

- 3/18/85, ENVIRON comm link timing fixed by PAUSE 5 SECONDS before TEST call.
- 1/25/86, ENVIRON comm link format modified per Problem Report 8.3.2-10.

Note that the user could also use the report-writing capability included with major commercial data bases to display information in a form that is more easily used.

These are an interesting combination of relationships. It seems reasonable now to look at what recent changes have been made to the system under test, NDF. Searching the change file for relationships involving NDF, we get the relationship:

- 1/31/86, NDF procedure TEST call deleted PAUSE 5 SECONDS.

It is now possible to make the association that the PAUSE 5 SECONDS should not have been deleted. The testing person would then likely try putting the PAUSE 5 SECONDS back into the procedure to see if that is what is needed to establish the communications link. It turned out that this was indeed the problem.

This example shows how the knowledge data-base concept permits a new topic or relationship type and a new field to be easily defined. It also shows how an analyst may extract knowledge without having to be familiar with the data-base structure. Next we show how we can use a M204 technique, the KTAG–KTERM technique, to build these files. Finally, we will briefly discuss data-base maintenance for the KDB.

10.3.4 Using M204

Large commercial data bases have techniques for inserting new relationships. In the case of M204, this is called the KTAG–KTERM technique. When an analyst needs to store information for which there is no existing slot, she or he may define two new fields. The first field, the KTAG, holds the description for the new data, while the second field, the KTERM, holds the actual data value. The KTAGs and KTERMs are unambiguously

```
KTAG1    =    PERSONNEL
KTERM1   =    KEN A. PERSON
KTAG2    =    DEPARTMENT
KTERM2   =    SYSTEMS ENGINEERING
KTAG3    =    ID#
KTERM3   =    555225555
```

Figure 10-10 KTAG–KTERM example.

paired. One way is to append the same number to the field names "KTAG" and "KTERM" as done in Figure 10-10. A problem with the KTAG–KTERM method is that the description in a KTAG may only be meaningful to the analyst who created it. For example, the value of KTAG3 in Figure 10-10 is ID#. This might refer to an employee number, social security number, or driver's license number. This problem is further exacerbated by the fact that KTAG–KTERMs may frequently be coded.

The KDB retains much of the flexibility of the KTAG–KTERM concept while controlling the proliferation of unidentifiable and unshareable data. In the Topics and Relationships records, actual M204 field names are drawn from a standardized set (e.g., PRI_KEY_01, DESC_01). The descriptive field names that the analysts see are paired with the actual field names and stored as field contents in the KDB Control File. A new Topics field is "defined" by adding the field occurrences containing the actual/descriptive field names to the appropriate control file record. Since the data-base administrator is the only one allowed to make changes to the KDB control files, the creation of new logical fields is under his or her control.

A third field occurrence the data-base administrator adds for a new logical Topics field is a long, meaningful description. This long descriptive field can be presented to an analyst on demand as part of a Help function. Thus an analyst can determine the unambiguous meaning of a field whether or not the fields were created on his or her behalf. Since the naming process is controlled by the data-base administrator, there is less chance of two different field descriptions being used to describe different instances of the same type of data.

10.3.5 Data-base and Software Maintenance

Typically, the following changes to a traditional data base can cause a significant delay for the analyst:

- Define a new field
- Create a file for a new subject of interest
- Create a new mechanism to link records from different subjects

These changes are called for when analysts receive new data that cannot be placed in an appropriate category within the data base or that call for correlation to other kinds of data in a manner not currently supported. Once these changes are identified, analysts must wait for data-base and software changes to be made before they can enter and use the new type of data.

For each of the types of changes listed, new software has to be created or old software has to be modified to allow the new data to be entered, changed, displayed, printed, and sorted. For the second and sometimes the third type of change, the data-base administrator must execute JCL commands to allocate new data sets for new M204 files.

Effecting these changes can cause significant delay and frustration to analysts who need to work with the new data and view old data in differing perspectives. The KDB eliminates the need to change software and to allocate new file space for most changes. The first type of change, defining a new field, is done by the data-base administrator when he or she adds a new field occurrence containing the new logical field name to the appropriate control files. When it is desired, for example, to print the record containing a new data field, the generalized KDB software "knows" that the new field exists because it always refers to the control file first to determine the format of the data it processes.

Completely new subjects of interest and relationship types are created by adding to the control file the appropriate records describing new logical record types for the Topics File and the Relationships File. Again, no software changes are necessary. Furthermore, since all Topics records are stored in the single Topics File and all relationships are stored in the single Relationships File, new M204 files and data sets need not be allocated for changes of the second and third type. This means that KDB changes should be neither as labor intensive nor as time consuming as changes to a traditional data base.

In summary, the knowledge data-base approach appears to be very promising. Its human interface is immensely better than the traditional data-base approach, and it permits users to share information. The maintenance of the data base appears to be simpler than maintenance for more traditional approaches. Unfortunately, only a concept is presented here. It remains to implement this concept to determine whether it is really valid.

REFERENCES

ATRE, S., *Data Base: Structured Techniques for Design, Performance and Management,* John Wiley & Sons, Inc., New York, 1980.

DEPARTMENT OF DEFENSE COMPUTER SECURITY CENTER, "Trusted Computer System Evaluation Criteria," CSC-STD-001-83, Aug. 15, 1983.

KENT, W., "A Simple Guide to Five Normal Forms in Relational Database Theory," *Communications of the ACM*, Vol. 26, No. 2, Feb. 1983, pp. 120–125.

LING, T.-W., F. W. TOMPA, and T. KAMEDA, "An Improved Third Normal Form for Relational Databases," *ACM Transactions on Database Systems*, Vol. 6, June 1981, pp. 329–346.

CHAPTER 11

Quality Assurance

According to Fife (1977), the delivered software of large systems has typically 1 error for every 300 program statements. How this translates into a mean time between failure, I am not sure, but the number is not encouraging. This means that about one of every two delivered software units contains an error. If these statistics were correct, then a newly developed ground station for processing satellite operations would have about 3,000 errors when it is delivered. Considering the cost of satellites, that seems like a worrisome number.

Perhaps this error rate has been significantly reduced with modern programming methods. Britcher and Craig (1986) report on the use of modern design practices by IBM to upgrade the FAA air traffic control software. In this effort, old code programmed in BAL and JOVIAL for the IBM 9020 (an IBM 360/50 with three extra operating instructions) was rehosted on IBM 3083 machines. During this effort, IBM rehosted over 1.5 million lines of code and added or modified 152,000 lines of code. "The software defect rate, determined through system acceptance testing was 7 defects per 1000 lines of code for the new and changed code, and 1.5 defects per 1000 for the total system software." Britcher and Craig give no indication of how many defects per 1,000 lines of code were contained in the delivered (i.e., accepted) software.

Petschenik (1985) claims that new releases of an inventory control system he has developed at Bell Communication Research have about 0.8 to 1.3 errors for each 1000 lines of code. He also states that AT&T Bell Laboratories has experienced one to two field defects per thousand lines of new and changed source code. These figures are impressive, but the inventory control system mentioned here is a mature system.

For many years, Bell Laboratories had not been motivated by profit considerations because they were part of a regulated monopoly. Consequently, they stressed quality.

This is apparent to anyone who has used an AT&T telephone or the 3B20 computer. During a visit to Bell Laboratories in 1985, I was told that the mean down time for the 3B20D system (i.e., the average amount of time a 3B20D was down due to hardware error, software error, or maintenance) was 4 seconds for the preceding year—and that they missed their goal of 2 seconds per year! It will be interesting to see whether this quality will continue now that AT&T is operating in a competitive environment.

The two preceding references were encouraging, but they are contrary to the results reported by *Software News* (1986). *Software News* reported that 25% of the projects to build software systems containing over 60,000 lines of code are canceled before they are completed. They also report that the average such system is completed one year late and costs almost double the original estimate. Defining a defect to be a fault that causes a program to produce unacceptable results, *Software News* reports that there are 60 defects per 1,000 lines of code in programs of over 512,000 lines. Results are somewhat better for small systems. There are 10 defects per 1,000 lines of code for systems of less than 500 lines of code. For medium-sized jobs (16,000 to 64,000 lines of code), the product defect rate is 40 per 1,000.

It seems appropriate to reference Poston (1986), the Software Standards editor for *IEEE Software*. He lists the approaches for improving software quality and productivity, in order of greatest payoff to least payoff as:

- Reusing software (code, documentation, or data)
- Buying commercial off-the-shelf packages
- Increasing work effectiveness (by providing policies, techniques, standards, metrics, tools, and training)
- Reducing rework (by using, e.g., modeling and prototyping to prevent errors, and by using testing and reviews to find errors early)
- Designing the product for change

Quality assurance for software usually implies the activities of a configuration control board or participation in major reviews. Most organizations group quality assurance with configuration management and place this group at the staff level. Making quality assurance a staff function is logical because the quality assurance group should report directly to the program manager and should have oversight responsibility for the quality of the products of all the line organizations. Unfortunately, these types of organizations generally do not attract top technical personnel. The real functions of these organizations are often reduced to ''bean counting.'' That is, they keep track of the configuration, participate in reviews, and make sure that all the developer produces all the required documentation.

I prefer to view the quality assurance group as a line organization with additional staff-level responsibilities. The quality assurance group should have broad responsibilities, which include quality control, configuration management, independent testing, and the development of quality assurance tools. These responsibilities are illustrated in Figure 11-1.

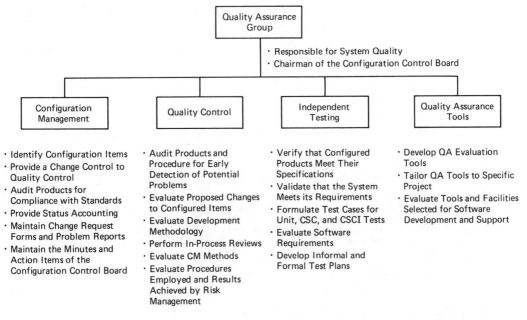

Figure 11-1   Recommended responsibilities for quality assurance groups.

The quality assurance tools include items like the electronic unit development folder and, in the case of a satellite ground station, a satellite simulator. The satellite simulator is considered a quality assurance tool because it is used to validate commands (an independent validation and verification function) to be sent from ground station to the satellite. Other functions of a satellite simulator include planning and training.

By including both independent testing and development of quality assurance tools as part of the quality assurance group responsibilities, there are enough interesting activities to attract good systems engineers to this group.

In Section 11.1 an introduction to configuration management is given. Next, in Section 11.2, quality evaluation is discussed. Some checklists that are useful in performing reviews are presented in Section 11.3. Finally, Section 11.4 provides an introduction to testing.

11.1 CONFIGURATION MANAGEMENT

Configuration management consists of four general activities: configuration identification, configuration control, configuration auditing, and configuration status accounting. The definitions of these activities given in DOD Directive 5010.19 are adequate for software engineering; by using them, we can simply blame the government if somebody doesn't like them. These definitions are:

- *Configuration identification*: selecting documents that identify and define the configuration baseline characteristics of an item.
- *Configuration control*: controlling changes to the configuration and its identified documents.
- *Configuration auditing*: checking an item for compliance with its configuration identification.
- *Configuration status accounting*: recording and reporting the implementation of changes to the configuration and its identification documents.

11.1.1 Bringing Software under Control

Software is deceptively complex. It is a challenge to our intellect to write a series of instructions that tell a machine what to do. It is tempting to think that software is simpler than hardware and easier to maintain because it is so easy to make changes. This quality of software is precisely what makes it so complex.

An analogous situation exists in writing. In the era of the typewriter, which ended in the early 1970s, an author had basically one chance of having his or her work typed. Incorrect spelling and other minor errors could be corrected by erasing the type and retyping the word, but this process diminished the appearance of letters and other documents. More extensive changes, such as correcting the grammar of a sentence or rewording a thought, required an entire page to be retyped. It was necessary to think through an entire document and to write it out by longhand before giving it to the typist.

Now that word processors are commonplace, authors often give secretaries rough drafts to type because they can easily review the typed material and make changes. When items are composed by a group of people, then everybody can review the document and suggest changes. This process leads to "wordsmithing." There are frequently multiple copies of a document, and it is not unusual to have to review several versions of a document to figure out which is the version you want to use.

Word processors are supposed to make typing cheaper because people can type much faster with a word processor than they can with a typewriter. However, uncontrolled revision makes it more expensive to produce a finished document. The added cost is due to both the increased time that the typist is revising documentation and the increased time of the author. Note that a controlled revision process leads to a better-quality document. Costs are saved when it is necessary to make a few changes on many pages or when we are able to "cut and paste" from one document into another. This is frequently the case when a document is produced for a client and changes are directed by the client. This is also the case for system documentation that needs to be revised because a new release or version has been developed.

Some of the software problems arising from this flexibility are:

- Corrections made to one version of a module are not made to other versions of the code.

- It is difficult to determine what changes were made, the order in which they were made, and when they were made.
- There may be uncertainty concerning which version the customer is using.
- Multiple versions or excessive dead code may consume critical resources.

As an example of problems with software control, the author is aware of a new weapon system that was developed and taken to the field for its first series of live tests. The tests were a failure; no missile could be fired. There were software problems compounded by the fact that when one bug was fixed something went wrong in a seemingly unrelated system. When a close inspection of the small real-time computer was performed, it was determined that the developer had left a copy of the game "Dungeons and Dragons" in memory. This was a system in which memory utilization was critical!

There is a tendency to think that a quality system is produced by putting together a small team of bright people and by letting them be creative. This process is very effective if the goal is to produce a set of system requirements or to produce a design. It is ineffective if the team is producing code or if the team is changing requirements to satisfy a clever design.

Complexity of software was discussed in Chapter 1. There the focus was on lines of code and attributes of the system, such as real time. Other items that complicate software are the existence of various versions of software, various releases of software, and variation of equipment with location. In commercial software, releases change as additional functional capability or processing capability is added to the software. For a given release, there may be various versions. For example, if a word processor is built, there may be separate versions for the Apple IIe, Apple ///, and the IBM PC. In the case of large operational systems located at multiple sites, it is common for the various sites to have different suites of equipment. Even if the equipment were the "same type," differences in the amount of memory, the operating system, the interfaces, and other attributes may exist. Thus, to know what software is operational, it is necessary to know both the release and the version of the software.

Since the subject of this section is bringing software under control, it seems reasonable to start by discussing how we lose control of software. The student may view the following discussion as somewhat incredible. An obvious question to ask is, "If we know how control is lost, then why did we ever lose it?" People with pragmatic experience on large systems will probably simply smile and think of a system on which they have worked or are working.

A glib answer to the question of how we lose control of software would be the same as the answer to the question, "How did we develop a one-year slip in schedule?" The answer is "one day at a time." Control is frequently lost because of time and budget constraints.

Disaster in the form of loss of control is obtained when any of the following rules apply:

- The customer will not pay for documentation.

- The schedule does not permit documentation—that will be done later.
- The selected hardware is overtaxed by the software application.
- Modern programming practices or guidelines regarding module coupling and cohesiveness are not followed.
- Mechanisms for configuration control and management are not established early in the development process (before the end of the requirements analysis).

Loss of control occurs in degrees; it does not mean that the system does not work. During a recent review of a space system, the following information was determined:

- The system consists of about 850,000 lines of code.
- Ninety percent of the code is written in Fortran V.
- The Fortran V code is poorly documented and spaghetti.
- The cost of this system is about $280 per line of code (Fiscal year 1986).

The other 10% of the code is structured and written in Fortran 77. Despite the fact that the code was written between 1980 and 1985, there is no evidence of modern programming methods. The code is difficult to maintain and must be used "as is." Any changes to the architecture at this time would cause massive reprogramming and design.

A lot of negative things have been said about this space system, but one very positive thing must also be said. The system works! In that sense, the system is successful. Successful operation is actually a key attribute about losing control of software. You can lose control of software of systems that work by making many "patches" or enhancements to the software to account for changing requirements. Under the pressures of the moment, these changes are inadequately documented. Eventually, the documentation no longer reflects the code.

If the system never worked, chances are good that the control of the software never existed. Unfortunately, it is not unusual for systems to never work. Even some major computer manufacturers have experienced being unable to get products to the marketplace because the software simply didn't work. By the time corrections could have been made to the software, the product would no longer be competitive.

A customer who cannot afford documentation really cannot afford the system. It is incumbent on the quality assurance people to convince the buyer that he or she *will* pay for documentation, the only question is when—and it is a lot cheaper to pay for it when the software is produced. As software support facilities are built, the cost of documentation should dramatically decrease. The use of a tool like the electronic unit development folder discussed in Chapter 3 provides for the automatic capturing of code and placing the code under configuration control.

This does not mean that the software is under control. It just means that you are tracking changes. If the sections of the electronic unit development folder related to design, requirements, and testing are not completed, you can still lose control of the software.

A very common excuse for not producing the documentation is that there is no time.

Some external constraint on the schedule exists, so we will have to produce the software as soon as possible and we will document it later. When this is the case, it is necessary to ask some difficult questions:

- Does this critical schedule also mean that there is no time to test the system?
- What if there is a 15% schedule slip in the development of the software; is there still time to test the system?
- What is the downside of fielding an untested or poorly tested system?
- Without the proper documentation, is it possible to construct meaningful tests?

It is frequently better to turn work down than to try to live with circumstances that will almost assuredly lead to a poor-quality system.

Suppose now that we are faced with a normal situation, the software is not well documented, and we have either lost control or are losing control of the software. The question is, how do we regain the control? It is surely not possible to use the following procedure:

- Go to a group of people who have produced, perhaps under trying circumstances, a system that works.
- Tell these people that they must immediately change the way they do business.
- Ignore existing schedules.

We cannot expect these people to be cooperative. In fact, if you do these things, you will probably be thrown out and told not to return.

The first step to regaining control is to convince the developers that *we* need formal reviews, documentation, and configuration management at some time in the future. Most senior software personnel will agree with you. After all, you are talking theoretically and not in a threatening tone. Good people are aware of what should be done and agreement in principle is not difficult to obtain. This is an excellent compromise. Their heart says that this approach is something that should be done. Their mind says that they don't have to do it now.

This approach is similar to the approach used to get people to agree to give a speech or run a charitable activity. If you ask the person to do it in two weeks, he or she will almost surely be too busy. If you ask the person to make a commitment for some date five months in the future, he or she will likely agree to it. It seems like the date is too far away to worry about; the near term pressures do not yet apply.

Having agreed in principle, it is necessary to start implementing procedures that will place the existing system under control. To get started, it is necessary to take stock of the documentation, management, and technical approaches. Ask to see the Software Development Plan and the Software Standards and Procedures. Chances are good that neither of these documents exists. Also ask for a review of the configuration control procedures and configuration management plans. These items may also not exist.

These were exactly the circumstances I observed when I began supporting a government customer on a system, which I will call System ASD. This case study will sound as if I brought the system under control, but the credit belongs to the customer. Without strong support by the top technical person and the top management in the customer's organization, it is virtually impossible to establish control of software that is out of control.

The initial set of activities that was improved consisted of:

- Configuration control and quality assurance
  - Develop an error-reporting mechanism
  - Support the establishment of CM procedures
  - Support the establishment of a QA program
- Project plans
  - Produce a software development plan
  - Produce a software standards and procedures
- Electronic unit development folder (EUDF)
  - Develop a proof-of-concept EUDF
  - Develop a prototype EUDF
  - Implement the prototype EUDF on a small segment of software (make sure that it is successful)
  - Implement the EUDF on the entire system

These activities are listed in order of their criticality; some activities were actually performed concurrently. Project plans are discussed in Chapter 7, so they will not be discussed here. The EUDF is a way of unobtrusively beginning the development of the software environment mentioned throughout this book. By reviewing the contents of the unit development folder, which include revision approval forms and status forms, it can be seen that this activity requires the establishment of most of the controls on which the software development environment is based.

The first step toward developing the error-reporting mechanism was the development of forms for software problem reports and software change reports. These forms are given as Figures 11-2 and 11-3. Note that the software change reports would more properly be named software change *requests*. The former name was selected for political reasons. The software developers were previously making changes "on the fly." These changes were not always documented. Since everybody was worried about imposing a bureaucracy and adding cost, the first step was to make it convenient to simply report the changes.

It is also a good practice to gather statistics related to the types of errors that are produced. Figure 11-4 represents a form that permits the programmer to simply check a box for the most common type of errors. When the forms given in Figures 11-2 and 11-3 are used (in paper media rather than electronic media), it is convenient to place the form in Figure 11-4 on the back side of the paper. This way, the user simply turns the form over and places a check in the appropriate box.

Configuration control should not impose significant changes in the general way people work. After configuration control is established, the controlled version or current baseline is under the control of configuration management. The developers and maintainers can still respond quickly to problems and make patches or changes. Weekly, the configuration control board would review the changes and either approve them (in which case they become part of the baseline) or disapprove them (in which case some other action is generally recommended).

The changes being controlled here are changes to baselines—not the changes made to a system between baselines. For example, after a detailed design specification is written, daily changes in the code are not controlled until after the code has been developed and tested by the developer.

Creating forms is necessary, but forms are inconvenient. People do not like to fill out forms. Forms are frequently lost and blank forms are always inconveniently located. When something is a bother to do, it is generally not done. Assuming that developers and maintenance personnel are usually working at terminals, an appropriate approach to the problem of filling out forms is to automate the forms.

One format for these automated forms is to have the users access them through a utility command. This permits the user to access the forms without getting up from his or her chair or performing a complicated series of commands. Ideally, with a split-screen capability, the user can view the problem on one part of the screen while making entries on another part of the screen. Data that can be entered automatically, such as software report numbers and the user's name, should be. Other data could be entered using a question and answer format. The forms as illustrated here (i.e., the paper version) could then be generated by request of the configuration manager.

Concurrently with the development of a convenient mechanism for reporting errors, the establishment of configuration management procedures and a quality assurance program was begun. An activity network for establishing configuration management procedures is given in Figure 11-5. For this particular case:

- The government customer was responsible for the development and test of a major segment of a larger system. Another government office, called the Program Office (PO), was responsible for the entire system.
- The customer had contracted the development of subsystems to a variety of companies.
- The customer had also contracted for systems engineering support and management support (including logistics).
- The developed products were to be delivered to the PO's prime contractor for system integration and test.

The activity network presented here needs to be modified to meet your specific circumstances. For the particular case under consideration, a configuration identification of the entire system was determined even though the customer was not responsible for the entire system. This was done because it seemed clear that the PO did not have appropriate configuration control for the system. If they did have the appropriate control, then the customer would have been receiving pressure from the PO.

There is really no problem in doing this from a system perspective. The prime contractor also needs a configuration item numbering system. The numbering system used

Software Problem Report

Number: _____

Problem ☐ Enchancement ☐ Date: _____, 19___   Time: _____ Tel: _____-_____-_____
Originator: Name: _____ Activity: _____

Software ID: _____ Version: _____ Date: _____

Problem Description

- -

- -

- -

- -

Suspected Cause

- -

- -

Urgency: Need Date: _____ Impact: _____

- -

Items Affected	Name and/or Document Number	Config. Number
Configuration Item		
System		
Specification		
Test Plan		
Other Item		

Action Assigned to: _____ Tel: _____-_____
Due Date: _____ Priority _____
Authorized signature: _____ Date: _____

Final Resolution

_____

_____

_____

_____

_____

Signature: _____ Date: _____

ATTACHMENTS: YES ☐   NO ☐

Figure 11-2 Sample problem report form.

Software Change Report   Number: _____

Date: _____, 19___   Time: _____   Originator: Name: _____   Tel: ____ - ____ - ____

Activity: _____

Software ID: _____   Version: _____   Date: _____

Change Description

_____
_____
_____
_____
_____
_____

Justification

_____
_____
_____

Other Items Affected	Reqd	Done	Name and/or Document Number	Config. Number
Configuration Item				
System				
Specification				
Test Plan				
Other Items				

Action

Assigned to: _____

Tel: ___-___-___

Due Date: _____

Priority _____

Change Approved ☐ or Disapproved ☐ & Reason _____

Authorized signature: _____

Date: _____

Comments

_____
_____
_____
_____
_____

Signature: _____ Date: _____

ATTACHMENTS: YES ☐ NO ☐

Figure 11-3 Sample software change request.

251

Type of Problem: ☐ Omission   ☐ Extra   ☐ Erroneous

Requirements	Design	Implementation	Operations
☐ Operating Rule	☐ Logic or Sequencing	☐ Decision Logic	☐ Documentation
☐ Performance Criteria	☐ Production of I/O Parameters	☐ Arithmetic Computation	☐ Overload
☐ Environment	☐ Recovery Procedures	☐ Branching	☐ Timing
☐ Systems	☐ Processing	☐ Other	☐ Capacity
☐ Conflicting Requirement	☐ I/O Data Attributes	....	☐ Recovery
☐ Derived	☐ Other	....	☐ Data Entry
☐ Other	....		☐ Record Error
....	....		☐ Operating System
....	....		☐ Other
....			....
			....
			....
			....

Figure 11-4   Classification of problem.

here could be based on the prime contractor's system, or a conversion matrix between the two could be generated. Note that it takes at least two months to establish the basic software controls. The schedule specified in the activity chart is optimistic. Don't be surprised if the effort actually takes over four months for your system. It takes a lot of time to visit each of the developers and to inventory the software.

Establishing things like CM plans, CCBs, and baselines is surely needed for software control, but these items do not in themselves provide software controls. There are many examples of systems that have all these attributes, but still have poor documentation and are not really under control from maintenance and enhancement viewpoints.

Many systems have evolved over a number of years; these systems have a design by default. The best that can be done is to continue patching and hoping that the system continues to work. In this case, one should also attempt to convince management to establish criteria for deciding when to redesign and rebuild the system.

System control can be reestablished by practicing configuration management. Dur-

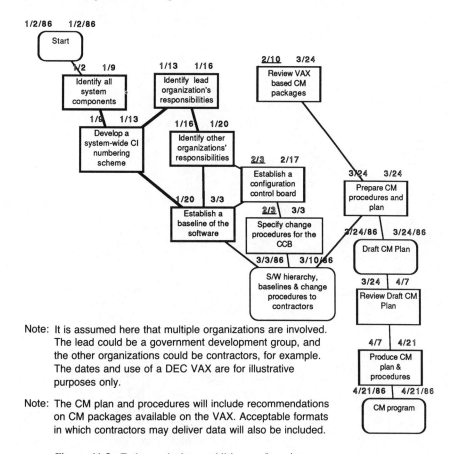

Figure 11-5 Tasks required to establish a configuration management program.

ing maintenance and enhancement activities, good documentation should be produced. Over a period of time, those portions of the system that have received the most attention (because they were trouble prone or were enhanced) become well documented, and should be better designed. Critical or error-prone sections of the system should be audited both from the functional viewpoint and the physical viewpoint.

Portions of the system that work are not redesigned. The fact that those portions may not be well documented and that the code may not be structured is of no consequence if the functions being performed and the data used are independent of the troublesome portion of the system.

A functional configuration audit (FCA) is intended to assure that the test and analysis data for a configuration item verify that the configuration item satisfies the performance specified in its requirements specification, and to assure that the technical documentation is available. Frequently, this documentation is either unavailable or incomplete. It is not uncommon for performance requirements never to have been specified. For an item to pass a functional configuration audit, the auditor should be able to indicate in the affirmative each of the items in the following checklist for the CSCI version and release under consideration:

- CSCI development specification is available.
- CSCI product specification is available.
- The qualification test plan has been approved.
- Qualification test procedures have been approved.
- The qualification test was completed.
- Qualification test results are available.
- Qualification test report is available.

FCA activities include:

- Compare the CI to the functional requirements.
- Compare test procedures with functional requirements to validate acceptance requirements.
- Review configuration status records.
- Examine PDR and CDR minutes.
- Review interface requirements.
- Develop a checklist for the physical configuration audit.

A physical configuration audit (PCA) is a formal review of documentation and code; its purpose is to establish a product baseline. The true purpose of the PCA and FCA is to make sure that the product is what it is supposed to be. Thus physical examination of the code and comparison of the code to the specification are suggested. The bottom line needs to be validated. That is, it is necessary to make sure that the code does what it is supposed to do from a requirements viewpoint.

The general activities of configuration control are summarized next by quoting Murachanian (1984):

- Separation of development and configuration management activities
- Version control of source
- Effectiveness of backup and archive systems
- Prevention of unauthorized modifications
- Reproducibility of software programs

11.1.2 Forming the Configuration Control Board

Among the various activities of the configuration management group, configuration change control is the most apparent. When forming a configuration control board (CCB), it is necessary to specify the responsibilities of the board and who should be on it. For the sake of simplicity, we shall assume that we are talking about a software configuration control board. For very large systems, there may be a Program CCB, Subsystem CCBs, Software CCBs, Interface CCBs, configuration control boards of subcontractors, and other special-purpose CCBs.

The configuration manager is a member of the CCB. It is his or her responsibility to perform the recording, tracking, and reporting functions of the board. It is the job of the configuration control board to review all software change requests and software problem reports. In the case of a software change request, the CCB either approves the request, assigns the request for further evaluation to an individual, or rejects the request. A decision for further evaluation may be required because of the potential impact of a change on other parts of the system.

Problem reports are reviewed and evaluated in terms of their urgency, impact, and magnitude. These problems may simply be recognized and not acted on. They may also be of sufficient magnitude to require an engineering change proposal (ECP). An executed engineering change proposal is a contract modification to permit the performance of additional work that is out of the scope of the existing contract. These are the two extremes. Problem reports usually result in the assignment of some resources to determine the cause of the problem. When the analysis is completed, a software change request is frequently generated.

To digress for a moment, it is common practice in the government contracting business for contractors to purposely bid a very low price to win a job. They do so on the assumption that they can find excuses to modify the contract through the ECP process, thereby generating profit and additional cash needed to do the original job. This type of process can easily get out of control. One way of keeping this process under control is to require strict cost justification both for the original contract and for the ECP. A traceability "data base" of requirements to specifications and modules should be maintained. This enables the program manager to determine every module affected when a requirement is changed. This limits the ability of the developer to claim an unreasonable fee for the change.

Another responsibility of the CCB is to determine the procedures for reporting problems and changes. The procedures illustrated in Figure 11-6 are based on those used by a large government organization that develops and maintains several related systems. This organization develops and maintains many millions of lines of code; its procedures are very formal and it has more configuration control boards than many other organizations can imagine.

Basically, the change control process has the following steps:

- *Submitting the problem report or change request (PR/CR) form to the configuration manager*: As indicated by the arrows labeled 1 in Figure 11-6, the system developer, system operator, testing personnel, or maintenance personnel can submit the problem report or change request form to configuration management by placing it in the PR/CR data-base file.

- *Retrieving problem reports and change requests from the PR/CR file*: The configuration manager retrieves new problem reports and change requests; he or she then produces a report on all new change control forms.

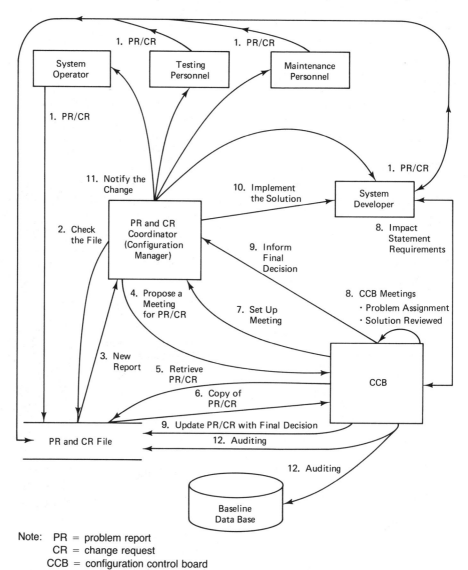

Figure 11-6 Procedure for handling changes.

- *Establishing a CCB agenda*: The configuration manager proposes an agenda and date to the chairman of the configuration control board for its next meeting (arrow 4), and upon direction of the CCB chairman (arrow 7), notifies both permanent and temporary CCB members of the meeting.
- *The CCB meeting*: During the CCB meeting (arrow 8), all issues that affect system requirements will be discussed; the CCB reviews the change requests and either approves, disapproves, or assigns for evaluation each change request.

- *The solution*: The final decision of the CCB is promulgated by the configuration manager (arrows 10 and 11), who will notify affected personnel of the results and assign the implementation of the solution as appropriate to the system development organization.

These series of steps assume that all problem reports or change requests are presented to the CCB. In practice this is not the case. During the second step, the configuration manager also evaluates the form. Many requests are small; their approval or rejection is immediate. In other cases, copies of problem reports and change requests are sent to a variety of people who can evaluate their effects. For these cases, the problem reports and change requests are presented to the CCB only if somebody does not agree with the request.

Deciding who should be on the configuration control board is not straightforward because it depends on the people and their skills. Generally, the following types of people should be permanent members of the CCB:

- The quality assurance manager; this person should be the chairman of the configuration control board.
- The configuration manager.
- A senior system engineer who understands the system, can communicate with users, and is familiar with project management.
- A test engineer with a good knowledge of the guts of the system.

In addition to the permanent members of the CCB, the chairman of the CCB should appoint temporary members to the board. The selection of these members depends on the problems and changes under consideration. Typically, these people include users, operators, and developers. The size of the CCB is variable. Committee meetings are generally very time consuming and nonproductive. The chairman of the CCB needs to use judgment to select the smallest possible number of people to participate, while being sure to include representatives of all affected parties.

A good strategy is to set a time limit for each meeting and to keep it! Each issue should be immediately resolved or turned over to somebody for action. If a particular subject requires a lengthy discussion, a separate special-purpose meeting for that subject should be scheduled.

EXERCISE 11.1   Suppose that software is categorized as in Table 11-1. Develop tables of the level of configuration management control versus software category for each of the following areas:

- Planning
- Documentation (subdivide this area in any manner of your choosing; an example would be test plans, test procedures, drawings, and unit development folders)
- Numbering and formatting

TABLE 11-1 Software Categorization

Category	Conditions	Examples
1	A CSCI Firware that is likely to change Complex security	Command and control Spacecraft ground station Control of nuclear devices Embedded critical processors
2	Contractual deliverable Low probability of change	Interpretation and control of hardware Display software
3	Used in qualification tests	Test programs for monitoring timing Simulations
4	Support software Test software (other than acceptance or qualification tests)	Software tools Automated test tools Management information programs
5	Scientific simulations Analysis tools	CAD tools Facility support software Structure simulations

- Document release
- Design reviews
- Baselines
- Records
- Library controls
- Change management
- Configuration reviews and audits

This type of level of control specification has been done by TRW, Inc., and is part of their configuration management manual (CM 100.2, September 1982).

   The authority of the configuration control board to approve changes generally depends on the cost and schedule impact of the changes. If either of these are greater than some specified limit, it is necessary for the CCB to get approval by some higher authority. In private industry, it may be necessary to gain approval from executive management. In government work, it may be necessary to gain approval from a high-level group, such as the Defense Systems Acquisition Review Committee (DSARC), a high-level group that must approve certain milestones for major systems acquired by the Department of Defense.

11.2 QUALITY EVALUATION

This section is based on the "IEEE Guide for Software Quality Assurance Planning" (IEEE Std 983-1986), the military handbook "Evaluation of a Contractor's Software Quality Assurance Program" (Mil-Hdbk-334) and the DOD draft "Joint Regulation: Software Quality Evaluation" (proposed DOD-STD 2168). Before establishing a quality assurance program, it is a good idea to read these documents. These standards specify criteria for evaluating quality assurance programs.

The proposed DOD-STD-2168 looks at the development life-cycle products and compares each product against the following set of criteria:

- Adherence to required format and documentation standards
- Compliance with contractual requirements
- Internal consistency
- Understandability
- Technical adequacy
- Appropriate degree of completeness
- Traceability to indicated documents
- Consistency with indicated documents
- Feasibility
- Appropriate requirement, design, and coding techniques used to prepare the item
- Appropriate level of detail
- Appropriate allocation of sizing and timing resources
- Adequate test coverage of requirements
- Adequacy of planned tools, facilities, procedures, methods, and resources
- Appropriate content for intended audience

Clearly not all these criteria apply to all activities in each phase of the life cycle. In the ''Joint Regulation,'' they have a series of tables, organized by life-cycle phase, indicating which criteria apply to the various products of that phase.

EXERCISE 11.2   For at least two phases of the life cycle, list the products. Next, create a matrix of products versus the preceding criteria. As elements of the matrix, enter either a ''blank'' or a ''check,'' the latter for the case in which the specified criterion applies to the specified product.

The IEEE standard and the military handbook specify the table of contents for a quality assurance plan. These contents are compared in Figure 11-7. The standards then specify criteria for each section. These criteria are summarized next.

EXERCISE 11.3   Compare the contents listed in Figure 11-7 to the top-level outline given in Figure 7-6.

In the following paragraphs some of the salient criteria for most of these sections will be specified. The scope or purpose section should specify all the software to which the SQAP applies. Sometimes firmware, software tools, and other nondeliverable software are inadvertently omitted from this list. In the absence of a section on management,

IEEE STD 983-1986	MIL-HDBK-334
• Purpose	• Scope
• Reference Documents	• Applicable Documents
• Management	• Tools, Techniques & Methodologies
• Documentation	• Computer Program Design
• Standards, Practices & Conventions	• Work Certification
• Reviews and Audits	• Documentation
• Software Configuration Management	• Computer Program Library Control
• Problem Reporting & Corrective Action	• Reviews and Audits
• Tools, Techniques & Methodologies	• Configuration Management
• Code Control	• Testing
• Media Control	• Corrective Action
• Supplier Control	• Subcontractor Control
• Records Collection, Maintenance, & Retention	• Preparation for Delivery

Figure 11-7 Comparison of the software quality assurance plan contents.

this section should include procedures for deviating from the software quality assurance plan (this information could be included in the software development plan rather than the SQAP).

The documentation section should specify the documents that should be produced and the general format of these documents. This section could present major problems in the contracting business if a contract is let before this section is completed. In this case, the contractor is bound to produce only the documents specified in the contract and only in the form specified in the contract. When no format is specified, the contractor can select the format of its choosing. On major procurements, it is a good idea to request the offeror to include a quality assurance plan with its proposal.

Other items that could be addressed either in this section or in the section on configuration management include provisions for controlling changes to documentation and for tracking these changes. It is also important to provide provisions for periodically auditing the documentation for consistency.

Program design methodologies, standards, procedures, and techniques are generally covered in a software standards and procedures document. The tools to be used are usually given either in that document or in the software development plan. The quality assurance plan should discuss how these standards are enforced. For example, are there tools that automatically capture software? Does the compiler include a mechanism that refuses to compile units exceeding 200 lines of code? When evaluating a quality assurance program, it is necessary to determine whether actions actually reflect what is written in the plan.

The reviews and audits section should identify each of the program reviews and baselines. The software quality assurance plan should also provide the type of information to be provided in each review. This information could be provided as a series of checklists like those in Section 11.3. Note that the SQAP is essentially defining a product, or data, perspective of the system development life cycle. The software quality assurance plan should pay attention to the details. It should specify, for example, who will document the proceedings of the reviews and who will be responsible for monitoring the subsequent action items.

The problem reporting and corrective action section should define both procedures and organizational responsibilities. This section should be evaluated in terms of potential conflicts of interest and vested authority. These procedures should specify how corrections are inserted into baselines. The procedures illustrated in Figure 11-6 would be included in this section of a software quality assurance plan.

11.3 CHECKLISTS FOR REVIEWS

It seems appropriate to include a section on checklists within a chapter devoted to quality assurance. Checklists are extremely useful for reviewing documents and for use during program reviews. In Section 7.2.3, the requirements phase is discussed. A checklist of topics to be covered in a system requirements review or a system design review is given there. Here other checklists are given. These checklists are intended to be used as guidance; they are neither exhaustive nor entirely applicable to every job.

Configuration item selection.   Management criteria for configuration item selection include:

- Visibility for control (e.g., relation to the work breakdown structure)
- The number of configuration items (since each configuration item may be separately baselined, their number affects configuration management)
- Impact on data management data (each configuration item has a separate specification, test plan, etc.)
- Test implications
- Impact on delivery

Technical criteria for configuration item selection include:

- Size of the configuration item ($\leq$ 15,000 SLOC)
- Residency of a CSCI on a single machine or at a single location
- Reusable or commercial software packages should not be split among CIs
- Functionality
- Interconfiguration item communications (a large amount of data, high data rates, or timing requirements may suggest a restructuring of the configuration items)
- Storage requirements
- Throughput requirements (this is especially applicable to determining items that should be performed at a local intelligent workstation as opposed to a remote mainframe)

Design reviews.   The preliminary and critical design reviews are similar in nature. They differ in the level of detail presented. The preliminary design review is a review of the design approach. The critical design review is a review of the design itself, just before production. Depending on the size of the system, there may be multiple PDRs and CDRs. There should be a review at the system level and a review for each configuration item. Sometimes a single review may cover several CIs.

I prefer to have these reviews at the subsystem level so that both hardware and software configuration items are considered. If done at the software configuration item level, the corresponding hardware should not be ignored. Likewise, a hardware review should not ignore the affected software. Interrelationships are especially important in the area of communications where items like timing and protocols affect both.

Items to be reviewed are:

- Functional flow
- Storage allocation
- Control functions (including start-up and recovery)
- Structure and organization of the data base
- Program structure
- Interfaces
- Security
- Special features
    - Parallel processing or tasking
    - Reentrant code
    - Double precision
    - Test features (not to be included in the operational system)
    - Development features (not to be included in the operational system)
- Development and support facilities
- Development tools
- Test tools
- Reusable or commercial software
- Trade-off studies
- Prototypes
- Performance requirements
- Management data (schedules, resources, dependencies)
- Risks and mitigation techniques
- Hardware- and communications-related items
- Comments on existing documentation
- Human factors
- Test and integration plans

Physical configuration audit.   The following checklist is taken from the military standard Mil-Std 1521B (December 5, 1985). Other forms for certification are given there. Some of the items in the checklist apply to hardware. Since the physical configuration audit refers to the entire system, this is unavoidable.

- Has the final draft of the CI product specification been approved?
- Is there a list delineating both approved and outstanding changes against the CI?
- Is there a shortage list of parts and documents?
- Is the shortage list complete?
- Have acceptance test procedures and associated test data been reviewed?
- Have all discrepancies with test procedures or results been documented?
- Have operating, maintenance and illustrated parts breakdown manuals been prepared and reviewed?
- Have manuscript copies of all CSCI handbooks and manuals passed review?
- Has each computer software version description document been reviewed?
- Are listings, flow charts, and other design documents current?
- Have action items from the FCA been resolved?
- Have all interface requirements been verified and validated?

11.4 TESTING

When a space shuttle blows up on national television, causing the loss of seven lives and over a billion dollars, we immediately ask how that could have occurred. What went wrong and why didn't we find it in our testing? (This may be a poor question; as it turns out, we should ask what went wrong with our quality assurance.) Obviously, for very large complex systems, testing cannot find every error. However, the design and testing should be good enough that all the catastrophic errors are found. This is a goal that is perhaps unachievable, but it should still be a goal.

If you are working on a large or complex system, one of your first testing activities should be the identification of high-risk items. These items could be coordination among groups or subcontractors, transmission of critical data, or incompletely specified interfaces. Having identified risk issues, you should relate these issues to the level of testing (e.g., system, element, or configuration item) and to the appropriate configuration items. For each issue, also indicate the level of risk (high, low, or medium) to the mission function and to the development. This information can be used in the definition of the testing program.

Popular cost-estimating models such as COCOMO, SLIM, and PRICE S indicate that more than 40% of a project's budget should be set aside for testing (Poston, 1985). Pressman (1982) says that ''In the extreme case, testing of human-rated software (e.g., flight control or nuclear reactor monitoring) can cost 3 to 5 times as much as all other software engineering steps combined!'' If we refer to the discussion of the Air Force Management Guide in Section 4.2, we see that the cost of validation and verification activities typically ranges from 25% to 50% of the development cost. For new, catastrophic software (i.e., software in which a failure could result in loss of life or severe economic impact), the recommended budget for validation and verification activities is 72% of the development cost. This may seem very high for your applications, but the percentages are more reasonable if you think in terms of space applications.

An appreciation of the significance of testing and the problems associated with testing becomes apparent by reviewing the software standards section of *IEEE Software*. Most issues seem to have something related to testing in this section. The IEEE has a variety of working groups devoted to various aspects of testing. For example, WG P1059 is devoted to Software Verification and Validation. IEEE Standard 830 is devoted to software requirements. A primary focus of this standard is to write the requirements for testability.

In this section, we discuss the testing life cycle, functional testing, and system testing. As we read the section it is important to keep in mind the testing viewpoint. Specifically, the purpose of testing is to find errors. The developer tests software to determine whether the software does what it is supposed to do. Testing personnel test software to determine whether it does something that it should not do.

11.4.1 The Testing Life Cycle

A considerable effort has been made throughout this book to depict each life cycle phase in terms of a black box—to think of each phase in terms of its input and output data rather than to focus on the activities inside. We showed how this viewpoint permitted us to debunk some myths about the life cycle and to show how prototypes can be used throughout the life cycle.

Here we will at least temporarily take a ''white box'' view of the life cycle. A white box viewpoint assumes that you know something about the contents or activities of the box. As we shall see later, the concepts of black box and white box apply directly to testing.

The system development life cycle is summarized in Figure 11-8. Beneath each phase are some of the testing activities that take place. An activity that is frequently ignored is the determination of acceptance criteria. These criteria are critical. Their absence is a primary cause of a contractor walking away from a ''cost plus fixed fee'' contract, claiming that the system being delivered satisfies the contracted requirements. In the case of ''firm fixed price'' contracts, disagreement over implicit acceptance criteria can lead to expensive court costs.

In a cost plus fixed fee contract, the contractor is reimbursed for his cost and receives a fixed fee or profit. In the absence of acceptance criteria, the job is over when the contractor claims to be done. Any further work must be reimbursed. Although a fee is not added, the costs include overhead, marketing, and administrative costs that are added to direct labor costs in accordance with accepted accounting procedures.

Firm fixed price means that the contract must be completed and accepted at the original price. Cost overruns are not allowed and a significant portion of the payment is withheld. Acceptance criteria are determined during the planning phase and refined during the requirements phase. They should be completed during requirements so that they are available at the time that the development contract is let. When acceptance criteria are not clearly stated, everybody loses.

Transition planning should be done early in concept development. It is important to decide whether the new system will operate side by side with the old system for a specified period of time. The test approach depends on the transition plan. For example, suppose that the transition plan calls for the development of a prototype test facility and requires the system and prototypes be available in a test bed for testing by system *users*. This requirement implies that the system users and their managers need to be trained on the system at an early date, before acceptance testing takes place.

Some of the testing activities not mentioned in Figure 11-8 are regression testing, functional testing, and stress testing. These are generally done during integration testing and acceptance testing. Debugging is performed during code and unit test.

It is necessary to be careful here to avoid the trap of viewing the life cycle in terms of activities rather than data. Exactly where various test activities take place depends on the test philosophy and the technical approach to developing the system. If we were to pursue the "build-a-little, test-a-little" approach, then many interfaces would be tested during the development cycle. Likewise, there is considerable testing associated with building prototypes. The message here is that it is necessary to have at least some of the test team in place at the start of the job. Testing activities exist in all phases of system development.

Mention of the operations and maintenance phase has hitherto been intentionally omitted. During this phase, we are either fixing errors that have been found the hard way (i.e., failures in the field) or doing enhancements, whose testing activities correspond to those done during development.

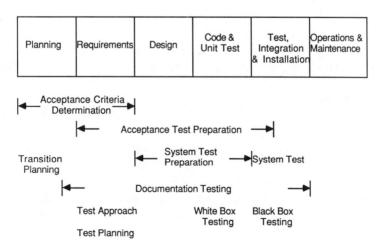

Figure 11-8   Test activities span the life cycle.

Returning to our philosophical approach to systems, it is necessary to capture software changes and errors in a data base. As shown by the heuristic approach to a knowledge data base, these data help problem solving and testing.

11.4.2 Functional Testing

The focus of functional testing is on locating processing errors rather than timing or performance errors. Thus, functional testing is generally done during module and intraconfiguration item integration testing. Timing and performance tests are generally done during system testing, the subject of Section 11.4.3.

Generalities are being made here. Allocated performance requirements are tested as part of module testing. This is especially true of real-time systems where timing, synchronizing, and tasking are critical.

In this section, we briefly discuss test coverage in terms of boundary tests, linear code/jump sequences, required elements, data context, and data-flow subpaths. Proof of correctness is also briefly discussed.

As an example of how not to test, I will relate a story about a student whose Ph.D. thesis was dependent on the results of a program he wrote. To check the student's work, his advisor ran the program for four special cases that I will simply call $n = 1, 2, 3$, and 4. The results were exactly correct. They corresponded to the analytically known solutions for these cases. The thesis was accepted and the student received his degree (from a prestigious university). After several years it was determined that the student's results were wrong. The test didn't reveal the error because the student had included in his program a check for $n < 5$. In those cases, the program branched to the analytical expressions that were known to be correct. Needless to say, everybody was too embarrassed to do anything about the erroneous thesis.

Testing every path of a large, complex system is impossible. This will be seen by those of you who perform the following exercise.

EXERCISE 11.4   Create a graph on a single piece of paper that corresponds to a program with at least 10 million paths. To accomplish this, use a DO LOOP with a variety of branches. What is McCabe's cyclomatic number for your graph? (Cf. Section 3.6.) How would you relate McCabe's cyclomatic number to the testability of a module?

By using McCabe's criterion that the cyclomatic number for a module should be under 12, we can test each path of each module. There are a couple of deficiencies with this approach. One is that we still cannot generally test all combinations of paths for the integrated configuration item. An infeasible path is not necessarily an error; the path could simply be a coincidence of program construction. Another aspect of path testing is that you should not assume that a program is correct just because all the paths have been tested.

Although it may not be possible to test all paths, under certain circumstances it is theoretically possible to prove the correctness of a program. Necessary conditions for this theorem are that the program be properly structured and that the data space on which a loop operates not be dynamically changed in the looping process.

Formal proofs of program correctness are made by inserting assertions related to:

- The state of the program data space as the program traverses an arc of its flow chart
- The outgoing data from a process given that the input data were true

This process is like cutting a program into small, single process pieces. Then you perform a test on the input data to make sure that they are correct. Finally, you test the output data to make sure that the process performed the calculation correctly. By doing this theoretically, you are frequently required to develop more than one algorithm for each process.

The number of assertions in this process grows linearly with the number of nodes in the program. Thus, this procedure for proving correctness cannot be done for very large programs. A procedure based on this approach, however, can be done for testing the control structure for programs.

EXERCISE 11.5   Develop a procedure for formally proving the correctness of the control logic of a program. [*Hint*: See Tausworthe (1979).]

If a module is properly documented, then the input, output, and internal variables are fully described. The description, which should be part of the data dictionary, includes an indication of the type of data, the acceptable range of values for the data, the accuracy of the data, the data representation (e.g., variable or array), the size of the data (e.g., in words or bytes), and the units of measurement. With this information, testing activities should include tests specifying:

- The boundary values of the data
- Input data that are very close to the boundary data (for both infeasible and feasible regions)
- Input data that differ, but are within the accepted accuracy (compare the accuracy of the product)
- Infeasible input data

Required elements testing is basically a physical inspection of the code, although some of the tests could be automated. The purpose of these tests is to assure that the attributes of the code are what is required by the specification. A checklist of these attributes, based on Myers (1979) and Pressman (1982), is:

- Are the input parameters the same as those specified?
- Are the output parameters the same as those specified?
- Are the units and accuracies of universal constants correctly specified?
- Does the implemented algorithm use mixed-mode operations?
- How can the module computations be influenced by other modules?

- What are the potential errors?
- How are errors handled?
- What machine-related problems could occur (e.g., are the units of storage allocated smaller than the units of storage addressed)?
- Are parameters named in a meaningful way (e.g., a system keyed to read only the first three letters of each command could have logical usage problems if both the commands <STORE> and <STOP> are needed)?

11.4.3 Acceptance Testing

FIPS PUB 101 (National Bureau of Standards, 1983) defines acceptance testing to be "formal testing conducted to determine whether a software system satisfies its acceptance criteria and to enable the customer to determine whether to accept the system." Acceptance testing is done by the customer or by an independent group working for the customer. When "acceptance" testing is done by the developer, it is called qualification testing.

Qualification testing is important to assure that acceptance testing will be smooth. If a system fails badly the first time it is used, the customer could lose confidence in the system. In this case, the system may never pass acceptance tests. It is not unusual for some requirements to include vagueness that could be exploited by a dissatisfied customer.

The key to acceptance testing is the assumption that acceptance criteria exist. These criteria should be the requirements to which the developer was building. In a sense, we have come full cycle. When requirements were discussed, it was emphasized that the requirements should be testable. Acceptance testing is the reason why.

In addition to functional requirements and performance requirements influencing the development, it is common to impose an acceptance requirement related to the period of time that the system must operate without failure in an operational environment. Before letting a development contract, the customer should decide the general procedures needed for installation and acceptance testing. For example, will it be required that the new system operate side by side with the old system for a period of time, such as 30 days? Will the installation be incremental?

The purpose of other testing is to find errors; the purpose of acceptance testing is to determine whether the requirements are satisfied. Tasks related to acceptance testing include defining acceptance criteria, developing a test approach, developing a test plan, designing test scenarios, executing the tests, analyzing the results, and determining whether or not to accept the system.

The specific type of tests to be performed include all the types of tests mentioned previously (e.g., functional tests and boundary tests). To make the acceptance testing as smooth as possible, it is suggested that the developer:

- Listen to the customer.
- Keep the customer informed during development.
- Make sure that the customer likes the user interface.

- The interface should *only* use words that are meaningful to the customer.
- Eliminate interface inconsistencies and irritations.
- Provide training for the customer; they need to know how to use the system.
- Be honest; the customer is smart enough to find hidden flaws.
- On large- and mid-sized jobs, there is usually somebody on the development team who likes to test systems by doing things that are unexpected; that person should be used wisely.
- Obtain agreement on acceptance criteria.

Remember, the customer who has confidence in the developer may accept a system on the understanding that the few gliches observed will be fixed.

REFERENCES

BRITCHER, R. N., and J. J. CRAIG, "Using Modern Design Practices to Upgrade Aging Software Systems," *IEEE Software*, Vol. 3, No. 3, May 1986, pp. 16–23.

DEPARTMENT OF DEFENSE, "Evaluation of a Contractor's Software Quality Assurance Program," MIL-HDBK-334, July 15, 1981.

DEPARTMENT OF DEFENSE, "Joint Regulation: Software Quality Evaluation Program," Apr. 26, 1985 (draft DOD-STD 2168).

FIFE, D. W., "Computer Software Management: A primer for project management and quality control," National Bureau of Standards, NBS-SP-500-11, July 1977.

IEEE, "IEEE Guide for Software Quality Assurance Planning," IEEE Std 983-1986, Institute of Electrical and Electronics Engineers, Inc., New York, 1986.

MURACHANIAN, N., "Software Configuration Management Plan," Jet Propulsion Laboratory, ASAS/ENSCE Document 7080-6, June 1984.

MYERS, G. L., *The Art of Software Testing*, John Wiley & Sons, Inc., New York, 1979.

NATIONAL BUREAU OF STANDARDS, FIPS PUB 101, "Guideline for Lifecycle Validation, Verification and Testing of Computer Software," June 1983.

PETSCHENIK, N. H., "Practical Priorities in System Testing," *IEEE Software*, Sept. 1985, pp. 18–23.

POSTON, R. M., "Improving Software Quality and Productivity," *IEEE Software*, Vol. 3, No. 3, May 1986, pp. 74–75.

POSTON, R. M., "Looking for a Test Comprehensiveness Measure," *IEEE Software*, Vol. 2, Nov. 1985, pp. 76–79.

PRESSMAN, R. S., *Software Engineering: A Practitioner's Approach*, McGraw-Hill Book Co., New York, 1982.

Software News, "The Productivity Report Card," Sept. 1986, pp. 19.

TAUSWORTHE, R. C., *Standardized Development of Computer Software*, Parts I and II, Prentice-Hall, Inc., Englewood Cliffs, N.J., 1979.

TRW, INC., "Configuration Management Manual," CM100.2, Sept. 1982.

CHAPTER 12

Some Analytical Techniques

Requirements are frequently stated in terms of the applications that need to be performed. These applications are expressed in terms of functions or data products. Unfortunately, it is not uncommon to omit specifications related to performance and reliability. Sometimes the need for expansion is stated in terms of ''modularity'' and ''expandability.'' The requirements generally do not express these qualities in terms of criteria that can be measured.

Contrary to popular belief, simply being able to add another mainframe to a network does not provide expandability. Alexander and Brice (1982) provide three case studies in which simply adding a computer was inadequate. They work with a network at Los Alamos National Laboratory that includes four Cray-1s, two CDC Cyber-73s, and four CDC 7600s. To put it mildly, that is a lot of computer power.

Specifically, on a distributed interactive graphics project, they added a front-end DEC VAX 11/780 to handle graphics terminal interactions and to drive the graphics screen. Designers could not find (by trial and error) a distribution of software functions that would provide adequate performance. What was needed was an analysis of the communication bandwidth and rates of CPU service.

This circumstance is not an isolated case. As mentioned earlier in this book, the FAA is updating the Air Traffic Control System. As a first step, they are rehosting the software on faster computers. The General Accounting Office (1985) found that ''vendor testing prior to acquisition . . . did not adequately simulate present or future operational requirements. . . .'' The GAO recommended that the production contract not be awarded until after realistic performance testing was made. They recommended stopping a multi-million dollar program because of inadequate capacity planning.

Capacity planning is the first subject of this section. Next a brief introduction to reliability is given. This is a subject that is well understood for hardware, but poorly defined and understood for software. Some new definitions of errors and faults are presented in Section 12.2.

Part of the problem with reliability of software is that software behaves differently from hardware. Hardware wears out, but software doesn't. Software errors usually occur because of design or programming flaws. Assume that we have two software items, each with 1,000 lines of code. The first item has one error in it and the second item has 10 errors in it. Which item is more reliable? The answer to this question is addressed in Section 12.2. Another problem with reliability of software is the occurrence of random software errors resulting from the change of one or more bits in a stored software program or data. These changes could occur from a poor data read during a power surge or, in some applications, from radiation. These types of errors are not generally considered in reliability analyses.

In Section 12.3, various aspects of fault tolerance are discussed. In the case of mission-critical software for embedded systems (fancy lingo for real-time systems in the DOD, such as space systems or weapon systems), we show how the maintenance of critical system state data in fault-free modules can be used to audit the health of the system and correct problems (i.e., to provide autonomous operations).

12.1 CAPACITY PLANNING

Capacity planning could result in the savings of millions of dollars. GTE claims to have saved over $100 million between 1974 and 1984 by careful capacity planning and volume purchasing (GTE, 1984). Factors affecting the price of hardware include the newness of the model, the manufacturer's backlog, the size of the purchase, how soon the equipment is needed, and the amount of time available for negotiating a price. These factors can be the difference between retail price and a 30% to 40% discount.

Related items that also could present significant savings are the procurement of building space, air-conditioning, and operations personnel. Excess capacity means excessive environment and operating expenses; having to procure space and air-conditioning quickly can be costly.

Despite these items, only 20% of the *Fortune* 1000 companies do serious capacity planning (Braue, 1984). The reasons are not completely clear, but they probably consist of a combination of factors, including:

- Most data-processing organizations are too busy putting out fires to worry about planning.
- Capacity planning cannot be successful unless the top MIS executive is involved with the process.
- Capacity planning activities include statistical analyses, modeling, and the use of detailed queuing models and simulations; data-processing personnel generally do not have the required mathematical skills for these activities.
- Data-processing personnel have not been trained for capacity planning.

Referring to the last item, it is important to note that top books on system engineering (e.g., Tausworthe's book or Metzger's book) do not even mention the subject.

For capacity planning to be effective, computer resources should be approached in the same way as other corporate or organizational resources. The purpose of purchasing computers is to perform functions that could not be performed manually, to perform functions that could not be performed with less capable machines, or to increase productivity. The bottom line is the value of these increased functional or production capabilities in terms of the return on investment.

The return on investment can then be compared to the return from other investments. For example, a food company will compare the return on investment from increasing computer capacity to handle universal bar code readers at the checkout counter to the return on investment from opening an additional store.

It is necessary to keep in mind that total central processor (CP) capacity is often not a driver. Giving every technical worker a microprocessor could increase productivity even if the microprocessors are idle most of the time. If a worker's burdened labor rate is $50 per hour and the person saves one hour per week, then a $2500 microcomputer pays for itself in less than a year. If tax benefits are considered, it probably pays for itself within six months.

Factors like personal computers should be part of the capacity planning process. It should be determined whether these computers will off-load processing requirements from the central computers or increase processing requirements.

The DP budget is very visible. This budget is a source of arguments among organizations. Nobody wants to pay for processing that he or she doesn't need, so charge-back schemes are common. Some of the pitfalls of these schemes are that:

- Computers generally do not pay for themselves.
- Charges become a source of irritation between the DP group and users.
- User organizations try to decrease their computer costs by buying their own computers for local processing.
- Overhead organizations, such as payroll, consider the central DP group as an overhead expense, so they have no qualms about consuming computer resources needed by line organizations.

One job of the top data-processing executive is to convince top management that running a computer center is like running a metropolitan bus system. You need this center for survival; it should not be expected to pay for itself.

There are five levels of capacity planning. These are shown in Figure 12-1. The first level of capacity planning basically consists of the use of static tools by the data-processing group. These tools include software monitors, a performance data base, statistics packages, and graphics packages. This type of planning determines trends based on workload parameters and historical records.

The second level of capacity planning introduces the user into the process. The primary tool added at this level is an accounting package that tracks computer resource utili-

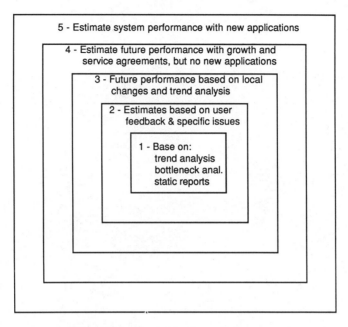

Figure 12-1 Five levels of capacity management.

zation by user. This type of package enables the data-processing group to institute charge-back schemes or, equivalently, for remote computing services to bill their customers. These packages are used to produce reports for both technical and management staff. Some packages (cf. Leavitt, 1985) produce performance data in real time. This enables network resource managers to immediately determine that system response is becoming sluggish and to determine which user is loading the system.

The third level introduces modeling into the planning process. This is the level that is very difficult for many organizations to attain because the modeling activities can involve sophisticated mathematics. Two general types of models are used for planning. One type of model is a queuing model.

In the case of queuing models, the system is modeled as a network. A typical network is shown in Figure 12-2. To evaluate the capacity of this network, it is necessary to specify:

- The type and frequency of input messages for each processor
- The processing time as a function of input message
- Output messages and their frequency as a function of the input message

These models produce statistics on the waiting time and queue length for each processor or node of the network.

In the case of the network portrayed in Figure 12-2, some of the key questions to be resolved were:

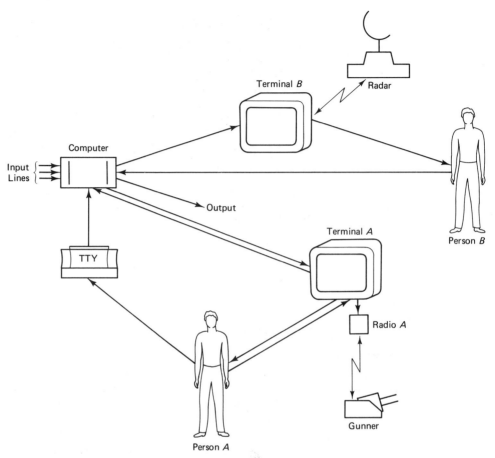

Figure 12-2 Symbolic representation of a hypothetical weapon system by a queuing network.

- How quickly does the weapon system receive cuing and alerting information?
- What are the quantitative benefits of enhancing the weapon system command and control?
- Are information timeliness requirements satisfied?
- What is the cost–benefits trade-off between increasing the ability of the radar to detect targets and increasing the ability of the computer to process data?

In Figure 12-2, people have been included as part of the system. To analyze this network, it is also necessary to perform a work task study to determine how long it takes somebody to do her or his job. One primary use of this approach is to determine which functions should be automated. A queuing model will determine whether the bottleneck is in the communications, the computers, or the people.

The input data are not generally easy to obtain. Workload statistics are frequently unavailable. This procedure is exacerbated by the difficulty in estimating processing time. Sometimes processing time is determined from very detailed simulations of the equipment.

Even when the problem is to redesign an existing system or to automate manual functions, data are generally unavailable. It is likely that it will be necessary to visit the operational site to collect data. This is a good idea even if statistics exist. Statistical data are frequently incomplete. Sometimes assumptions have been made during the gathering of the statistics to make the results biased. To paraphrase Disraeli, there are three kinds of lies—lies, damn lies, and statistics.

Closed-form solutions to queuing networks exist for only a few special cases. Many people have developed programs based on these special cases. Some people have developed simulations based on approximate methods for general queuing networks (e.g., Kuehn, 1979).

Several accepted commercial queuing models are available. It is nearly always much more expensive to build and validate a queuing model than to buy one. Even when commercial models are used, considerable personnel time may be required to run these models. It is not unusual for large computer operations to require one or two people to work full time on models and simulations.

Commercial simulations are also available. These simulations model equipment produced by major vendors. The equipment modeled includes disk drives and CPUs. They require information on the number of inputs and outputs, accesses to disks, and program lengths. Some simulations take network architectures into account.

Product surveys of queuing models and simulations periodically appear in trade magazines such as *Computer Decisions*. The prices vary among packages by more than an order of magnitude. Likewise, the computer and human resources required to use these models vary widely. Before making a commitment to purchase any of these models, talk to people who have used them. Determine whether and how the models have been validated. The vendor should be able to provide you with a list of satisfied customers. Check the assumptions used in the model; make sure that you understand them and find them satisfactory. Also, try to get a thirty-day free trial period so that you can determine whether the package really applies to your problem.

Surveys of the state of the art of performance modeling or queuing networks occasionally appear in professional journals. A tutorial and survey is given by Reiser (1981).

In the case of hardware, performance is sometimes measured by building production prototypes. This approach generally does not work for software. One reason for this is that there is no such thing as a production prototype in software. Other problems associated with the use of prototypes to predict performance are (Alexander and Brice, 1982):

- Memory size, communications loading, communications processing, disk utilization, and functional interactions in the prototype are different from those of the actual system—this makes extrapolation difficult.
- Changes in performance due to changes in the environment are not predicted by prototypes.

- Prototypes are not as flexible as models. This makes prototypes more difficult to use when considering fundamental design changes or when considering a variety of potential designs.

The fourth level brings user service agreements into the set of tools used for capacity planning. At this level, the future capacity required to process increased workloads from existing applications is determined.

A user service agreement is an agreement between an operations group and the MIS group. The MIS group works with the operations group to determine the factors that are critical to the success of the operations group. The MIS group then translates these factors into required computer resources as a function of time (the time scale may be in months or years). An agreement is then made between the two groups for the MIS group to provide these resources.

It is important to note that the operations group should not be expected to think or talk in terms of CPU speed (MIPS or millions of instructions per second), disk size, baud rates, or other computer terms. That is not their expertise. The operations group will talk in terms of how they do their job. They can talk in terms of how often they need to access categories of data, how many messages they receive during peak and off-peak periods, the average length of a message, and how long it takes to perform certain tasks.

User agreements are a good way to institute charge-back schemes. Get the user to agree to pay for the availability of resources (like paying a retainer to a consultant) whether or not they are used. This becomes a planned expense; the users will make sure that they get ''their money's worth'' from the MIS group before buying their own equipment. With this agreement, it is necessary to provide utilization reports to the user. Additional details on the contents of user service agreements and procedures for reaching these agreements are given by Emrick (1983) and Koltes (1982).

The key ingredient of the fifth level is the introduction of processing estimates required for new applications. The general approach used by GTE for their capacity planning (which occurs at this level) is (GTE, 1984):

- Quantify the current workload in terms of applications categories grouped by growth predicted from statistical data.
- Estimate the impact of future developments by interfacing with applications development groups.
- Identify future growth in terms of forecasting units, and use these units to predict impact on computer demand (e.g., determine how much additional processing is required by the payroll system if the number of employees were to increase 10%).
- Combine current and estimated usage to predict resource requirements for the next five years.
- Plan hardware upgrades.
- Select appropriate hardware.

The last two steps in this approach are oriented toward hardware planning. It is also necessary to plan for the development of software, which may, for example, be needed to off-load some of the functions from one processor to another.

With the current availability of commercial and reusable software, many more systems are being built as systems engineering and integration jobs rather than as systems development jobs. The lead time to build some systems, such as office automation systems, is less than two years. This is a very short time. In the case of government systems, this is shorter than the budget cycle of some maintenance and operations centers.

In planning for capacity management, the MIS group must take into account the fact that users often are very familiar with computers. It is common for high school graduates to know how to program. Summer camps are run for ten-year-old children to teach them BASIC, LOGO, and other languages. Given the appropriate tools, many users are capable of building their own applications software. This knowledge presents problems. It could result in a lot of uncontrolled and untested software. It also could result in considerable user impatience with the MIS group. The capacity planners should take advantage of this user knowledge to determine latent resource requirements. Latent resource requirements are those requirements that don't surface until certain capabilities are in place. Sophisticated users are capable of understanding the use of computers and addressing the ''what if'' questions.

12.2 RELIABILITY

Since the remaining sections of this chapter are devoted to reliability and fault tolerance, it seems appropriate to begin by defining some terms. The definitions used here were developed by Schwartz and Wolf (1985).

A *fault* is an erroneous state of hardware, software, or data base. It can be the result of component malfunction, environmental events, mistakes in design or operation, and errors in information transfer. A fault that is permanent is called a *hard fault*. If the fault is correctable, it is called a *soft fault*. A fault can be evident in each use of the system (a *persistent fault*), or it can be evident only sporadically (an *intermittent fault*).

An *error* is the conveyance of erroneous information from one location to another. For example, errors can occur in reading memory and during communications. If a software fault exists due to an incorrect design or incorrect coding, its use generates an error. That is, incorrect information is generated and conveyed somewhere. Errors can result from faults (*systematic* errors) or from noise (*random* errors).

A *failure* is the omission of specified performance. A system can provide its expected performance despite faults and errors. A malfunction is not classified as a failure unless its effect is evident at an external interface. A system can provide its expected performance despite errors in its output when it operates within specified error limits and rates.

EXERCISE 12.1   Give an example of each type of fault, error, and failure just defined. Provide an example of a fault and an error that does not result in a failure.

These definitions lend themselves nicely to systems engineering. We can define the reliability of a system as the probability that a system performs successfully (i.e., that a failure doesn't occur) for a specified period of time.

A suitable definition (and the one we use here) for reliability of a software item, such as a program, is the probability that the software item does not fail for a specified period. The period may be defined in terms of time (e.g., CPU time or calendar time) or number of runs. This definition of reliability is consistent with the engineering measure of reliability in terms of "mean time between failure" and "mean time to repair."

Failures of a software item may result from:

- Incorrect input
- Incorrect data stored in memory
- Changes in the machine representation of the software
- Incorrect design

Reliability models of application software ignore failures due to the operating system, hardware, reads from or writes to memory, and the environment. They also generally ignore the probability of adding errors while fixing an error. When computing system reliability, these types of failures need to be taken into account.

It is generally a good practice to check the feasibility of input data before using it. This practice prevents many failures resulting from noisy transmissions. Techniques used to determine the validity of input data and data stored in memory include straightforward *checksums* and complicated error-correction schemes. The latter are briefly discussed in Section 12.3. Error-correction schemes can also be used to verify that software stored in memory is not changed; this is also a subject of Section 12.3.

The reliability of a collection of software is calculated from the reliability of its components by representing the software as a network and using the standard reliability formulas. A network is composed of parts that are run in series [Figure 12-3(a)] and other parts that are run in parallel [Figure 12-3(b)].

In Figure 12-3, assume that the probabilities that a failure does not occur in the interval $[0, t]$ for the three parts are $PA(t)$, $PB(t)$, and $PC(t)$, respectively. If three parts are run in series, then the probability of no failure for the series is

$$P(t) = PA(t) \times PB(t) \times PC(t)$$

If the three parts were run in parallel (i.e., were redundant), then

$$P(t) = 1 - \{[1 - PA(t)] \times [1 - PB(t)] \times [1 - PC(t)]\}$$

In the case of redundant processes, you can determine the formula by observing that a failure does not occur unless it occurs in all processes.

Ramamoorthy and Bastani (1982) classify reliability models in accordance with the life cycle as follows:

- Development (debugging) phase
  - Error-counting models

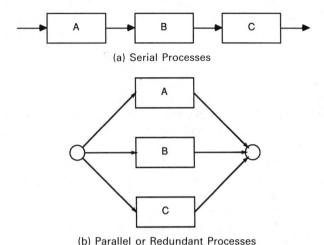

(a) Serial Processes

(b) Parallel or Redundant Processes

Figure 12-3   Network representation of parallel and sequential processes.

Deterministic (Poisson models, Musa, Schick–Wolverton)
Bayesian
Markov
- Nonerror-counting models
  Deterministic
  Stochastic
  Bayesian
- Validation phase
  - Nelson's model
  - Shooman (path reliability)
  - Input-domain-based model
- Operational phase
  - Input-domain-based model
  - Markov processes
- Maintenance phase
  - Input-domain-based model
- Correctness measures (test reliability)
  - Error seeding
  - Phenomenological (Halstead)
  - Statistical
  - Input domain

Ramamoorthy and Bastani provide a set of 114 references on these models. Most of the models involve complex statistics or probability. They share a focus on software errors that have been detected. Although errors are related to failures, the relationship is not really identified in these models.

Also, for many of the models, the assumptions need to be questioned. Error seeding, for example, is based on techniques developed for fisheries and forestry. Suppose we want to determine how many fish are in a lake. One way of doing this is to catch a bunch of fish, mark them, and release them back into the lake. Assume that we marked 100 fish. After the fish have had time to mingle with the other fish and become distributed among them, we go fishing again. Now suppose we catch another 100 fish and that 10 of these fish were previously caught (i.e., they are marked). We then conclude that we have caught 10% of the fish, because 10% of the marked fish were caught. Thus, there are 1000 fish in the lake.

In the case of testing software, we create errors and insert them into the code. We then count the errors found during testing to estimate how many more errors may exist in the code. A major problem with this approach is that it assumes that we know what type of errors exist. This logic is unfortunately somewhat incorrect. The errors that will be the most difficult to find and correct (those with the greatest mean time to repair) are precisely the types of errors we don't expect.

My own experience with software reliability has been very disturbing. For example, while working on a major proposal (worth at least $50 million), we hired as a consultant somebody with a well-known reputation in software reliability. This person provided absolutely no information that was used in the proposal. I do not know whether the reason for this failure was due to the fact that our reliability engineers were hardware oriented or because the expert could not apply to real problems what was preached in academia. If the problem was with our reliability engineers, then the expert was still at fault. It is up to the consultant to talk to the engineers in a language that they can understand. The bottom line is that I have seldom seen reliability models successfully used, even by experts.

This problem should not be interpreted as a condemnation of the experts. A major reason for the absence of systematic reliability analyses is that they are not required by the system procurement personnel. They do not provide requirements that include reliability metrics and criteria.

Even in those few cases where reliability criteria and metrics are specified, these criteria are rarely given in terms of the state of the system. There are many systems that operate in various states. The reliability requirements vary widely with the state. A multi-purpose radar may perform both search and target tracking. During the search mode a failure is not good, but the impact is not nearly as great as a failure while it is tracking a target.

Being able to measure reliability is important for both operational and cost reasons. We need to understand reliability to understand the risk associated with using a system. We also need to understand reliability to determine its cost. Like hardware, software reliability is also related to cost. Without good measures it is not possible to perform trade-offs of reliability versus schedule and dollars.

EXERCISE 12.2   Go to the library. Look up at least two different methods for computing software reliability. Write a paper showing how you would apply one of these methods to a real project. A good place to start is Stankovic (1985).

A good discussion of the assumptions in reliability models and a derivation of mean time to failure (MTTF) are given by Musa (1980a; this is a revision of his 1975 paper). In a subsequent paper by Musa (1980b), he discusses some practical aspects of parameter estimation. The ensuing discussion summarizes Musa's results.

Musa develops two models for the MTTF. One is based on execution time and the other is based on calendar time. His basic assumptions are:

- Tests are representative of the environment . . .
- All failures are observed . . .
- Failure intervals are independent . . .
- . . . hazard rate is constant [between failures]
- The hazard rate is proportional to the number of faults remaining
- Fault correction occurrence rate is proportional to failure occurrence rate . . .

A constant hazard rate is equivalent to assuming an exponential distribution. Using these assumptions, Musa presents the formula for mean time to failure, MTTF (which he derived in his 1975 paper):

$$n = N' [1 - \exp(-Ct/M'T')]$$

where n is the net number of faults detected and corrected, N' is the number of faults (uncorrected) in the system at time $t = 0$, M' is the number of possible failures at time $t = 0$, t is the execution time with $t = 0$ being at the beginning of the test interval, and T' is the MTTF at $t = 0$. Because of the fifth assumption, $N' = BM'$, where B is a constant.

C is the time compression factor; it is the ratio of equivalent operation time to test time. If m is the expected number of failures experienced, then $m = Bn$, and the preceding equation becomes

$$m = M' [1 - \exp(-Ct/M'T')]$$

Here m and t are measured parameters. M' and T' are determined from maximum-likelihood estimates. For the details of how to calculate M' and T', the reader is referred to Musa's work.

EXERCISE 12.3   Musa's work is available both in the journals in which they were originally published and in the *IEEE Tutorial on Models and Metrics for Software Management and Engineering* (V. R. Basili, ed.). Read these papers. How would you use these results to determine the amount of testing time required as a function of the desired reliability? How else can you use these results?

12.3 FAULT TOLERANCE

Regardless of the system reliability, every large or complex system has faults. The purpose of fault tolerance is to continue to operate without a failure despite the occurrence of a fault. Historically, the subject of fault tolerance has been approached from the viewpoint of "how can we keep the system running continuously?" Since reliability concepts for hardware are better understood than for software, it is no surprise that the initial efforts related to fault tolerance have been dominated by hardware approaches.

A primary example of a fault-tolerant system that has influenced this approach is the telephone systems. The telephone systems use fully redundant computers (such as the AT&T 3B20D) with uninterrupted power backup (four 12-volt truck batteries in the case of the 3B20D; the telephone is a 48-volt system). Typically, one computer is used for processing and the other is a hot backup. If something goes wrong with the first, it is automatically shut off and the second machine automatically takes over without failure of any system functions. In the case of peripherals (such as disk drives and disks) and networks, redundancy is built into the system so that there is no single point of failure. A difficulty associated with redundancy is knowing when a fault has occurred.

Another approach, pioneered by August Systems [e.g., Wensley (1982)] is referred to as triple modular redundancy. The general idea behind this approach is to use three modules or processors to perform parallel, redundant operations. The results are periodically compared. If all three do not agree, then a decision is made to use the majority opinion. It would be unusual (i.e., a very low probability of occurrence) if at least two modules did not agree. The minority opinion is assumed to be wrong and corrective action for that processor would begin.

When using triple modular redundancy, the voting mechanism also has to be tripled to make sure that the fault is not in the voting mechanism. Tripling your hardware and storage adds a lot of cost, but it does produce extremely high reliability.

In the case of fault-tolerant software, redundancy approaches are more complex. Unlike machines, simply manufacturing another processor doesn't work. Hardware of the same model are different, and each item wears out differently. A copy of software is exact. Thus redundancy is obtained by producing different software that performs the same function.

This could be achieved by forming two teams that work independently, but from the same specifications. This approach increases the development costs by at least two. Another approach is to develop multiple algorithms for the same functions. A problem with these approaches to fault tolerance is that they do not detect mistakes in the design specification. Also, many modules are easily coded and verified to be correct. Major causes for problems in software occur in the interfaces and in changing or misunderstood requirements. Redundancy does not generally find these problems.

As we shall see later, this approach does not address some of the major problems associated with:

- Real-time systems
- Systems that do not have to operate continuously, but do have periods when operations are critical
- Remotely operating systems that are difficult or impossible to fix

An example of a real-time problem not addressed by redundancy is sequencing. Timing is critical to real-time systems. In real-time systems involving multiple processors, the workload of one of the processors may be unexpectedly high. This could slow the processor and cause a timing error. This error can lead to a failure despite the fact that the software and hardware operated correctly.

Accounting systems are generally batch oriented, and faults do not present major problems. However, when the payroll is being run on a Thursday night for issue on Friday, the operations are critical. Faults that delay the payroll are simply unacceptable. In many cases, the workers would walk off the job if their checks were not delivered on schedule. Residual ill will could be significant.

Space systems are examples of both systems that do not have to operate continuously (but have critical periods) and systems that operate remotely. Although a couple of satellites have been repaired during space shuttle flights, it is normally not possible to replace satellite hardware. Because of the relation between software and hardware, it is important to consider the effects of software errors and to control those errors that would be disastrous.

It is convenient to define the duration of error effects in three categories (this discussion follows Schwartz and Wolf, 1985):

- *Long-duration effects:* These effects degrade a system for an indefinite period of time relative to the system mission (e.g., an error resulting in loss of attitude control of a satellite; or an error that takes 30 minutes to fix, but results in loss of a life-support system in use during an operation).
- *Temporary effects:* These effects degrade or jeopardize system performance over a modest period of time. Errors causing temporary effects can frequently be purged by a reinitializing procedure or through remote maintenance procedures. These errors may be software errors or may result from the environment (e.g., cosmic rays or an electrostatic discharge affecting the bits in memory). Sometimes, hardware errors should not be handled by automatic turnover to redundant equipment. If the associated fault is uncorrected, it may cause failure of the backup equipment also. Thus, a strategy may be to transition the system into a ''safe'' mode. After the cause of the fault is determined, some new software may be required for the system to continue to satisfy its mission with the existing hardware and fault.
- *Transient effects:* These effects are short and occasional. They are anticipated in the way the information is processed and used. Transient errors typically occur from noise. For example, transmission errors in message systems are generally handled by asking the transmitter to resend the message.

Having looked at the various types of error effects, the original goal of keeping a system running continuously can be reexamined. The goals of fault tolerance could be modified to:

- Maximize performance during critical periods (in some systems we can determine these periods in advance)
- Protect against indefinite-term damage

The techniques used are influenced by the goals. When we discussed data-base design in Chapter 10, we were concerned with recovering the data base when errors occurred, such as a system going down in the middle of a transaction. To protect ourselves, commercial data bases are designed so that transactions are logged and relatively few data should be lost due to these failures. A goal of data-base design is to protect the data base against indefinite damage.

Fault- and error-control strategies can be categorized as follows:

- General programming techniques
  - Periodic restarts
  - Watchdog timers
  - Algorithms for noisy data (filters)
  - Error-tolerant algorithms
  - Diagnostic routines for hardware, software, and stored data
- Error-control coding
  - Failure-free module (FFM) design
  - Refreshing working memory from a FFM
  - Error control during execution
  - Diagnostic aids
- System design
  - Feedback techniques for minimizing error effects
  - Redundancy
  - Overall strategies

It is interesting to compare this categorization of errors with the categorization developed by Anderson and Knight (1983) for software fault tolerance for real-time systems. They specified the following:

- *Internal error:* an error that can be handled by the process in which it is detected.
- *External error:* an error that cannot be handled by the process in which it is detected, but whose impact is limited to that process.
- *Pervasive error:* an error that cannot be handled by the process in which it is detected and whose effect is promulgated to other processes.

Anderson and Knight also distinguish between transient errors and persistent errors.

Anderson and Knight are concerned primarily with techniques for recovery and continued service. If the sequencing of processes were specified (e.g., by using SREM, discussed in Chapter 9), these data could be used to determine timing and sequencing violations and may be used to recover from them.

Error-control coding techniques are discussed for the remainder of this section. This discussion continues to follow the work of Schwartz and Wolf.

EXERCISE 12.4   Write a two- to five-page paper on one technique from each of the other two fault and error control categories. Be sure to specify your references.

A failure-free module is a portion of a system (module, component, subsystem, etc.) that is reliable enough to handle data with error effects in the permanent or indefinite categories. These modules should have a reliability such that the mean time to failure is on the order of ten times the mission or system lifetime. A failure-free module can be used to check the integrity of information produced or contained in memory. In spacecraft applications, a failure-free module could be used to verify that software contained in memory has not been affected by environmental conditions and to correct the software if it has been changed. It can also be used to reset the system to some initial conditions.

The failure-free module itself must be designed to prevent internal faults from affecting its mission. For example, consider a Kalman filter used to estimate vehicle position in a real-time, on-board navigation computer. The vehicle may be a spacecraft, airplane, or missile. The typical filter will include a force-field model that is stored in a failure-free module (perhaps a ROM) along with software defining the filter. The filter has periodic inputs of two kinds: (1) low-rate observations at intervals of minutes or greater to account for low-frequency effects, and (2) high-rate sensor information to track high-frequency perturbations.

Errors in the high-rate data are transient; the filter is designed to smooth these data. Errors in the low-rate data are temporary. A good filter design will keep these effects out of the indefinite category and will minimize degradation due to these errors. Errors in the force-field model are probably of the indefinite category. With a correctly defined failure-free module, these indefinite errors should not occur.

Having introduced the concept of failure-free modules, how do we code with them? The answer is complicated, and the application of failure-free modules to software fault tolerance could be a good topic for a master's thesis. The application given here is to errors in memory, called *soft upsets*. These errors are errors in memory bits; usually only one or two bits in a word may be in error. The contents of the memory may be programs, system attribute data, or other data. When dealing with real-time systems, we may select to keep a copy of the code in volatile memory (which is quick but susceptible to soft upsets) and another copy of the code in a failure-free module.

When a correct copy of the information is contained in a failure-free module, one approach to correcting errors in the soft-upset memory (SUM) is to periodically refresh the information by transferring it from the FFM to the SUM. On the surface, this process appears wasteful in that almost all the bits that are refreshed do not contain errors. It violates the dictum "*If it works, don't fix it.*" The process certainly is suspect if the refresh operation itself can introduce errors, if the refresh operation takes too much time, or if it absorbs excessive power or capacity of a communications channel.

An alternate procedure to the periodic refresh strategy is to test the contents of the soft-upset memory and locate portions of the contents that contain errors. Then we would only refresh those portions that contain errors. This process is called *selective* refresh. This approach both reduces the mean time to correct errors due to soft upsets and locates the fault in the soft upset memory.

One approach to locating errors in the SUM is to assume that the SUM is divided into words, each word being protected by an error-detection parity check code. Such codes are linear and have the property that the modulo-2 summation of a set of code words is also a code word. Thus you could module-2 add the words in a block to form a single composite word and then check the parity digits of this composite word. If all the words are error free, the composite word will also be error free. The converse is also true. If the composite word does not pass a parity check, some word of the block contains a fault. This summation and error-detection operation could be hard-wired in the memory or could be performed by a peripheral circuit.

Another approach is to assume that the soft-upset memory contains no redundancy, so errors must be found by comparing the contents of the SUM with the contents of the failure-free module. If this comparison were made on a word basis, it would require as much data transfer as an entire refresh operation.

To make this comparison, first hash each block to a small number of bits (say 30). Add modulo-2, the hashed bits in a treelike fashion, as shown in Figure 12-4 for 16 blocks. In Figure 12-4, the block labeled i ($i = 0, 1, 2, \ldots, 15$) represents 30 bits; the box labeled A represents the 30 bits that are the sum of 0 and 1, and so on. One would initially check the 30 bits corresponding to END against the same information in the FFM (which could be precomputed). If there is a disagreement, then we backtrack along the tree until the faulty block is determined.

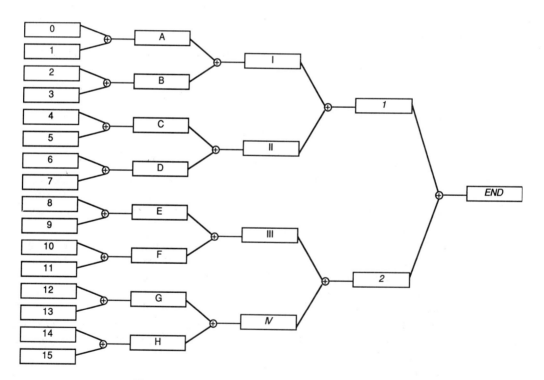

Figure 12-4 Tree structure for locating subblocks in error.

EXERCISE 12.5   Using this second approach, minimize the number of tests needed to locate an error in a block.

EXERCISE 12.6   Look up the subject of error-correcting schemes (see, e.g., Krol, 1982) and summarize that approach. If you were to use four error-correction bits for each eight-bit word, how many errors could be corrected? How could you incorporate this approach into the triple redundant module (TRM) concept? What are the advantages and disadvantages?

REFERENCES

ALEXANDER, W., and R. BRICE, "Performance Modeling in the Design Process," Los Alamos National Laboratory, LA-UR-82-1819, Dec. 1982.

ANDERSON, T., and J. C. KNIGHT, "A Framework for Software Fault Tolerance in Real Time Systems," *IEEE Transactions on Software Engineering*, Vol. SE-9, No. 3, May 1983, pp. 355–364.

BRAUE, J., "Capacity Management Part I: It Keeps You Running," *Computer Design*, July 1984, pp. 129–137.

EMRICK, R. D., "Capacity Management of End User Processing," *Proceedings of the Capacity Management Group (CMG) XIV International Conference*, Dec. 6–9, 1983, pp. 252–256.

GENERAL ACCOUNTING OFFICE, "Federal Aviation Administration's Host Computer: More Realistic Performance Tests Needed Before Production Begins," IMTEC-85-10, June 6, 1985.

GTE's COMPUTER SYSTEMS TECHNOLOGY GROUP, "Compacity Management Part II: We've Never Run Out of Gas," *Computer Design*, July 1984, pp. 138–145.

KOLTES, J. C., "The User Service Agreement," *EDP Performance Review*, Vol. 10, No. 9, Sept. 1982, pp. 1–6.

KROL, T., "The '(4,2)-Concept' Fault Tolerant Computer," Fault Tolerant Computer Society (FTCS) *12th Annual International Symposium on Fault-Tolerant Computing*, June 1982.

KUEHN, P. J., "Approximate Analysis of General Queuing Networks by Decomposition," *IEEE Transactions on Communications*, Vol. COM-27, No. 1, Jan. 1979, pp. 113–126.

LEAVITT, D., "CPE Use Pays Off in the Real World," *Software News*, Apr. 1985, pp. 53–56.

METZGER, P. W., *Managing a Programming Project*, 2nd ed., Prentice-Hall, Inc., Englewood Cliffs, N.J., 1983.

MUSA, J. D., "A Theory of Software Reliability and Its Application (Revised)," Tutorial on Models and Metrics for Software Management and Engineering (V. R. Basili, ed.), IEEE Computer Society, Silver Spring, Md., 1980a, pp. 147–156.

MUSA, J. D., "Software Reliability Measurement," *Journal of Systems and Software*, Vol. 1, 1980b, pp. 223–241. (Reprinted in *Tutorial on Models and Metrics for Software Management and Engineering* (V. R. Basili, ed.), IEEE Computer Society, Silver Springs, Md., 1980b, pp. 157–193.)

RAMAMOORTHY, C. V., and F. B. BASTANI, "Software Reliability—Status and Perspectives," *IEEE Transactions on Software Engineering*, Vol. SE-8, No. 4, July 1982, pp. 354–371.

REISER, M., "Performance Evaluation of Data Communications Systems," IBM Research Report RZ 1092, Aug. 19, 1981.

SCHWARTZ, J. W., and J. K. WOLF, "Control of Faults and Errors in Satellites: Error Control Coding Techniques for Memories with Soft Upsets," Avtec Systems, Inc., May 1985.

STANKOVIC, J. A., "Reliable Distributed System Software," IEEE Computer Society, Silver Spring, MD, 1985.

WENSLEY, J. H., "Reliability Comparison of Dual and Triple Systems," August Systems, Technical Report 009-3400-00, June 1982.

CHAPTER 13

Case Study: Design of an Office Automation System

In recent years I have frequently hired bright young honors students from good schools. Over 90% of these recent college graduates had degrees in computer science and were eager to make their mark as a programmer. Two things were very apparent to me:

- These students knew more about languages and operating systems than the sum of what I know and have forgotten (despite my head start of over two decades); their knowledge of data bases was also very impressive.
- None of the computer science graduates knew anything about systems engineering.

These circumstances meant that I had a significant training problem. They are also part of the motivation for this book. Not only has it been necessary to train these people in systems engineering, but it is also necessary to change their career goal orientation from being a programmer to being a systems engineer. Simply put, I do not recommend a career as a programmer to a twenty-two-year-old person—as a systems engineer, yes, as a programmer, no.

To understand the reasons, we just need to look around at the current state of the art. Microcomputers today are readily available and cheap. Users are generally computer literate. They know how to program in BASIC, and if they wanted they could easily learn how to program in LISP-like languages. There are many commercial software packages available that perform many functions for which there is a large demand. Some software integration packages are already on the market. These packages enable us to tie various other software packages together and to display various results using window techniques.

The biggest problem remaining in integration of commercial packages is data exchange. Some steps to solve this problem have been taken. The data interchange format

(DIF) is used in many programs for file storage. This means that any program using this format can access the files of any other program using this format. Another major step is the action by IEEE to develop a data standard.

Now, try to imagine the state of the art in twenty years. These bright young college graduates will be in their early forties at an extremely productive point in their careers. On whatever job they are working, they should be either the lead technical person or the manager, or both. Now let's ask the question again. What should their career goals be and how should they prepare for the achievement of these goals?

Until this chapter, we have been discussing systems development from the viewpoint that it is necessary to develop and integrate nearly all the software. Periodically, reusable and existing software have been discussed in terms of their influence on the design and in terms of the need to test these packages.

This chapter takes a very different approach. A case study is presented for an office automation system. In this situation, nearly all the software already exists. Also, all the hardware already exists. Thus, this case study focuses on a problem that is primarily a system integration rather than a system development. When you are done with this chapter, I suggest that you compare the approach to the techniques of Chapter 8, the other case study.

Beware of drawing a conclusion that systems integration jobs like the office automation being described here are small. The cost for building and installing the office automation system described here is about $15 million.

13.1 SYSTEM REQUIREMENTS

The system requirements are given in Figure 13-1. Only a couple of items require special mention here. The remote systems are actually named in the government requirements, but for the purposes of this presentation it is not necessary to state them. All the equipment was required to satisfy government emissions standards for processing classified information.

Many large corporations have office systems that handle extremely sensitive competitive information, which could literally cost them many millions if the information became available to their competition, yet these corporations are not concerned with emissions. Electronic spying seems to be a very remote possibility to them. Considering the state of electronic advances and availability of electronic equipment, this possibility does not seem very remote to me. This perception is enhanced when we consider that an office automation system installed today will be in use for ten to twenty years.

Closely related to the subject of emissions is the inverse problem of electromagnetic interference (EMI). This subject is generally ignored in systems design. The results of ignoring EMI can be catastrophic. For example, there was an incident in 1984 in which a steel worker died and several people were severely burned when molten steel in a vat was spilled on them. The vat was being transported along a rail under the control of a person using a walkie-talkie device. When this device got too close to a 30-foot vertical cable, it transmitted an erroneous signal. This signal caused the vat to tip.

Category	Requirements
MIS	Operate in local mode and remote mode concurrently
	Interfaces with Hewett-Packard, Sperry, and Prime mainframes/minicomputers (specific model numbers were given)
	Interface with Kurzweil optical character reader
	Hard-copy devices are a shared resource
	Workstations shall be able to operate in a stand-alone mode
	Backup of local files by the HP shall be provided
	Electronic mail, including the passing of files between workstations, shall be provided
	The system shall be independent of remote central computers
	Hardware shall satisfy the government emissions requirements for security (TEMPEST) or be placed in a screened room
Workstation configuration	IBM AT with 1-MByte RAM
	Advanced graphics adapter
	One 10-MByte removable hard disk (or cartridge)
	Support the 80287 mathematics coprocessor
	One port interface with a front-end processor (FEP) or switch
	Two additional serial ports
Workstation software	Word processor
	Graphics
	Spread sheet Note: Equivalent Commercial
	DBMS packages were specified.
	Program planning
	Desktop organizer
	The above software must be integrated.
	A key disk should not be required (i.e., the local software should be stored on the hard disk and not require the use of a floppy).
	Workstation shall be able to emulate the existing terminals so that they can operate with existing software packages.
	The software must be compatible with the specified output devices
System connectivity	One port outlet per office
	Six port outlets per bay
	Workstations shall be able to act as a terminal to access remote devices mentioned
FEP	Interfaces to support 380 workstations, 178 peripherals, and two HP computers
	Configuration shall be controlled from a single point
	No single point of failure

Figure 13-1 System requirements for office automation.

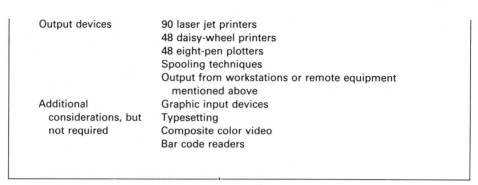

Output devices	90 laser jet printers
	48 daisy-wheel printers
	48 eight-pen plotters
	Spooling techniques
	Output from workstations or remote equipment
	mentioned above
Additional	Graphic input devices
considerations, but	Typesetting
not required	Composite color video
	Bar code readers

Figure 13-1 (continued)

13.2 ANALYSES

As we look at the requirements, we note that the primary constraints on the system configuration relate to the hardware. The workstation is specified in great detail. The only leeway concerns the method of controlling emissions. The keyboard and monitor are generally source protected (i.e., each source of emission on their integrated-circuit boards is determined and protected). The microcomputer could be either source protected or placed in a protective box.

The protective box permits the addition of any board at no extra cost, but it adds to the footprint of the machine, making it less desirable from a human factors viewpoint. The procedure for source protection requires an engineering charge of about $50,000 for each board not previously protected; however, if the engineering were done, the cost of protected boards would be less than the cost of the "emission proof" box. A box that satisfies the government emissions standards is called a TEMPEST box. The cost of this type of product depends on the size of the buy and the shrewdness of the negotiator.

Since the peripherals need to be compatible with HP graphics packages on the minicomputer, only the daisy-wheel printers provide the opportunity for brand shopping. The minicomputers and mainframes in the client's computer room already existed. Interfaces to these computers were required, but this existing equipment was not to be considered as part of the office automation system.

The software suite also contained little flexibility. The types of applications programs at the workstations were specified. Trade-offs were conducted between the brand name mentioned in the requirements and competing commercial products.

The greatest flexibility in the system architecture was in the network communications. The decision of whether to go with a central switch or a front-end processor was left to the designers. It was also necessary to decide what type of wiring should be used (twisted pair, coaxial cable, or fiber optic) and what type of network to design. Options include:

- A central switch with a star architecture (i.e., all workstations and peripherals direct

wired to a redundant switch; redundancy is needed because of the requirement for no single point of failure; twisted-pair or fiber-optic cable may be used).
- A baseband local-area network (like Ethernet) with a central controller; this type of network may use either twisted-pair or fiber-optic cable.
- A broadband local-area network using coaxial cable.

To help organize ourselves, one of the first steps taken was to separate the hardware and software into configuration items. This step was straightforward; the results are shown in Figure 13-2. The further division of these configuration items into components was also straightforward for the workstation (CI 1.1), the shared peripherals (CI 1.3), and the workstation software (CI 2.1) because these components are specified in the requirements. This breakdown is shown in Figure 13-3. The division into components of the network hardware and software (CI 1.2 and CI 2.2) depended on decisions relative to the system architecture, so this could not be done until later.

Referring to Figure 13-3, the following observations are made:

- A configuration item for the TEMPEST box was included (CI 1.1.10) to allow for a decision that has not yet been made (i.e., whether or not a box will be used).
- Some of the items included under the workstation software (CI 2.1) required more thought and analysis than simply looking at the requirements list provided in Figure 13-1. The need for the session profile, for example, comes from an architectural analysis of the system.
- Some of the configuration components need additional layers of specification. These include CI 2.1.8, security, CI 2.1.5, terminal emulation, and CI 1.3.4, cables.

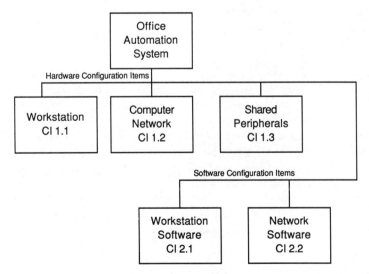

Figure 13-2 Configuration items for an office automation system.

Workstation H/W 1.1.___	Shared Peripherals 1.3.___	Workstation S/W 2.1.___

1 Processing unit
  and keyboard
2 Enhanced graphics
  board
3 Color monitor
4 Color adaptor
5 1-MByte RAM
6 10-MByte disk
7 80287 mathematics
  coprocessor
8 Cabling
9 Serial port board
10 TEMPEST box
	1 Laser printer
	2 Daisy-wheel
	  printer
	3 Eight-pen plotter
	4 Cable
		1 Word processor
		2 Spreadsheet
		3 Graphics
		4 Desktop organizer
		5 Terminal emulation
		6 Integration
		7 Program management
		8 Security
		9 Database management
		  system
		10 File transfer
		11 Operating system
		12 Diagnostics
		13 Printer driver
		14 Session profile
		15 Higher-order
		  language compiler
		16 Interfaces
		  (special)

Figure 13-3 Initial guess at configuration components.

Observe that we are beginning to add the system-oriented requirements to the requirements specified by the user in Figure 13-1.

EXERCISE 13.1   What other configuration components need further specification?

EXERCISE 13.2   Assume that a star architecture is selected using fiber-optic cable. That is, all terminals and peripherals are hardwired using fiber-optic cable to a central redundant front-end processor. How would the components specified in Figure 13-3 change? Generate a list of components for the computer network, CI 1.2, and for the network software, CI 2.2. Is all the network software resident on the front-end processor? *Note:* If you have trouble with this exercise, you may want to finish reading this chapter and then come back to this exercise.

Having discussed some of the limits imposed on this integration of an office automation system, we now ask what analyses have to be done. A partial list of analyses follows:

- A survey of software vendors' literature to determine comparable workstation software packages.

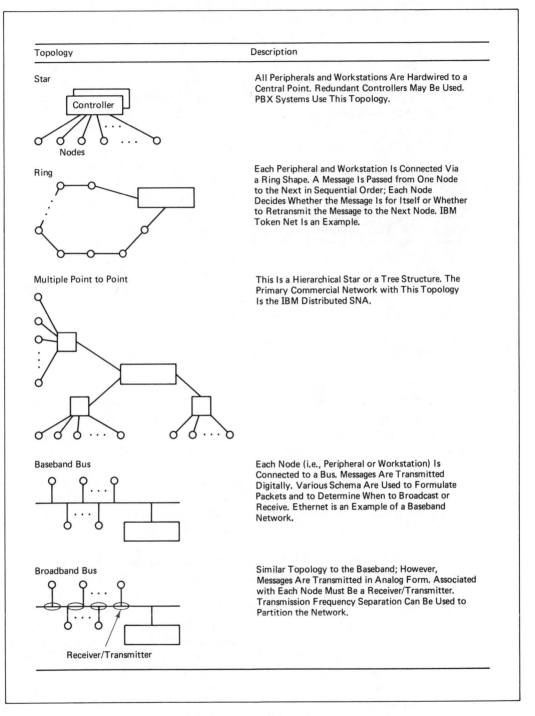

Topology	Description
Star	All Peripherals and Workstations Are Hardwired to a Central Point. Redundant Controllers May Be Used. PBX Systems Use This Topology.
Ring	Each Peripheral and Workstation Is Connected Via a Ring Shape. A Message Is Passed from One Node to the Next in Sequential Order; Each Node Decides Whether the Message Is for Itself or Whether to Retransmit the Message to the Next Node. IBM Token Net Is an Example.
Multiple Point to Point	This Is a Hierarchical Star or a Tree Structure. The Primary Commercial Network with This Topology Is the IBM Distributed SNA.
Baseband Bus	Each Node (i.e., Peripheral or Workstation) Is Connected to a Bus. Messages Are Transmitted Digitally. Various Schema Are Used to Formulate Packets and to Determine When to Broadcast or Receive. Ethernet is an Example of a Baseband Network.
Broadband Bus	Similar Topology to the Baseband; However, Messages Are Transmitted in Analog Form. Associated with Each Node Must Be a Receiver/Transmitter. Transmission Frequency Separation Can Be Used to Partition the Network.

Figure 13-4 Description of alternative communications topologies.

• After selecting candidate packages, the integration package and some compatible packages should be obtained and tested on the specified workstation or a compatible workstation. These packages could be purchased; however, when such a huge buy is being competed for, the vendor may simply lend you a package for evaluation purposes for thirty days. Packages should not be eliminated just because they are incompatible with the selected integration package. Some vendors may be willing to invest their own development dollars to make their package compatible if it were selected; however, this does introduce an element of risk.

• Trade-off of network topologies. Candidate topologies are star configurations, ring configurations, multiple point to point, baseband bus, and broadband bus. These topologies are illustrated in Figure 13-4. Tradeoffs should take into account security, expected communications load, and cabling options.

EXERCISE 13.3   Specify other trade-offs that you think are necessary.

EXERCISE 13.4   For each of the preceding trade-offs (including the ones you specified in Exercise 13.3), specify the parameters and/or measures of effectiveness that you think should be evaluated.

13.3 TRADE-OFFS

In this section, the results of the analyses are presented. No brand names are specified because the names are not relevant. With the rapidly changing and improving software and hardware capabilities, it is simply not possible to publish features of specific software packages or hardware in a book. Even the trade magazines are frequently obsolete at publication time—and they combine very good people who are aware of the latest product capabilities with very short delays in publication.

First, we will discuss software trade-offs. Since this is an integration problem, we begin by selecting the parameters to be evaluated in the trade-offs. Concurrently, we select the actual products to be compared. The initial product selection is based on vendor advertisements and brochures. The list is then paired to be consistent with the requirements of the RFP.

It is very unlikely that a $250 project management package would compare favorably to a $5,000 project management package that runs on the same machine. As we shall see, this does sometimes happen, so caution is recommended. The parameters selected are given together with the results of trade-offs for the data-base management software and the desktop organizer software in Figure 13-5. The "functionality points" specified there refer to another analysis in which the functional attributes of each type of product were listed in terms of required and desired. The functionality of each candidate software package was compared to the functional attributes list. A package received a certain number of points for each required attribute it satisfied and another number of points for each desired attribute it satisfied.

Parameter	DB Management S/W			Desktop Organizer S/W	
	Product A	Product B	Product C	Product D	Product E
Relative cost	N	1.2N	8M	M	3M
Number installed	5,000	3,000			—
First shipment date	—	—	Apr. '85	Apr. '85	???
Company established	1977	1977	1984	1983	???
Listed in requirements	Yes	No	Yes	No	No
Floppy key required	No	No	No	No	No
Data security	Files	Files, records, fields	No	No	No
Natural language query	No	Yes	n/a	n/a	n/a
Source language	Pascal	C	n/a	n/a	n/a
Upward compatible	No	Yes	n/a	n/a	n/a
Functionality points	83	98	141	178	35
Literature reviews	Poor documentation	Well known	Overpriced and poor technical support	???	Widely acclaimed
Integrates with Product I	Yes	Yes	No	Yes	Yes

Figure 13-5 Sample trade-offs of software packages.

Of particular interest in this system integration job is the ability to store the primary software packages on a hard disk. The "floppy key required" parameter refers to the need to insert a floppy disk into a disk drive in order to use the software for the first time during a session. Users don't like this feature, but manufacturers often include this feature to prevent people from copying the software onto many hard disks.

Like other analyses, this one is somewhat cyclic. First, the individual packages were evaluated. Next, integration packages were evaluated. Finally, we returned to the individual packages to include the attribute of whether or not they integrate (with only minor further work) with the selected integration package. This attribute is the bottom one listed in Figure 13-5.

The parameters on which the trade-off for the integration packages was based are:

- Graphics supported (yes or no)
- Keystrokes to change windows
- Compatibility with software packages listed in the requirements
- Compatibility with software packages selected as a result of the trade-offs
- Supports mouse or other data-entry devices
- Maximum number of windows that can be simultaneously open
- Availability of help commands at all levels

The results of the trade-off on the peripherals are presented in Figure 13-6. Two laser printers, five daisy-wheel printers, and three 8-pen plotters are compared. The commercial products are simply identified as P1 to P10. Note that only vendor V1 sold a peripheral in all three categories. Coincidentally, the laser printer, daisy-wheel printer, and 8-pen plotter it sold were the best selections in each category. All requirements are satisfied. Risk is not a big concern here because vendor V1 is a well-known company with extensive experience in producing TEMPEST computer equipment.

The final set of trade-offs that will be discussed relate to the system architecture. Specifically, trade-offs were performed to determine the system topology and the transmission media (fiber-optic cable, coaxial cable, or twisted pair). In the event that a bus architecture is selected, trade-offs on the type of local-area network (i.e., baseband or broadband) were conducted.

A prerequisite to the trade-offs on the topology is a system workload analysis. Without knowing the performance requirements, significant portions of the topology trade-off would be meaningless. The system workload analysis is done by listing the types of transactions, the average number of bytes in each type of transaction, and the total number of transactions that occur in an average time period (such as an hour).

Assumptions regarding the number of users that are active during the average hour and during the peak hour are also made. Typically, the peak hour is 30% more active than an average hour. It is also necessary to take into account factors such as the first hour of the working day. During that period people report to work, log onto the system, read messages that have been sent to them, and print files needed "the first thing in the morning." This is a period of a great deal of activity.

Parameters	Laser Printer		Daisy-wheel Printer						8-Pen Plotter	
	P1	P2	P3	P4	P5	P6	P7	P8	P9	P10
Relative unit cost	N	2.5N	1.3M	1.3M	1.3M	1.2M	M	R	1.2R	1.2R
Quantity	90	72	44	44	44	44	44	44	44	44
TEMPEST certified	Yes	Yes	Yes	Yes	Yes	Yes	Yes	Yes	No	No
Delivered TEMPEST units	None	Yes	Yes	Yes	Yes	Yes	Yes	Yes	None	None
Production risk	Low	No	No	No	No	No	No	No	Medium	Medium
Mainframe graphics compatible	Yes	No	n/a	n/a	n/a	n/a	n/a	No	No	Yes
Output capacity	8 ppm	12 ppm	22cps	58 cps	44 cps	45 cps	40 cps	22 ips	n/a	31.5 ips
Vendor	V1	V2	V3	V4	V3	V4	V1	V4	V3	V1

Figure 13-6 Trade-off of peripheral equipment.

299

For this particular office automation system, the primary types of transactions are as follows:

- Electronic mail (550; 500)
- File transfer
  - Workstation to workstation (120; 10,000)
  - Workstation to host (240; 1750)
- Security/network administration (30; 27,000)
- Access control (970; 100)
- Host file spool (80; 50,000)
- Host file print (80; 50,000)
- Workstation file print (120; 10,000)

Next to each transaction are two numbers. The first number is the estimated average number of transactions per hour; the second number is the estimated average number of bytes per transaction.

Thus, the network capacity must handle an average of 12.8 Mbytes per hour or 30 Kbps. This average is fairly low and is deceiving. A queuing model was developed and run for the peak hour. The results showed that the network may exhibit bursts of up to 4 Mbps.

The trade-off for the network topology is shown in Figure 13-7. The results show that the choice is between a star topology and a bus topology. The ring topology was eliminated because of the difficulty in reconfiguring the network, and the multiple point-to-point topology was eliminated because of cost and complexity concerns. The star topology was judged to be adequate for the current workload, but was questionable for the worst-case projected workload. The other two drawbacks of the star topology are its inability to handle video data (although fiber optic may be able to handle video in the future) and the very high cost of cabling.

EXERCISE 13.5   Define what is meant by the representative networks of Figure 13-7. That is, define PBX, token, SNA, and CSMA/CD.

Among the bus topologies, the broadband bus has capacity to handle the worst-case workload while using one channel. If this estimate is off by 20%, a second channel could be used. In fact, at least five channels can be used with the coaxial cable. A broadband network is generally installed by a cable TV company. Video data can be transmitted over a broadband network using one channel for this purpose. The 3-Mbps effective channel capacity of a baseband network makes this network questionable for the worst-case load.

Because of the expandability and the ''other considerations'' of the requirements, the broadband network topology was selected. One problem that has to be evaluated in an integration problem like this is the client's views of security requirements. In the case of the broadband network, a subnet can be formed by changing the frequencies of the corresponding bus interface units. This technique provides complete physical data separation

Parameter	Star	Ring	Multiple Point to Point	Baseband Bus	Broadband Bus
Representative network	PBX	Token	SNA	CSMA/CD	CSMA/CD
Effective channel capacity					
Data	57.6 kbps	n/a	n/a	3 Mbps	5 Mbps
Voice	64 kbps	64 kbps	64 kbps	64 kbps	64 kbps
Video	None	None	None	None	5 Mbps
Must preconfigure data paths	No	Yes, time slots	Yes	No	No
Add node without interrupting network	Yes	No	Yes	Yes	Only if a tap exists
Reconfigure without interrupting network	Yes	No	Yes	Yes	Yes
Broadcast capability	No	Yes, re-transmit	No	Yes	Yes

Figure 13-7 Network topology trade-off.

because of frequency separation. To accomplish frequency separation, an RF technician must adjust each node of the desired subnet. The remainder of the network cannot physically interface with this subnet.

This type of separation may not be acceptable to an organization that is very security conscious. In that case, a star topology should be selected. The star topology allows complete physical separation of a subnet. It also permits the use of fiber-optic cable, which cannot be tapped without electronic detection.

While on the topic of security, note that fiber-optic cable also provides no electromagnetic emission. Twisted pair is noisy and must be placed in shielded containers to prevent measurable emissions. Coaxial cable provides measurable emissions at distances very close to the cable, but generally does not require additional shielding.

13.4 ARCHITECTURE

Having completed the trade-offs, we can begin to specify the hardware and software architecture. The office automation system of this particular case study has some difficulties relative to very strict security requirements. Specifically, there are up to 380 users with multiple security accesses. These accesses are categorized by both people and physical location of the hardware.

One implication of this requirement means that every access to a data base on a mainframe and every transmission using electronic mail must be checked to assure that the data recipient is cleared (i.e., approved for that data) and the location of the recipient is approved for the access at the level transmitted.

A centralized security module, co-located with the bus controller, was selected. This approach required that all transactions among workstations, between a workstation and a host computer, and between printers and either workstations or hosts must be approved before they occur. A general flow chart of the transactions is given in Figure 13-8.

The system functions are then allocated to hardware and software configuration items. The stand-alone user applications (1.0) clearly are allocated to the workstations hardware (CI 1.1) and the workstation software (CI 2.1). The file transfer functions (2.0) involve both workstations and the network. Some aspects of the host computer software and hardware may be affected by this function, but it is not mentioned here because that system is not considered as part of the office automation system; the host interfaces with the office automation system. This interface should be standard and not require any additional hardware or software, but without an inspection of the actual system, a firm conclusion cannot be drawn.

The hardware functions are allocated to workstation hardware (CI 1.1) and network hardware (CI 1.2). The workstations require hardware to interface with the network; the network hardware is the medium for transferring messages. File transfer software is needed at the workstation; this is identified in CI 2.1.10. The remaining software required for the software transfer file is included in the network software, CI 2.2.

Similar logic applies to the remaining functions. The network software (CI 2.2) needed to perform these functions were determined to be:

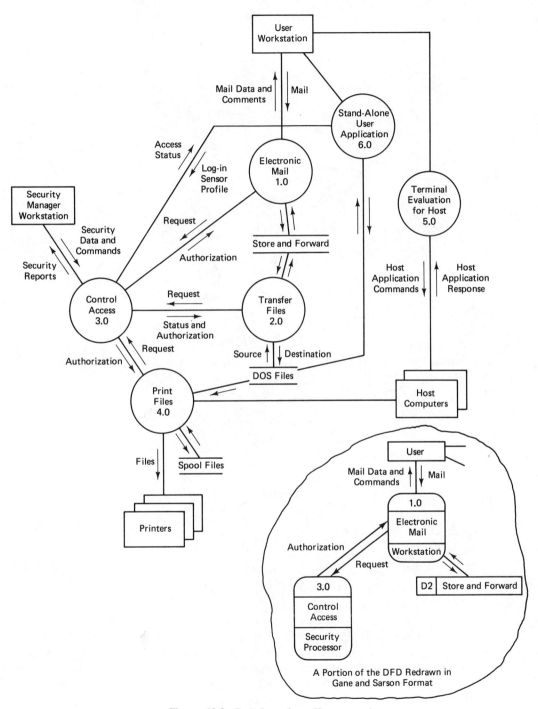

Figure 13-8   Data flow of an office automation system.

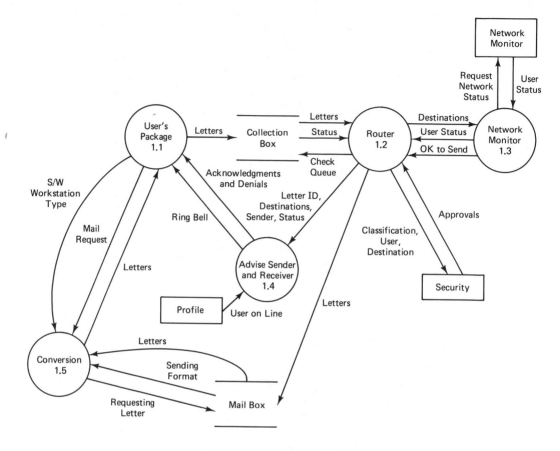

1. Electronic mail
2. Network services
3. Security (flow control, authentication, and administration)
4. Failover
5. Output interfacing
6. Printer allocation
7. Spooler functions
8. Operating system and utilities
9. Cluster software

Determining the configuration items for the network hardware (CI 1.2) is a bit more complicated. It is necessary to know the building layout to specify the hardware, because the cable layout and interface equipment depend on the building architecture. The network interface units selected depend on how far the unit is from the bus or network controller transmitter because of the dissipation of energy along the cable.

The equipment layout is depicted in Figure 13-9 (which is not to scale). The building consists of two floors plus a basement. The minicomputers and mainframes are located in the basement. The cable is laid in the ceiling over the center corridor of each floor. Each office and bay area denoted by a rectangle consists of six offices and one bay. The network interface units are mounted in the ceiling and connected to the cable through coaxial taps. Cable is then run from the network interface units (NIUs) to the wall outlets. Each outlet is identical and can be connected to the RS232 port on either the workstation or the printers. This provides maximum flexibility for moving equipment. An exploded section of a typical office and bay area is shown in Figure 13-9.

When designing a broadband network, it is recommended that you work closely

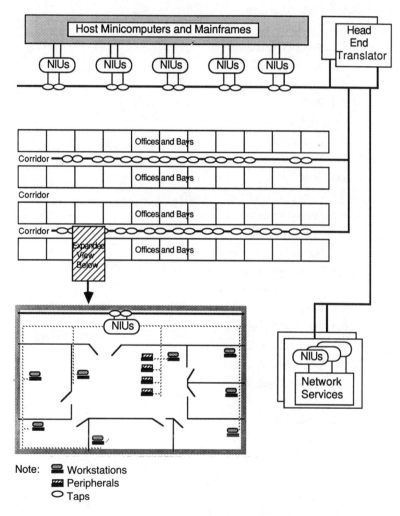

Figure 13-9 Schematic of the office automation system.

with one of the manufacturers. They have the engineering personnel with the skills needed to specify all the necessary equipment; they also provide consulting services and will frequently specify a network design when they feel that a major purchase is possible. A partial list of the network hardware configuration (CI 1.2) is:

1. MIS service network

1.1 Network processor

1.1.1 Cabinets

1.1.2 Disk drive

1.1.3 Eight-megabyte ram

1.1.4 Disk controller

1.1.5 Console

1.2 Security processor

2. Network cabling

2.1 Cables

2.1.1 0.750-inch network coaxial cable

2.1.2 NIU to outlet cable

2.2 Connectors

2.3 Terminators

2.4 Taps

2.4.1 Four-port multitap (12 dB)

2.4.2 Four-port multitap (14 dB)

· · ·

2.5 Bus interface units

2.5.1 Eight-port network interface

2.5.2 Eight-port unibus interface

2.6 Conduit

2.6.1 One-half-inch tubing

2.6.2 Compression couplings

2.6.3 Compression connectors

2.6.4 Junction box

2.6.5 Outlet box

2.6.6 Outlet cover

2.6.7 Hanger strap

2.6.8 TEMPEST box

2.7 Splitter

· · ·

3. Network monitor system

4. Broadband equipment

4.1 TEMPEST box

4.2 Head end

4.2.1 Channel translator

4.2.2 Network power supply

4.2.3 Redundancy switch

4.2.4 Amplifier circuit breaker

. . .

4.3 Network maintenance equipment

4.3.1 Signal analysis meter

4.3.2 Spectrum analyzer

4.3.3 Sweep generator

The configuration item number for each network hardware element listed above is defined by placing the number 1.2 before the number in the list. For example, the configuration item number for three-quarter inch coaxial cable is CI 1.2.2.1.1.

Observe that the network hardware configuration appears to be specified in far more detail than the software architecture. This is true because the hardware configuration is more concrete; the hardware already exists and we can specify it in detail. In the case of the software, not all of it already exists. Most of the workstation software is available off the shelf. The configuration items for these software packages are at the same level of detail as the hardware. For example, CI 2.1.1, word processor software, is just as specific as CI 1.2.4.3.2, spectrum analyzer. Corresponding to CI 1.2.4.3.2 is a model number and brand name, something about which a purchase order can be written. Likewise, corresponding to CI 2.1.1 is the name of the word processor package and the vendor, also something about which a purchase order can be written.

Other software configuration items are of a less specific nature because these items have to be developed.

Let's review for a moment what has been accomplished so far in the design of this large office automation system. Commercial integration packages and application programs were reviewed and evaluated. This evaluation was done functionally and experimentally. Copies of the software were obtained and run together. Trade-offs relating to the network topology were determined. After settling on a topology, a specific hardware configuration was determined and the system-level functions were investigated to further specify network and security software.

There are two remaining items to be presented with the design of this system integration project. One is the control structure and the other is a specification of the modules that will have to be built rather than bought. Both of these items are specified in Figure 13-10.

EXERCISE 13.6   Referring to Figure 13-10:

1. How are these software components related to configuration items?

2. Are any functions missing?

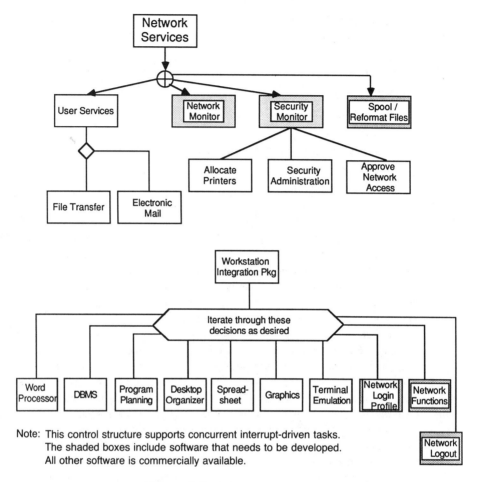

Figure 13-10 Software control structure.

3. How would you further decompose these functions?

4. Where, for example, do the workstation print requests appear?

13.5 MANAGEMENT PLANS

Showing how we determine the design of a systems integration job is important, but it is only part of the entire job. The importance of management planning was emphasized in the beginning of the book, but little has been said about this subject since Chapter 7. The case study in Chapter 8 served as an introduction to engineering design techniques, and that has been the focus for the subsequent chapters.

In the preceding sections of this case study, the techniques discussed in Chapters 9 to 12 were used. The trade-off studies included capacity planning by running a queuing model of the configuration with anticipated workloads. A prototype had been developed. Some of the software packages considered were either purchased or loaned to us; we already owned a microcomputer that satisfied most of the workstation hardware requirements. The software packages were then tested on the workstation with the integration package selected to determine whether they really worked. Although not explicitly stated, this testing did require some test plans and procedures to be developed. Structured analysis techniques were used to specify the data flow and the software control structure. The design information presented in Sections 13.1 to 13.4 includes most of the information required for a preliminary design review.

EXERCISE 13.7   Create a checklist of the material that should be presented at a preliminary design review. Place a check next to each item that has been covered so far for the office automation system. If you were given the go ahead to start the job today, how soon would you be prepared to give a PDR? What activities would you have to perform and how much effort would each activity take?

The requirements of Section 13.1 were limited to design requirements. Some of the other requirements of this system are:

- The system must be completed within twelve months.
- The thirteenth month must be devoted to acceptance testing.
- Six months after contract, a test bed must be available to the users (note that the design was done as part of the *proposal* prior to receiving the contract).
- People need to be trained so that a minimum of work interruption is incurred.
- Transition plans and other management plans are required deliverables (these are indicated in greater detail later when the contract data requirements lists, CDRLs, are scheduled).
- Maintenance will be provided for months 13 to 25.

EXERCISE 13.8   Generate a work breakdown (WBS) structure for this case study. Begin by selecting major categories like systems engineering or installation. Then partition each of these areas into subareas. It is suggested that you write a definition of each first-level WBS element. Later in this section a WBS that I generated for this case study is presented. There is no right or wrong answer to this exercise; when you get to the work breakdown structure I prepared, compare it to yours. Have either of us forgotten anything? To fully answer this question, it is necessary to consult the WBS dictionary.

In a system engineering and integration job like this office automation system, there are a wide variety of activities to be planned. These activities include systems engineering, system development, installation, system test and integration, integrated logistics support, development of engineering plans, procurement and contracting, and program management. To understand and plan these activities it is necessary to determine how we are going to put the system together and how we transition from the current way the client is doing business to the new way the client will operate with this system. We also have to figure out how this is accomplished with minimal disruption of the client's operations.

There are lots of items to be considered. The vendor who is producing the TEMPEST workstations may only be able to deliver sixty per month. This means that we have to start accepting delivery of the workstations in month 5 and store them until month 12, when the installation occurs. Some of the activities arising from this delivery schedule are:

- Our acceptance testing of the vendor hardware starts very early.
- A one-year vendor warranty on the workstation begins to expire with eight months remaining on the maintenance portion of the contract; thus, either we have to provide hardware maintenance or we have to issue a subcontract for hardware maintenance.
- The workstations and peripherals require a lot of storage space; it is probably necessary to rent a small warehouse.
- The stored equipment has to be retested before installation.

The installation itself is a problem. The cable and local-area network need to be installed and tested before any workstations or peripherals are installed in the offices or bays. The installation schedule is part of the larger problem of how to transition from the current system to the new system.

The transition period for this case study was defined to be the period of time from establishment of the test bed until system acceptance (months 6 through 13). A topical outline for the transition plan is:

- Purpose of the plan
- Detailed schedule with dependencies and milestones
- Activities to be performed (including specifying the critical path)
- Required staffing as a function of the schedule and activities
- Subcontractor and vendor activities (such as delivery schedules)
- Installation practices and procedures
- Acceptance procedures for operational test and evaluation (OT&E) (*Note:* Specification of acceptance criteria and procedures is critical to the success of the effort; the friendly user who helped with requirements and made lots of useful suggestions during development generally, and suddenly, does not know you when it comes to acceptance.)
- Documentation and reporting requirements

Topics included as appendixes to the transition plan include training, supply consumption, transportation and handling of hardware, certifications, guarantee and warranty data, and acceptance testing of the vendor products. Remember, there are two levels of acceptance testing that occur for this program. It is up to the system integrator to perform acceptance testing of the vendor-supplied hardware and software. It is up to the client to perform acceptance testing of the office automation system.

Documents that provide key inputs to the transition plan are the systems specification, the operations and maintenance plan, the training plan, and the test procedures for operational test and evaluation. For this case study, the specific activities that have to be scheduled include:

- Performing the test bed demonstration
- Supporting OT&E
- Installing a test site
- Training of the test team
- Training the initial users, operators, and managers
- Installing the product baseline
- Disposing of the existing site equipment
- Performing configuration management

This digression into transition planning has been intended to stimulate thought about the variety of activities that must be planned. A work breakdown structure of the required activities is given in Figure 13-11. This WBS is specified to three levels. These categories were selected because they represented a logical division of the activities and because each expected cost can be allocated to an element of the work breakdown structure. The cost for each of these activities is estimated in terms of labor and other direct costs. These other direct costs include computer time and travel expenses. The WBS elements within Procurement and Contracting (WBS 12) are grouped in accordance with the expected purchase orders to be let. The production cost of documents like the user manuals is given under WBS 13, Data Production. These costs include the cost of photocopying, artwork, and delivery.

The technical work breakdown structure elements are defined at the top level in Figure 13-12. It is important to have each element clearly defined at the top level because WBS elements at this level are generally assigned to specific managers. At the lower levels, the manager may want to define the elements to suit his or her purposes. When defining the work breakdown structure, the definitions should be clear enough so that each activity is counted precisely once. If it is too vague, we have two dangers. One is that an activity may be omitted because each manager thinks that somebody else is doing that activity. The other danger is that the same activity is performed more than once because more than one manager thinks that he or she has the responsibility.

The schedule of activities associated with this work breakdown structure is given in Figure 13-13. Note that the WBS number for each activity is given. If we were to assign job order numbers in accordance with the work breakdown structure, we could track actual versus budgeted costs for each item. For example, the time charged could be charged

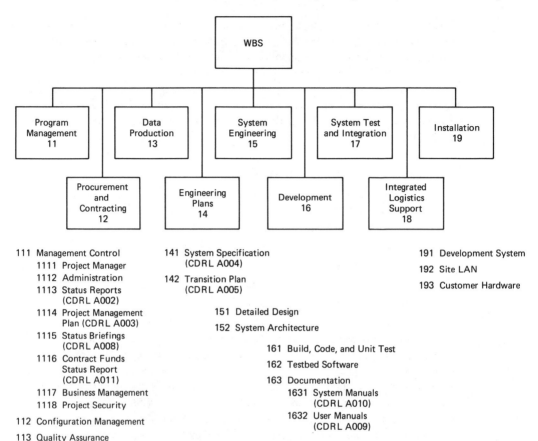

111 Management Control
    1111 Project Manager
    1112 Administration
    1113 Status Reports
         (CDRL A002)
    1114 Project Management
         Plan (CDRL A003)
    1115 Status Briefings
         (CDRL A008)
    1116 Contract Funds
         Status Report
         (CDRL A011)
    1117 Business Management
    1118 Project Security
112 Configuration Management
113 Quality Assurance
114 Other Direct Costs

    121 Workstation Hardware
    122 Network Hardware
    123 Software
    124 Cable Tuning
    125 Other

141 System Specification
    (CDRL A004)
142 Transition Plan
    (CDRL A005)

    151 Detailed Design
    152 System Architecture

    161 Build, Code, and Unit Test
    162 Testbed Software
    163 Documentation
         1631 System Manuals
             (CDRL A010)
         1632 User Manuals
             (CDRL A009)

    171 Acceptance Testing
    172 Net Services
    173 Integration
    174 System Testing
    175 Test Procedures

    181 Training
         1811 Training Plan
             (CDRL A006)
         1812 Instruction Design
         1813 Conduct Training
    182 Operations and Maintenance
         1821 Use Studies
         1822 O&M Plan (CDRL A007)
         1823 Logistic Support Reports
         1824 Support System Standards
         1825 Post Production Support
             Plan

191 Development System
192 Site LAN
193 Customer Hardware

Figure 13-11 Work breakdown structure for the office automation system.

Technical Task	Description
Engineering Plans WBS 14	Produce the system specification (A004)
	Produce the transition plan (A005)
	Specify the post-test-bed activities, finishing with full operational capability (FOC)
Systems Engineering WBS 15	Perform detailed design; specify development methods
	Define inter- and intrainterface controls for hardware and software
	Specify the person–machine interface
	Specify PDL for software modules
	Develop the workstation rapid prototype
Development WBS 16	Code and unit test of modules
	Develop systems manuals and user manuals
System Test and Integration WBS 17	Perform acceptance testing of vendor hardware and software
	Perform integration and testing of subsystems and components
	Test and integrate test bed and development facilities
Integrated Logistics WBS 18	Perform all training activities
	Specify the O&M plan
	Perform all O&M activities
	Arrange for the storage, packaging, and handling of all hardware and software
Installation WBS 19	Remove existing equipment
	Install new hardware and software

Figure 13-12   Definition of top-level technical WBS elements.

to Cnnnnn.wwwww, where C denotes a charge to a contract, nnnnn is the number of the contract, and wwwww is the WBS number. If this were contract number 12345, then a charge of C12345.141 would correspond to generating the system specification for this office automation system. This procedure provides complete cost accounting and tracking.

EXERCISE 13.9   Using the information given in Figures 13-10 through 13-13, develop a detailed activity network for the system transition. Note that you need to specify the WBS in greater detail than is given here. For example, WBS 172 system test and integration of network services, can be further partitioned into test and integration of the security module (WBS 1721), test and integration of the network control software (WBS 1722), test and integration of the electronic mail unit, and test and integration of spooling software. Specify additional levels of the work breakdown structure as needed.

Months After Award of Contract

WBS	Title	Schedule (Months After Award of Contract, 0–25)
11	PROGRAM MANAGEMENT	▲ Design Review
114	Program Management Plan (A003)	▲ (month 1)
113	Program Reports and Briefings	
1112	Contract Closeout Schedule (A001)	No Later Than 120 Days after Contract End Date
1113	Status Reports (A002)	As Required for Missed Deadlines →
1115	Status Briefings (A008)	Monthly →
1116	Contract Funds Status Report (A011)	Monthly →
112	Configuration Management and QA	
114	Other Direct Costs	Monthly →
12	PROCUREMENT AND SUBCONTRACTING	
121	Procurement Administration	As Required →
122	Subcontract Management	As Required →
13	PROJECT DATA PRODUCTION	As Required per CDRL and System Documentation Requirements →
14	ENGINEERING PLANS	
141	System Specification (A004)	▲ (month 1)
142	Transition Plan (A005)	▲ (month 2)
15	SYSTEM ENGINEERING	
151	Detailed Design	◄ ◄
152	Performance Assessment	◄
16	DEVELOPMENT	
161	Code and Unit Test	▲ (month 3)
162	Test Bed	▲ (month 5)
	Test Bed Demonstration/Acceptance	▲ (month 8)
163	System Documentation	
1631	User Manuals (A009)	▲ (month 6)
1632	System Manual (A010)	▲ (month 6)

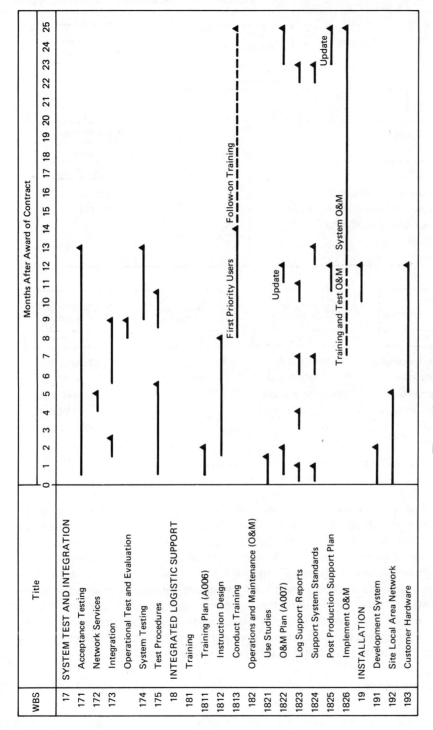

Figure 13-13 Schedule of activities.

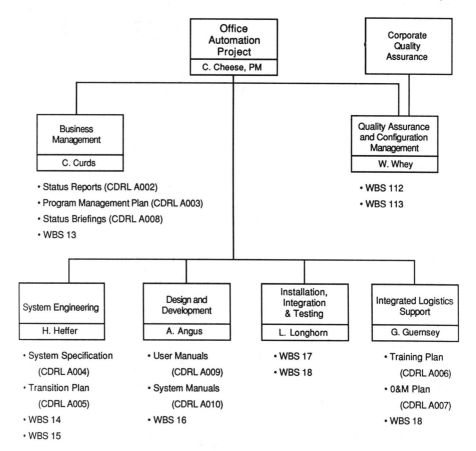

Figure 13-14 Organization structure and responsibilities for development of an office automation system.

There remain two aspects of the management plan to be presented. One is the project organization with designated responsibilities and interfaces. The other is a discussion of the risk and associated risk mitigation. The project organization is given in Figure 13-14. Responsibilities related to the deliverables (contract deliverable requirements list, or CDRL) and WBS elements are also specified in this figure. Note that the manager of project configuration management and quality assurance has dual reporting responsibilities. The manager reports to the project manager just as any other manager; however, she or he also reports to the corporate quality assurance manager. This second reporting responsibility is specified to assure that the project manager does not hide quality problems or subvert configuration management because of schedule pressures.

13.6 RISK MANAGEMENT

The development and installation of any new system entails a degree of risk associated with acquisition, technical issues, scheduling, and cost. The overall risk for this case

Critical Area	Impact	Mitigation Approach
No existing TEMPEST certified 8-pen plotter compatible with required graphics.	The TEMPEST certification process could delay installation.	A vendor was selected to perform TEMPEST engineering and certification with extensive experience in these areas. Request temporary waivers if needed.
Government-furnished cable installation.	If not completed by date specified in schedule, it will cause a day for day slip in delivery.	Deliver the required cable layout at the preliminary design review. Use an experienced cable TV company to test cable and isolate faulty segments.
Performance of vendor integration software.	User friendliness and performance.	Selected the most flexible integration package. Developed prototype of workstation software. Schedule integration activities early.
Required activities in the first three months.	Slip in early activities impacts entire schedule.	Arrange for early delivery of equipment. Complete integrated logistics planning for PDR. Careful management planning.

Figure 13-15 Office automation risk matrix.

study is characterized by low technical risk and moderate-to-high scheduling risk. An array of risk areas, their impacts, and mitigation techniques are given in Figure 13-15.

The assessment of a low technical risk is based on extensive use of off-the-shelf hardware and software, use of commercial local-area network technology, and a relatively small amount of new software to be developed. As indicated in the risk matrix, the schedule risk is based on the density of the activities in the early part of the schedule and the dependence of the schedule on factors outside the control of the contractor, specifically, dependence on the cable installation (to be government furnished) and the TEMPEST process, which is complicated and always takes more time than planned.

With this early identification of the critical areas, the risks can be reassessed at each monthly review meeting.

13.7 CONCLUSION

Although this case study has emphasized system integration rather than system development, the system development life cycle remains unchanged. This case has illustrated that software engineering is a way of thought. It is necessary for the software engineer to understand something about hardware and to work with hardware and communications engineers.

CHAPTER 14

Designing an Integrated Home Computer: A Challenge to the Reader

The intent of this chapter is to get the reader to use most of the material in this book. This goal can be accomplished in several ways. If this book is being used for a training course, this chapter can form the basis for a six-hour workshop on applying software engineering. In a college course, the last week of the semester could be based on this chapter, or it could form a take-home final examination. It could also simply be used as a challenge to the reader.

The chapter is written as if it were being used for a workshop because software engineering is generally a group activity.

Assume that the client is a multimillionaire who knows nothing about computers. He has an idea that he would like to invest in a complete home computer package for mass marketing. The system would be a total, integrated system for the home. He is not sure of the requirements, but feels that it should do things like:

- Activate a home security system
- Regulate the heating system
- Turn lights on and off at any prescribed time
- Provide word processing, tax packages, and the like
- Provide access to outside computers for catalog purchases, bank accounts, and so on

The client thinks that the system should be modular so that it could be bought in increments. He plans to market the system to new-home builders, security-system companies, computer stores, and first-class department stores. The end users are expected to be people aged 35 and older with at least one child and a family income of $40,000, and people with two-family incomes.

As you can tell, the client's ideas are a bit fuzzy. He does know that IBM, Apple, and other manufacturers have been selling individual computers and software packages. These packages are neither complete nor well integrated.

In a training course, the class should be split into groups of six to eight people. The groups will be competing for the job of building the totally integrated home computer system. The following is a schedule of activities:

- 0:00 to 0:30 hours
  Organize your group. Formulate ideas and questions. Organize your activities for the proposal generation. Delegate responsibilities.
- 0:30 to 0:40 hours
  A bidder's conference will occur. You can ask any question you want. (Assume that you will not get any technical information; in fact, you will probably not get any useful information. Do not give away your ideas to the other groups.)
- 0:40 to 1:25 hours
  Develop a written concept of operations. Be prepared to present your ideas to the client.
- 1:25 to 1:40 hours
  Present your ideas on the concept of operations. If there are two groups, you each have 7.5 minutes. This presentation should be made to qualify for continuing with the effort (everybody qualifies in a workshop setting). Do not be too upset if your ideas are presented in the presence of the other groups. In a real competition, the chances are good that your ideas will be obtained by the competition.
- 1:40 to 3:15 hours
  Perform a requirements analysis from a systems-oriented viewpoint. Establish your system configuration. You are preparing for a system design review. Figure out what other information you need. Are there existing software packages or hardware that could be used? Is your approach an open architecture or a closed architecture?
- 3:15 to 3:45 hours
  SDR presentations occur at this point.
- 3:45
  Personnel changes occur. The instructor will switch one or two people from each team to another team. This process simulates industrial practice of hiring the competitor's top talent.
- 3:45 to 5:00 hours
  Design as much of the system as you can. Review your assignments. Prepare for your preliminary design review. Earlier you were told that the client knew nothing about computers. Do not assume that he is stupid; he may have an independent consultant with him to ask you hard questions. These questions will be related to

development and production costs, schedule, and all aspects of the design. The scope of the questions need not be limited.

- 5:00 to 6:00 hours

  Present your proposal to the client. This is a preliminary design review. The client will select a team for development and production based on this review and any written materials submitted to him at this time.

APPENDIX A

Conceptual Design of Part of the SDDB

The SDDB contains management, financial, personnel, maintenance, documentation, and technical data. A conceptual design of the portion of the technical data that details the design is given in this appendix. For these data we have indicated where in the life cycle the data are generated, required as input, or modified.

SDDB Elements as Input–Output to System Development Life-cycle Phases

System Development Life-cycle Phases / System Design Data-base Elements	System Planning	System Requirements		System Design		System Development		Configuration Item Integration		Configuration Item Qualification Test		System Integration and Validation		Operations and Maintenance	
	Output	Input	Output	Input	Output	Input	Output	Input	Output	Input	Output	Input	Output	Input	Output
SYSTEM-LEVEL ELEMENTS															
System name	X														
Client (A Spec.) requirements	X	X												X	X
System context/scope documentation	X	X												X	X
System-derived requirements			X											X	X
Definition of functional areas	X	X												X	X
System test requirements			X	X	X							X		X	X
System test plans			X	X	X							X		X	X
Inter-CSCI interface documentation			X	X	X							X		X	X
Inter-CSCI interface source code													X	X	X
System test results													X	X	X
CSCIs			X	X	X									X	X

323

SDDB Elements as Input–Output to System Development Life-cycle Phases

System Development Life-cycle Phases / System Design Data-base Elements	System Planning Output	System Requirements Input	System Requirements Output	System Design Input	System Design Output	System Development Input	System Development Output	Configuration Item Integration Input	Configuration Item Integration Output	Configuration Item Qualification Test Input	Configuration Item Qualification Test Output	System Integration and Validation Input	System Integration and Validation Output	Operations and Maintenance Input	Operations and Maintenance Output
CSCI-LEVEL ELEMENTS															
CSCI identifier			×	×	×									×	×
Descriptive name			×	×	×									×	×
Brief description			×	×	×									×	×
CSCI functional area			×	×	×									×	×
Applicable requirements			×	×	×					×				×	×
Applicable specifications (B5, C5)			×	×	×	×	×			×				×	×
Applicable derived requirements			×	×	×					×				×	×
CSCI test requirements			×	×	×					×				×	×
CSCI test plans			×	×	×					×				×	×
CSCI qualification test results											×				×
CSCI performance test results											×				×
Incoming data flows			×	×	×			×		×		×		×	×
Outgoing data flows			×	×	×			×		×		×		×	×

Element												
Functional descriptions	X	X		X		X		X			X	X
Process descriptions	X	X		X		X		X			X	X
Inter-CSC interface documentation	X	X		X		X		X			X	X
Inter-CSC interface source code	X	X					X					X
CSCI data stores	X	X				X		X			X	X
Estimated total CSCI lines of code	X			X		X		X	X		X	
Allocated total CSCI lines of code	X					X		X	X		X	
Actual total CSCI lines of code	X				X		X				X	
Subordinate CSCs	X	X				X					X	X
CSC-LEVEL ELEMENTS												
CSC identifier	X					X					X	X
Descriptive names	X					X					X	X
Brief description	X					X					X	X
Containing CSCI	X					X					X	X
Subordinate CSUs	X					X					X	X
Applicable requirements	X					X				X	X	X
Applicable specifications (B5, C5)	X					X					X	X
Derived requirements	X					X					X	X

SDDB Elements as Input–Output to System Development Life-cycle Phases

System Development Life-cycle Phases / System Design Data-base Elements	System Planning	System Requirements		System Design		System Development		Configuration Item Integration		Configuration Item Qualification Test		System Integration and Validation		Operations and Maintenance	
	Output	Input	Output	Input	Output	Input	Output	Input	Output	Input	Output	Input	Output	Input	Output
Test requirements			×	×	×			×						×	×
Test plans			×	×	×			×						×	×
Test results									×						×
Incoming data flows			×	×	×									×	×
Outgoing data flows			×	×	×									×	×
Functional descriptions			×	×	×									×	×
Process descriptions			×	×	×									×	×
Inter-CSU interface documentation					×			×						×	×
Inter-CSU interface source code					×				×						×
Estimated total CSC lines of code			×	×	×										×
Allocated total CSC lines of code			×	×											×
Actual total CSC lines of code							×		×						×
CSU-LEVEL ELEMENTS															
CSU identifier					×									×	×

Element									
Descriptive names	×	×							×
Brief description	×	×							×
Containing CSC	×	×							×
Subordinate CSMs	×	×							×
Test requirements	×	×				×			×
Test plans	×	×				×			×
Test results	×				×				
Functional descriptions	×	×				×			×
Process descriptions	×	×				×			×
Inter-CSM interface documentation	×	×				×			×
Inter-CSM-interface source code	×	×			×				
Estimated total CSU lines of code	×					×	×	×	×
Allocated total CSU lines of code						×	×	×	×
Actual total CSU lines of code	×	×			×				
CSM-LEVEL ELEMENTS									
CSM identifier	×	×							×
Descriptive names	×	×							×

SDDB Elements as Input–Output to System Development Life-cycle Phases

System Development Life-cycle Phases / System Design Data-base Elements	System Planning	System Requirements		System Design		System Development		Configuration Item Integration		Configuration Item Qualification Test		System Integration and Validation		Operations and Maintenance	
	Output	Input	Output	Input	Output	Input	Output	Input	Output	Input	Output	Input	Output	Input	Output
Brief description					X									X	X
Containing CSU					X									X	X
Module test requirements					X	X								X	X
Module test plans					X	X								X	X
Module test results							X								X
Functional descriptions					X	X								X	X
Process descriptions					X	X								X	X
Programming language			X											X	X
Source code module							X							X	X
Estimated total CSM lines of code					X	X									X
Allocated total CSM lines of code					X	X									X
Actual total CSM lines of code							X							X	X
DATA FLOW															
Data-flow identifier			X	X										X	X

Descriptive names		✕	✕	✕								✕	✕
Brief description		✕	✕	✕								✕	✕
Containing data flow		✕	✕	✕								✕	✕
Subordinate data flows		✕	✕	✕								✕	✕
Applicable requirements		✕	✕	✕								✕	✕
Applicable specifications		✕	✕	✕								✕	✕
Derived requirements		✕	✕	✕								✕	✕
Source data store		✕	✕	✕								✕	✕
Sink data store		✕	✕	✕								✕	✕
Source CSCI		✕	✕	✕								✕	✕
Sink CSCI		✕	✕	✕								✕	✕
Source CSC		✕	✕	✕								✕	✕
Sink CSC		✕	✕	✕								✕	✕
Data Flow Documentation		✕	✕	✕									
DATA STORE													
Data-store identifier		✕	✕	✕								✕	✕
Descriptive names		✕	✕	✕								✕	✕
Brief description		✕	✕	✕								✕	✕
Containing data stores		✕	✕	✕								✕	✕
Subordinate data stores		✕	✕	✕								✕	✕
Subordinate data bases		✕	✕	✕								✕	✕

SDDB Elements as Input–Output to System Development Life-cycle Phases

System Development Life-cycle Phases / System Design Data-base Elements	System Planning Output	System Requirements Input	System Requirements Output	System Design Input	System Design Output	System Development Input	System Development Output	Configuration Item Integration Input	Configuration Item Integration Output	Configuration Item Qualification Test Input	Configuration Item Qualification Test Output	System Integration and Validation Input	System Integration and Validation Output	Operations and Maintenance Input	Operations and Maintenance Output
Subordinate data structures			X	X	X									X	X
Applicable requirements			X	X	X									X	X
Applicable specifications			X	X	X									X	X
Derived requirements			X	X	X									X	X
Incoming data flows			X	X	X									X	X
Outgoing data flows			X	X	X									X	X
Data-store documentation			X	X	X									X	X
Estimated storage			X	X	X									X	X
Allocated storage			X	X	X									X	X
Containing CSCI			X	X	X									X	X
DATA BASE															
Data-base identifier			X	X	X									X	X
Descriptive names			X	X	X									X	X
Brief description			X	X	X									X	X
Containing data store			X	X	X									X	X
Subordinate data structures			X	X	X	X		X	X			X	X	X	X

Item														
Subordinate primitive data elements										X		X	X	X
Access keys	X	X	X	X	X	X	X	X	X	X	X	X	X	X
Applicable requirements	X	X	X	X									X	X
Applicable specifications	X	X	X	X									X	X
Derived requirements	X	X	X	X									X	X
Estimated storage	X	X	X	X						X		X	X	X
Allocated storage	X	X	X	X						X	X	X	X	X
Access time requirements	X	X	X	X		X	X	X		X	X	X	X	X
Access time test plans	X	X	X	X	X	X	X	X		X	X	X	X	X
Access time test results					X	X	X	X		X	X	X	X	X
Data-base documentation	X	X	X	X						X		X	X	X
DATA STRUCTURE														
Data structure identifier	X	X	X									X	X	X
Descriptive names	X	X	X									X	X	X
Brief description	X	X	X									X	X	X
Containing data store	X	X	X									X	X	X
Containing data structure	X	X	X									X	X	X
Containing data base	X	X	X									X	X	X
Subordinate primitive data elements			X								X	X	X	X
Subordinate data structures	X	X	X								X	X	X	X

331

SDDB Elements as Input–Output to System Development Life-cycle Phases

System Development Life-cycle Phases / System Design Data-base Elements	System Planning	System Requirements		System Design		System Development		Configuration Item Integration		Configuration Item Qualification Test		System Integration and Validation		Operations and Maintenance	
	Output	Input	Output	Input	Output	Input	Output	Input	Output	Input	Output	Input	Output	Input	Output
Access key			×	×	×							×	×	×	×
Referencing modules					×									×	×
Source code names					×	×	×							×	×
Data structure documentation			×	×	×									×	×
Frequency of access			×	×	×							×	×	×	×
Frequency of update			×	×	×							×	×	×	×
Access time requirements			×	×	×			×	×	×	×	×	×	×	×
Access time test plans			×	×	×	×		×	×	×	×	×	×	×	×
Access time test records							×	×	×	×	×	×	×	×	×
PRIMITIVE DATA ELEMENT															
Primitive data element identifier					×									×	×
Descriptive names					×									×	×
Brief description					×									×	×
Containing data store					×									×	×
Containing data structure					×									×	×

Containing data base	X								X	X
Referencing modules	X								X	X
Source code names	X	X	X						X	X
Units	X	X	X						X	X
Precision	X	X	X						X	X
Value range (min/max/average)	X	X	X						X	X
Length range (min/max/average)	X	X	X						X	X
Frequency of access	X					X			X	X
Frequency of update	X					X			X	X
Primitive data element documentation	X								X	X
Data type	X	X	X						X	X

APPENDIX B

Tables for Computing Programming Time as a Function of Vocabulary

The tables of this appendix provide programming time and program length as a function of vocabulary size. The time is specified in worker-hours. This table is calculated using Halstead's formulas presented in Chapter 5. Case 1 corresponds to the assumption that the number of operators is equal to the number of operands. Case 2 is the "very complex" case in which it is assumed that the number of operators is half the number of operands.

Case 1: NUMBER OF OPERANDS = NUMBER OF OPERATORS
$S = 18, L = 1$

VOCABULARY	LENGTH	TIME (HOURS)	VOCABULARY	LENGTH	TIME (HOURS)
10	24	0	110	635	10
20	68	0	120	708	13
30	119	0	130	782	16
40	176	0	140	858	20
50	236	1	150	934	24
60	299	2	160	1011	28
70	364	3	170	1089	33
80	432	4	180	1168	39
90	501	6	190	1248	45
100	572	8	200	1328	52

334

VOCABULARY	LENGTH	TIME (HOURS)	VOCABULARY	LENGTH	TIME (HOURS)
210	1409	59	570	4648	763
220	1491	66	580	4744	797
230	1574	75	590	4840	832
240	1657	83	600	4937	867
250	1741	93	610	5034	904
260	1825	103	620	5131	942
270	1910	113	630	5228	980
280	1996	124	640	5326	1020
290	2082	136	650	5423	1060
300	2168	149	660	5521	1101
310	2255	162	670	5619	1143
320	2343	176	680	5718	1187
330	2430	190	690	5817	1231
340	2519	205	700	5915	1276
350	2607	221	710	6014	1322
360	2697	238	720	6114	1368
370	2786	255	730	6213	1416
380	2876	273	740	6313	1465
390	2966	292	750	6413	1515
400	3057	311	760	6513	1566
410	3148	331	770	6613	1617
420	3239	352	780	6713	1670
430	3331	374	790	6814	1724
440	3423	397	800	6915	1779
450	3516	420	810	7016	1834
460	3608	444	820	7117	1891
470	3701	469	830	7218	1949
480	3795	494	840	7319	2008
490	3888	521	850	7421	2067
500	3982	548	860	7523	2128
510	4077	5/6	870	7625	2190
520	4171	605	880	7727	2253
530	4266	635	890	7829	2317
540	4361	666	900	7932	2382
550	4456	697	910	8035	2448
560	4552	729	920	8137	2515

VOCABULARY	LENGTH	TIME (HOURS)	VOCABULARY	LENGTH	TIME (HOURS)
930	8240	2583	1290	12039	5778
940	8343	2652	1300	12147	5889
950	8447	2723	1310	12255	6000
960	8550	2794	1320	12363	6113
970	8654	2866	1330	12471	6227
980	8757	2940	1340	12579	6342
990	8861	3014	1350	12688	6458
1000	8965	3090	1360	12796	6576
1010	9069	3167	1370	12905	6695
1020	9174	3245	1380	13014	6815
1030	9278	3324	1390	13122	6936
1040	9383	3404	1400	13231	7059
1050	9487	3485	1410	13340	7183
1060	9592	3567	1420	13449	7308
1070	9697	3651	1430	13558	7434
1080	9802	3735	1440	13668	7562
1090	9908	3821	1450	13777	7690
1100	10013	3908	1460	13887	7821
1110	10119	3996	1470	13996	7952
1120	10224	4085	1480	14106	8085
1130	10330	4175	1490	14216	8219
1140	10436	4267	1500	14326	8354
1150	10542	4359	1510	14436	8490
1160	10648	4453	1520	14546	8628
1170	10754	4548	1530	14656	8767
1180	10861	4644	1540	14766	8907
1190	10967	4741	1550	14876	9049
1200	11074	4839	1560	14987	9192
1210	11181	4939	1570	15097	9336
1220	11288	5040	1580	15208	9482
1230	11395	5142	1590	15319	9628
1240	11502	5245	1600	15430	9776
1250	11609	5349	1610	15541	9926
1260	11717	5455	1620	15652	10077
1270	11824	5561	1630	15763	10229
1280	11932	5669	1640	15874	10382

VOCABULARY	LENGTH	TIME (HOURS)	VOCABULARY	LENGTH	TIME (HOURS)
1650	15985	10537	1790	17552	12843
1660	16096	10693	1800	17664	13018
1670	16208	10850	1810	17777	13194
1680	16319	11009	1820	17890	13372
1690	16431	11169	1830	18002	13551
1700	16543	11330	1840	18115	13731
1710	16655	11493	1850	18228	13913
1720	16766	11657	1860	18341	14096
1730	16878	11822	1870	18454	14281
1740	16990	11989	1880	18567	14466
1750	17102	12157	1890	18681	14654
1760	17215	12327	1900	18794	14842
1770	17327	12497	1910	18907	15033
1780	17439	12670			

Case 2: NUMBER OF OPERANDS = 2 * NUMBER OF OPERATORS
S = 18, L = 1

VOCABULARY	LENGTH	TIME (HOURS)	VOCABULARY	LENGTH	TIME (HOURS)
10	24	0	170	1103	34
20	68	0	180	1183	40
30	119	0	190	1263	46
40	176	0	200	1345	53
50	236	1	210	1427	60
60	299	2	220	1509	68
70	364	3	230	1593	76
80	432	4	240	1677	85
90	501	6	250	1761	95
100	572	8	260	1847	105
110	644	10	270	1932	116
120	718	13	280	2019	127
130	793	17	290	2105	139
140	869	20	300	2193	152
150	946	24	310	2280	166
160	1024	29	320	2369	180

VOCABULARY	LENGTH	TIME (HOURS)	VOCABULARY	LENGTH	TIME (HOURS)
330	2457	194	690	5873	1255
340	2546	210	700	5973	1300
350	2636	226	710	6072	1347
360	2726	243	720	6172	1395
370	2816	261	730	6273	1444
380	2907	279	740	6373	1493
390	2998	298	750	6474	1544
400	3090	318	760	6575	1596
410	3182	339	770	6676	1648
420	3274	360	780	6777	1702
430	3366	382	790	6878	1757
440	3459	405	800	6980	1812
450	3552	429	810	7082	1869
460	3646	453	820	7184	1927
470	3740	479	830	7286	1986
480	3834	505	840	7388	2045
490	3928	532	850	7491	2106
500	4023	560	860	7593	2168
510	4118	588	870	7696	2231
520	4214	618	880	7799	2295
530	4309	648	890	7902	2360
540	4405	679	900	8005	2426
550	4501	711	910	8109	2493
560	4598	744	920	8213	2562
570	4694	778	930	8316	2631
580	4791	813	940	8420	2701
590	4888	848	950	8524	2773
600	4986	885	960	8629	2845
610	5083	922	970	8733	2919
620	5181	960	980	8837	2994
630	5279	1000	990	8942	3070
640	5378	1040	1000	9047	3147
650	5476	1081	1010	9152	3225
660	5575	1123	1020	9257	3304
670	5674	1166	1030	9362	3384
680	5773	1210	1040	9468	3466

VOCABULARY	LENGTH	TIME (HOURS)	VOCABULARY	LENGTH	TIME (HOURS)
1050	9573	3548	1410	13455	7307
1060	9679	3632	1420	13565	7434
1070	9785	3717	1430	13675	7563
1080	9891	3803	1440	13785	7692
1090	9997	3890	1450	13896	7823
1100	10103	3978	1460	14006	7956
1110	10209	4068	1470	14116	8089
1120	10316	4159	1480	14227	8224
1130	10422	4250	1490	14337	8360
1140	10529	4343	1500	14448	8497
1150	10636	4437	1510	14559	8636
1160	10743	4533	1520	14670	8776
1170	10850	4629	1530	14781	8917
1180	10957	4727	1540	14892	9060
1190	11065	4826	1550	15003	9204
1200	11172	4926	1560	15114	9349
1210	11280	5027	1570	15226	9495
1220	11387	5129	1580	15337	9643
1230	11495	5233	1590	15449	9792
1240	11603	5338	1600	15560	9943
1250	11711	5444	1610	15672	10095
1260	11819	5551	1620	15784	10248
1270	11928	5659	1630	15896	10402
1280	12036	5769	1640	16008	10558
1290	12145	5880	1650	16120	10715
1300	12253	5992	1660	16232	10874
1310	12362	6105	1670	16344	11034
1320	12471	6220	1680	16457	11195
1330	12580	6336	1690	16569	11357
1340	12689	6453	1700	16682	11521
1350	12798	6571	1710	16794	11687
1360	12907	6691	1720	16907	11853
1370	13017	6811	1730	17020	12021
1380	13126	6934	1740	17133	12191
1390	13236	7057	1750	17245	12361
1400	13346	7181	1760	17358	12533

VOCABULARY	LENGTH	TIME (HOURS)	VOCABULARY	LENGTH	TIME (HOURS)
1770	17472	12707	1850	18379	14145
1780	17585	12882	1860	18493	14331
1790	17698	13058	1870	18607	14518
1800	17811	13236	1880	18721	14707
1810	17925	13415	1890	18835	14897
1820	18038	13595	1900	18949	15089
1830	18152	13777	1910	19063	15282
1840	18266	13960			

APPENDIX C

Partial Data Dictionary for Use in Chapter 8

Data Dictionary

No.	Identifier	CSC No. Source	CSC No. Sink	Description
1	Departure	6.2	1.1	Input after takeoff, absence causes FP drop.
1	Departure	8.2	1.1	Input after takeoff, absence causes FP drop.
2	Amendment, flight plan	6.2	1.1	Altitude, aircraft type, beacon code, equipment, airspeed, 3D-trajectory.
2	Amendment, flight plan	8.2	1.1	Altitude, aircraft type, beacon code, equipment, airspeed, 3D-trajectory.
3	Flight plan	8.2	1.1	Filed flight plan: beacon code, filed route, filed airspeed, departure time, souls on board, equipment, pilot's name, aircraft type.
3	Flight plan	6.2	1.1	Filed flight plan: beacon code, filed route, filed airspeed, departure time, souls on board, equipment, pilot's name, aircraft type.
4	Bulk flight plan	1.3	1.1	As 3, but without pilot's name and souls on board, used for scheduled flights.
5	Handoff flight plan	1.3	8.2	As 3, but only route remaining portion of the filed route.
5	Handoff flight plan	8.2	1.1	As 3, but only route remaining portion of the filed route.
6	Environment A	9.3	1.1	Message format requirements, assignable beacon codes, logic rules.
9	Route amendments	1.1	1.2	The latest amendment. The route conversion process will reconvert the route to incorporate the new amendment.
10	Flight route	1.1	1.2	That portion of the flight plan (3) required by route conversion: aircraft type, beacon code, route, airspeed and altitude profile, and departure time.
11	Clearance	1.3	8.2	Directives to pilot. Usually as flight plan (3), but accepted by the ATC system.
11	Clearance	1.3	6.2	Directives to pilot. Usually as flight plan (3), but accepted by the ATC system.
11	Clearance	1.3	4.3	Directives to pilot. Usually as flight plan (3), but accepted by the ATC system.
12	Initial beacon code	1.1	1.2	Initial assigned beacon code.
14	Filed flight plan text	1.1	6.2	Flight plan information requested by controller.
16	Environment B	9.3	1.2	Airspace definition: fixes, boundaries, and routes.
22	Winds aloft	2.1	5.5	Wind direction and velocity for different altitudes.
22	Winds aloft	2.1	6.2	Wind direction and velocity for different altitudes.
23	Environment C	9.3	5.5	Fixes, posting codes, priorities, etc.
23	Environment C	7.2	5.5	Fixes, posting codes, priorities, etc.
24	Flight strip output	1.3	6.2	Fix times, s/s location, aircraft ID, posting points, aircraft speed, altitude, and other posting data delivered in a time-dependent fashion.
24	Flight strip output	1.3	8.2	Fix times, s/s location, aircraft ID, posting points, aircraft speed, altitude, and other posting data delivered in a time-dependent fashion.

No.	Name			Description
25	Parameter times	9.3	1.3	Parameter times for strip output, etc.
27	Remove strip	6.2	1.1	Controller command to remove all flight data for a flight from system.
31	Filed FP data	1.1	1.1	Flight plan as filed but format checked, put into the FP data base for use by RC in maintaining amendments/updates received from PDA.
31	Filed FP data	1.1	1.2	Flight plan as filed but format checked, put into the FP data base for use by RC in maintaining amendments/updates received from PDA.
32	FP text	1.2	1.1	Text retrieved from the flight plan data base in response to queries or requests for flight plan data.
32	FP text	1.1	1.1	Text retrieved from the flight plan data base in response to queries or requests for flight plan data.
33	FP amendments	1.1	1.1	Data used to modify the flight plan data base, includes altitude, route, speed, profile, and departure time amendments.
33	FP amendments	1.1	1.2	Data used to modify the flight plan data base, includes altitude, route, speed, profile, and departure time amendments.
33	FP amendments	1.1	1.3	Data used to modify the flight plan data base, includes altitude, route, speed, profile, and departure time amendments.
35	Released beacon codes	3.2	1.1	Beacon codes that have just become available for assignment due to a flight terminating or leaving a facilities airspace.
36	Bulk FP store	8.2	1.3	Flight plans for regularly scheduled flights (stereo flight plans) that are delivered by flight status alerts to FDPE in a timely fashion.
36	Bulk FP store	9.3	1.3	Flight plans for regularly scheduled flights (stereo flight plans) that are delivered by flight status alerts to FDPE in a timely fashion.
37	Handoff initiate/accept	1.3	3.2	A flag delivered in a timely fashion to instruct the track display processing function to start or stop handoff processing.
37	Handoff initiate/accept	6.2	3.2	A flag delivered in a timely fashion to instruct the track display processing function to start or stop handoff processing.
37	Handoff initiate/accept	8.2	3.2	A flag delivered in a timely fashion to instruct the track display processing function to start or stop handoff processing.
38	Flight strip and clearance	5.1	1.3	Posting prompt and clearance directives to ensure that flight strip data (see 24) is delivered at predetermined times to the controller and/or pilot.
39	FP updates	1.2	1.1	Updates to the flight plan data base originating from changes made by PDA; these data will be in both converted form and in a deliverable clearance form.
41	Flight plan request	6.2	1.1	Controller request for specified flight plan data.
42	Flight strip data	1.1	1.3	Data are retrieved from the flight plan data base, upon receipt of a prompt for flight strip data or clearance directives (38), for delivery to the controller and/or pilot (37).

Data Dictionary

No.	Identifier	CSC No. Source	CSC No. Sink	Description
42	Flight strip dta	1.2	1.3	Data are retrieved from the flight plan data base, upon receipt of a prompt for flight strip data or clearance directives (38), for delivery to the controller and/or pilot (37).
43	Strip request	6.2	1.1	Request by controller for an extra flight strip.
44	Route display request	6.2	1.1	Request for graphic projection of route on situation display.
45	Aircraft data update	1.1	6.2	Updates on aircraft data.
46	Route display	1.1	6.2	Graphic representation of planned flight path.
47	Stereo flight plan	6.2	1.1	Initiates previously stored bulk FP. Contains FP ID and flight ID.
47	Stereo flight plan	8.2	1.1	Initiates previously stored bulk FP. Contains FP ID and flight ID.
48	Graphic track reroute	6.2	1.1	Route amendment by using the trackball on the situation display.
49	Cancel FP	6.2	1.1	Used before flight departure. After departure use "Remove strip."
49	Cancel FP	8.2	1.1	Used before flight departure. After departure use "Remove strip."
50	Discrete code request/mod.	6.2	1.1	Controller selection/modification of a flight's assigned beacon code.
50	Discrete code request/mod.	8.2	1.1	Controller selection/modification of a flight's assigned beacon code.
51	Actual departure time	1.1	5.1	Time aircraft actually left ground. Used to update, fix times.
101	Environment E	7.2	2.1	Sector suite configuration, message formats, logic rules.
101	Environment E	9.3	2.1	Sector suite configuration, message formats, logic rules.
101	Environment E	7.2	2.2	Sector suite configuration, message formats, logic rules.
101	Environment E	9.3	2.2	Sector suite configuration, message formats, logic rules.
102	Derived winds	2.3	2.1	Derived winds aloft.
102	Derived winds	2.3	8.2	Derived winds aloft.
103	WX messages	8.2	2.1	SIGMETS, weather reports, requests, observations, and forecasts.
103	WX messages	6.2	2.1	SIGMETS, weather reports, requests, observations, and forecasts.
104	PIREPS	8.2	2.1	Pilot-reported weather.
104	PIREPS	4.3	2.1	Pilot-reported weather.
104	PIREPS	6.2	2.1	Pilot-reported weather.
105	Weather alert	2.1	6.2	Nonrequested weather reports (SIGMETS, PIREPS).
105	Weather alert	2.1	8.2	Nonrequested weather reports (SIGMETS, PIREPS).
106	Requested weather data	2.1	6.2	Requested weather reports
107	Primary radar weather	4.1	2.2	Primary radar WX messages in system coordinates.

ID	Name			Description
108	CWP WX maps	8.2	2.2	T3.5 replaces item 107.
109	Weather display	2.2	6.2	Weather maps, either primary radar or CWP, possibly overlayed on PVD display.
110	Tracking data	3.2	2.3	A/C position, velocity, planned position, times.
111	A/C trajectory	4.3	2.3	A/C-supplied trajectory, position, heading, vector (T4).
112	Weather map requests	6.2	2.2	Message requesting specific weather maps on controller's display.
113	Weather text requests	6.2	2.1	Controller requests for weather data.
114	Winds request	6.2	2.1	Controller requests for winds aloft.
115	Altimeter request	6.2	2.1	Controller requests for altimeter settings.
116	Altimeter settings	2.2	6.2	Altimeter settings from various reporting stations.
201	Radar messages	8.2	4.1	All seven radar messages from CD.
202	Barometric pressure	2.1	4.1	Used for mode C correction.
203	Environment F	9.3	4.1	Radar sort boxes, format logic, coordinate system parameters, configuration.
203	Environment F	7.2	4.1	Radar sort boxes, format logic, coordinate system parameters, configuration.
204	Bias correction	4.2	4.1	Bias error in range and azimuth computations for each radar for registration and collimation correction.
205	Modify filters	4.2	4.2	Mods radar sort box filter to change preferred radar source.
206	Primary, beacon, strobe hits	4.1	3.1	Filtered, sorted, corrected targets.
208	Radar counts	4.1	4.2	Count of targets and target errors.
209	Reg. and coll. targets	4.1	4.2	Selected target returns for registration and collimation analysis.
210	Status/test messages	4.1	4.2	Results of self-test.
211	Environment G	7.2	4.2	Error thresholds (TBD).
211	Environment G	9.3	4.2	Error thresholds (TBD).
212	Radar status	4.2	7.1	Radar site status, coverage status, current registration and collimation error values, data counts, test results.
213	Radar status request	7.2	4.2	DSO request for radar status.
215	Mode S downlink	4.1	4.3	Air-to-ground telemetry extracted from mode S beacon reply.
216	Mode S uplink	4.3	8.2	Ground-to-air telemetry to be sent with radar signal.
217	Data request	6.2	4.3	Controller requests for information such as heading, IAS, temperature.
218	Acknowledgment	4.3	6.2	Pilot's response to ATC instructions or queries.
301	Environment H	9.3	3.1	S/S assignments, correlation parameters, special beacon code list.
301	Environment H	7.2	3.1	S/S assignments, correlation parameters, special beacon code list.
302	Velocity vector modifications	6.2	3.1	Requests for velocity vector with system coordinates (match to a track).
303	Track initiate/terminate	3.2	3.1	Controller drop, hold, coast, initiate, terminate messages resulting in target initiation/termination.

Data Dictionary

No.	Identifier	CSC No. Source	CSC No. Sink	Description
304	Special beacon output	3.1	3.2	Emergency or military beacon codes requiring special output to display.
305	Velocity vector	3.1	6.2	Vector derived from track history. Requested by message 302.
306	Correlated tracks	3.1	6.2	Primary and beacon targets correlated to be same track plus mode C and beacon code.
306	Correlated tracks	3.1	3.2	Primary and beacon targets correlated to be same track plus mode C and beacon code.
306	Correlated tracks	3.1	3.3	Primary and beacon targets correlated to be same track plus mode C and beacon code.
308	Track status modifications	6.2	3.2	Controller or remove strip requests to initiate, terminate (drop), coast, or hold a track.
308	Track status modifications	1.1	3.2	Controller or remove strip requests to initiate, terminate (drop), coast, or hold a track.
309	Environment J	9.3	3.2	S/S sector assignments, spatial boundaries, association threshold limits, auto handoff status.
309	Environment J	7.2	3.2	S/S sector assignments, spatial boundaries, association threshold limits, auto handoff status.
310	CA/MSAW alerts	3.3	3.2	Conflict alert and/or minimum safe altitude warning. Conditions needing special outputs.
311	Longitudinal errors	3.2	5.1	New velocity data needed to update fix times for tracks out of longitudinal association limits.
312	Data blocks	3.2	6.2	Data output for free and flat tracks, including special outputs for emergencies, CA MSAW, military, hijack, etc.. Also handoff outputs.
313	CA/MSAW control	6.2	3.3	Controller/DSO inputs to suppress or allow by target, sector, or center CA and MSAW processing or output.
314	Environment I	9.3	3.3	Spatial coordinates for MSAW and CA threshold values.
315	Handoff messages	8.2	3.2	Message initiating or updating handoffs to/from another facility. Results in track data being transmitted/received and a track initiation/drop.
315	Handoff messages	3.2	8.2	Message initiating or updating handoffs to/from another facility. Results in track data being transmitted/received and a track initiation/drop.
316	CA/MSAW status	3.3	7.2	Current parameter settings for CA/MSAW processing. Modified by message 313.
317	Reported altitude	6.2	3.3	Pilot-reported altitude for non-mode C targets.
317	Reported altitude	6.2	5.1	Pilot-reported altitude for non-mode C targets.
318	CA/MSAW alert/resolution	3.2	6.2	Attention-drawing prompt and suggested vector for CA/MSAW.

No.	Name			Description
401	All trajectories	5.1	5.1	All data (4D trajectories) maintained in the trajectory model. This will be used for FLAT tracking and to generate a 20-minute snapshot of the traffic situation to be scanned to ensure no conflicts.
401	All trajectories	5.1	1.3	All data (4D trajectories) maintained in the trajectory model. This will be used for FLAT tracking and to generate a 20-minute snapshot of the traffic situation to be scanned to ensure no conflicts.
402	Tentative 4D A/C trajectory	5.1	5.2	A proposed A/C trajectory in four dimensions. It will be checked against all probes to ensure no problems exist.
402	Tentative 4D A/C trajectory	5.5	5.1	A proposed A/C trajectory in four dimensions. It will be checked against all probes to ensure no problems exist.
403	Snapshot frequency	9.3	5.1	Preset parameter time dictating the frequency of conflict scans (approx 2 minutes).
405	Manual resolution	6.2	5.1	Manual resolution to problems that have not been resolved by PDA. This can also be used to override a PDA directive. It will usually be input in response to message 407.
406	Approved modification	5.1	1.2	Modified 4D trajectory that has no conflicts for the required period of time (20 minutes) and satisfies metering constraints.
406	Approved modification	5.1	5.1	Modified 4D trajectory that has no conflicts for the required period of time (20 minutes) and satisfies metering constraints.
407	Unresolved problems	5.1	6.2	A request for manual intervention due to a failure by PDA to resolve a conflict situation in a satisfactory way. This message will prompt response message 405.
408	20-Minute snapshot	5.1	5.3	A 4D trajectory situation map used for conflict probing.
408	20-Minute snapshot	5.1	5.4	A 4D trajectory situation map used for conflict probing.
409	Metering constraints	8.2	5.2	A list of metering constraints to be used when allocating aircraft arrival times and keeping controller workload below a parameter level.
409	Metering constraints	9.3	5.2	A list of metering constraints to be used when allocating aircraft arrival times and keeping controller workload below a parameter level.
409	Metering constraints	7.2	5.2	A list of metering constraints to be used when allocating aircraft arrival times and keeping controller workload below a parameter level.
410	Metering lists	5.2	8.2	Metering lists for fixes, airports, etc.
410	Metering lists	5.2	7.2	Metering lists for fixes, airports, etc.
410	Metering lists	5.2	6.2	Metering lines for fixes, airports, etc.
411	Metering list request	5.2	8.2	A request for specific metering lists for airspace/airports external to the facility.
412	Time stop and 3D trajectory	5.2	5.5	A 3D trajectory including A/C speed profile, route, altitude profile, and an arrival time. The fix time calculation process will fill in fix time data by working from destination to departure.

Data Dictionary

No.	Identifier	CSC No. Source	CSC No. Sink	Description
413	Time start and 3D trajectory	5.3	5.5	A 3D trajectory including A/C speed profile, route, altitude profile, and a start time. The fix time calculation process will fill in fix time data by working from departure to destination.
413	Time start and 3D trajectory	5.4	5.5	A 3D trajectory including A/C speed profile, route, altitude profile, and a start time. The fix time calculation process will fill in fix time data by working from departure to destination.
413	Time start and 3D trajectory	1.2	5.5	A 3D trajectory including A/C speed profile, route, altitude profile, and a start time. The fix time calculation process will fill in fix time data by working from departure to destination.
414	A/C performance	9.3	5.3	Aircraft performance characteristics: airspeeds for different flight configurations, turn rates, descent rates, endurance, etc.
414	A/C performance	9.3	5.4	Aircraft performance characteristics: airspeeds for different flight configurations, turn rates, descent rates, endurance, etc.
415	Reroute rules	9.3	5.3	Hierarchy of allowable changes to aircraft trajectory in order of preference, such as speed change, metering vector, and holding pattern.
415	Reroute rules	9.3	5.4	Hierarchy of allowable changes to aircraft trajectory in order of preference, such as speed change, metering vector, and holding pattern.
416	Blocked airspace	9.3	5.3	Airspace to be avoided. Permanent forbidden airspace such as minimum safe altitude, occasional forbidden airspace such as military training areas.
416	Blocked airspace	6.2	5.3	Airspace to be avoided. Temporary forbidden airspace, such as thunderstorm areas input by controller based on PIREP.
417	Change OK	5.2	5.1	Tentative trajectory (402) approved without modification.
418	Facility traffic count	5.2	6.2	Current traffic loads.
418	Facility traffic count	5.2	7.2	Current traffic loads.
418	Facility traffic count	5.2	8.2	Current traffic loads.
419	Progress report	6.2	5.1	Aircraft-reported position used in lieu of radar data.
419	Progress report	4.3	5.1	Aircraft-reported position used in lieu of radar data.
507	Graphic instructions	6.2	6.1	A hierarchical description of the graphical representation.

ID	Name			Description
508	Display input	6.1	6.2	Inputs used to modify the display.
509	Task input	6.1	6.2	Inputs to be forwarded to some other process.
510	Application model	9.3	6.2	A description of both graphical and nongraphical properties of display.
602	Self-test results	All	7.1	Self-explanatory.
603	Self-test prompt	7.1	All	Initiates tests in H/W or S/W modules.
604	H/W faults	All	7.1	H/W-generated fault indication.
605	Anomaly reports	7.2	7.1	Electronic mail about observed anomalies.
606	Future load requirements	7.2	7.1	Notification to ACs operator of expected peaks or valleys in system load.
613	Resource status reports	7.1	8.2	Current utilization and availability of resources.
613	Resource status reports	8.2	7.1	Current utilization and availability of resources.
622	Current activity report	7.2	8.2	What is happening?
622	Current activity report	8.2	7.2	What is happening?
623	Airspace assignment mods.	7.2	6.2	Modification to S/S coverage.
624	Airspace assignment status	6.2	7.2	Current assignments.
625	Important event notice	7.1	7.2	Notice of degraded or expected lower capability.
626	System startup messages	H/W	7.1	OS-type message during start-up.
630	Resource Performance Records	7.1	7.3	H/W failures, configuration changes, test results, radar status reports, system initiate/reinitiate report, resource status reports, resource configuration modifications.
631	Operational performance records	7.2	7.3	Operational changes, environmental changes, adjacent facility activity report.
632	Legal Recording	TBD	7.3	Interfacility messages, all interfacility messages(?), S/S actions, trajectory model, flight plan data base.
701	Simulator/pilot input	6.2	12.1	Additions or modifications to developed situations in real-time during ATCS training.
702	Simulator/pilot output	12.1	6.2	Responses to modified situations, plus progress to ATCS training.
703	Dynamic simulation input	12.1	12.2	Generated situation data and also simulator/pilot prompts.
704	Dynamic simulation output	12.2	12.1	Various prompts regarding progress and current situations of the various operating procedures.
705	Option trace settings	12.4	12.2	Instructions to the various operational CPCIs (1.0 to 9.0) to begin operating in the trace mode.
706	Historical recorded input	7.3	12.3	Recorded situation data to provide the AAS system with the requirements to meet the preplanned operational situations.
707	Generated input data	12.4	12.3	A combination of the data extracted from the baseline situation data and data entered by the situation developer to generate preplanned situations.
708	Situation developer input	6.2	12.4	Instructions to the operational CPCIs (1.0 to 9.0) to engage the trace mode of execution to provide additional data in generating preplanned situations.

Data Dictionary

No.	Identifier	CSC No. Source	CSC No. Sink	Description
709	Situation developer outputs	12.4	6.2	Prompts to the situation developer while developing trace options and preplanned situations.
710	Situation intiate data	12.4	12.1	A combination of data extracted from the baseline situation data base and data entered by the situation developer to provide ATCS training scenarios.
711	Situation developer data	12.3	12.2	Data provided by the situation development generator (12.4) reformatted to build the simulation development data base.
712	On-line recorded input data	1–9	12.1	Data extracted from the 20-minute recorded data base to provide the simulator/pilot instructor with restart capability during the ATCS training program.
713	Baseline situation input	TBD	12.4	Baseline situation input consisting of skeletal situation data to assist the situation developer in providing planned situations.
714	Driver input	12.2	1–9	Simulated radio messages, flight data inputs, etc., necessary to drive CPCIs 1.0 to 9.0, plus any trace options set.
715	Operational output	1–9	12.2	Mode S uplink and interfacility data.
716	CPE configuration	7.1	6.2	Instructions issued by the resource manager to direct the device manager of a CPE as to what function that CPE will be performing (e.g., simulator pilot, controller PVD, controller planning unit, training unit, etc.).
717	Manual configuration commands	7.1	6.2	Commands issued by the system controller, via dedicated workstation, to initiate a manual reconfiguration.
719	Configuration reports	7.1	6.2	Reports issued to the system controller, via dedicated workstation, to inform him or her of completion of manual reconfiguration commands (716) and automatic reconfiguration actions.
720	CA/MSAW status reports	7.2	6.2	Data showing the completion of a CA/MSAW status modification request.

Bibliography

ADRION, W. R., M. A. BRANSTED, and J. C. CHERNIAVSKY, "Validation, Verification and Testing of Computer Software," *ACM Computing Surveys,* Vol. 14, No. 2, June 1982, pp. 159–192.

ALEXANDER, W., and R. BRICE, "Performance Modeling in the Design Process," Los Alamos National Laboratory, LA-UR-82-1819, Dec. 1982.

ALFORD, M., "SREM at the Age of Eight; The Distributed Computing Design System," *Computer,* Vol. 18, No. 4, Apr. 1985, pp. 36–46.

AMERICAN NATIONAL STANDARDS INSTITUTE, "Flow Chart Symbols and Their Usage in Information Processing," ANSI X3.5-1970.

ANDERSON, T., and J. C. KNIGHT, "A Framework for Software Fault Tolerance in Real Time Systems," *IEEE Transactions on Software Engineering,* Vol. SE-9, No. 3, pp. 355–364.

ATRE, S., *Data Base: Structured Techniques for Design, Performance and Management,* John Wiley & Sons, Inc., New York, 1980.

BOEHM, B., *Software Engineering Economics,* Prentice-Hall, Inc., Englewood Cliffs, N.J., 1981.

BOHM, C., and G. JACOPINI, "Flow Diagrams, Turing Machines, and Languages with Only Two Formation Rules," *Communications of the ACM,* Vol. 9, May 1966, pp. 366–371.

BOURDON, G. A., and J. A. DUQUETTE, "A Computerized Model for Estimating Software Life Cycle Costs (Model Concept)," USAF Electronic Systems Division, ESD-TR-77-253, Apr. 1978.

BOWEN, T. P., and others, "Software Quality Measurement for Distributed Systems: Guidebook for Software Quality Measurement," Boeing Aerospace Company, RADC-TR-83-175, Vol. II, July 1983.

BRACKETT, J., and C. L. McGOWAN, "Applying SADT to Large Systems Problems," Softech TP059, Jan. 1977.

BRAU, J., "Capacity Management Part I: It Keeps You Running," *Computer Design*, July 1984, pp. 129–137.

BRITCHER, R. N., and J. J. CRAIG, "Using Modern Design Practices to Upgrade Aging Software Systems," *IEEE Software*, Vol. 3, No. 3, May 1986, pp. 16–23.

BROOKS, F. P., JR., *The Mythical Man-Month: Essays on Software Engineering*, Addison-Wesley Publishing Co., Reading, Mass., 1975.

BURNS, R., and others, "On-Line Documentation," *The DEC Professional*, Nov. 1985, pp. 32–38.

CHAPIN, N., "New Format for Flowcharts," *Software—Practice and Experience*, Vol. 4, No. 4, Oct.–Dec. 1974, pp. 341–357.

CODD, E. F., "A Relational Model of Data for Large Shared Data Banks," *Communications of the ACM*, Vol. 13, No. 6, June 1970, pp. 377–387.

CONNOR, M., "Structured Analysis and Design Techniques, Introduction," 9595-7, SofTech, Inc., Waltham, Mass., 1980.

DELP, P., and others, "System Tools for Project Planning," Program of Advanced Studies in Institution Building and Technical Assistance Methodology (PATSITAM), 1977 (ISBN# 0-89249-021-7).

DEPARTMENT OF DEFENSE, "Evaluation of a Contractor's Software Quality Assurance Program," MIL-HDBK-334, July 15, 1981.

DEPARTMENT OF DEFENSE, "Joint Regulation: Software Quality Evaluation Program," DOD-STD 2168, Apr. 1, 1987 (draft).

DEPARTMENT OF DEFENSE, "Requirements for High Order Computer Programming Languages: 'STEELMAN'," June 1978 (DTIC AD# A059444).

DEPARTMENT OF DEFENSE, "Software Technology for Adaptable, Reliable Systems (STARS)," a series of 12 reports, March 1983.

DEPARTMENT OF DEFENSE COMPUTER SECURITY CENTER, "Trusted Computer System Evaluation Criteria," CSC-STD-001-83, Aug. 15, 1983.

DEPARTMENT OF NAVY, "A Software Engineering Environment for the Navy," Report of the NAVMAT Software Engineering Environment Working Group, Mar. 31, 1982 (DTIC No. AD A131941).

DEMARCO, T., *Structured Analysis and System Specification*, Prentice-Hall, Inc., Englewood Cliffs, N.J., 1979.

DIJKSTRA, R. W., "GOTO Statement Considered Harmful," *Communications of the ACM*, Vol. 11, Mar. 1968, pp. 147–148 (also cf. pp. 538 and 541).

EMRICK, R. D., "Capacity Management of End User Processing," Proceedings of the CMG XIV International Conference, Dec. 6–9, 1983, pp. 252–256.

FEDERAL CONVERSION SUPPORT CENTER, "Review and Analysis of Conversion Cost-Estimating Techniques," GSA/FCSC-81/001, Apr. 1981 (NTIS PB81-207854).

FELDMAN, C., K. SCHOMAN, and D. SNYDER, "Structured Analysis Model for Naval Telecommunications Procedures," Naval Research Laboratory, NRL Memorandum Report 3086, July 1975.

FIFE, D. W., "Computer Software Management: A primer for project management and quality control," National Bureau of Standards, NBS-SP-500-11, July 1977.

FITZSIMMONS, A., and T. LOVE, "A Review and Evaluation of Software Science," *Computing Surveys,* Vol. 10, No. 1, Mar. 1978, pp. 3–18.

GANE, C., and T. SARSON, *Structured Systems Analysis: Tools and Techniques,* Prentice-Hall, Inc., Englewood Cliffs, N.J., 1979.

GENERAL ACCOUNTING OFFICE, "Conversion: A Costly, Disruptive Process That Must Be Considered When Buying Computers," FGMDS-80-35, June 3, 1980.

GENERAL ACCOUNTING OFFICE, "Federal Aviation Administration's Host Computer: More Realistic Performance Tests Needed before Production Begins," IMTEC-85-10, June 6, 1985.

GILB, T., *Software Metrics,* Winthrop Publishers, Inc., Cambridge, Mass., 1977.

GOLDEN, J. R., J. R. MUELLER, and B. ANSELM, "Software Cost Estimating: Craft or Witchcraft," *Data Base,* Spring 1981, pp. 12–14.

GOMAA, H., "A Software Design Method for Real Time Systems," *Communications of the ACM,* Vol. 27, No. 9, Sept. 1984, pp. 938–949.

GROH, H., and K. LUTZ, "Outside-in Instead of Top-down: Industrial-scale Software Production with CADOS," *Data Report,* Vol. XII, No. 4, 1984, pp. 19–25.

HALL, N. R., and S. PRESIER, "Combined Network Complexity Measures," *IBM Journal of Research and Development,* Vol. 28, No. 1, Jan. 1984, pp. 15–27.

HALSTEAD, M. H., *Elements of Software Science,* Elsevier North-Holland, Inc., New York, 1977.

HIGGINS, D., *Designing Structured Programs,* Prentice-Hall, Inc., Englewood Cliffs, N.J., 1983.

HULL, T. E., "Would You Believe Structured Fortran?," *ACM SIGNUM Newsletter,* Vol. 8, No. 4, Oct. 1973, pp. 13–16.

IBM CORPORATION, *HIPO—A Design Aid and Documentation Technique,* Manual No. GC20-1851, White Plains, N.Y., 1974.

IEEE, "IEEE Guide for Software Quality Assurance Planning," IEEE-STD 983-1986, Institute of Electrical and Electronics Engineers, New York, 1986.

IEEE, "IEEE Guide to Software Requirements Specifications," ANSI/IEEE-STD 830-1984, Institute of Electrical and Electronics Engineers, New York, 1984.

JACKSON, M., *Principles of Program Design,* Academic Press, New York, 1975.

JENSEN, R., and C. TONIES, *Software Engineering,* Prentice-Hall, Inc., Englewood Cliffs, N.J., 1979.

KATZAN, H., JR., *Systems Design and Documentation: An Introduction to the HIPO Method,* Van Nostrand Reinhold Co., New York, 1976.

KENT, W., "A Simple Guide to Five Normal Forms in Relational Database Theory," *Communications of the ACM,* Vol. 26, No. 2, Feb. 1983, pp. 120–125.

KNUTH, D. E., "Structured Programming with GOTO Statements," *ACM Computing Surveys,* Vol. 6, Dec. 1974, pp. 261–301.

KOLTES, J. C., "The User Service Agreement," *EDP Performance Review,* Vol. 10, No. 9, Sept. 1982, pp. 1–6.

KROL, T., "The '(4,2)-Concept' Fault Tolerant Computer," *Fault Tolerant Computer Society (FTCS) 12th Annual International Symposium on Fault-Tolerant Computing,* June 1982.

KUEHN, P. J., "Approximate Analysis of General Queuing Networks by Decomposition," *IEEE Transactions on Communications,* Vol. COM-27, No. 1, Jan. 1979, pp. 113–126.

LANO, R. L., "The N^2 Chart," TRW-SS-77-04, Nov. 1977.

LEAVITT, D., "CPE Use Pays Off in the Real World," *Software News,* Apr. 1985, pp. 53–56.

LING, T. -W., F. W. TOMPA, and T. KAMEDA, "An Improved Third Normal Form for Relational Databases," *ACM Transactions on Database Systems,* Vol. 6, June 1981, pp. 329–346.

LIPOW, M., "Comments on 'Estimating the Number of Faults in Code' and Two Corrections to Published Data," *IEEE Transactions on Software Engineering,* Vol. SE-12, No. 4, Apr. 1986, pp. 584–585.

MASTERS, T. E., II, "An Overview of Software Cost Estimating Methodology at the National Security Agency," NSA, May 18, 1983.

McCABE, T., *Software Quality Assurance: A Survey,* McCabe & Associates, Columbia, Md., 1980.

McCALL, J. A., and M. MATSUMOTO, "Software Quality Metrics Enhancements," General Electric Company, RADC-TR-80-109, Vol. I, Apr. 1980.

McCALL, J. A., M. A. HERNDON and W. M. OSBORNE, "Software Maintenance Management," National Bureau of Standards, NBS Special Pub. 500-129, 1985.

METZGER, P. W., *Managing a Programming Project,* 2nd ed., Prentice-Hall, Inc., Englewood Cliffs, N.J., 1983.

MILLS, H. D., "How to Write Correct Programs and Know it," *Proceedings of the International Congress on Reliable Software,* IEEE Computer Society, Apr. 1975, pp. 363–370.

MISEK-FALKOFF, L. D., "Software Science and Natural Language: A Unification of Halstead's Counting Rules for Programs and English Text and a Claim Space Approach to Extension," IBM Research Report 4/19/82 RC9426 (also, SCORES Proceedings, ACM, 1982).

MURACHANIAN, N., "Software Configuration Management Plan," Jet Propulsion Laboratory, ASAS/ENSCE Document 7080-6, June 1, 1984.

MUSA, J. D., "A Theory of Software Reliability and Its Application (revised)," *Tutorial on Models and Metrics for Software Management and Engineering* (V. R. Basili, ed.), IEEE Computer Society, Silver Spring, Md., 1980a, pp. 147–156.

MUSA, J. D., "Software Reliability Measurement," *Journal of Systems and Software,* Vol. 1, 1980b, pp. 223–241. (Reprinted in *Tutorial on Models and Metrics for Software Management and Engineering* (V. R. Basili, ed.), IEEE Computer Society, Silver Spring, Md., 1980b, pp. 157–193.)

MYERS, G. L., *The Art of Software Testing,* John Wiley & Sons, Inc., New York, 1979.

NASSI, I., and B. SHNEIDERMAN, "Flowchart Techniques for Structured Programming," *ACM SIGPLAN Notices,* Vol. 8, No. 8, Aug. 1973, pp. 12–26.

NATIONAL BUREAU OF STANDARDS, FIPS PUB 106, "Guidance on Software Maintenance," June 1984.

NATIONAL BUREAU OF STANDARDS, FIPS PUB 101, "Guideline for Lifecycle Validation, Verification and Testing of Computer Software," June 1983.

NATIONAL BUREAU OF STANDARDS, FIPS PUB 38, "Guidelines for Documentation of Computer Programs and Automated Data Systems," Feb. 1976.

NATIONAL BUREAU OF STANDARDS, "Validation, Verification and Testing of Computer Software," NBS Special Pub. 500-25.

NATIONAL SECURITY AGENCY, "NSA/CSS Software Product Standards Manual," NSAM 81-3.

NEUGENT, W., and others, "Technology Assessment: Methods for Measuring the Level of Computer Security," National Bureau of Standards Special Pub. 500-133.

NG, N., "A Graphical Editor for Programming Using Structured Charts," IBM Research Report, RJ2344, Sept. 19, 1978.

ORR, K., *Structured Systems Development,* Yourdon Press, New York, 1977.

PARNAS, D. L., and D. P. SIEWIOREK, "Use of the Concept of Transparency in the Design of Hierarchically Structured Systems," *Communications of the ACM,* Vol. 18, No. 7, July 1975, pp. 401–408.

PAUL, M., and H. J. SIEGERT (ed.), *Distributed Systems: Methods and Tools for Specification,* Lectures in Computer Sciences 190, Springer-Verlag, New York, 1985.

PERRY, W. E., *A Standard for Testing Application Software,* Auerbach Publishers, Inc., Pennsauken, N.J., 1985.

PETERS, L., *Software Design: Methods and Techniques,* Yourdon Press, New York, 1981.

PETERS, L. J., and L. L. TRIPP, "Comparing Software Design Methodologies," *DATAMATION* Nov. 1977, pp. 89–94.

PETSCHENIK, N. H., "Practical Priorities in System Testing," *IEEE Software,* Sept. 1985, pp. 18–23.

POSTON, R. M., "Improving Software Quality and Productivity," *IEEE Software,* Vol. 3, No. 3, May 1986, pp. 74–75.

PRESSMAN, R. S., *Software Engineering: A Practitioner's Approach,* McGraw-Hill Book Co., New York, 1982.

RAMAMOORTHY, C. V., and F. B. BASTANI, "Software Reliability—Status and Perspectives," *IEEE Transactions Software Engineering,* Vol. SE-8, No. 4, July 1982, pp. 354–371.

REISER, M., "Performance Evaluation of Data Communications Systems," IBM Research Report RZ 1092, Aug. 19, 1981.

ROSS, D., "Structured Analysis (SA): A Language for Communicating Ideas," *IEEE Proceedings,* Vol. SE-20, Jan. 1977, pp. 6–24.

SCHKOLNICK, M., and P. TIBERIO, "A Note on Estimating the Maintenance Cost in a Relational Database," IBM Research Report RJ3327, Dec. 9, 1981.

SCHWARTZ, J. W., and J. K. WOLF, "Control of Faults and Errors in Satellites: Error Control Coding Techniques for Memories with Soft Upsets," Avtec Systems, Inc., May 1985.

SHERE, K. D., "Myths Related to the Software Development Life Cycle," *Fourth International Workshop on Software Specification and Design,* Computer Society Press of the IEEE, Washington, D.C., 1987.

SHERE, K. D., "Structured Decomposition Program: A New Technique for System Analysis," *DATAMATION,* Oct. 1979.

SHOOMAN, M. L., *Software Engineering,* McGraw-Hill Book Co., New York, 1983.

SIEVERT, G. E., and T. A. MIZELL, "Specification-Based Software Engineering with TAGS," *IEEE Computer Magazine,* Apr. 1985, pp. 56–65.

Software News, "The Productivity Report Card," Sept. 1986, p. 19.

STANKOVIC, J. A., "Reliable Distributed System Software," IEEE Computer Society, Silver Spring, Md., 1985.

SUMMERS, R. C., "An Overview of Computer Security," *IBM Systems Journal,* Vol. 23, No. 4, 1984, pp. 309–325.

TAUSWORTHE, R. C., "Deep Space Network Software Cost Estimation Model," Jet Propulsion Laboratory, JPL Publication 81-7 (also NASA-CR-164277), Apr. 15, 1981.

TAUSWORTHE, R. C., *Standardized Development of Computer Software,* Parts I and II, Prentice-Hall, Inc., Englewood Cliffs, N.J., 1979.

TEICHROEW, D., and E. HERSHEY, III, "PSL/PSA: A Computer-aided Technique for Structured Documentation and Analysis of Information Processing Systems," *IEEE Transactions on Software Engineering,* Vol. SE-3, No. 1, 1977, pp. 41–48.

TELEDYNE BROWN ENGINEERING, "IORL: Input/Output Requirements Language: Reference Manual," July 1984.

THIBODEAU, R., "An Evaluation of Software Cost Estimating Models," Rome Air Development Center, RADC-TR-81-144, June 1981.

TRACHTENBERG, M., "Validating Halstead's Theory with System 3 Data," *IEEE Transactions on Software Engineering,* Vol. SE-12, No. 4, Apr. 1986, p. 584.

USAF Space Division, "Management Guide for Independent Verification and Validation," Aug. 1980.

WARNIER, J. -D., *Logical Construction of Programs,* 3rd ed., translated by B. Flanagan, Van Nostrand Reinhold Co., New York, 1976.

WARNIER, J. -D., *Logical Construction of Systems,* Van Nostrand Reinhold Co., New York, 1981.

WEINBERG, V., *Structured Analysis,* Prentice-Hall, Inc., Englewood Cliffs, N.J., 1978.

WENSLEY, J. H., "Reliability Comparison of Dual and Triple Systems," August Systems, Technical Report 009-3400-00, June 1982.

WHITE, D. R. J., K. ATKINSON, and J. D. M. OSBURN, "Taming EMI in Microprocessor Systems," *IEEE Spectrum,* Vol. 22, No. 12, Dec. 1985, pp. 30–37.

WOLBERG, J. R., *Conversion of Computer Software,* Prentice-Hall, Inc., Englewood Cliffs, N.J., 1983.

YOURDON, E., *How to Manage Structured Programming,* Yourdon, Inc., New York, 1976.

YOURDON, E., *Techniques of Program Structure and Design,* Prentice-Hall, Inc., Englewood Cliffs, N.J., 1975.

YOURDON, E., and L. CONSTANTINE, *Structured Design: Fundamentals of a Discipline of Computer Program and Systems Design,* Yourdon Press, New York, 1978.

Index

A

Abstraction, 56, 200
Acceptance criteria, 264
Acceptance testing, 268, 310
Access keys, 214
Anomaly, 215
APCE, 57
Architecture, 292, 302 +
Atomic transaction, 222
Auditing, 242

B

Baselines, 43, 46, 247
  Product, 120
BEST/1, 76
Black box, 39
Bottom up, 25, 117
Bugs (*see* Errors)

C

Capacity management, 42, 110
Capacity planning, 75, 271 +
CDRL, 124
C5 Specification, 119
Change procedures, 256 +
Change request, 33, 35, 246, 248
Checklists. 309

Acceptance testing, 268
Code inspection, 267
CSCI, 254, 261
Design reviews, 262
FCA activities, 254
Physical configuration audit, 263
Quality evaluation, 259
SRR, SDR, 153
COCOMO, 95
Code and checkout phase, 157 +
Cohesion, 28 + , 244
Commenting standards, 27 +
Commercial off-the-shelf software
        (COTS), 55, 289 +
Complexity, 7 + , 65, 86, 92, 243
  Complexity class, 93
  Complex systems, 7 + , 33, 105, 242
  Metrics, 8, 65, 73
Computer resource management plans,
        123
Computer software component, 23, 51,
        54, 154
Computer software configuration item,
        23, 51, 54, 80, 117, 121, 169,
        293
Configuration control, 242
Configuration control board (CCB), 59,
        240, 247, 254 +
Configuration identification, 242
Configuration management, 77, 113,
        144, 241 + , 260
Configuration management plan, 122,
        123, 129 +
Contracting, 61, 96
Conversion, 86 + , 89 +